Norbert Blei

DOOR WAY

DOOR WAY

NORBERT BLEI

THE PEOPLE IN THE LANDSCAPE

Dave Etter's poems "The Tree Chopper," "Snow Country," and "Two Beers in Argyle, Wisconsin" from *Go Read the River* (University of Nebraska Press), "Barn Dreams" and "Why I Don't Go to Parties Anymore" from *Open to the Wind* (Uzzano), "Yale Brocklander" from *Cornfields* (Spoon River Poetry Press) and "Fishing" from *StoryQuarterly No. 10*, all reprinted with permission of the author.

Parts of this book appeared in slightly altered form in the following publications: *Midwest Magazine*, the Chicago *Sun-Times*, *Insight* Magazine, the Milwaukee *Journal*, *Chicago* Magazine, and the Door County *Advocate*. "Charley" was adapted as an award-winning radio play produced by the Wisconsin Educational Communications Board. The author wishes to acknowledge his gratitude to these publications and the ECB.

Photographs on pages x, 18, 26, 47, 56, 83, 93, 98, 100, 108, 142, 152, 168, 186, 201, 203, 204, 241, 247,and 286 by Norbert Blei. Photographs on pages 12, 51, and 297 by Ross LewAllen, used by permission. Woodcuts on pages 35, 52, 114, 126, and 212 by Louis Smolak, used by permission. Photographs on pages 75 ("Old Man Winter"), 170 ("Emma Toft"), 178 ("The Clearing in Winter"), 254 ("Bay in Winter" and 298 ("The Fishermen") by Frank Pechman, used by permission. Watercolor on cover by Charles Peterson, used by permission, for which the special thanks of author and publisher.

Published by The Ellis Press, P.O. Box 6, Granite Falls, Minnesota 56241. Printed by Thompson-Shore, Inc., Dexter, Michigan

ISBN: ISBN: 978-0-944024-59-9

1   2   3   4   5

with love for my father, George Blei, in his way
and my mother, Emily, in hers

and for
Charley Root
Bill Beckstrom
and Chet Elquist

. . . How can a man's life keep its course
If he will not let it flow?
Those who flow as life flows know
They need no other force . . .
                    —Lao Tzu

Door Way

I came to live in Door in the spring of 1969. I came deliberately to this landscape where I had experienced a kind of private peace in place for three summers before, a stillness bordering on the serenity some men find in religion. I could neither explain it nor express it at the time and knew it would take some amount of living here to begin to know it.

It was an alienated landscape to me, a starkly beautiful peninsula, more like an island encircled by water. There never seemed to be much doing, and that was its secret allurement. It pulled you in, made you almost non-existent when you least expected it. It could be a field of wildflowers. It could be a spring rain, a stand of birch, an old farm, a stone fence, a herd of deer. Most certainly it was water everywhere enchanting the eye, reflecting, working the oldest mystery within us.

I came to Door, though, uncommitted, unsure, even somewhat afraid of what it might take to live a daily life in such a place. Never having felt comfortable making any decision, especially one that could certainly affect the entire course of a man's life, I did not care to act upon a decision as drastic as the choice of country life over city.

I see now that I have lived a life of indecision from the very beginning. Somehow the choice has already been made for you. So this has happened, and now you are here or there . . . and now you proceed to whatever else you must do, wherever else you may find yourself. But this kind of knowing came later — it was something else I was to discover by withdrawing into this landscape.

I remember almost buying this house in the spring of 1968, then going back to Chicago exhilarated because the decision had been postponed. Days passed. I thrived on the stimulation of the city, the openness and complexity of city-type people, the nearness of neighborhood, friends, relations.

Something about the scene up there in Door, something about that old house buried in the woods left me with a feeling that I could never inhabit that landscape. I could never make a home there.

I could handle night in the city with bright lights, neighborhood bars, all-night coffee shops, movie houses, and daily editions of all the newspapers, but night in the country had all the intimations of death.

Possibly a month of such feelings occupied my mind in the city. Who knows just how, or why, or even if we make a choice? Things began to close in on me. City life was changing, sometimes for the worse. My wife and my two children needed the possibility of a life lived closer to the land. I needed space. I needed quiet. I found myself buying the house and land in the spring of 1968. I spent the summer there, and made a permanent move a year later, the spring of 1969. I knew that very first night I had lost my sense of place—I was nowhere. I began living, in mind and heart, the life of an exile.

The contradictions of my personal existence began almost immediately. That's understandable but unexplainable. I would woo friends and relatives to Door, regale them with personal tours and insights concerning the magnificent countryside, the color of fields, the woods bountiful in beech, birch, maple, pine, and always, from beginning to end, the water which cradled the preciousness of this landscape like a nest, lavishing a light upon it almost liquid in sunrises and sunsets that could lead a man to walk water to be nearer the source.

It was an enviable life, they all agreed—though to this day I am convinced the visitor never partook of this feast to the fullest. And I am always at a loss trying to reveal my vision to others. So many come, but so few see.

It was an enviable life here, indeed, but I lived it best only when others came to visit. Upon their departure I felt stranded.

I could not deceive myself. In my mind I did not live here at all for at least the first five years. Chicago was truly my address; the old neighborhood was my home. And so the journeying back and forth began. It was a bizarre existence, a schizoid way of life. I was a man who lived, and began to thrive in a dual existence: neon and nature.

Even in those summers spent vacationing here, Door County spoke to me, but I had neither the time nor the desire to decipher the message entirely. Like many tourists and summer people, I merely skimmed from the top, celebrated surface pleasures only—the beaches, the back roads, the parks, the restaurants and gift shops—both the natural and the manufactured quaintness the county exudes in July and August at best.

Often during those summer months I thought it could all be captured in painting, so tried my hand at that, only to realize it was a landscape far beyond my ability to define by color, form, and line.

Photography also called me—or rather, the fields, the old farms, the fishing tugs, all of it. Everything here addresses itself to whatever degree of imagination a man possesses, and asks, damn near begs, to be made something of. "Paint me, photograph me, render me in poetry," whispered the landscape; "Do what you will to me; make even more of me, more of yourself."

This was a considerable part of the original attraction, though I did not comprehend it completely at the time: possession in all its forms. Wanting to have it all, take it all for keeps, for personal satisfaction. It would take a hell of a lot of living here for me to realize that truth is found in the opposite way.

I did not try to write of this immediately, for I knew it was all too close, too new. I stayed with fiction set in an urban, often ethnic culture, though I soon found images of my rural experience slowly emerging. I wrote articles celebrating city and neighborhood culture, where I felt most at home. But the realities of the rural experience seemed to demand a voice as well.

I quietly began a journal the first year in Door. Slowly this place and I began a dialogue on paper that I knew would someday produce a book. I have been at this ever since.

I found a good part of meaning here amongst natives and outsiders. Some came to me at first by the very nature of their proximity. Later I began to look for them.

The first natives I met —Chet Elquist and his wife, Flossie —became my closest friends. We rented an apartment above the garage on their small farm in Ephraim for two summers before moving here.

Down the road from my house lived the Carlsons and their son, Carly, whom we came to depend on for all manner of house repairs. Alongside of me, in a back 40, lived an old man all alone but for his dogs, a man named Charley Root.

It was a strange mixture of people I was attracted to, and it was to grow even stranger in the years to come. I felt continually frustrated in my feelings toward many of the natives. They seemed to give only so much of themselves before pushing a "do not enter" sign in my face. I have never met a more difficult people to know, either in cities, other parts of America, or foreign countries.

Unless you were born and raised here, subjected to the intricacies of family relations, religion, local education, and common labor, you will never know what it is to be a native. I ignored this at first, made fun of it later, felt threatened by their overwhelming sullenness, feigned pieties, dependencies on "good old time religion" in judging others, not to mention living an entire life without asking questions (minds at the mercy of ministers) under the pretense of hear no evil, see no evil, speak no evil.

Goddamn it, they all made me so angry, professing one thing but doing the other! I respected, I missed the honesty of "fallen" friends back home. I longed to listen to down-to-earth people who told you exactly how they felt, using language as if it were alive and made for them, not the niceties they'd been taught in Sunday School.

The outsiders were easier to relate to, but there were not that many here nine years ago. As I came to know them, there was inevitably the common bond of city life. We all seemed to know and share where we came from; most of us seemed confused, unsettled, as to where we found ourselves now.

I have spent years here looking for the realness in people, both natives and outsiders. And they have all taught me much about myself.

I began, then, to live and make my way in this landscape —people and place —from a superficial appreciation of spring, summer, and fall, to an in-depth struggle with winter, a season of solitary confinement that I still fight, yet manage to survive each year with fresher insight.

I learned to love and hate the uniqueness of this landscape. And strangely enough, as the county began to move toward greater and greater development in the '70s, I found myself, such a lover of the city and all its attractions, suddenly hating, fighting every aspect of urban thinking: condominiums, housing developments, prefabs, paved roads, more restaurants, more gift shops, more tourists—everything destined to desecrate this land.

Who can explain the dichotomy of his own desires? It is almost as if I wish the county to be left empty, impoverished, desolate, as uninhabitable as it seems at times, so I can go on hating it because I've come to love it so for what it is.

Philosophically I came to Door as an existentialist, a lapsed Catholic, Protestant, all-around Christian. I came with a cynical urban writer's attitude, a tendency to question everything. I came, too, with much success and satisfaction in ten years of teaching. What I best taught others was to discover and trust their own feelings . . . and to question everything. I was rewarded by seeing students come alive, begin their own quest (hopefully creative) for values in life far greater than money and security.

But I was thwarted here in continuing self-revolution (realization) through writing and literature. There was no way the local school system would let me—an outsider, a writer, a long-haired looking hippie who didn't even send his own children to church—near a group of students at that time. To keep my hands in teaching, I would have to return to Chicago to do writing workshops, discuss writing with kids in class, and teach at a community college for a winter's quarter. Not until The Clearing, in Ellison Bay, found me did I have a place where I might continue to learn and practice the art of teaching. The Clearing has added much to the quality of my life here ever since, and to it, and its people, I am forever grateful.

If I came here somewhat irreligious, believing only in myself and the act of writing, I gradually allied my deepest feelings with Thoreau in a deliberate attempt to better understand and identify with the natural life all around me. I began to withdraw from people—the natives in whom I found no comfort. I sought solace, found peace in burrowing into these fields around me, merging into woods, studying birds, plant life, and constantly watching the drama of sky from season to season . . . even the effect of sun on my own state of mind. There was much to mull over, perhaps even meaning enough for me to stay for years to come.

A visit with Wisconsin author August Derleth in Sac Prairie one fall served only to intensify the need for meaning and truth, for a life of roots in the common earth. Here was Derleth, who had made his mark in the world of literature, who had lived and explained a life, yet hadn't gone anywhere. He simply stayed home.

I bought that whole attitude, a life of woods, water, plants, animals, and local people, just as Derleth described it. I tried living it myself for a good period of time, only to realize many months after his death, that I was wrong, that Derleth, too, had been possibly mistaken.

I had no roots in Door and never would. My history here was all now—and I seem to prefer it that way. History is fine for old age, for people who have settled within themselves, but there was a personal history of one's own to be explored. There were too many other lives in other places I still wanted to live. Derleth, I decided, had gone only so far, and then stood still. Either he had found out all there was to know in Sac Prairie (and I rather doubt that) or there were areas of his own psyche which for personal reasons he feared to probe on the home grounds or any other regions of the real and unreal world that might reveal yet other truths.

It was time to move on philosophically once again. This was not a conscious decision. It never is. Visitors arrive from far out regions of the mind. Strangers come. Old friends tell of different ways they've found upon the land. Books find you. Dreams speak. Nature, men, women suggest a unity of earth and heaven you have always known. And you journey yourself. I visited Greece again, and New Mexico, where I thought I should be headed after here. But some places, including Door, just won't let you go.

All the while you seem to be the same, yet all the while you are changing. The people, the landscapes of your life appear the same as before, though they are telling you other things now because of where you've been and the way things move within us in the slowest dance.

If I was a fallen-away Catholic, Protestant, existentialist, it became clearer and clearer to me that I was still everything I had seemingly rejected, passed through. Where I suddenly found myself philosophically, and where this book on Door began to lead me, was a silent, sunny, snowy region of the inner landscape that I had been called to many times before, even as far back as grammar school, when I wanted to be a priest, even as far back as summer on my grandparents' farm in Michigan, where I first became acquainted with the incredible mysteries of earth, even as far back as high school when I read my first book on Zen. That region was Eastern religion. And everything up to now had lead and brought me back to this, including a continued pursuit of native American Indian ways where I begin to see East and West, the circle once again.

And the Way of Door is the way I came to see how all of this works: the way it is.

Winter in Door

"What do the natives do around here in winter?" is the standard summertime Door County joke. I don't care to answer it, because you're expected to smile and give them the anticipated reply: "Nothing." This is only part of the truth. Those who make enough money off the tourists all summer usually manage to get out for a good part of the winter. Those who can't afford it, or have no vision of what life outside Door could be, remain fixed in place, an immovable part of the landscape. There is something to be said for that too, but not now. Back to summer.

The sad thing about summer here is that it is so unreal, never quite long or hot enough, and more like the final edge of spring. Summer in Door enters surprisingly sometime after the 4th of July and disappears almost as suddenly before the end of August. That's just the "Door condition" that one must learn to live with.

"It's a short growing season," some of the farmers will tell you. Tomatoes hardly have enough time to understand they're supposed to turn red, melons may grow as big as golf balls, and then lie there to mock you the rest of the season, and green peppers sometimes don't even get off the ground. Gardening here can be as frustrating as raising grapes on the polar ice cap. If it's not the poor weather, then it's the rocky soil, which seems ideal only for raising more and more rocks to the surface. As for the famous cherry orchards of Door, that's country comedy at its best, a kind of rural theater of the absurd to be saved for a long winter night's entertainment.

Yet before leaving summer, before closing the door completely, I should confess: Door County, in the purity and essence of each season, is one of the most satisfying places for a man to find himself anywhere in the world. It has less to do with people than with place . . . and hardly anything at all to do with the tourist industry, which in the long run will destroy it.

But enough of summer. This is my third winter here, and I am as un-resigned a Door resident as ever. I continue to wonder what I am doing here at this time of year and expect to get the hell out as soon as possible. But I remain motionless.

The first winter I stayed because I wanted to. The second winter I stayed because I had to. The third winter I escaped to Greece and vowed in the sun again never to spend a winter in Door. And here I am, actually my fourth winter here, though I missed last year's rerun.

So you see, it's forever in and out with me. Perhaps that's my problem, my own peculiar nature that is so out of tune at times with this natural cycle of place: staying, but not belonging; ready to sell, but unwilling to put up the sign for fear that I never will find a better setting for "home"; loving the place with a solitary intensity of oneness that at times I consider every phone call, every visitor an intrusion, but hating the "Door condition" at other times with a passion that knows no bounds.

"Going anywhere this winter?" It's the question everyone asks this time of year. I've heard it a hundred times since Labor Day. "I don't know," is the usual reply; "I'd like to go someplace warm. But I suppose I'll stick around."

He'll stick around. Most people do. They kid themselves with *Farmer's Almanac* games: "It's supposed to be a pretty mild one this winter. Then there's the January thaw. February's the bad one. After that, things should be looking, up."

But the snow keeps pummeling them till March, and the ice sometimes doesn't break in the bay till April. My neighbor, Charley Root, 88, remembers snow in Bailey's Harbor on the 4th of July. I believe it. I believe the worst weather imaginable can happen here at any time of the year.

With Lake Michigan on one side, Green Bay on the other, the whole tundra waiting to pounce in the north, what the hell chance does a struggling sun have in these parts? No wonder the forecasters usually throw their hands to the winds when trying to predict the weather in Door.

Call it the Door condition, or call it the Door County consciousness: white on gray. The spirit, of a people is affected by weather, I am sure. It's a consciousness of little hope and much resignation, come winter. "You have to learn to live with it."

Most of the young people spend most of their growing years looking for a way to get out. Most of them never do, except for the few who get away to college, and then beyond. Carly Carlson, a young friend across the road, has plans with his wife for an indefinite stay in Europe, beginning next week. "We'll be in Spain for winter," he tells me. "Come on over." He's attempted one or two final breaks from Door but never made it. The odds among the locals are that Carly and wife will be back in Door before they're even missed.

How much sweeter to come and go than to stay; that by way of judgment upon Wisconsin.
                                        —Glenway Wescott, *Good-bye Wisconsin*

And so what do you do in Door County in winter, besides endure?

You get struck with what they call "cabin fever" about the middle of January and begin climbing the walls, resting momentarily, perhaps, to study a spider web in the corner. And you wonder about that spider all balled up, and how he handles winter in the web.

You nurture and thrive on every medical symptom known to man and Doc Farmer. You've got arthritis, gout, a brain tumor, a bad heart, or whatever. One thing's for certain, you'll never make it through the winter. Doc Farmer probably prescribes some natural vitamin C, a good stiff drink, and maybe a copy of *Playboy*. For good measure, he throws in a slightly risqué joke.

You go to church and play the role every Sunday. Then you discover you've got to live with your same old self the rest of the week and, damn it, it just doesn't work, especially in winter. Thoughts of raising hell someplace else seem a little warmer and consoling. I could tell you more about Door County Christians, but I won't. We're all the same everywhere. You know the story by now.

And I could tell you Door County tales of the whole human condition, from saintliness to infidelity to eccentricity to madness to courage to murder to truth and beauty. But I won't. Not now.

I could tell you about my concern for young people. How many of them turn to drink, too early, and stay with it till it's too late because . . . because? To use the answer they use so often, "What else is there to do around here?" It's the same problem in suburbia, where drugs are the easier way out.

Yet the court report for these parts is frightening at times, and the number of young people killed on the roads is a bit much. A bit much.

Maybe the rural imagination (unchallenged in the schools, dead in the villages, unexpressed in the countryside) is best expressed at night, on the road, the empty highways and county trunks, pushing 100 m.p.h. under whatever influence might be handy, or even stone sober, just for the hell of it. Running wild and free through a deadening, solitary landscape that seems determined to hang there in front of you the rest of your life and remind you that things will always be the same. So maybe this one time, this moment, this Saturday night, you fly, and maybe you live to laugh and tell about it tomorrow. Maybe the act to define yourself spreads through gossip, and could, in years to come, end in legend. But maybe you die and are remembered in other ways.

I could tell you about rural male chauvinism and The Hunt, but I won't. I could tell you about the desolation of women in this county, but I won't. I could try to tell you why I hang on here despite everything, even winter, but I can't explain it all just now. Or maybe I already have.

I could tell you about some fine people here in Door, friends and neighbors like old Carl Carlson, the plumber, and his brother John; the

Tills, Johnny Gonzales, Bill Beckstrom; Darlene Cooper—good woman, guitar teacher—and her fine kids.

I could tell you about many real people in these parts, like Chet Elquist and his wife; Doc Farmer, the last of the old time country doctors; Gust Klenke, garage man, beekeeper, all around mechanic and good man who has a reputation for never quite telling you exactly what you owe for his services; never reminding you of your debt to him; so consequently, you forget you owe Gust something. "Either way you look at it you lose," he told me over coffee the other afternoon. I think he was talking about the difficulty of doing all the things he must do without any help, including coming to the aid of a neighbor who runs out of fuel oil in the middle of the night. "You gotta do something for people or there's no use doing anything," he explains.

So, where are we finally? In Door. In winter. In a time and place to pause, to reflect. Call it more conflict bordering on contradiction. As much as I hate the soft white death of such a season, I respect the silence it affords and try to learn to live through it once again. For I am not so sure that it wasn't an earlier winter here that gave me my first—and now lasting—love and awe for what the earth holds and does, and how the universe works with man.

Remembering an ice storm that turned my woods to glass; remembering snow-smothered days of empty blue sky with a sun the shape and color of a lemon; remembering afternoons and so many nights rocking in the chair, looking out on the wonder of birds scratching out a living in ice, trees determined to their very depths; dozing off into the landscapes of Vivaldi's "Four Seasons," the symphonies of Sibelius— remembering all of this, I wonder: where else in the world can a man be?

In the night, in the nagging absence of friends and good times, some great ethnic dinner, a memorable French wine, a good cigar, some decent pipe tobacco, I pull down books from the shelves to remember that even here I run not alone.

A man deserves whatever landscape he finds himself in, I reflect, even a landscape like Door. Jens Jensen knew this. Though an outsider, he was one of the first to recognize the true value of land in Door. This was a place for a man to come to terms with himself in a natural setting. So Jensen, a landscape artist from Chicago, set up a school in Ellison Bay and called his final landscape The Clearing. It was the most revolutionary thing that ever happened to Door County, and that was done in 1935. In years to come, The Clearing, along with a few state parks, may be all that will be left of the natural landscape of this place.

A people might live amongst beautiful surroundings and fail to understand the message of these surroundings.
—Jens Jensen, *Siftings*

Ah, Jens, thou shouldst be living in this hour! I've seen your Clearing, taught and learned your lessons there, and could talk for hours about the magic it works in the souls of men and women. But still I remain restless here, especially in winter.

> What does it all mean? That you need a village, if only for the pleasure of leaving it. Your own village means that you are not alone, that you know there's something of you in the people and the plants and the soil, that even when you are not there, it waits to welcome you. But it isn't easy to stay there quietly. . . .
> —Cesare Pavese, *The Moon and the Bonfire*

So I rock in place with the world, and wait and wonder whether to leave at winter's end . . . or before. Or should I call this place "home"? Stay in Door, or leave for good? There is plenty to read, more to write, the Czech language to study, the guitar to learn, paintings to try, children to raise, so much worth a man's while to do. A few friends will no doubt make it through the stillness.

And so, in the face of winter moving through Door, I dream the unsettled dream of maybe getting out, maybe hanging in . . . Grecian islands in the sun, the sound of ice cracking in the bay, the woods and fields of Door opening up to spring.

Charley

I keep a watch on the old man living alone with his dogs on the back 40: Charley Root, 88, a neighbor and native of Door County, born in Baileys Harbor in 1884.

1884! I take that down in my notes, though the year means nothing to me. I keep a watch on the old man. I try to preserve him.

The fashion today, in a plastic society where nothing is supposed to last very long, is to preserve old buildings, old furniture, old clothes, anything that speaks, however silently, of days when life depended upon the use of a man's own hands, and there was a simplicity and softness about the earth.

The moon was doing what it was supposed to do. The sun was a wonder. A man set his time by the seasons.

There were animals, of course, and all the elements that would take a daily adjusting to. So, very simply, there were good things and bad things; here and there; up and down; heaven and earth; and a man worked somewhere in the middle and made his feelings known mostly to God.

But of what use are the old people? I ponder that under "Charley" in my notebooks. In the cities, mostly, we hide them. No one grows old anymore.

What's to become of us? Eighty-eight years (that a man should live so long!) will never measure up to all the days and nights of Charley.

So I ask the old man questions, the same questions with each season. And he gives me answers, the same answers, like he's never thought of them before. I try to make sense out of him. I tell my children to listen. I don't want the old man to die, because he has lived so much and accomplished so little—if you judge a man's life the way most men do. Yet a simple man's life is not to be overlooked.

Charley hears, but not so clearly. The local Rural Route Hearing Aid Man came through one day and fleeced him of almost $800 for a set of twin devices that only gives him headaches. So the years have taken away some of the subtle sounds, like the birds at daylight, the hoe slicing the earth, the wind singing through the empty barn. I shout to Charley and act natural:

"HAVE YOU EVER SEEN CHICAGO, CHARLEY?"

"I left the county a couple times only," he says. "Went to Chicago once about 1918, 1920. An uncle of mine said, 'Charley, you come down here. I'll get you a job on the streetcars.' Well, I stayed 'bout a week. 'I'm goin' back to Door County,' I says to him."

In summer, when the woods are thick and I cannot see Charley's place from my house, I follow the road to his open field at night and look for the light in his windows. In fall and winter, I can see clearly through a woods wide open.

Charley retires early. When you are 88 years old, alone, surrounded by a personal, inconsequential history and silence of rock earth that never gave you an even break, of land you can no longer try to work even though you want to, there is not much else for an old man to do.

"I bought this place in 1917. It was nothing but rocks and stumps then. I blasted 'em like I did the cellar. I was pretty good with dynamite. I put a stick right near the corner a the house, and I said to my wife, 'Jenny, you better get out of the house. I'm gonna blow it up.' You never saw such a nice cellar. I kept diggin' at it by hand and dynamitin' what I couldn't get a hold of."

For supper you break bread into a bowl of milk and cover it with maple syrup. You can barely hear, but you must feel the thrust of an autumn wind that hits the house with its own history of seasons — a floor that has settled into a graceful slant, a roof that leaks in a driving southeastern rain, windows that will never keep out all of a wild winter.

You sit in complete silence in a dimly lit kitchen, your back arched over the table, suspenders stretched, wrinkled red hand moving in and out of a bowl of sweet milk and bread. Spots is gone. Mittens is gone. Only Happy remains, still making pups, still under your feet waiting for scraps.

Notebook entry: Charley and His Dogs. "I had to kill Spots this mornin'. She was out all night chasin' porcupines again. I told her the last time she came home with a mouthful of quills, 'I'm not pullin' these outta your mouth with pliers again. It's too much work for an old man. If you can't learn to leave porcupines alone, then I'll have to take a gun to you."

When you are 88 years old and wait for another winter, you put your supper bowl in the sink, let the dog out, and move into the living room where it's warmer. You put the space heater up a little higher and check to see if the flame is burning "a nice blue." You may took out the front windows toward the fields and woods as you have all your life, but you will see nothing now because darkness begins to descend early at this time of year, and you are too tired to see what a harvest moon will do.

It's a slow moon anyway, as you remember. You will catch it in the morning about sunrise outside the window, above the kitchen sink. There will still be time enough for it in the early blue sky, the both of them then—the moon in front, and the sun at your back as you rinse the bowl for breakfast and fill it with Wheaties. And then you feed Happy.

So you sit in the red cushioned rocker at night, or the straight-backed chair, and you wait. Maybe you put on the TV and search for Lawrence Welk again, or tune in the news and try to understand.

"I think, by golly, in a few years from now, the whole world'll be black. So goldarn much going on, a fella can't keep up with it. I don't think the moon was ever put there for the people to go climbin' up on it. The Lord made the earth for people."

When you're 88 years old, you wait. You wait till it's time to turn off the lights. If it's cherry season, the month of July, you still harbor a native fear and suspicion of outsiders—the dark-skinned pickers working the orchards: Mexicans, Indians, blacks—maybe coming to your door at night and causing you concern, though they've never found you yet. But just in case, before going to bed, you rest Jenny's old 16-gauge shotgun quietly against the wall alongside you. When you are 88 years old, you do not give up the gun.

> *Notebook entry: Charley and His Dogs. "I killed my Mittens yesterday. I had her locked up in the pump house last night, and I went in there this mornin' and Carlson's old black dog was in there with her, by God. They been at it all night, I suppose. Her with another bellyful of pups. I can't handle 'em. I should a shot Prince, that black thing. That's what I should a done. But then Carl 'ud be mad at me."*

"HOW DID YOU DO IT, CHARLEY? WHERE DID YOU BURY HER?"

"I just tied her up with a rope by the pump house and shot her in the head. It only took but one shot," he laughs. "I'm still a pretty good aim. I dragged her on down there in the hollow in the woods. But by God, I miss my Mittens. Happy's sniffin' around the house lookin' for her. Mittens was her pup, you know. They was good friends, and she's awful lonesome now."

When you are 88 years old, you do not give up your manhood. Charley takes a child's delight in telling my wife what he's going to do to Prince someday.

"If I can catch him! I'll set a bear trap for him, I will. Then I'll club him a few times. If only I could catch him. I'd put turpentine on his tail, then you'd see him run! Then he wouldn't go botherin' my dogs no more!"

When you are 88 years old, sleep comes all of a sudden at night, and you rely mostly on stories during the day to explain yourself. . . .

Notebook entry: Charley and His Dogs. "How many pups you think my Happy had last night?"
"SIX," my wife guesses.
"TEN?" I ask.
"Thirteen!" laughs Charley. "Kept me up half the night the way they kept comin'. Drowned 'em all this morning in a bucket. There weren't no pretty black and white ones like my Spots, else I might a kept one. Goshsakes, all the work. "
"HOW COULD YOU DO SUCH A MEAN THING, CHARLEY?" asks my wife.
And once again, with a brightness in his eyes, a suddenness of laughter around his mouth, Charley explains, "Ah, you'd be surprised how much I've killed with these hands."

Killing, I explain to my son, to myself, is a common thing to men like Charley. To survive, to keep going, a man had to kill. Charley killed only what he could eat. That was the neat thing about the old man.

"But what about the dogs?" asks my son.

Yes, what about the dogs? He's just a lonely old man, I try to tell myself. And maybe at 88 there's more of life than an old man can handle. Maybe there's such a thing as being overwhelmed by it all: the weeds taking over the flower garden, the grass growing faster than you can push a lawn mower, more apples hanging on a tree than you have ever seen in your life. How's an old man to keep up? Does he just give up, move into a home for the aged, and settle down to do some slow dying? Or does he continue to function like a man, and keep on top of it all?

"I used to go around and do butcherin' for all the farmers. I did a lot of alterin' too. Charley Anderson had a butcher shop here in Ellison Bay. 'Charley,' he said to me one day, 'you got to come down here and help me. I'm gonna start a meat market.' Well, goshsakes, I did everythin', even went out to the fields to fetch the cows for slaughter.

"Sometimes I'd hit 'em in the head with an ax or hammer. Other times I'd use a .32 revolver. I got the gun here yet. I used to be pretty good with it. Jenny'd say, 'Charley, go out and get us a chicken for supper,' and I'd go out near the barn there and most nearly always blow the head off a chicken with one shot.

"Can't use it on a pig, though. A pig's head's too thick. At the meat market, sometimes the sows was so old they didn't have teeth in their head. But that don't mean the meat was tough. I always gave the cows a quart of vinegar the night before I butchered 'em. An old Indian butcher told me that once.   Why, the meat's just as juicy and tender as anybody could want."

When you are 88 years old, there is no end to all the stories tied up inside of you. Everything seems a memory of what the land was able to give you, whatever the season, however little it all added up to.

"Jenny and me used to always gather maple syrup. There must be more 'n 200 sugar maples in them woods. The middle of March is best, when a frost comes at night and then a warm day so the sap'll run. You need that kind of weather for maple syrup.

"Deer used to come right up to the house to feed, there was so many of them then. I could drop one with my gun right here through the kitchen window, and often I did. We would a starved some winters if it weren't for deer.

"My wife said to me once, 'Charley, I think we best put in a crop of peas.' We owed somethin' on the place then, and by golly we pretty ne'r got enough on the peas that year to pay for the whole place.   There weren't nearly enough years like that.

"We made more money out a makin' fish boxes than anythin' else, once I got my saw rig going. I made fish boxes for all the fishermen here. About three feet long, with handles, about seventeen inches deep, if I remember. Sold them for fifty cents at first. Toward the last, it jumped up to as high as a dollar. Jenny and me both made 'em. Whenever we had slack times on the farm, we made fish boxes."

You do not dream the big dreams at age 88. When dreams come at all, they are small, dry little things like straw flowers, and mostly they are memories of the one woman you loved for so long.

"We had dances around here then. Jenny would play her mandolin, and one of my friends would play the concertina. I can't remember his name no more. We had good times right here in the house. They'd get up on the kitchen table to play, and we'd dance. I was a good dancer. All the women would want to dance with Charley. Most of us is gone now. Gee whiz, I miss 'em.

"Jenny's garden was somethin' to see. I had to let it all go the last few years, but the flowers kept comin' anyways. Look at them red poppies, will ya. They're bigger 'n a man's fist."

When you are 88 years old, your heart can still break for unrequited love.

"Yeah, we was supposed to be engaged. I bought her a ring an' everything. 'Charley,' she says, 'just in case anythin' should ever happen to either of us, so we'll be able to handle it.' So I went to the bank and got hold a the money for her. Then one night she calls me and says, 'Charley, I'm a-leavin' in the morning.' And she ups and goes and marries someone else, and plays a dirty trick on me like that. I didn't sleep pretty n'er a whole month after that. I sure got a foolin', didn't I?"

When you are 88 years old, you know a man never stops being a fool.

When you are 88 years old, you make conditional plans with your neighbor, who for some reason you call "Herb."

"You're too much in the woods there, Herb. Nothing'll grow. We'll put in a garden next to my old barn. That's good ground there. I'll get the cultivator fixed. We'll put in a patch of strawberries for the two of us . . . if I'm still around in the spring."

Notebook entries: Charley.

—Charley's old barn collapses under the weight of heavy snow. "As long as it didn't fall on our garden. Maybe we'll put in some squash this year."

—Charley on the telephone:"Can you get me out, Herb? It's been blowin' all night. There's snow piled to the top of my door. I climbed out the porch window, but there's more snow than I can shovel."

—Old Charley and his hippie-looking neighbor, how they all stare at us in the store. What ever brought the likes of them together? Old Charley with his cap pulled down over his ears. That neighbor of his with hair down to his collar. "I think next winter I'll let my hair grow long like yours," says Charley.

When you are 88 years old, you let your neighbor, your friend, write a story about you that you will never understand and very likely never read, for you never had much time or patience with the written word. What's more, your life never needed any explaining . . . to you.

When you are 88 years old, the dog barks at the first sound of a bird in the morning darkness, and you do not hear. You awake when the bedroom is light, pull on your clothes, harness into your suspenders, and wait to see what you will do today.

Uncle Tom: Socrates at Newport

It is winter in Door. The old Greek, all alone, looks out the windows of his house and store (built inside the old Newport school) and reflects: "I must watch myself in loneliness so that I don't get too eccentric." He remembers a line from one of his own poems: "All raindrops will not go down to sea but have other callings like you and me."

We leave him to his musings for the moment. First, some definitions in the Greek tradition: SOCRATES, Greek philosopher, father of the dialogue, compelling men to speak to each other in the mutual search for truth and beauty. PISCES, 12th sign of the zodiac symbolized by two fish . . . pisces, interesting minds, generous to a fault, dreamers. PROTEUS, the Greek sea-god who could change into any shape, but if seized and held, could tell the future. KOLOKOTRONIS, great leader in the fight for Greek independence. PHILOTIMO, love for strangers, hospitality. UNCLE TOM COLLIS, all of the above.

He's a cosmic man, he will tell you; "I'm a Pisces, born March 6, 1904. And I can always pick out another Pisces." Spiritually, the old man is made of stars, and the heavens are his stomping grounds.

So I speak of the Greek, and I speak of the Christian. I speak of the politician, philosopher, mayor, milkman, patriot, poet, candy maker, pancake man, Uncle Tom Collis, going on 74, owner of Newport School, resident of Ellison Bay (and Elmhurst, Illinois) and unofficial ambassador to Door County, the human heart, the universe.

If you know this sweet Greek of a man, you know how difficult it is to get any word in once he begins. You listen to Uncle Tom and then you go away, sometimes with the gifts of candy and popcorn this old Greek insists in showering upon you, sometimes with new insights into yourself, and almost always feeling a lot better than when you stepped into the warmth of his kitchen.

Fragments of the Pancake Man: Tom Collis, born in 1904 in Newark, New Jersey. His father came from Greece, his mother from Germany. At the age of three, Tom and the family moved to Gary, Indiana, where his father opened the first candy store on Broadway.

Candy, in the beginning, of course. Ah, the Greeks and their sweet shops and restaurants. What do you remember, Tom, about the candy store? "I remember a chute going down into the basement with huge blocks of ice coming down to freeze the ice cream; I remember fifty-gallon barrels of maraschino cherries; I remember making ice cream, my folks working around the clock—ice cream, ice cream, ice cream—and cherries at their best!"

His face, like a great actor's, going through all the motions, reflecting all the feelings of whatever he describes: sadness, pity, anger, love, laughter, concern, confusion, peace. The hands flying, the eyes rolling around, widening, narrowing, closing. Greeks are all emotion; they invented acting, too, not to mention comedy and tragedy. Drama has always been a part of their life.

What is it, anyway, with the Greeks, Tom?

"They were always good cooks . . . special flavoring and spices. They love people. They have always been able to draw people. That's the number one ingredient: love people! They took time to talk to people. Their generosity is tremendous. If you're a friend of a Greek, you're King! You're King, buddy! They say, 'Beware of Greeks bearing gifts.' Ha. No, not at all. If a Greek can't give you something, there's something wrong."

From Indiana Tom moved to Chicago—the old Halsted area, a Greek enclave—where "Pa worked in candy factories and Ma taught English to the Greek children. Pa had the formula for Cracker Jack, but he got rooked out of it because he couldn't speak English. Then Pa borrowed $300 from Uncle Alex and we built a house in Forest Park, Illinois. Around Prohibition, Ma found an empty store in Forest Park, the Belkow Saloon, and Ma said, 'Now we're going to start our store again.' We had nothing, you know. Nothing in those days. But then a fella came along and said to Pa, 'Tom, here's a hundred pounds of sugar to get started. Here's a hundred pounds of peanuts, fifty pounds of chocolate.' I always remember that. You can't forget that. When I had my own pancake business, I didn't forget that. Whenever I saw someone starting a business, I'd say, 'Here, forty pounds of pancake flour. You get that cash register jingling, buddy.' I've been criticized all my life for giving too much.

"The Busy Bee Confectionary, Pa's place was called. It went six years till our lease ran out. Pa saved $65,000 on 5¢ ice cream sodas and 15¢-a-pound candies! When he died, he left $100,000 in four envelopes for all the kids. But it was never found. You see why I can't worry about money?

"When we lost the lease, there was a lot for sale three doors east, and we put up a three-story brick building right on Madison Street. I said, 'Pa, I know a German clockmaker. We'll make an animated candy shop.'

This was before Disney! I had these ideas. I wanted to buy a machine that made lollipops, but Pa wouldn't listen. He took all the old fixtures and put them in the new store. Pa was an old handmade candy maker. I knew then, at age eighteen, my future with Pa and the candy making business was very limited.

Then I fell in love with a cute little hat maker next door, and I knew the candy business couldn't support two families. So I became a milkman. I went to work for the Standard Dairy of Maywood, 1926. I was just married. There were twenty routes. I was given three cases of milk, 36 bottles, and had to build it up to 200 bottles a day to make any money. In one year I brought the route up to the second highest in commission!

Tom stares at an old photograph of his milk wagon and horse. "My horse. I contended with that horse! Frank was his name, a little mustang with one nut. He would bite and kick. The real job was taking care of that horse, not selling milk. He would cut through everybody's petunia patch. He'd eat the gardens. I was always paying people off in milk for Frank. Then he would sit down in the middle of the street and not move!

"I stayed with the milk business thirty-three years. I started my own milk business in 1932? '39? Collis Dairy Products. During the Depression, two quarts of milk for 15¢ delivered, and nobody could pay. $100,000 in bills outstanding. I traded in my pleasure car to a farmer for milk. Yes, yes yes.

"Then Mayor. Mayor of Forest Park, 1939-1943. The war years. Oh yes, mayor. I wanted to run for mayor to make a better town. There was corruption in the whole town. I could never have got elected if I didn't take a stand. Campaign! I put a bottle of milk down in the kitchen, and I was campaigning! From 1929 to 1939 I was selling Tom Collis for mayor and nobody knew it. I won the primary without any organization! I had to defeat both the Democratic and Republican machines of Proviso Township. That was great personal satisfaction. 'This milkman won't get elected!' the said. That milkman was elected. The Greek community loved me. I could have been anything. They called me Kolokotronis. Kolokotronis, the George Washington of Greece. A revolutionary leader in the Greek War of Independence. I'd walk down the street and they'd yell, 'Hey, Kolokotronis!'

"I served four years as mayor, the rockiest four years of my life. It broke up my home. My wife left me. The thrust of the impact was too big, too big! I did all right for the people, though. I got the Navy to come in. They built the torpedo plant there, which created 5,000 jobs. That was my memorial to being the mayor of that town. And all this while I was still delivering milk—government to the door! Don't tell me it can't be done. It can!"

The ups and downs of Uncle Tom are a Greek epic in itself. "Turn me off if I talk too much," he says. So I turn him off temporarily—just not enough time, not enough space. How he lost his help and went out of the milk business. How he went to work in the very torpedo plant he helped establish. "I don't want any political job," he told the Navy. "Just give me a broom." How he started as a factory hand and, before long, helped redesign the gyroscopic parts for torpedoes, making them more effective. "Not knowing a thing about it, I created my own department from that with close to a hundred men working under me. That's why I encourage all these young guys who come here to see me: You can do it! You can do it!"

The ups and downs of the old Greek. "As mayor, I saw I was pursuing futility; war clouds started coming into my home. I could see my marriage was disintegrating." Even his success at the torpedo plant brought no peace. "I wanted to get out of there. I saw death, only death, in every torpedo." There were other job offers far away, "but I decided I was a homebody and moved to Glen Ellyn, built a house and opened a candy shop."

The candy shop, which became as famous there as his present candy shop at Newport School, was more than just a candy shop: it was a community center of sorts for the people, the students of Wheaton College and the local high school. "All found a home under my roof."

At this time he came under the influence of Dr. Raymond Edman, the president of Wheaton College, who helped Tom through the rough times. "He became the most important spiritual influence in my life, next to my mother." With his wife gone, his world was not so sweet a place on the inside, the old Greek candy man admits. "I blacked out for ten years. My whole life fell apart." Out of the candy business again, back into the milk business, and eventually out of that again, Tom began working nights at a food plant in Chicago, where he started to experiment with his own pancake flour.

"I used the formula my mother left me, but I was still experimenting. The first pancakes kept sticking to the grill. I had no laboratory. It was all trial and error. Finally I perfected it and began selling it to my milk route customers. It took ten years to make it profitable. The pancake is the biggest thing that ever came into my life. I sold out in 1972, but I still have an interest in it."

And through it all, the Greek as giver remained. "Right down the line, whoever needed help got it—fund raisings, what have you. I never charged for my time."

As for his love affair with Door: "I was married in 1926 and spent my honeymoon up here. I saw the place with young eyes. I went to Egg Harbor, Bertschinger's [Alpine Resort]. I saw in Door County what I saw in the Illinois prairie—unspoiled, untouched. I saw this picture out of my window here, fifty years ago [Tom pointing to the snow-covered fields and orchards, a herd of horses in the distance].

"But everything, everything has been a revelation to me. I knew in 1926 I was coming back here to stay." And here he is, finally, his first winter. "I could predict the future. [Ah, Proteus.] There has never been any doubt in anything I've done here. Everything has fallen in line. I bought this schoolhouse in 1962 and came up weekends, working on it. I knew what it was! I might be Thomas, but I'm not a doubting Thomas. I knew that success was here." Tom and his wife, Alecia Marquardt, now have a new home near Newport School.

Define yourself, Socrates. Success—what is it to you, Mr. Candy Man? "Very simple. Be a success as a man first, as much as the frailty of the flesh will permit! [The old Greek pounding his fist on the table, standing up.] Other success will be laying there for you to pick up off the street like gold! Understanding the trials and tribulations of other people. You can't be any better than the best you see in the other man. Take time to find out why that other man acts as he does—justifiable allowances. Only at such time as I can understand another man's troubles, can I offer compassion. I can offer that much: compassion. That leads to understanding."

Uncle Tom has been known to come on too strong. He's well aware of this, especially among the rather taciturn natives. "The average native here says, 'Cool it.' They have a tendency to be complacent. I have a tendency to come on heavy and back off hard. I'll take the middle of the road and break the loaf." But to strangers. . . .

"First I say, 'Welcome! Welcome!' [often running out the door and sweeping them off their feet]. 'Come in! Come in!' I show them around the candy shop. 'Where you from?' I ask. We get closer, closer. I not only aggravate conversation, I irritate it! People are frozen when they come in here. The world is cold, cold. People are troubled, hungry, trying to find a refuge, getting away from that rolling surge of greed. Have some popcorn, have some candy. The good Lord put everything in full measure—the lake, the trees, the flowers—but we stupid people haven't learned the capacity we have. You can do it! Anything! I tell you, they come in here small, and they go out like giants! Giants!

"The one basic thing that is needed by everybody is love of person. I'm not embarrassed to say that I love all these people. I pray for them. And I can truthfully say they love me. Where I can fit in the giving of myself, I do. There's no giving but giving out of sacrifice. It's the only evidence that you're giving."

Tom recently hosted a pancake breakfast at his place for seventy-five senior citizens from Washington Island. He has been known, all summer long, to serve breakfast on the spot to complete strangers. The Greeks have a word for that too: *xeni* which means both *stranger* and *guest*. In Greece they say the stranger is a god.

"Maybe I am running a kind of church here," he continues. "The things that I know, the things that I am, have not come from man.

"This is my first winter here alone. Yes, yes, I'm very satisfied. I've planned fifty years for this moment. The whole world that I've planned for fifty years lives right outside the windows here: my many, many smiling windows. Lonesome? No. I have letters to write, poetry to write, work to do. I'm teaching Marge Larson to make candy. Marge will be the one to take this all over eventually. There's a history of her and her family in this school. I'll stay open weekends. It's Saturday nights I have to watch out for: Saturday night blahs.

"I have no desire to settle down. And I will never give this up. I will not go back now to Elmhurst even for a pair of socks. This is it, yes. This is only the third act of a five-act play. I'll go down to the beach every morning and take care of my physical body. Reverend Aymond Anderson down the road will take care of my spirit. I have a 70-year-old body but a 30-year-old attitude. The best day is still unused, still out there.

"Yes, I'll stay open weekends now in the winter. I'll make candy and popcorn and hot chocolate. Skiers, snowmobilers, friends, please come in and say hello. You don't have to purchase, just visit! That's what I'm here for. This could be the Door County Hospitality Center. The real value is friendship, love.

"Too many people get too tired, want to give up. I hardly sleep at all. My mind is always working. I get up, look at the clock, thinking it's 7:30 in the morning, but holy cow! It's only 1:30! So I stay up!

"Over at the park, you know, where you can see Ephraim over the water: what a sight! You see eternity; you just want to grab it, grab it!"

The old Greek gesturing, holding the waters of the bay and Ephraim in his arms like the sweetest hunk of candy in the whole world.

Gerhard Miller: Dean of Door County Painters

This county begs to be painted, photographed, shaped, expressed in so many ways by the man and woman of art. It is difficult to merely pass through this landscape without feeling the need to possess it, and Door is a paradise for painters, creative people of all sorts: Lou Smolak, Pam Burns, Joan Champeau, Charlie Lyons, Andy Redman, Austin Fraser, Fred Johnson, Lionell and Bettie Wathall, Ruth and Phil Philipon, Karsten and Ellen Topelmann, Jon Dietrich, Dave and Jeanne Aurelius, potter Abe Cohn, leatherworker Mary Sisulak. So many other craftsmen and artists.

I don't know who captures Door County best. Some say Austin Fraser. Some say Phil Austin. One man whose work is constantly praised, even by artists themselves, is Charles (Chick) Peterson of Ephraim. More than once I've heard someone say, "He can do it all."

Yet before any of these artists entered the scene, a native was already hard at work: Gerhard Miller, master, and Dean of Door County Painters. The man's output is difficult to estimate, his appetite for life/art (one and the same to him) remains insatiable.

Thirty-three years ago he published a book, *Residue*, containing the poem "Drink Deep of Happiness":

> Whence comes this driving force that sends me on
> though buffeted by storm
> And oft thrown back against my will?
>
> For strength I pray, that I may for another day
> Paint racing waves
> Or birches in a quickening April breeze.
>
> And thus, in my small way, partake
> Of God's great universe.
> For then my soul can drink its fill of happiness.

Though he has been confined to a wheelchair the past few months as the result of a recent fall, Gerhard Miller, 74, persists in his art as he has always done. He has turned difficulty to strength before in his life; in fact, that is the way his life as an artist began.

"When I was a kid, eleven years old, I had polio. I didn't walk for a long time. Grandma taught me how to crochet washcloths. After a million washcloths, I turned to painting."

Miller was born in Sturgeon Bay in 1903. His father came here from the small town of Alimeth, near Bay City, Michigan, in 1896, and started a clothing business in 1901, a business which in time Gerhard himself took over. Most of his life Gerhard has been both businessman and artist—an unusual combination, especially achieving success in both.

"I went to the University of Wisconsin for several years, majored in Business Administration. Then Dad became ill and I had to come back and run the store. I was in the business full time in 1927, retired in 1960."

After his washcloth period, the desire to paint stayed with him. "I painted more or less through high school and college. I had paintings in the county fair and all that bit. I painted in oils then, landscapes around here. The sort of thing all the amateurs do—painting birch trees. Oh, you better not put that down."

Miller is very conscious of the feelings of others. It is difficult to imagine him ever hurting any living thing, or saying anything unkind about the work of amateurs or professionals alike.

"I didn't really get seriously interested till after I was married, but I always had a studio, even when I was a kid. After I married, we lived on Memorial Drive in Sturgeon Bay, and I apportioned an attic and made my studio there. It's important to have a place where you can sort of cloister yourself, leave things be. A place where you're more apt to get your work done."

In 1936/37 he built "Nordlig" ("the most northerly") on North Bay Shore Road. It is the home/studio and gallery where he and his wife Ruth still reside, reflecting her concern with home as a living art in itself, reflecting the painter's intimacy with the Door landscape: water, trees, light, all the natural resources which keep the artist aware of a sense of spirit in his work.

First success is never entirely forgotten. "You always hope that sooner or later you can sell something. I finally sold a little painting for $15. I must have been around thirty when I sold that painting. Oh, before that . . . I must have been fifteen or sixteen when I sold the very first painting for $4.50. It was a little flower painting of cyclamen. The painting I sold for $15 was a little landscape from over in Potowatomi Park. It had a couple of pretty birches in it."

Recalling the first $15 he made, he explains, "I always told my wife we'll use some of it for materials and put the rest in a kitty for travel. The kitty grew, and I never took a nickel out of the clothing business for these things. Our trip to Greece this year was my 26th crossing to Europe. I've been to Canada, Guatemala, Mexico, Yucatan, Africa, Egypt, Morocco, Lybia, Syria, Jordan, Yugoslavia."

One of the very first "serious painting trips" he made, to Nova Scotia, was most important to his artistic career. "I wanted to meet a painter, Roy M. Mason, who was living at that time in Batavia, New York, on a place he called Woodchuck Hollow. I wrote to him asking if he would criticize some of my paintings, and he answered and said he would be happy to. We packed the two kids in the car, stopped at Roy's on the way, and he couldn't have been nicer. He had us stay with him. I got my first criticism from Roy, my first lesson. I was probably about forty at the time. He said to my wife, "This guy is on the right track. Don't let him study with anyone. He has to paint a thousand pictures.' "

Gerhard's wife, Ruth, whom he married in 1957, after the death of his first wife, remains closely by his side, so much a part of Gerhard's world, his art, that it is difficult at times to even separate the two in conversation. "We go together," he says. She anticipates his reactions, he relies upon her impressions and memories.

When I ask about the artist's painting habits, his ability to proceed as an artist and run a business at the same time, Ruth answers. "He would paint in the morning before he went to the store, paint at noon when he came home for lunch, and paint at night. He's a perfect example of 'If it's in you, it'll come out.' Gerhard always earned a living, and in addition he painted."

"I could get in an hour in the morning," Miller continues, "a half hour at noon, then a couple of hours in the evening. If you do that consistently, you can get in quite a bit of time."

"He put his whole mind on whatever he was doing," adds Ruth. "His work at the store was another thing entirely."

"I learned one thing from Jens Jensen," continues Gerhard: "the importance of singleness of purpose. I always wanted to paint. I must have had it in mind that I would always do it. It was just a matter of when the time would come. I always enjoyed the clothing business, though."

"He knows everybody in the county because he either sold them a shirt or a pair of socks," laughs Ruth.

In the 1940's, he gradually turned the garage he had built into a little shop and then turned the carport into a little gallery where he "began to hang a few pictures. Then the war came along and things got blocked off, so we just closed up till after the war. When we reopened, it just became a gallery. Ruthie is the one who does the great job in handling the gallery. She's more knowledgeable about art than at least twenty other people," he smiles.

There is no mistaking one of Miller's paintings of the county for anybody else's. He has a native grasp for the mystique of the landscape. He has the talent, the diligence, the craft to focus on a scene, take it inside himself, and render it into something beautiful, something personal, something timeless.

He defines himself through his work habits. He explains his early attempts in painting the county as "drawing on the spot. I never painted on location, I don't believe in it. You get too overwhelmed with detail on location that you forget what it takes to make a picture. I have to concentrate on what I'm doing, like a doctor, in a controlled light situation with no interference.

"Painting outside is too precarious. I like to spend more time thinking about a painting, planning it. That's what I do when I got out sketching.

Ruth interjects: "He develops his morgue, frankly" (the morgue: a collection of very rough sketches, akin to a writer's notes). "Most of his paintings are composites, not anything special."

"From the sketch I go to the finished drawing, and from there, to the painting. But at this sketch stage I establish all lines, make my mistakes, think about composition and values. At the second step, I can really establish my values. The final step is the color. You're pretty much discovering yourself by then."

Miller has some very definite opinions on what it takes to make good painting. "There are certain things that become prerequisites in art. You have to exercise your imagination. You develop a good memory. Then you have to have a sense of color. Color to a painter is as important as perfect pitch to a musician."

Although Miller began as an oil painter, somewhere around 1939 or 1940 he turned to watercolor. "I think I did it pretty much for the time element. For watercolors all you need to cleanup a brush is to soak it in water. I could do more in the limited time I had. Then I found out I liked it. Later I began to get a little disenchanted with watercolors because they had certain limitations."

In 1965 both Gerhard and Ruth received fellowships from the Huntington Hartford Foundation in Pacific Palisades, California—she in writing, and Gerhard in painting. "I began experimenting with egg tempera then, about the early '60s. That's the important medium for me now. But that was an outgrowth from watercolors."

He attributes his disenchantment with watercolors to a number of things. "There's a cult of watercolor purists who use the page for white. They limit themselves. I don't want to be hampered by any rules. For instance, you need white in a sky. It lends a solidity to the sky that helps you create atmosphere. Another thing, if you want anything reproduced, a transparent watercolor reproduces poorly. The main point is, I don't want to be limited."

"With egg tempera, you can do much more definite painting," adds Ruth.

"I'll do anything to get the results," Miller says. "Also, I don't mean that I don't have respect for purists. I do."

For an artist whose work is so synonymous with the essence of Door, a discussion centering on his native landscape lends light to just what this particular artist sees. When did he become aware of this special atmosphere? How do things really look?

"I was aware of it at a very early age," he explains, "because I got out an awful lot. It was a much more exciting place then than it is now. We used to stay up at Newport at Pete Knudson's boarding house. There was a long dock there, it must have been six hundred feet or more, where they loaded the schooners with lumber. Jacksonport was quite a fishing village. I used to drive up there to deliver oilskins and southwesters to all the fishermen. But that's all gone. If I want to paint a fishing village now, I have to draw upon my imagination, my memory.

"When I was a kid, the schooners used to come in and anchor off our house on Memorial Drive. The minute we came home from school we'd hop on a boat and go out. We'd sit on the decks of these schooners and listen to the skippers tell us stories. They would give us fresh baked bread, and we would sit there and listen. My mother, who had a mega-phone, would then call us back.

"There were dead bones of old sailing vessels sticking out of the water by the ship company. I used to roam the woods, but you see, there really isn't enough left to paint in the county as it used to be. You've got to paint whatever's left. At the rate it's going, it'll be gone.

"I used to be the only painter around here, and I had a lot to paint. Now there are more painters and less to paint."

His trips to so many different parts of the world—do they influence his Door county paintings in any respect? "One influences the other in this respect: you sharpen your perceptions. You're always holding them at a certain level of perception back home, so you see things more clearly when you come back home. It's all part of an exercise in training to be more perceptive."

When it comes to the particulars of the home landscape, the things a painter sees and loves which make his particular patch so different from other places, Gerhard pauses for a moment then says, "We live in a rather rugged part of the world. Not the most comfortable, but very dramatic. Complete changes in season. Complete changes in weather, from hot sun to thick ice. I can't imagine waking up every morning to the same kind of thing. We get a thrill from the first flower to the first snowfall."

"There is nothing bland about the peninsula," adds Ruth.

"We're surrounded by water," continues Gerhard. "We have a varying terrain. We've got about as much variety as you can hope to get in a concentrated area."

His paintings, however, do not necessarily portray the people of Door, because, he explains, "I haven't had any academic training. I haven't had any experience at it, on that particular score. I'm not as knowledgeable as one who can. Whatever I got, I had to get out of books or these people who were kind enough to criticize my work.

"I know the people, though; I can still remember many of the people who have strong pioneering traits. I know so many nationalities—the Belgians, the Germans, the Swedes—such a tremendous variety here, and each different.

"One of the reasons we were so interested in giving the art gallery [the Miller Art Center in the Sturgeon Bay library] to the county was mainly because we have such a love for the place. We could move to Florida or Arizona and pay less taxes, but we would be deprived, giving up a lot of the joy that we love. "

In analyzing his own work, his own drives, his personal theories of art and success, Ruth is quick to point out, "Gerhard has never accepted a plateau. People always ask, 'Aren't you sad to see a painting sold?' But once Gerhard has painted them, he forgets about them. He's so concerned about the next one."

There is no end to learning for the true artist. All experiences become part of the man, and sooner or later, part of the art. Ruth again points out how both she and Gerhard study in every museum they visit. "He reads more books than anyone can imagine."

"I don't think I've changed in my thinking, really," explains Gerhard. "I'm basically interested in imaginative realism. I believe that art is something that has to be very well planned. I don't believe the Creator did what he it without some very good planning. Things just do not happen. There's always a cause and effect."

"Gerhard always says, 'If you aim low, you will hit low. If you aim high, you will have a chance," smiles Ruth.

Growth, then, continues to occupy the man and his art, though his goal, at the outset, may seem a very simple one: "to just paint a better picture. You don't always do it. If you can think to the point where you can see where you can make a little improvement over the last one, if you're going to indulge in life, you're going to have to grow.

"This whole wheelchair business has turned out to be quite an experience the last three months. It's surprising how I've learned to do things. I've got a bunch of drawings done, got half of them framed, and I'm doing all this in the normal way, only slower. I find I can manage these things from a wheelchair. As a matter of fact, I've even learned to do a wheelie!" Gerhard laughs as he pops the old wheelchair in the tradition of a biking enthusiast. "I get outside; I've learned so much."

Religion, as Gerhard concedes, "is always a good question."

"We support churches," suggests Ruth, "because we wouldn't want to live in an area without churches."

"Any picture that you do has to have a certain spiritual quality about it," adds Gerhard, "otherwise it is not going to ring a responsive bell as far as other people are concerned. Religion to me is like art, and art is like religion. It is part of life, to the extent that one has to continually grow."

"We can't become part of a church that becomes too authoritarian," explains Ruth.

"Fortunately, the Moravian church doesn't let that happen," says Gerhard. "The Moravian motto is: 'In essentials, unity. In nonessentials, liberty. And in all things, charity.' We can live with that."

Planning is important to Gerhard in both life and art. His year follows a definite pattern. "I'll first work on a lot of drawings in the fall. Then I go to the small paintings, doing quite a few in one long session. If I work steadily at them, I get progressively better. After I put in a couple of months on all this exercise business, then I'm ready for the important pictures, big pictures I have been subconsciously planning all that while. My major output is from winter to spring.

"I can't do anything in the summertime. Most of the time is for the gallery. The summertime is not the time to paint anyway. Everything's too green, overloaded with foliage. You can't see the anatomy of the trees properly. Fall, winter, spring are the seasons to paint."

"I like to roam around the farm areas. I still like to look through red barns, regardless of what these sophisticates say. If I have to paint a manure pile, I'll put the stink into it! "

Miller declines to play the numbers game when it comes to "how many hours/days/weeks/months/years does it take to do a painting?" or "how many paintings has he done?" It takes any artist his entire life to create any piece of work. Time has no meaning in that respect.

"When I kick the bucket, the county will be so overloaded with my paintings that the county will be glad to see me go," laughs Gerhard.

Not true. There will never be enough Miller paintings, for each is unique, each a separate vision of one man and one instant of love. The question of an artist doing too much, weakening, losing his true perspective, perhaps, and turning to mere potboilers for tourist consumption, intrigues Miller, though he is certainly not guilty of it.

"What your aim is, that's the only thing. I think the thing to do is to give more thought to what you're going to do. Some people are very knowledgeable [in judging good from bad paintings] but on the whole, they've got a lot to learn."

His mention of Jens Jensen earlier brings us back to that time in his life when he knew Jensen well, taught for him at The Clearing, in Ellison Bay. "That was probably in the middle 1940's," recalls Gerhard. "I taught up there for seven or eight years. You couldn't help but absorb some of his philosophy. That's when some of us became converts to conservation—before anyone heard about it."

Jensen did some painting too, and here and there about the county (mostly at The Clearing) evidence of his work remains. Did Jensen and Miller ever discuss painting? Did Jens ever approach Gerhard for a critique? A lesson? "He never asked me about painting. I never saw him paint. No, we never talked about it. We just talked about the things in nature. He did most of his painting in early spring, when the sap begins to run. I noticed one of his paintings the other night at The Clearing. You could just spot it was done about the middle of March. He could see things in nature that other people didn't see. His philosophy was very simple, very straightforward—just fighting to correct the mistakes that other people made."

Gerhard Miller's paintings have gone far beyond Door, to galleries and museums across the country, including the Metropolitan Museum in New York. They can be found in private collections here and around the world. There are private collectors in this country who each own twenty or thirty or more of his paintings. "Vincent Price must have bought over a hundred paintings from me."

And though the price of his work has risen somewhat beyond the first flower painting for $4.50, or the Potowatomi landscape for $15, the question of fame, of value of art, is difficult to answer.

"If you make too much of that," says Ruth, "people will buy a signature rather than a painting. It's what it does for you; that's the most important thing. The only reason for buying a painting is because you love it, not because it's an investment."

"The important part as far as I'm concerned is to paint the picture," says Gerhard. "Jens Jensen gave me a very profound appreciation of just plain nature. That's where perfection lies: if a painting is well done, it will gradually enhance itself in the eyes of the beholder. It'll just get better and better all the time. If there's something wrong with it, it can only depreciate in time. It has to have the mood, the spiritual impact. And that will carry it."

There's another poem in his book titled "Ad Infinitum." The first line reads, "Happy is he who is prophet of the beautiful."

And the last line reads, "An artist is he who of life hath made use."

Roy Lukes: Naturalist

I first became acquainted with Roy Lukes—naturalist, student of plants and animals—through his column, "Gone for the Day," which appeared weekly in the local paper. Although I am a city man—with a city consciousness that feasts on a steady diet of metropolitan newspapers with foreign and Washington correspondents, book critics, and columnists like Mike Royko and Sydney J. Harris in particular—I soon discovered that I needed Roy Lukes and his common celebrations of the great outdoors as much as I needed all the Washington analysts rolled into one . . . and certainly more than the front pages of all the major newspapers with their daily renditions of the same old story, man against man.

If I found his columns a little bit hokey at first, I now attribute this to my own ignorance of the "genuine country boy," an "innocent" in a way, an extraordinary man still given expressions like "Yikes!" "Wow!" "Holy Smoke" and "Lo and behold."

"Chickadee number 106-74490 has returned to our yard" may not be the greatest opening line for a column, but the fact that it's a chickadee that Lukes banded himself on April 4, 1967, gives both him and the reader cause for wonder. . . .

"This means that the bird had to have been born during the summer of 1966 or before. Simple arithmetic will show that here is a chickadee at least seven years and four months old (born in about June). You're correct. This is very old for a black-capped chickadee, such a tiny bird. And perhaps, if we're lucky, he'll return next fall to prove that chickadees can live to be eight years old too!"

Startling? Perhaps not for some people, but somehow I find that the lifespan of the chickadee is more comforting than the lifespan of the American presidency during the past years.

In column after column of utter simplicity and down-home writing, Lukes leads you quietly into his own world, his own sanctuary. And whether he's talking about Franklin fireplaces, snowflakes, gentians, wild cranberries, redpolls, snowshoeing, skunks or swans, it's all there free, if only you'll take the time to look around. (One of Lukes' favorite and fairly simple messages is that hardly any of us experience enough.)

In every column, season through season, there is always this quiet joy of simple things, of a man in place, which he invokes so effortlessly in his opening lines: "Happy Days! The woodcocks are back! Rather I should say happy ducks, for this is when the males' unusual aerial sky dance and song take place." "The fox sparrows are coming through now. Have you seen them at your feeders?" "Spring wildflowers are beginning to carpet the woods these days." "How much is one evening grosbeak worth?" "A rosy pastel sky greets me at 5:15, a beautiful good morning. By 5:45 Old Sol shows himself down east through a narrow slot of open sky, shows himself only briefly as though to say, 'Hello down there, you lucky people!' "

It's been some time, perhaps, since many of us considered ourselves lucky people, yet with this attitude, a naturalist's attitude, Lukes looks upon our natural world as a place we somehow deserve and must learn to respect.

Sometimes a man is more than his writings, and in some cases, a different person altogether. Not so Roy Lukes. He is what he writes. He knows who he is, as I discovered for the first time, some three summers ago during one of his 5:30 a.m. bird walks at the Ridges.

"Good morning," he said as he approached us from the upper range light residence where he lives, "I'm Roy Lukes. It looks like a swell morning for bird watching. Well, here it comes," he said, pointing to the eastern sky. "Here comes the Old Haymaker!" And indeed it did, right on schedule, almost summoned by Roy's hand as he coaxed the sun above us.

He had a telescope already fixed in place as I recall. What I recall more than anything that morning was the constant consideration he afforded my seven-year-old son, always giving him first crack at the telescope or his own pair of binoculars. "After all," he told us, a group of about ten adults and one child, all strangers, "this little guy is the most important member of the group. He's the fella we're going to have to depend on someday."

"What a valuable man to have around," was all I could think of that morning, and for years to follow, as I continued to read his columns, follow his tours at the Ridges, attend some of his lectures and slide shows, and see him occasionally in town. There was always something else, it seemed, to ask Roy Lukes about. (His phone rings constantly with local people and friends questioning him about birds and plants, reporting some strange sighting in the bird world.)

What time of the year do rose-breasted grosbeaks come through? Where do juncos winter? Where can I find the morel mushroom? Must ask Lukes about the pileated woodpecker sometime . . . Indian paint-brush . . . whip-poorwill and wintergreen.

Consider now the Naturalist as Teacher. We talked about this recently—his background, his education. Does a man just wake up one morning and call himself a Naturalist, or is it something like an artist, something that takes hold of a person and directs his whole life to the point where there is no distinction between what a man does and what a man is?

Lukes was born and raised in Kewaunee, Wisconsin. He has fond boyhood memories of the great outdoors, outings with friends, picnics with parents, a setting conducive to natural explorations. He went to Door-Kewaunee Normal for two years, followed by a two-year stint in the Army during the Korean War, and then completed his education at Oskosh where he received a Bachelor's degree in elementary education.

"I was going to enter the masters program at Madison then," he recalls, "but I was offered a job teaching seventh and eighth grade in Shorewood, which was a good break for me. Of all the places I've taught, Shorewood was the most satisfying. The parents took a genuine interest in their children. Not only were they fine people, but I learned so much from them. I could see what they were doing for their children. These were professional people, many of them very interested in nature. In a way, it was the parents who got me interested in nature. They belonged to all kinds of clubs. I formed several nature clubs at school with their help. When you can see people take such an interest in you, then you can do something. I don't think I've ever been happier teaching than I was in Shorewood."

He reviews his own early education to see if there might be some clue there as to where it all began for him. "No, I never had any guidance from teachers at school. I never remember taking field trips. My father, though, was quite interested and knowledgeable in the outdoors. My father was a mushroom hunter. In spring my folks liked to pick wild-flowers. We would frequently take a picnic lunch and spend the whole Sunday along the Kewaunee River.

"At Oskosh I had a Professor Talbot for biology, probably the most inspirational teacher to me. He would bring animals to class, bats from the attic. He was the first person to seriously interest me in nature study. He was the kind of teacher that you wait to come along, and he finally does.

"Also, a Dr. Owens, an ornithologist who led us on bird walks. He had a real background in ornithology. He knew just what birds to look for and where they were. He was a very dynamic person."

Lukes went to Madison for his Masters in Elementary Education in 1958, taught junior high in Wisconsin Rapids for two years, then returned to Madison. "I missed Madison, the Audubon Society, my friends there. You could go just a few miles out of the city and be in the countryside. I have to admit that Madison was an excellent place to start teaching. But then I got wind of an opening at the Door-Kewaunee County College in Algoma. This was my first chance to teach in my home area, so I grabbed it. That was 1962.

"It's funny how things work, almost like fate. I had gotten my bird banding license by that time, and I remember I went bird banding with Harold Wilson [of Ephraim] and Murl Dusing [president of the Ridges Sanctuary at that time]. The three of us went on this banding trip, herring gulls on Jack Island, one of the Strawberry Islands. We set a record that day, banding 1,100 gulls in three hours.

"That day was a key day in my life. The Ridges board had been talking about a summer educational program, and it was like all of a sudden the three of us looked at one another and Murl asked, 'Say, how would you like to work at the Ridges next summer?' Holy smoke! Well, I got to thinking about it, and I decided to give it a try.

"I really set myself the task of learning about the area from that summer till next summer. I had to teach myself all the natural history of the place. When I came here, the Range Light Residence had been vacant for a few years. I've been here now for ten years.' "

An opening developed at Fish Creek Junior High in 1966, and Lukes taught science there for four years. "During my last year there I began to look into the idea of going into teaching on my own, being a sort of environmental education specialist. So I set up this program. I simply outlined the types of things I would like to do with teachers and students. I gave teachers an idea of ways I thought I could help them."

Lukes, born teacher that he is, began to reach out beyond, a single school building, a restricted grade level set-up. He had the summer program at the Ridges to "teach" adults about birds and botany, the unique history of that marvelous preserve in Baileys Harbor. He had the weekly column in the *Advocate* too, as a teaching device. And he was preparing to reach all the way down to the very young—kindergarten, first grade, second grade, third grade and on up as well—because he knew instinctively that preservation and appreciation of natural wonder had to begin there. So he divided his time among the various school districts that saw fit to hire him.

Kindergarten? How do you teach environment to five- and six-year-olds? "I give them a lot of things that they can handle. That's important: handling, feeling, touching rocks and leaves. We go outside and look at these things. I have models of birds they can hold."

His program for the various grades reads like a Whitmanesque poem, a veritable catalog of natural beauty. Kindergarten: rock & fossil awareness, spring birds, spring wildflowers. First grade: trees, their wood, bark & leaves, etc. Second grade: marshes, fields and woods, cottontail & red fox, soil study, terraniums, planting seeds & growing plants. Third: tree identification, rabbits, raccoons, porcupines & skunks, rocks of Door Co. & their study, birds of Door Co. & their songs. So it goes, from one grade to the next, one subject more fascinating than the other, a growing awareness of the natural world.

Which age group does he prefer? He almost hates to have to make a choice, to be put on the spot. "To me there seems to be an age when all this begins to jell a little bit, all of it come together like a puzzle. I'd say the third or fourth grade. It's a kind of magical age."

On the education trail with Roy Lukes, I follow him to Southern Door Elementary School one morning just to catch his act with a group of fifty third-graders. It is not so much an act as an incantation to nature.

The minute we step into the building, kids from all grade levels drift up to him. "Good morning, Mr. Lukes. What are you going to tell us about today?" "Hello, Mr. Lukes. Are you going to show us some slides?"

Southern Door has one of those special open classroom situations where five or six classes meet simultaneously in a huge area comfortably carpeted and furnished with learning situations and stimulations, it would seem, at every child's fingertip. It's an atmosphere where a child couldn't wait to go to school and see what was happening today. The presence of Mr. Lukes this morning intensifies the atmosphere with even more excitement.

"Good morning boys and girls," he says.

"Good morning, Mr. Lukes," they politely reply. The kids sit everywhere, on chairs, at desks, but mostly on the floor, semi-circled beneath his feet.

Lukes notices a shelf fungus that the regular teacher has displayed near the blackboard and launches immediately into the meaning of its name—shelf, bracket. "Isn't this a beautiful thing?" he asks, as he takes it into his hands and discusses it with the children. "There's a name I like even more than *shelf fungus*," he says. "What else does this remind you of, boys and girls, when I hold it like this? Notice the shape of it." Hands fly up everywhere.

After a few long guesses, someone finally comes up with "turkey." "Yes, the turkey tail fungus," says Lukes. "Or some people call this the partridge tail fungus."

"They grow on old trees," another kid ventures by way of a little more explanation. "In our woods, sometimes we see them on old trees."

The topic for today, though, is not fungus. "We're going to talk about wild animals today," says Lukes. "And the thing that I would like you to imagine this morning, boys and girls, is that all of you are wild animals. Now here are some clues as to what particular kind of wild animal I would like you to imagine today.

"You are about this big," he gestures with his hands, and you're furry, with a bushy tail. . . ." Hands again fly up all over the place.

"A fox," one kid says, two kids say, three, four.

"Correct," smiles Lukes. "A red fox. Now, if we're going to be foxes, that means we're going to live outdoors: no stores to buy our food from, no cars or buses to take us everywhere. Think of how you're going to have to live. What are you going to have to do to stay alive? What are you going to need?"

"Shelter?" volunteers one kid.

"Yes," says Lukes. "Describe it. What kind of shelter?"

Once again all hands shoot up, and answers of all sorts pour forth: a rock, a tree, a tunnel, a barrel, a cave, a bush.

"A tunnel is good," he says. "What else would we call this?"

"A fox hole." "Good." "A den?" "Yes." "A burrow." "Yes, yes. And how do you get this den for a shelter, since foxes don't like to dig burrows?"

"You're going to have to chase out some other animal?" asks a kid.

"That's right," says Roy. "As a fox you're probably going to have to look for what kind of a hole?"

"A badger hole," answers another kid.

"Very good. Now, what else do you need besides shelter?"

"Food," says a little girl.

"Tell me: what kind of food would like to eat if you were a fox?"

"Rabbits," answers a boy.

"Do you think a fox can run fast enough to catch a rabbit?" asks Lukes. "How many of you think that foxes are faster than rabbits?" Not too many hands go up. "Right. Rabbits are a little too fast for a fox. Yet, how can you find a rabbit if you want one?"

"Well," says one kid as he goes into a long "supposing" situation, "You can learn where the rabbit lives. And then one night you can hide behind a tree and wait till the rabbit sticks his head out and then catch him!" He gestures the swift capture, much to the delight of his classmates.

Roy doesn't deny the kid/fox his rabbit in this way, but he does deftly slide into the matter of wounded and crippled animals, and how nature handles this. "Along the highway," he explains, "a fox might find a wounded rabbit for food."

Within a few minutes you can tell Lukes understands the learning process and knows what effective teaching is all about: not giving answers from the standpoint of omniscience, but letting kids discover their own answers, weighing them out loud in an atmosphere of complete freedom, under the guidance of a teacher who is no more than a person with a little more experience, imagination, patience, and with great love.

I reflect on this while nearby a teacher of the old school lectures her charges on behavior, keeping their desks neat, keeping quiet, listening, not making a mess in the classroom, and on and on into the depths of boredom and deadly learning situations. To have open classrooms, you must have open teachers. Perhaps, for only an hour, you must allow your children the freedom to fantasize that they are foxes.

Lukes this morning is a bit of a fox himself, an environmental fox. Unbeknownst to the kids, he's slowly leading them to conclusions and wonder about their own relationship to the good earth. By the end of his session with them, he is turning the tables on them, trying to get them to re-examine the role of the fox in nature's pattern, to compare the needs of the fox—shelter, food, water, sun, protection, transportation, air—to the needs of man. "Who's the user; who's the abuser?" is the message underneath. He gets them to re-think the attitude that "all foxes should be shot because they kill chickens," a particularly ingrained rural attitude.

"Not necessarily true," claims Lukes. "Do you know what men have found in opening up the stomachs of dead foxes? Mice. More field mice than anything else. And you know how field mice can bother the farmer's grain." Chalk one up for the preservation of the red fox.

"Now how many of you think foxes are good?" he asks. "How many of you think foxes are bad? You know what I think? I think foxes are better than people! Why?"

And then the teaching begins to show, from third-graders no less. "Well, they don't use gasoline like people," claims one kid. "They don't waste electricity." "They don't waste food." "They don't dirty the air." "They don't smoke."

Ah, Lukes, you old fox, you've got them, I smirk to myself.

"Do they use plastic?" he asks in a mild evangelical manner.

"No!" the kids chorus.

"What about iron, steel, tin cans?"

"Noooooooooooooo."

"As a fox, you have learned to use the things that are right near you, the things that will grow back again. Maybe this is one of the most important things to know, not to waste anything, to pattern our lives after the fox, to keep our lives simple."

End of lesson.

Yet even Lukes, as naturalist, as teacher, as "fox" is not entirely accepted for his full value in the schools, the community, and parts of the county. I've never met a kid he taught who hasn't admired him and wished for more. As for adults, well environmentalists everywhere continue to have problems with people who feel the natural landscape is theirs to exploit rather than preserve, understand, and take only spiritual sustenance from. Call them illegal hunters, call them land developers, call them plain ignorant in most instances. And color them all greedy.

One would think that in these ecologically aware times, the value of one Roy Lukes in any school district would be immeasurable. In Milwaukee, Madison, Chicago and suburbs, one Roy Lukes would be worth a fortune to any school system. The county would be lucky to hold on to him in the coming years. Yet one local school district has never considered hiring him, while another quietly dropped him this year using lack of funds as some sort of excuse. We buy new school buses instead, new equipment of all sorts, and continually fail to invest in the best teachers to be found.

Lukes remains silent about this, but you can tell he's hurt. He is not a one given to making big waves, but I have a young son who reveres the knowledge and excitement this man brought to the classroom in the last few years. Now he is to be denied this for "lack of funds" . . . and this in one of the juiciest school districts around, as far as tax money goes.

"How much is one evening grosbeak worth?" he asks in one of his columns. The question we should be asking ourselves is, how much is one Roy Lukes worth to all of us?

"Since most my life has been teaching, I'd really like to think of myself as just going along, doing this in different ways. I find a great deal of pleasure in teaching and writing about these things, giving programs. It's the best way I can meet people, influence the most people, in a way. I wouldn't be doing this if I didn't feel there was a need for it, even though the destruction of nature is practically a losing battle."

The end? Not quite. First back to the Ridges, the beginning, back to Lukes' own natural habitat, looking for the real ending, yet knowing with such a man, it's all the same, just a change of seasons, that's all.

Should I end with a note on Lukes' latest joy, the creation of a Nature Center in the Ridges in the very near future, a place for "continuing education" for both young and old? "I'm just trying to get people to be more aware of their surroundings—animals and plants—learning from them. I think I'm trying to get people more and more away from artificial enjoyment of life to real enjoyment of the outdoors. Obviously I'm against most mechanical things in life."

Should I end with our discussion of the spiritual? "I've only had one deep discussion with this minister once—seeing God in nature. I'm a firm believer in plant evolution, yet it really doesn't make much difference how all this came about. I'm interested in the here and now. It's so much more important to take an interest in the things we do have. We should be interested in caring for these things. Obviously, and my wife won't like this, I don't have a very strong religious background. Yet I know very religious people who are totally ignorant of the natural, of the way the outdoors is. To be outdoors with nature and people, that's what religion is to me. I feel I can go out and spend an hour sitting under a tree, and reflect, and feel I've spent as valuable an hour as sitting in church."

No, I'll end with our short hike through the Ridges, down Winter Wren Ridge, with Lukes himself in the lead, the constant teacher, pointing to all manners of wonder around us.

"How fresh it smells here, how invigorating: deer tracks, deer ruttings, mating season. This is high bush cranberry here. Ruffed grouse like these seeds. This is running club moss. People tear it up and use it for Christmas wreaths; they shouldn't. Here, winterberry . . . taste it." Lukes bends down. "At times I almost feel that I'm anthropomorphic; these plants are like old friends. I know just where to find them, year after year."

He stands before a balsam fir and cradles a branch. "This is the tree where I stopped with the blind woman. She was the first blind person I had ever taken through the Ridges. What could I do for her? What could I possibly do for her? I wondered how I could help her see what was here. I led her to this balsam fir so she could touch it, and she took a branch and rubbed the needles to pieces in her hands. For the rest of the tour I watched her bring her hands to her face, smelling the fragrance of the pine."

The End, I guess. Except that that particular experience eventually led to a Trail for the Blind, still under construction at the Ridges. And even this is not the end for a naturalist, teacher, or of Roy Lukes' character as he ponders the real problems of blindness. "What I have in mind is for people with sight to also use the blind trail, to blindfold them, to lead them in, to sharpen their senses. . . ."

That's as good a beginning as any.

John Henderson: The Dark Man of Door

He is much like the character in Ralph Ellison's novel, *Invisible Man*: you see him, but you don't see him. He often appears where you least expect to see him, then fades fast in your eyes. He's everywhere and nowhere.

Once he turned up as a guest at a gathering of the Clearing-in-Winter. One summer I saw him in the stables of the Birchwood Farms Riding Academy introducing his city nephews to the wonder of horses.

In summers past, he could often be seen hanging around Wilson's, in Ephraim, with the young people, always raising a few eyebrows amongst the tourists. (He is not *that* invisible).

He was, and still is, quite popular, quite approachable—an oddity perhaps. Friends are very important to him. He claims he has many, though he is most often seen alone. I've talked with him, even joked with him occasionally through the years. Many of us do.

John Henderson, 36, is one of a kind. If there were ever a minority, it is he: the dark man of Door, resident since 1965.

Questions persist in the mind of anyone with the slightest interest in human survival in the county, in the country, in this day and age. What's a black man like you doing in a place like this? How deep are the friendships? And if the quality of loneliness is measured by the extent of being outside of things, isolated in one's own skin, how does one man, one black man, hack it alone in these parts?

We may all know *what* John Henderson is, but *who* is he?

His physical presence, of course, reflects the features of his race, even its history. He is "as black as the ace of spades," as John himself might say without anger or shame or any of the slogans of the '60s.

"I'm proud of myself," he'll tell you. "I'm proud of my heritage. I wouldn't want to change it any other way. Mankind was created by God. He created us all. If I'm dissatisfied, I'm saying God was wrong. I can't do that. He made me the color I am, and I'm proud of it. I always will be."

He's slight in stature, with hands so large as to be almost out of proportion for his size, and the tip of one finger missing. His head is vaguely skeletal, with a high boniness to his face, stretching the skin to a sheen, making his whole expression hard at times, mute, resigned . . . until John Henderson meets a friend, breaks into a laugh, or talks about the way things are with him.

"I came up here the summer of 1965 from Milwaukee. Worked there in hotels as a busboy, a cook. I went to visit an uncle in Missouri one winter. He was going to come here to pick cherries. I said I'd go with him, but I finally came up with some guys I met there who had been here before. I got to work for Dale Seaquist, and that's where I stayed."

His first reaction to Door? "I don't think I had any. Always just wanted to be outside, could never stand being inside much. More or less I wanted to be out of the city. Too much of a rat race. There's just got to be a place that's more peaceful. After the cherry season, Dale said he needed me to help pick apples. I said I'd stay and help him, and that was it. I stayed seven years with him working on the farm. I enjoyed the work. It was outside. He was a good guy to work for. I really loved working for him. He fixed up a cabin for me. Everything. It was well insulated, it was livable, it was comfortable."

Either time passes very quickly here for John Henderson, or it doesn't seem to move at all. He left Dale Seaquist after seven years to take a job (salesman-driver) at the lumberyard. "I needed to make more money," he confesses. "We're still good friends. I've helped [Dale] out a couple of times since then. I'll have five years in at Lamperts [in Sister Bay] in February."

There's an amazing calmness about the man, an acceptance of things—manmade or natural—just being what they are. Winters are just winters, "the same here as in Milwaukee." And even with the absence of family (his mother, father, one sister, and four nephews back in Milwaukee), there's a concern, but not a desire to return. "Ever since I was eighteen years old, I've been on my own, making my own decisions."

His life seems simplified to the acts and possessions of daily living—a job, a car, a dog, friends, a place to stay—with little thought of wanting or expecting a great deal more. He once had a phone, but had it taken out. "I'd get a call maybe once a week, or every two weeks. What do I need a phone for?

"I get home from work, either make supper or go out to eat. Oh, once in a while I'll go out with a couple of friends—maybe just to eat, listen to music someplace. And there's always fishing. Tweety [Chuck Tveten] and I have a lot of places to fish. We enjoy fishing together because it's always a contest—who's going to catch the most fish, the biggest fish. It makes it more fun.

"Usually, though, if I go out, it's alone. Other friends I meet out. You sit down and chew the fat for a while. I think if you keep your mind occupied, you don't get lonesome. I do a great deal of reading—*Popular Mechanics, Workbench*—not so much television. I like working with wood—mostly knickknacks—anything I feel like with a scrap of wood. I took a course at Gibraltar with Bill Beckstrom. He was a real craftsman.

"Walking in the woods, long walks on the beach. I think in the County here you have a chance to stretch out. You're not crowded—room to move and breathe. You can lay out at night and watch the stars. You can see things here that you can't see in the city. There's a closeness to nature.

"I can't think any man is really satisfied with his life, because he's always trying to do better. Right now all I want to do is be happy, healthy . . . just to live. I have a lot of friends, but I want just time to be myself."

For the second summer now he has brought his four nephews up from Milwaukee. "I try to show them something about nature. It's good for them to be out of the city for awhile. I worry about them back there. How easy it is for young kids to fall in with the wrong type of people, make the wrong friends. Of course, you can find that any place. I love kids. A kid is funny. He can sense instantly someone he can trust. He'll automatically take a liking to that person. I've been able to get along with all the young people here."

As for meeting other blacks in the county: "Once in a while in summer. It makes me feel good to see another black, just to talk to him. But he's still a stranger, and there's not much to say. I'm not in the habit of it being an everyday thing."

There's a religious side to John, too (Baptist), which at one time he testified to rather openly, as excessively religious folk have been known to do. John's calmed down a bit the past year or so. Something personal he'd rather not talk about. He still has the faith, though. He's just grown beyond the organization.

"I got interested through Dale and his dad, John Seaquist. I think they were the biggest help in my spiritual life, more than anyone else. They would explain things to me, why Christ was important in our lives, things I couldn't understand. They were more than helpful.

"Once you have something, you can never lose it. You can get away from it. If I was to say every time I need guidance I would turn to the Bible, that would be lying. But whenever I want it, it's there. And it's good reading material."

John Henderson has lived a history of names. He's kidded a lot at work. They call him "nigger," "Black John," damn near all the tags we attach to someone different than ourselves. In CB lingo, he calls himself "Rusty."

"It never bothers me," he smiles. "You know the guys you work with. It's done out of kidding and joking with one another. We never think anything of it because there's no harm meant by it. I guess anywhere you go you're going to find prejudice. If it's not against blacks, it's against someone else. But I can't say I've really been bothered by it here."

As for the television series *Roots*, "There were parts I liked, parts I didn't like. It told some of the truth. I can't believe everyone in the South was mean and cruel toward the blacks, 'cause then if I said that, I would be lying. I've always looked at life this way: you can make it good, or you can make it bad for yourself. I've never been prejudiced. What happened in the past, really, I can't do anything about that. Why should I hate anyone for the way they treated slaves? That was their lifestyle at the time."

John Henderson is either years behind the times, or light years ahead. The "invisible man" wears a green work shirt around the lumberyard with LAMPERTS on the back. Over a front pocket is stitched, in yellow, yet another name for him, for easy identification: "Good John."

John smiles. "When I first started at Lamperts, there was another guy working there. They called him Bad John."

Albert Zahn: The Man Who Carved Birds

Though the birdman himself, Albert Zahn, has been dead since 1953, the "birdhouse" which he built—where he lived and where he carved—still haunts that dark green cove of cedars off the main road in Baileys Harbor in glorious dereliction, weathered shadows of birds and all.

It is the one building in the entire county that compels an almost spiritual attention, not to be missed or forgotten—even, sad to say, by vandals and thieves. But it remains a living museum in a way, the daily transformation of a reality into dream, myth, and art itself.

Its presence begs explaining—and painters, photographers, story-tellers have all had a hand at it. "What is that place?" "Who lives there?" "Look at those strange birds."

Albert Zahn was a simple farmer, woodcutter, with a native intelligence for form which he expressed almost mysteriously, reverently, in an obsessive carving of birds, most of these in his later years when he turned over the 160-acre farm down Meadow Lane to a son and retired to the house he built in Baileys Harbor. He fathered ten children, six of them still living, three of them still in Door County.

"He was born around Pomerania, in Germany," says his son Elmer Zahn, sixty-seven, "and came over here at the age of sixteen to dodge the army." The youngest daughter, Evelyn Langohr, claims he settled first in Forestville where he worked as a well digger, which brought him to the Baileys Harbor area where he eventually settled.

"Dad died in 1953 at the age of eighty-nine," she says. "We left the farm when I was ten years old, 1924. My oldest brother took over then. The farm has never been out of the family."

But the carving: when did it begin?

"He carved already in Germany as a boy," she recalls. "In Germany he was like a sheep herder. I remember his talking about taking care of sheep and how he whittled while he did this. He carved a few things on the old farm. I remember there were some birds on the post railings of the porch. He did this just to trim things up. I just remember there were birds, and I don't think they were painted. That came when we moved to the house."

Don Langohr, her husband, remembers the old man's skill. "Sitting there, talking in the evening, he'd carve three birds, small ones. He used cedar: the body was one solid piece of wood. The wings he'd wire, putting the wire in there with an awl. He used nails on the smaller stuff. He carved with just a jackknife, a handsaw to cut the wood, and a hatchet. He could take a hatchet and chop a piece of wood to shape like nothing. I've never been able to figure out how he could do that, but most of it was done with a jackknife."

And those first birds that began to appear on the farm? What became of them? Evelyn shrugs her shoulders. "I don't know. The old house isn't even there anymore."

Do you have any of his work?

She disappears into another room and comes back with a large wooden bird painted in gray, brown, and yellow, which she sets down on the kitchen table. "The kids used it for a chair for years," she laughs, explaining its rockiness on the perch and a broken wing which Don has repaired with a nail.

"It's a hawk," she explains. "Mother did all the painting. Dad didn't know nothing about painting. But this came later on when he moved to the house, when the birds began to sell. My mother bought a small book with pictures of birds so she would know how to paint them."

The house—what about the house, the unusual design?

"He built the house with the family," she remembers. "There was dad, mother, me, and brother Albert. It was all poured concrete, all mixed by hand. I don't know where he got that design. It must have been something he picked up from a house in Germany. There are no others like it around here that I know. It used to be painted blue and white. What is it now? On the columns outside was a bird on each one. He built that little cupola on top later. He called it his penthouse. He even had a bed in there. But he really built it so it would be easier for him to get on the roof and fix all the leaks."

The purity of the artist is such a rare thing these days, and if the work of Albert Zahn continues to fascinate us, it is primarily because of the combination of purity and primitiveness in the man, the art. There is something incredibly ancient and refreshing about a man "making art" (for "trim" as Evelyn says) just for the sake of making art (like American Indians), unconscious of artistry, value, or fame in the world of art.

"He had no interest in selling birds when he built that house," says Evelyn. "It started when he began putting birds outside and people began stopping and asking to buy them from him. Evidently it was the house with the trimming that made them stop. He thought that was okay. He let people roam around. He never put up a private sign. Everybody was welcome. He would sell the birds off the pedestals, and then he would replace them.

"He had no workshop as such, nothing close to a studio. He carved right alongside the kitchen stove," laughs his daughter. "Mother would get so mad because of the mess he made. The stove, an old-fashioned range, stood out this far. The wood was piled right behind it. He used to pick wood right out of the pile sometimes."

Though he occasionally carved other animals—deer, lions, even toy boats—birds seemed to occupy the heart and hands of the man. It is difficult to discover why.

"Nobody ever asked him about it," as far as his daughter can recall. "Nobody was ever that interested in it in the family. He never taught any of us to carve. It was just a pastime, a little extra money coming in. That was all."

"He used to go into the swamp there," Don begins remembering, "and cut wood all by himself. We'd go in there and sometimes find him sitting on a stump watching the birds."

So there was that and . . . "They had canaries," Don remembers. "He used to make canary cages."

"And I remember back on the farm an eagle used to come every once in a while," says Evelyn, "and he knew where the nest was."

And that is all. Nobody knows just how many birds the old man ever carved. Nobody is quite certain what ever happened to all of them.

Another son, Bill Zahn, seventy-seven, says, "He just done it for a hobby and made a living at it: 25¢ for the smaller birds, up to $5 for the largest. He was strict," he recalls. "He knew that Bible pretty ne'r by heart."

The man continues to elude us: only a glimpse here, a glimpse there.

"As far back as I can remember, Dad had gray hair," says Evelyn. "He always looked old—chin whiskers, goatee, mustache. He loved kids. He had to have something for them. He'd give away lots of the smaller birds to kids if they didn't have money. He was strict, but he was good hearted."

As for fame? Neither Evelyn, Bill, nor Elmer ever heard of his work being exhibited in a gallery or museum. "I know artists used to come and paint the house," says Evelyn. "Then their paintings would be exhibited at the county fair. But the house got the attention, not my father. Some of the birds are in Chicago, I heard. I remember a man, a Mr. Fritz, bought a lot of them for a kiddieland outside Chicago, but he must be dead by now."

"A lot went to Chicago," agrees Elmer; "to the Merchandise Mart for display, I think."

Chicago artist Bill Stipe, a Zahn enthusiast for years, recalls some of his work in private collections, some of it once displayed in the windows of Marshall Field's. As for the old man's obsession with birds, "He was a primitive," Stipe explains. "He worked it all in his head."

In 1965, twelve years after his death, some of Zahn's work was purchased and exhibited by the Benjamin Gallery on Michigan Avenue in Chicago. A sketch of the birdhouse and the birdman by famed artist Aaron Bohrod appeared in a 1975 a book, *Wisconsin Sketches*.

Who knows where it all ends, or the value of an old man's carvings? His son Elmer can only say, "Because there won't be any more, they must be worth something."

Whatever the disposition of Zahn's handmade birds, there is still the birdhouse and some of his birds to ponder, to enjoy. Though the house was sold more than twenty years ago, whatever the old woodcarver (perhaps Door County's only primitive artist) was and what he did lingers in that area of Door, adding yet another dimension to the essence of so intriguing a setting.

You can turn to the family for answers—and find some. You can look at the birdhouse—and find a few others. Or you can stare at the carvings up in the windows, discover a veritable tree of colored birds, including one piece, a haunting, mystical work painted white, with eight woodpeckers harmoniously clinging to the base and trunk, with the uppermost birds looking up, paying homage to what appears to be an angel with a crown and white wings encompassing all.

Whatever he was about, Albert Zahn, in the true way of the artist, never explained. He left us only the secrets of birds, the evidence of angels.

Bill Beckstrom

He was already a living and local legend in his later years, though he didn't flaunt it, was not aware of it entirely, and received far less attention than he deserved. I regret I was unable to do more for him, with him, but what is there to say about an ordinary plant lover? Except that in his case, he was an extraordinary man.

His name came into the conversation again the other evening as I am sure his name will continue to be acknowledged around the county for years to come whenever there is any discussion of plants—or woodcraft, music, landscaping, Jens Jensen and the Clearing, Viking history. His interests were infinite, his experiences astounding. The question that evening concerned the purple flower that graces the fields and roadsides of Door in the fall. What is it? A thistle? No. Is it called "napweed"?

"If Bill were around, he'd know," I thought aloud. That's just one of the things about him that we've lost, that I already miss. Beckstrom could tell you the common name, the Latin name, the history of the plant, and throw in a few personal experiences he might have acquired in his own green and growing years.

"Where is Bill?" somebody asked that same evening. Silence. I found it hard to believe that anyone was unaware that Beckstrom was gone. But Bill always kept a low profile even to the very end. He rarely came to you; you came to him.

"He's dead," I answered, shocking myself with the terseness of the reply. "Beckstrom's dead," I repeated, trying to confirm the fact in my own mind.

"That which I should have done and did not do" is a haunting refrain over the loss of anyone, and a terribly haunting refrain in this instance over the loss of a friend, an intellect, an incredible source of natural history. I doubt any man alive knew as much about native plant life in Door County as Bill Beckstrom. I sincerely doubt any other man ever will. I don't mean a field guide mentality, being able to identify one wildflower from another. I mean an intimate knowing and caring for the total life and history of the most inconspicuous of plants. That kind of a man and a mind is gone.

He could tell you exactly where witch hazel grew, high-bush cranberry, native anemone, all manner of mushrooms, every kind of tree. He constantly surprised you with species which grew here that you never knew existed.

"There are succulents [cacti] you know, native to Wisconsin," he'd say offhandedly. No, I didn't. Then he would begin on yet another adventure with plants. An encyclopedic mind, a born storyteller, a natural teacher who thrived outside the deadliness of classrooms. For a self-taught man with a sixth-grade education, the merits of formal education leave a lot to be desired. (And we worry about school bus routes and hot lunch programs.)

His classroom was his shop, the Red Barn Plant Farm, his house, his garden, and, more and more in the final years, his corner table against the north wall at Al Johnson's restaurant. When Beckstrom sat down, you could not help but learn something. People were always picking his brain. He began his ritual of coffee and a cigarette, fingers yellowed and stained from years of nicotine, and inevitably the comments, the questions, the answers, the observations would unfold. "Well, gentlemen, I think we've solved enough of the world's problems for today," he'd say before leaving, but he'd be back two or three or more times in the course of the day and night. For me, he helped make winters bearable. There were times in February when the only thing to look forward to was meeting Beckstrom for coffee at Al's.

With his gray crew cut, a facial expression both sharply distant and intensely open, he cut a distinct figure dressed, as he frequently was, in a wool shirt, a Scandinavian sweater, and checked pants. He had flair. He had taste. There was never any doubt that he dressed or looked or thought like anybody else but Bill Beckstrom.

He was thin, he was wiry, and though the years of hard living had undoubtedly taken their toll, he was tough as hell. Bill Beckstrom in his sixties was still a very young man. Or so he thought, and so he lived, often despising others of his age or older who had given up, who lived in the past, who let their brains go soft.

Enough. I can hear the Beckstrom critics already whispering in themselves: "But he was a scoundrel. He was a drinker. He was an irresponsible family man." I seldom heard a person credit Beckstrom for his artistry and his intelligence, who did not discredit him in the same breath for his drinking habits. It seemed an unexpressed satisfaction that a man of such talents had a weakness which might lessen his stature in the eyes of ordinary people.

He was morose at times. He could be arrogant. His personal feelings were not something he shared with everyone. But he did admit to me that he did not like to cook and eat by himself, that *that* was loneliness.

When he was really down, he disappeared for days, weeks, always working it out himself in the solitariness of his room with the two truths he sought most at these times: alcohol and classical music. Dvorak symphonies and Slavonic dances blared from his confines at all hours of the day and night till eventually a friend would have to go in after him and see that he received help. What was it that plagued the man so? And why must we judge?

He never was honored as Chieftain of Ephraim's annual Fyr Bal festival, though he probably knew more about the Vikings and local history than all the past Chieftains lined in a row. Some say that bothered him: the holier-than-thou attitude of some villagers in denying him that honor each year because of his habits. (Beckstrom had a singular dislike for self-righteous people: "They're all a bunch of goddam hypocrites.")

Some say he never achieved all the fame and success he felt he deserved or was capable of, and that plagued him. He was unsatisfied with his lot—a very human trait. But he was, in this man's opinion, a very old, old soul. The next time around, he'd make it.

So you honor him now for all that he knew about the natural life and all that he freely shared. You honor him for all the woodworking artistry he left in the county, shaped with his hands. You honor him for the legacy of fine craftsmen who came under his influence. (He had a strange attraction for society's dropout culture: hippies, wanderers, the back-to-nature cult. He identified with them for all his sixty-eight years, finding them just as impressive as leaders of industry, society, and the arts.) You also honor him because at the age of sixty-six he told the boys at Al's one morning, "The hell with you guys. You're beginning to bore me. I'm going to Europe. A person needs a change of climate." And he picked up and went, all alone. You honor him for putting on a pair of ice skates last winter, at the age of sixty-seven, and cutting a mean figure on Al Johnson's pond. (He was a champion skater in his youth.)

And you honor him for the dreams deferred: a projected trip to South America just before he fell ill ("There's incredible plant life down there"). A future trip to Greece to do, perhaps, a book on the plants that made a habitat in the crevices of the ancient ruins.

But you honor him mostly for sharing his presence and friendship, frequently with complete strangers. I speak for all of us at Al's who spent a special part of the morning with him—Lou Smolak, Ossie Burstrom, Lew Pillsbury, all the waitresses, Al himself, and so many others.

Beckstrom is dead. The man will be missed. The coming winter will seem considerably longer and more boring. Waitress, more coffee, please. And by the way, do you happen to know the name of the purple flower that lights the fields in waves of lavender at this time of year?

Beckstrom would have known.

Ernie Anderson: Woodworker

He's a relatively young craftsman, thirty-two, though old in his ways, preferring hand tools to power equipment. He is very quiet, very retiring, a man who literally fades into his work. Summer finds him escaping in his homemade sailboat on sunny afternoons; in winter, cross-country skiing through the back areas caters to his stillness. That's Ernie Anderson.

Under the proper conditions and given the right medicine, the man's passiveness fades, and he talks, he laughs himself crazy, he tells grand and almost perfect stories far into the night. A man with a true sense of humor, a great lover of classical music, an omnivorous reader, and a very keen mind "for sure," as the natives say. How does the old line go? "To look at him, you wouldn't think so." First impressions are dangerous indeed.

Unruly hair, scraggily beard, red bandanna, worn clothes, a pickup truck, and the saddest looking dog in the world, named Moses. Let's confine him to that subculture of Door called Hippiedom, or the "dropout people" (a much larger subculture than some would care to admit). Pockets of them here and there in the county, more visible in summer than winter, hold down the odd-job market. Hippie carpenters and builders, some of them are called. Yes, artists and craftsmen among them as well. Like Ernie, for example, who couldn't care less what you thought of him or what class of Door County he belongs to, though he'd appreciate it if you valued his skill.

He works in almost cave-like conditions of an old apple storage building that once belonged to Sid Telfer's "Driftwood Farms" and now is owned by John Dietrich, the potter, who lives and works upstairs. There is Ernie down below, ankle-deep in sawdust, shaping wood; John up above forming clay: what one might call a creative "centering" of sorts, for the north end.

Ernie began making furniture about six years ago. Prior to that he ran the usual Door County gamut of ungainful employment from odd-job carpentry to the famous Sister Bay Sewer Project. "I made a dinner table for Dar [Darlene Cooper] for a Christmas present and really enjoyed that. Then the Langs [Merlin] saw it and wanted me to make one for them. Then I made some small cabinets for a while." And then it slowly began happening: with some guidance from Bill Beckstrom, an increasing personal awareness of design and technique in the handling of wood, and an overall desire to be in charge of his own life, Ernie Anderson began developing into one of Door County's finest craftsmen.

"I get the feeling that real craftsmanship takes a long, long time. I consider myself just beginning to become accomplished. The mechanics of it are just practice and forethought. The real difficulties are controlling the material. I like the design part of it, and I don't have too many problems with it."

The County itself affects his work in interesting ways. "There's a surprising amount of timber here, a good variety of hardwoods and softwoods, birch, cherry, even butternut, although that's getting scarce— almost everything but walnut. One of the reasons I got into woodworking is that it enables me to make a living here, where it's really difficult to find any kind of satisfactory job. The economic opportunity is still very low.

"I got into Scandinavian design when I first got started with Al Johnson. I designed things for Ingert [Al's wife] which specifically fit into her boutique. She became sort of a patron for me, and I really think that ought to be said." (Some of the finest examples of Ernie's work are to be found in Al's today—from the stools at the counter to some of the furniture in Ingert's butik.)

Scandinavian design? "It's heavier, thicker materials. The construction techniques are very similar to Early American country furniture, except that the Scandinavians are not as austere. There's a little more ornateness and a lot of curves and things."

The Ernie Anderson trademarks are trestle tables, benches and chairs—all of his own design. "I take a special pride in my tables and benches, in that I can construct them entirely without metal fasteners. They can be assembled and held tight with wooden wedges and pins." Though Ernie does not have the time or, perhaps, the incentive to submit his work to art shows and national competitions, there is little doubt that his craftsmanship measures up to some of the finest being done in the country today. One might even project that years from now, whatever might become of the County, a piece of Ernie Anderson furniture will be a good find indeed, and a part of the local history. (Just as the work of the late Bill Beckstrom is beginning to be more and more appreciated.)

Still, the dollar and cents factors of everyday existence are a constant reminder that craftsmanship of the kind Anderson practices is a precarious existence at best.

"For my part, it's been easy to get business lately, but still, at times it's damn hard to make any money. My type of woodworking has a very heavy cost factor. Most of the gross income I make is taken away by cost of materials and my time." Unlike other craftsmen/artisans, Anderson cannot make two dozen tables in an afternoon.

"I haven't been able to find any nice, handmade wooden pieces that can be made with any rapidity at all . . . no bread and butter items. It all takes a lot of time. My experiments with mug racks and pipe boxes all proved too time consuming in the end. When you begin to cut the time down, you end up with an unsatisfactory object. The only solution— raise my prices. But there's another dilemma I go through.

"For example, I was engaged to make a large round table and six chairs. After the bargain had been made, the people, on second thought, wanted everything stained. The original figure I gave them was too low anyway—$650. Then I had a lot of trouble with the stain. I had to strip two chairs completely, which took a lot of time. I think I came out making maybe less than a dollar an hour on that one.

"Another dilemma is that I don't really think that the crafts are booming, yet every craftsman in these parts must pay the same cost of living that the people pay who come up here with their inflated city dollars. Consequently, I can't buy an old rundown farm to live and work like some of these people did ten years ago." Nor can he come close to even touching an acre of Door County land today.

Any serious artist or craftsman, in addition to the monetary reward for his work, appreciates (sometimes even more than money) the person, the "customer" who recognizes and values the essence of the work itself. Ernie, in particular, is aware of this. I recall him once finding it very difficult to part with a beautiful cherry wood chest because he was certain that the people who wanted it couldn't care less about all the time and art he had put into it. "There are some people, customers, who are quite wealthy, who scarcely glance at the craftsmanship, choosing something just to 'fill up' their summer home. They need a table, so they go out and buy a table. You hate to let it go under those circumstances, especially when the work gets down to the final stages, spending a lot of hours sanding and finishing. It's dispiriting to know that the possessor is going to be more or less oblivious to it.

"The second type of customer I call the 'romantic.' He likes the idea of something handmade. He likes solid wood, appreciates its being good wood, but doesn't have any real glimpse into the workings of it, or what is really good and might just have a good appearance. But I like the romantic. Sometimes you find yourself trying to do a little bit more for him, like picking boards with attractive grains, more character. You tend to pick these out of a pile for people who are really decent, appreciative.

"The third type is very rare: someone who has a real understanding of working with wood. Someone who will be very critical, know the aspects of joinery. I don't really meet too many people like this, and they're not always customers. Sometimes they just come in to talk. I'm always glad to see them. You can learn from these people."

The values of a craftsman? Pride of workmanship, of course: "If it looks fine to me when I finish. I'm paid like a tradesperson, money per hour. I like it all, though. I like to be standing in shavings. I like the smell of it all. I like my tools to be shiny and sharp. And I like to receive just a reasonable amount for my work.

"I don't know so much about the other artists here, but the young craftspeople are here for the most part because they have an intense dislike for the city—and I am able to make sacrifices for that in order to live here. And that goes hand in hand with my style of life because I don't have to be working all the time."

Speaking for some of the other young craftspeople, Ernie contends, "They're all embittered by the rate of commercialization and development going on here. They're discouraged by the rising costs. Yet most of them do own a place. The market here is good, but still strictly seasonal. That's one way in which I'm more fortunate. I can take a dozen orders and be busy all year. Actually, I can only handle less than a dozen a year. The last set I did—a table, a bench, and four chairs— took about 135 hours."

Looking again at the people he deals with, Ernie claims, "I possibly see only one or two personally: older/wealthy and young professionals. Almost all of my customers are outside the County. I found that really surprising. I thought I'd be making furniture for summer homes here, but very few of my things have stayed. Almost all of them have been taken back to the city. I'd really prefer my work to stay up here. In my designs, I always sort of had places up here for them in the back of my mind. They fit better into a rural home with their massive, clear finishes. They blend in a lot with the local cedar people are using in their buildings up here."

As a native of the County, born in Ephraim and educated at Gibraltar, Ernie may be more aware than others of the changes going on. Maybe it's the fact that he left the county twice (once for Vietnam, once again to kick around Europe) that he sees and feels a little differently about the place than those who never left at all, and certainly those who just arrived. Then too, pretty much a loner with no family to speak of, he remains quite apart from the native way of life and more in tune with the subculture of drifters, dropouts, that whole new generation of back-to-the-land people with their wood stoves, natural foods, organic gardens, and homemade lives.

"Natives," he remarks; "you know, you hardly see any natives anymore. You sort of wonder what's happened to them." The subculture he describes as "people living on very little money. They're all around, and they get by. The county still provides some cubby holes for these people. They get enough wood for their fires. They own a few pairs of old blue jeans. It's very easy to find a little work here and there, but very difficult to find anything that's really decent. The tradesman here still makes wages that were made in the city fifteen years ago. But there's always something to do, somewhere to make a hundred bucks that'll carry a guy into the next month. Dropouts? I often wonder if the dropouts are not the ones who get the most pleasure out of this place. There are hundreds of them, I suppose, so many of them between Egg Harbor and Ephraim. I was in Omnibus back some time ago one night, and I'll bet there were twenty faces there I'd never seen before. I don't see a lot of them. For the most part a lot of them do carpentry. Some of them even get it together and contract themselves for jobs. Waiters, waitresses, kitchen help. The whole thing really seemed to start in the early seventies."

Ernie, too, drifted in again about that time. His story was the return of the native, only he was a native who almost got away, having graduated from the University of Wisconsin, Madison, with a major in English, intent on teaching on the university level. "I was going to go to grad school, but never did. I just got tired of going to school after all those years." After serving in Vietnam as an aerial observer, "I sort of dropped out. Came back here to live. I had a little cabin by the shore— Hedgehog Harbor in Gills Rock. I took a very long, extended vacation which I enjoyed thoroughly. Then I went to Europe and traveled extensively, spending all my army savings—Spain, Morocco, Algeria, Italy, Switzerland. Came back again, got to Milwaukee. Interviewed for jobs, the kind of job someone with a liberal arts education thinks he might get. I ended up working in some really crummy factory job just to get a few bucks. I saved enough to come back here. I've been here ever since."

He has not noticed much resentment on the part of the natives over his lifestyle, though he himself is part of the past and part of the changes going on. He doesn't like all that he sees, and harbors a natural pessimism that the land is closing very quickly. "Everywhere you look another area is closed up. One thing I especially find disturbing—urban people who come up here, buy property, and have this highly developed sense of property rights and privacy. It took me a few times of being bawled out for trespassing for this to sink in. Such an overdeveloped sense of property! It seems they're obsessed with the idea that something's going to be carried away from it, even though it's been standing here untouched for years. I remember walking around Garret

Bay in heavy woods, in wet land totally unsuitable for building, and suddenly coming across an enormous sign in the middle of it, in big red letters: PRIVATE. Someone's acre of heaven, I guess. "

Still, he doesn't see himself or too many of the craftsmen moving out, regardless of the inevitable changes taking place. "I've got into this conversation several times, even willingly: 'To hell with this place; I'm going to some place that's country!' But if it's really country, how the hell are you going to make a living? And crafts are a good way to make a living.

"If there are enough people coming up here who are wealthy enough to buy a tract of land and hang on to it, that'll help to keep the land open. Even if you can't walk on it anymore, when you're driving down the road at least you don't have to look at a house every fifty yards."

So the craftsmen, perhaps, will remain for a while, and the craftsmanship will continue and hopefully contribute to this special landscape. I toss Beckstrom's name out at Ernie Anderson at the end in the hope of making a connection, bringing it all full circle. What part does a man, an artist, an individual of the past play in the present life?

"Here's another thing about growing up here: some of those few, incredible people who were around. I always refer to them as the 'exotics': out of place, very different, very well educated people. I worked for Beckstrom all the way through late high school and college, every summer. For the most part it was landscaping, and in the shop as well a little later. But aside from learning landscaping and woodworking, just being exposed to someone like Beckstrom who had an enormous collection of books, classical records . . . he was just a whole different breed of humanity which you certainly didn't find at Gibraltar High School.

"One of the things I always admired and liked him for was from the time I was sixteen years old, he was always willing to talk to me on any subject. And no matter what you were discussing, by the end of the day he would always appear with a whole armload of books, which was all sort of incongruous at times, because he could really be sort of an irascible fellow. Yet I don't think I ever found him ignorant of anything, from Gothic architecture to Alpine plants or how to leave a butternut log lay in the woods for a couple of weeks so it gets wormy."

The Chicago Run

"How far are you from here?" It depends, it depends.

Door County, Wisconsin, to Chicago . . . a feeling for distance.

Chicago is about 275 miles from my place in the woods. It depends upon conditions, physical, psychological, climatic. I've made the journey hundreds of times in the past few years. Hundreds of times, particular times, under the guise of a man who seems to know where he is going, but is usually lost in the shortest distance between two points.

"How far are you from home?" It depends. At times it seems I step out the door and I'm here (or there?). At other times, I anxiously eye the slow procession of highway markers and damn near weep, wishing the journey were over. "When the hell am I going to be there already?" It's like a steady rerun of that old dream: running, never arriving, yet extremely conscious of the loss of time.

I speak of solitary journeys: a man on the road alone. Those journeys remain quite distinctive. Sometimes adventure, sometimes dream, sometimes nightmare, and often heightened by both excitement and despair.

To stay on top of it all, you discover it's best not to dwell upon where you're at. You consult neither watch nor mileage indicator. You remain oblivious to road signs or the various guide markers you habitually set up along the way to remind you of near and far in your constant coming and going.

You just get into the car, you turn on the radio, you light up some tobacco, and you move in the direction of home . . . where you have to be, where you should be later the same day or night.

Home is supposedly the real destination of all our journeys, but am I leaving it, or still looking for it? Is there really such a place on earth at all? I moved from a Chicago neighborhood to the countryside some years ago to find the answer, I've dug into Europe twice, and I still don't know. Sometimes I think nobody's ever home. Sometimes I feel all the real meaning lies in the frenzied movement between places. "I must be going" means more than goodbye.

So I prepare to return again to that other life I exchanged years back for "life in the country," a life of sidewalks and newsstands and corners and alleys, tangible settings I miss so much at times that I walk here through an open rural landscape visualizing Chicago neighborhoods, bars, restaurants, and streets all hours of the day and night. I can walk into a forest of birch and maple at midnight and see myself on lower Michigan, heading for the red door of the Billy Goat.

"Gentlemen, I am sorely in need of nourishment on this frosty night. A double brandy and a beer should do it."

Now I am up again at 5 a.m. in the winter darkness, throwing a suitcase and notebooks together, filling a thermos of coffee, saying goodbye to a family asleep. I have a couple of stories to work on back there, and as this is my livelihood for now, the journeying must continue. Chicago means survival for me. So I go, too, to keep those fires burning.

And journeying is conducive to all sorts of wild imagining. My homing stories are peopled with fantasies and projects. I have authored thousands of stories, pictures, poems, letters, and books in the miles in between here and there. Most of them are now forgotten, though I ride now with a notebook always open to capturing whatever image, vision, or object might lead to further discoveries.

The conflict is felt the moment I step outside to begin the journey. Sometimes the moon looms close enough to take a chunk out of it with your teeth. Sometimes the density of stars whirl in such wonder a man can lose his footing if he stares too long. The stars just don't shine down upon Chicago like that anymore. The air, too, is purer here than anything you'll taste in the Midwest, though the pollution of paper mills and from Green Bay is beginning to take effect.

I dwell on these natural things awhile because they do make a difference. They have made a difference in me.

There will be wind, too. There is always wind here to be either seen or heard in the branches of trees. It is too early yet for the birds, but they are roosting in the cedars and bushes around the house, waiting for dawn and me with my bag of sunflower seeds. I fill their feeders with a double measure against my absence.

Silence now in the starry morning, except for the foghorn on the lake a few miles away near Death's Door. It is the only unnatural sound in the landscape, yet in absolute harmony with the soft feel of things. Besides, it's good for a man to live close to water and be always reminded of it. I revere the sound of the foghorn even more than the sound of church bells.

The conflict, it would seem, has disappeared in the natural habitat I am tempted to call home. Yet as I back the car toward the road, a quiet excitement for the city begins churning in my gut. I slowly pull away and soon lose sight of my home in the woods. I'd like to think I don't look back, but I do. And I keep hearing all the old arguments breathing down my neck. "Don't you *hate* going back to Chicago?" "How can you leave this place?" "Oh, you're so lucky to be living here. None of the crime and dirt of the city." "Door County? We love it! As soon as my husband retires, we're going to move here for good." "What a perfect place to raise kids." "At least you don't have the Black problem."

"Wonderful Wisconsin . . . We Like It Here" goes the current hype. I can understand that, but I can't accept it completely. There's a certain arrogance to it which is unnatural to me. I am not a bumper sticker person for any person, place, or thing. If you like it here or there, fine, but don't remind me, or ram your homilies down my throat. Place is at best personal, and always imperfect. And one man's home can be another man's prison.

I moved here because I could no longer afford to write fulltime and live in the city. I moved here because the untouched wonder of the landscape intrigued me, and I wanted to experience it and be part of it to see if a man could live with it for good, or for as long as either one did not change.

Right now, I've got the juices going as I barrel my way through the darkness. Chicago, here I come. The radio is blaring out John Denver's "Back Home Again," and the pipe tobacco's smoking real fine. Home— Chicago—still lies somewhere ahead in a bit of a haze. You just don't shake off Door County and the still beauty of the countryside that easy.

To see the lights on in a barn, to know a farmer and his cows are deep inside the hay and warmth and animal-smelling atmosphere of that particular setting, to partake in such rural rituals in whatever way, creates a special feeling and reassurance about "place" that cannot be denied. There's a certain faith in that scene that does my own soul good, even though I appear to flee from it this morning for the welcome uprootedness of days and nights in the city.

Here and there a few people are up as I pass by, faces and shadows moving around in the kitchens. Neighbors, I would like to call them, though neighborliness here between outsiders and natives is difficult to describe. We nod hello and small talk the weather to death whenever we happen to meet at the post office or local store. We know, in fact almost all there is to know about each other. What we don't know, we imagine. Gossip is our lifeline, our soap opera, our evening news, our literature, and damn near our religion. We check the county newspaper occasionally just to get the facts straight—though we prefer our version to the printed word.

Even at this hour, on the road, I laugh to myself again in the realization that I will probably never make it even to the next town without somebody recognizing me or my car and speculating about my destination.

Security, I guess. You can't knock it. There's very little crime in these parts. People do mind their own and everybody else's business. Is that what it takes to make the streets habitable once again? Reducing faceless humanity to recognizable numbers? That is the way it once was in my old neighborhood, where the setting was a containment, a history of families, a system of checks and balances in the blood.

I think about that, too, and where I'm headed. Maybe I am just an Old-World, village peasant at heart, though I know in my blood that an overdose of that way of life must be a slow kind of dying.

As I pass these houses and farms along the highway of my adopted rural neighborhood, I recall the faces and read the stories behind the darkened doors and windows. The comedy and tragedy, the love and hate, the hope and despair, all of it so accessible, so meaningful and meaningless, a stark landscape for the dark and light sides of the human heart for any writer with the desire to put it all down.

I lecture myself again, as I do almost every journey to the big city: "Why the rushing back and forth for a mere piece of short-lived journalism to satisfy the Sunday soul? Why that, for enough bucks to maybe get you through the month, when there's so much here above the realm of journalism? Stay. Sit on your ass. Gamble. Settle for good and maybe make something lasting of all these lives around you."

But I can't. Not now, anyway. Maybe never. Maybe I'm still too close to it. Maybe someday if I can get away from here for good. But maybe, just maybe, these really aren't my people; this truly is not my setting. I will never feel at home here. I could satirize life here till it hurts, but I can't seem to be able to love and accept it. I've felt more at home in a Greek village 5,000 miles away than I do here.

I stop to drop off a letter at a village post office. I have yet to meet an-other car this morning. The place is still asleep. There is only the sound of wind and the mailbox as it squeaks open and clunks shut to receive my letter.

Sister Bay, Baileys Harbor, Jacksonport: the towns drift in and out of the scene. I follow Lake Michigan's edge for the pure sake of privacy and poetry, nothing else. This is one of the rare natural settings that pulls a man in and holds his attention till he questions his own place in time. Few scenes in urban Americana are so compelling.

Besides, I'm waiting for a sunrise, the most mind-blowing event on this part of the journey for me. I keep a constant eye over the lake. I like to catch every second of the performance, from the moment the sky begins to lighten to the first touch of the sun above the water. Time and space: the movement is miraculous. The pure wash of light—to keep a knowing eye on it all is something like trying to watch a flower open. You know it's happening, though it doesn't seem to be. But there, suddenly, it is!

I keep abreast of world events, though, through all this mystical meandering. My head isn't gone completely. The radio remains a special kind of reality connection to keep me on the beam, to bring me back to where I'm at. The Green Bay Packers are always news here, and I do love those early morning farm reports on cows and pigs and cattle. What the dairymen are doing is of some news, too. Frankly, I prefer to ponder the problems of Wisconsin cheese-makers than to swallow the hard facts of Chicago's progress in crime.

Yet my hand is itchy on the dial. I long for the distance (another hour or two?) when I can bring in the Chicago stations. I wonder what Studs is up to this morning. WFMT, where are you? And WSDM, smack dab in the middle, the station with all the girls and all that jazz . . . I miss you.

Another glance at the lake, another insignificant touch of light. The waters, all black of blue, turn slightly steely gray with the horizon now clearly discernible, as water and sky part and define each other. Come on, sun, do your stuff.

A light on in the window (the same light, the same window) in Jacksonport, where a husband, probably going to work in the shipyards, sits down for breakfast with his wife at the kitchen table. They look toward the road as my headlights drift by.

Soon I am in Sturgeon Bay, not a particularly beautiful town, the largest on the peninsula and the least aesthetic. Shipbuilding keeps it alive and growing. Mainly it is one of those towns, like so many in America, that you *have* to pass through in order to arrive at something better. And the bridge, the singularly scenic focal point of the whole town, signals in many ways both the entrance and exit of Door County, even though a few miles still remain to the south and west. Going or coming, the bridge is the best place to be in Sturgeon Bay, suspended in anticipation.

Time now to break out the thermos, to head down County Trunk S toward Algoma for the final stretch of natural wonder, and to somehow balance it all: the approaching sunrise, fields lightly dusted with snow, the sound of radio, the sight of blackbirds sweeping, and a steaming cup of coffee on the dashboard.

This is the finale to Door. With each turn of the wheel, I feel less and less attached to the place, more and more a stranger to all I've left behind. There's a burning band of dark orange above the gray horizon. Solitude and silence in this unique Wisconsin landscape of barns, fields, windmills, water, as it gradually yields to more traffic, more towns, more business.

And so the continuity of scenic wonder begins to break up into smaller, unforgettable shots which somehow stick in a man's memory: the fishing boats just beyond the small bridge in Algoma, country church steeples, cows moving out of the barns after milking, the rhythm of snow fences, a hawk wheeling above the earth in search of breakfast. Now, finally, here comes the sun! I break into a little song for a morning meditation. To bid goodbye with a sunrise to a place of such perfect peace is perhaps only fitting, and the only way to go, to merge into the mainstream of urban landscape which awaits me, where both sunrises and sunsets have all but disappeared from the eyes and hearts of men.

Within a few miles, even I will forget the significance of such natural events and concentrate instead on the energies of the city. By the time I hit the Illinois Tollway, a sunrise will be the least of my concerns. Either the sun is out today in Chicago, or it's cloudy. You learn to live with those conditions. Anyway, they don't really affect your spirit because you spend most of your time in one building or another. Survival is more important than sunsets in a city.

Kewaunee (small town, Midwestern beauty at its best), Two Rivers, Manitowac. I am picking up speed. The true fading point for me comes somewhere around Sheboygan, where a new stretch of four-lane, divided highway seems to capture both my momentum and imagination, sweeping me, mind over matter, at a terrific rate of speed toward Milwaukee and a growing Chicago consciousness.

Psychological? Yes. Four lanes, for one thing, seem to cry out for speed. "You're not driving down a quiet country road anymore, boy. Now get a move on." It's just one of the voices of the city I subconsciously seem to act upon. I have all the time in the world, yet I am increasingly anxious to be there. Why? Well, there are so many things to be done! So many people to see! Back in Door, everything can wait, but now, there is not enough time.

So I settle into a different driving pattern as I near Milwaukee, as I begin to fight for survival on the expressways. Not that I reject my rural vision, just that I have grown more aware in the past few years that I am not the same driver in Door County that I am in Chicago. I am more anxious at the wheel on Interstate highways, expressways, city streets. I am more verbal, more physical. I may even be a better driver under such circumstances. I am more aware, though less secure. I lock the doors, even while driving. Back home, I don't even remove the key from the ignition.

From Milwaukee on, pollution is another powerful reminder that I live in two different worlds. Air pollution, noise pollution, people pollution. I breathe differently, I see differently, I am constantly making minor adjustments in an environment that has suddenly become all concrete and electric, hard instead of soft. I find myself thinking ahead to what will happen, rather than what is happening. The Illinois toll booths will be coming; I lay the change out on the dash. I notice a driver tailgating me and shout, "Dumb bastard!" at him through the back window. I even start playing little games with him, including obscene gestures. I remind myself that I'm in a different world again. He could have a gun. He could be drunk or crazy or high. Men have been killed on Chicago streets for less than the stupid games we play in our automobiles.

I erase him, though, by breaking the speed limit and forgetting about him. For the blood is circulating fast now. Should I go straight to the Loop, check with the newspapers, have lunch? Should I call some friends and stay down there for a night on the town? I wonder what movies are on. I wonder if there's enough time to catch a play. I've got to stop at Kroch's and Field's for sure. Typing paper, envelopes, tobacco, records. I should call J. and have a beer. I haven't seen him in so long.

No, I'll do all that tomorrow. Get everything lined up on the phone in the morning, then start on the stories and save part of the night for myself. I'll make some phone calls this afternoon. Or as soon as I am in.

So I end up headed where I always seem to be headed: the old neighborhood, Cicero and Berwyn. I can't explain the pulling power of that place. Maybe it's my real home after all because I know where things are and where to find my people. I know just exactly where to find my in-laws and my parents at any time of the day or night. I know which of the many fine Bohemian restaurants serve tripe soup and on what day. I recognize the people on the streets. I'm a little differently alive here.

I begin living by phone once again. I start to walk the hard streets, getting at the ground work for stories. I have a coffee, I have a beer, I stay in touch. I maybe land in Oak Park or Oak Brook in the late afternoon, browsing for books.

Food is on my mind; it's always on my mind in the city. I can taste a Big Mac for supper, or a couple of Italian sausage sandwiches. It's visceral thing, my time in the city. I live in my skin. I think with my appetites. I make too many appointments, see too many people, eat too much, think too much, smoke too much, spend far more money than I have. I run myself ragged, but I seldom tire. Back in Door, I can fall asleep watching a snowfall. At midnight, 1, 2 a.m. in the city, I am probably in the Hotel Norland in LaGrange, buying the latest magazines, newspapers, paperbacks and then heading out for an all-night restaurant—probably the Seneca, back in Berwyn—for coffee and breakfast and the peace of just slowly perusing a morning newspaper.

I run because I know that in a few days, all this will be gone. In a few days I will probably look forward to the sanity of the solitary existence once again . . . though the conflict of where a man's roots are will still be the same, knowing that as long as I consider myself a writer, I am doomed to live a life separate and apart, somewhere halfway between home.

Frank Pechman:
Shadows and Light in the Landscape

A winter's afternoon. A solemn sky, the color of light held in stone fences still preserving the old fields. The stillness of fallen snow and then the suddenness of a child's red crayon on paper. Frank Pechman, master photographer, at the wheel of his bright red International Scout, a camera behind him, searching down the back roads of Door with a friend—the two of us looking for images and answers. If you know this man's kindness, humor, courage, concern for nature, beauty, and people, you know some of the light inside this good and interesting man. If you have seen his photographs, you recognize some of the harmony of his composition, the clarity of his vision, the necessity of light for him to show meaning.

But unless you have traded questions, answers, doubts, hopes, secrets and fears with a friend such as he, you can never be certain just where you are and what you see. So in the dark times of winter, with their negative images of the soul, there is some consolation in camaraderie, in landscape both inner and outer.

We, the outsiders, find ourselves here for different reasons—fear and congestion of cities, the sameness of suburbias, the chance for a new way of life, the possibility and security of a natural landscape.

This was to be the answer. It is for many of us, yet questions remain, and the restlessness persists. (And in the windy darkness of the coldest nights, whatever our age or background, one question haunts the unsettled soul: given whatever life is still to be lived, is this all? Given the peace, given the beauty, is this it? Is there any more to do? Could there be another, a better place to be?)

Some of us pursue art for an answer, only to discover more questions. Pechman and I this afternoon focus on the countryside, looking, seeing. A photographer and a writer, we have nothing in common. But we have everything in common: some Hungarian blood for one thing (along with that inherent central European tendency toward brooding), and also a hunger for fine food, movies, books, drink, travel, ideas, an appreciation of feminine beauty . . . all those things in life some men deem good.

And a mutual restlessness in winter with Door's intimations of death all around us. Anxiety in the midst of too much calm—a common affliction of many outsiders whose big city energies take time to adapt to the rural wave length.

"Let's talk. Let's go. Let's do *something!*"

I'm interested in the moment in what the photographer sees, what the man, Frank Pechman, sixty-seven, has focused on since he moved to Door in 1971 from Kaukauna after having bounced back from a paralyzing stroke in 1969. The brush against those dark wings was close enough to make Frank reach for that golden ring of early retirement at age fifty-nine instead of just talking an early retirement as most men do.

Pechman, born in Oshkosh in 1911, came to understand the significance of shadows early in life. Felled by tuberculosis at the age of twenty-one, he has never quite forgotten that introduction to the dark side of existence. "I went into the hospital when I was twenty-one and came out when I was twenty-seven. Man, if you don't think that's a period of depression. All your friends going out, doing things. Why me? Why am I here?"

He attributes his early interest in art to a commercial artist who lived in his neighborhood. Frank ran errands for him and was fascinated with his work and way of life. "I've always been interested in art, studied it all my life—not a heck of a lot of formal training. My hospitalization, you see, was really a blessing in disguise. I was able to take correspondence courses through the University of Wisconsin's extension division. This was a real break—to be able to study with people from the university. They would write long, personal notes. I took all the art courses they could give me by correspondence. I spent about six years in the tuberculosis sanitarium.

"I find those times, like my stroke years later, were strong stepping stones, a definite demarcation in the path along life. But I think it leaves its mark on you in others ways as well. One of the bad things: you have a habit of thinking about death very much. I die every day, you see. You constantly think about it, so many little occasions in a day, a week. When you get to be my age, it's really common to see that hole in the ground ahead of you."

His roommate in the hospital was an amateur photographer, and it was at this time in his life that Pechman's interest in art spilled over to photography—a combination he was to explore to this very day. Borrowing the money to buy his first camera, he actually began with portrait photography by photographing all the nurses and patients in the hospital. In 1939 he opened his first studio in Kaukauna. Upon his retirement in 1971, he was president of Frank J. Pechman, Inc.—three photo portrait studios and a professional color finishing lab.

Awards and honors of all kind mark Pechman's career. In 1947 he received the degree of Master of Photography; in 1968, Craftsman, plus numerous awards from various photographic associations, including the Professional Photographers of America, and, just recently, induction in the Hall of Fame of Wisconsin's Professional Photographer's Association.

Yet at this stage in life, this particular winter's hour in Door, Frank finds himself at a kind of crossroads with his photographic art. That early interest in painting continues to gnaw at him.

"When I retired at fifty-nine, I thought I'd do a lot of pictorial photography, but you don't sell a lot of that in Door County, not with all the painters around. By the way, I had always intended to retire at sixty-two, but you don't just suddenly stop. You keep on going.

"It's hard to photograph Door County. It's such an immense thing. It's like trying to paint a sunset. Take that view from the top of the Ellison Bay hill. It's just immense . . . too much. I'll bet thousands of dollars in film are wasted there every year. You have to isolate it, reduce it. If it doesn't tell a story, don't put it in there. The county is too vast."

We're driving down County T now, east of Egg Harbor. The scene is winter, December, desolation, yet a definite beauty hovers in the air. The immensity of the County still on his mind, Pechman makes a comparison to a fall he experienced in New England.

"Here you have patches of color in fall; in New England you have mountains of it. You can't do justice to this. The camera can't. That's why the artist has it all over us. He can reduce it to a paintable image. I still think a painter looks at this with a 100 millimeter lens, to isolate, to eliminate all the unnecessary elements. He doesn't take everything in."

We park beside some deserted farm buildings—scenic Door, just waiting to be rendered into art. This is the real stuff that both Door and art are made of, why many of us live here, why the tourists keep coming: the past and the poetry in the landscape.

But Frank does not move to pick up his camera. "I'm almost beyond making a good photograph of this," he explains. "I don't think the camera can do justice to any of it anymore. I'm really turning away from it. The camera—to mirror nature—I don't know if that's all you want to do. Oh, you can get a couple of lovely shots here and there, but the painter can put so much more of himself into it than the photographer."

The journey down the back roads continues. The red Scout burrows through the bare bones of the landscape, marked by leaning fences, naked trees and black crows. Melancholia lingers.

Frank recalls the stroke which almost destroyed him, the despair, the months and months of physical therapy. He recalls a therapist who came in the very next day, "and we began working immediately. Everything was dead. I couldn't feel a thing. My whole left side, dead. 'It's all in your mind,' the therapist said. 'There are other nerves and blood vessels that can take over if you will make them take over.'

"We started with my fingers. You look at that finger and you try to make it move. I was bending fingers, thumbs, for months after I left the hospital. You can't imagine how many times you must manually manipulate the fingers with your other hand . . . thousands, hundreds of thousands of times. I would look at my hand with all my life and try to make it move with all my might. I kept looking at that finger and finally . . . it moved . . . maybe just a sixteenth of an inch. I called Marvis [his beautiful wife, once a model]—'Marvis, look what I can do!' I did that for weeks and weeks, joint by joint, finger by finger. It took about a year. The leg came back last, but when the leg came back . . . to know I could walk in the woods, that was it!

"I've always been a pretty happy man. Mentally, though, I can't accept complete annihilation. Twenty-five years ago I accepted a philosophy of life: something to love, something to do, something to look forward to. I added one more—to have some beauty around you. This really works out for me. I believe it very much. Family, friends—that matters. My kids, I just love them. Kids, they're the real beauty of life. I think growing old is a horrible experience. Emma Toft said to me the other day, 'Mr. Pechman, it's hell to grow old.' "

With his health returned, his photographic studio sold, the move to Ellison Bay gave him the time and place to continue his interest in photography. "But I could not start a portrait studio anywhere for as long as I lived. That was in the contract. So I thought pictorial photography would be the answer. I've taken everything around here by now, but what are you going to do with it? I think every photographer dreams of someday retiring and making a living off his pictorial photography. Here I have the ideal opportunity for that, and it can't be done."

Although the camera is still an extension of the man himself (only less so these days) what Frank Pechman has begun to do in the past year is perhaps what he really meant to do in the very beginning: paint. And that has sharpened his eye even more, while the dialogue within him—artist or painter?—persists.

"I've painted only fifty-two paintings in my whole life, and I've sold twelve or fifteen of those, which makes me feel good. I've only painted seriously for about two years.

"I've always had a tremendous affinity for artistic, creative people. The first thing I did when I moved up here was to get to know them. I came up here knowing Door County by two names: Emma Toft and Gerhard Miller. They were Mr. and Mrs. Door County to me.

"Artists are always very curious . . . like children. I think that's great, to be always open, always wondering, always explaining, always so much more tolerant than the average person. I admire them. I have a deep respect and regard for their abilities, and wish I could do likewise."

What does he see here?

"There is so much more natural beauty here than anywhere else — the bluffs, the water, the trees, the abundance and variety of wildflowers. Forty acres of daisies. The beautiful harbors. As a painter you have a feeling that you're sort of preserving a little bit of the natural beauty. You try not to just mirror it, but put something of yourself into it. I think what a photographer needs more than anything else is patience. To wait for that particular time of day when the hour is right, the time is right, the mood is right. Then to capture it! The painter can put in shadows, light, wherever he wants to, but not the photographer. I've been watching this particular red door at Fandrei's for some time now. The west rays of the sun just going down over the woods, only the last fifteen minutes of the day in June, in one particular week. I would say there are only maybe five days out of the year when that shot could be made.

"You paint with light when you photograph. Your brush is your camera. There is no question in my mind that it is an art form. But the subject matter for a photographer is much more limited. I think I get a bigger kick out of finishing a painting, though, because I know it's something that's completely me, more of myself than a photograph ever can be. I wish now that I had started as a painter."

"Retiring to Door County" is the cry of so many all around us. Onward to God's country and eternal peace, as if this, in itself, is all a man can live for. For some, it seems to be. For Frank Pechman, though, it is not the final answer.

"All these people coming up here making birdhouses, leather wallets," Frank shakes his head. "I call them bead stringers," he laughs. "Like the kid in kindergarten, you know, who comes home after his first day of school, and his mother asks him, 'How was kindergarten?' 'OK if you want to be a damn bead stringer all your life.' Well, I don't want to be a damn bead stringer here. There is such a thing as happiness in retirement, if you work at it; to create something, to do something. You've got to be involved with something productive. I think there's a tremendous amount of waste, boredom, self-deception in retirement."

The day grows, strangely enough, a little lighter, though the afternoon grows late. It will be dark soon. Not a single photograph has been taken. Images, though, of all sorts linger in the mind's eye.

Turning down Townline Road he points toward the western horizon with a photographer's eye, a painter's eye . . . the spirit of a man wanting to transcend his own place and time, given all the inevitables, like the very movement of this afternoon toward night.

"The thing I don't like about Door County is the winter, probably the most beautiful of all seasons. As you grow older, you feel it more. I shiver like a wet pup. The beauty is here, but you've got to be young to absorb it. Spring, summer, fall—I wouldn't want to live anywhere else in the world. Hey, look at that sky!

"I love the skies here. You'll see any formation of clouds. Just look at it now. Look at what you have here in 100 degrees—mauves, blues, golds. There, a little deepening. Where else do you get that vista? The sky is beautiful in Door. The sky and the water. The only other thing a man might request is a little mountain. Then you'd have it all."

"Clean Piece Wally": The World's Greatest Car Salesman

A light covering of snow dusts the downtown drag of Sister Bay this morning, and there he stands, outside of Lundh Ford in the used and new car lot, a habitat of horse trading he has made legendary on the local scene. There he stands waving and smiling: the world's greatest car salesman. Another Door County original.

"I'm gonna have some fun this morning," he laughs. "Bruce Hanson is coming to look at that old green pickup back there, that '66 Ford. I call that a stone-crusher, heh, heh, heh . . . a field piece, heh, heh, heh. I'm asking $500, he says $400. He'll probably try to get me to go halves, $450. We're gonna have some fun, heh, heh, heh. . . ."

"Clean Piece" Wally, they call him, among other things. For damn near every old heap he shows you, he closes his eyes in that Wally Mickelson way, puts on that infectious smile (actually a grin that I'm not at liberty to describe), and maybe even doffs his hat in adulation of the four wheel wonder that sits or leans or coughs in front of you: "It's a cleeeean piece," he tells you. (He also has the entire local history of its owner at his fingertips: just who he or she was/is, who they're married to, how he himself may or may not be related to them, something else about them that calls another story to mind . . . and probably how much money they have in the bank. You don't just buy a car from Wally; you buy a chapter of local history and hearsay as well).

"Reeeeeeeal cleeeeean," he says. And then that machine gun laughter of "heh, heh, heh's" which catches you into the manner and style of the man—his humor, his storytelling, his friendship—till you find yourself laughing with him, exchanging stories, bargaining in between, and very likely writing up papers on a car you maybe didn't even want in the first place, but you've been Wally Mickelsoned . . . heh, heh, heh.

A baron of bargainers that echoes at times the early days of horse trading, Wally's a natural. As real as they come in Door County, with a fine line of bull he's developed into art after twenty-seven years of keeping half the home folks rolling. (What President Carter really needs is Wally Mickelson sitting between Menachem Begin and Anwar Sadat and in his own inimitable Door county drawl, an up and down sing/song

Scandinavian rhythm, telling stories, smiling, laughing, but all the while scratching figures on paper, all of a sudden hitting them with, "Well, fellas, I'll tell you what. We're gonna make a reeeeal good deal here . . . and we'll all come out smelling like a rose, heh, heh, heh. Fair enough? Sure. Let's write up the papers.")

He was born in the county in 1916, "raised on a farm one mile east of the Cities Service station on Scandia Road in Sister Bay—now Voyager Auto Sales, but you don't want to say that, he's my competitor, heh, heh, heh. I went to Appleport university, next to the old cherry plant. Eight grades, then two years of junior high, two and a half miles away. I walked to Wildwood, then went by car pool to Gibraltar High School. I graduated there in 1935. It was a four-room school with five teachers. My favorite teacher, heh, heh, heh, was Oswald E. Massey, my math teacher. Don't forget the E. He was my favorite 'cause he always chewed paper. He'd always have this wad of paper going in his mouth, heh, heh, heh. But he was a good teacher."

Following high school, Wally went to Chicago and worked as an elevator operator and bellhop at the Bismarck Hotel, which is about as ripe a story-telling scene as one could hope to find Wally in.

He smiles and he laughs, but there's no way we get The Adventures of Wally the Bellhop into the local paper. Let's just say he learned people there, all kinds of them, high life and low life, and he learned the city, which he still knows today, almost forty years later,

"But a person didn't earn enough money to enjoy it then," he says; "$22 a week plus room and board." What he remembers most about the Bismarck were the German chefs telling him about their letters from home, how the mothers would write and tell them, "Hitler is marching."

He came back to Door in '40 or '41 and went to work in the shipyards in Sturgeon Bay till 1945, when he went into the service. The war ended shortly after he entered. "I spent exactly three months and two days in the service. I was going to say when I ran for school board, 'I never had any initials before or after my name [Ph.D., M.A. etc.] except one: Pvt.' Heh, heh, heh"

We're inside the cubbyhole of his office now, locked in for privacy except for a tiny talk-through opening above his desk where he's posted the sign "Exit." Periodically he answers questions to any and all voices out there. Suddenly Bruce Hanson's voice can be heard.

"Wally?"

He's come to check out that 1966 stone-crusher Wally wants to sell him.

"Bring your checkbook along?" Wally asks.

"You got the keys? I want to try it out."

"Sure, take it out as long as you like."

"And Gene's interested in that other pickup" (another clunker).

"Well, you buy two, by golly, you make a better deal," laughs Wally.

After his brief stint in the service, Wally went into the floor sanding business. "I didn't like it though. I had this sinus problem, and the dust was too much. For four seasons, I was the summer traffic patrolman in the village of Ephraim, 1947 to 1950 by golly. Yes, sir. You bet. I kept law and order in a village that didn't even have a tavern. I had a star and a suit and everything. I didn't arrest too many people, though. Mostly I was there for speeders. The idea was more or less a warning. Ephraim was the greatest for pedestrians years ago. People walking everywhere. There was no 'hips' in those days. 'No 'joints,' none of that. The college girls were so meek they even found pastors to marry, heh, heh, heh."

With the advent of tile floors and wall-to-wall carpeting, he sold out the "See Wally to Sand Your Floors" business and fell into a number of pick-up jobs common to the area: the Sturgeon Bay shipyards, construction work.

"I spent quite a few years working with the stone masons—stone mason's helper—with Johnny Landstrom. Off and on a number of years. I carried mud [mortar] up to my. . . you better not say that, heh, heh, heh.

"I was married in June 1942 to Helen Ohman of Ephraim. It was a double wedding, Clyde Logerquist and Helen's sister, Lucille. We went on a double honeymoon, too.

"The 1950's? Well, first it was back to the shipyards. I was a ship fitter, only that's not what my dad called it, heh, heh, heh. And in June, 1951, I began to drive a bus for the Bayview Busline. That lasted until the first major snow storm in Green Bay, and that terminated my bus driving days. Back to the shipyards for the third time, heh, heh, heh.

"Then one evening Leonard Swenson of the Ford dealership here in Sister Bay stopped by the house and approached me if I would be interested in selling automobiles. I'd only been back at the shipyard a week. I told him I'd let him know, but I'd already made up my mind. I didn't want to act too anxious, heh, heh, heh. I began here on Monday, Dec. 10, 1951. I just had my anniversary, twenty-seven years.

"In the fall of '67 I left here and went to Sturgeon Bay because this was such a small operation at that time. They had Lincolns and Mercurys in Sturgeon Bay [then Kestner Ford, later Bosman]. I left there on March 15, 1978, and came back here to work for this new dealership, for Jeff Lundh. The smartest thing I ever did."

But it was Swenson, back there in 1951 who must have seen the salesman's potential in Wally Mickelson. And Clean Piece Wally found his place in the sun almost immediately.

"I came in here on a Monday morning, took a little briefing from Mr. Swenson for a few days. On Wednesday I took out a car to Egg Harbor and made my first sale. I took another car up on Thursday, also to Egg

Harbor, and sold that one to the postman up there. I gained a little confidence right away, you see. I started with $60 a week and 5% commission, but the commission worked against you at first in a small dealership like that. It took a while to figure these things out. I worked for $60 a week from '51 to '54 and finally said, 'I got to have more than this.' I got $75 a week then till 1957. Then I was told I was making more money than the dealer was, heh, heh, heh. I've sold a lot of cars in my day, but I was never rewarded for it the right way. Here it's strictly commission. It's the best deal I've ever had.

"A good month? Oh, I've had several months where I've sold 30, 31 cars, average of one a day. That usually happens in May or June. I'd say so far, all together, I've sold about four thousand pieces at least."

There are cars and there are cars. As far as the worst hunk of junk Wally ever pawned off on anyone . . . well, the honesty of the man shines through: "I've never taken that attitude . . . laughed when a man drove away. I've sold a lot of $25 cars, sure.

Customers? There are all kinds. "I see customers that you have to be very careful with, just listen. Others have to be goosed or bulldozed into deals. Customers are changeable. They come in and want to spend $5,000 for a car, and you wind up selling them one for over $6,500. Ladies still want a nice appearing car—better than their neighbor's. It's crazy. You sell a nice looking automobile to people, they think they're getting a dandy deal, and you have nothing but trouble with them. Everything's wrong with it, they say. Sometimes it's all in people's minds—every time the wheels go around, they think it's going to go. But you just got to try and keep calm with it."

How does a used car man judge a used car?

"First, appearance. I walk around the car and judge it by its paint. I then look under the hood and see how clean the engine is, if there's any rust spots around the cooling system, any oil on the pan, the valve covers, things like that. I look very closely. And I look for rust spots in the inside fenders. Then I inspect the trunk for rust, interior panels, the floor. I look inside the car, the interior, the upholstery, for tears and stains. I look at the brake pedal—any undue wear. The right hand lower part of the brake pedal is where the wear is. It tells you if there are a lot of miles on that car. Then I listen to the car. I start it. I drive it. Listen to the transmission."

The "deal" involves everything from his inspection of the trade in ("I'll give the man more for his beautiful creampuff with 15 or 16,000 miles on it"), to the bluebook price, to whatever numbers he can come up with within the range of dollars he can play around in, to the actual bargaining. (Watching Wally figure out deals—percentages, pluses, minuses—on his desk pad shows just how much he learned from his old paper-wad-chewing math teacher. "The lower I can steal that thing, the better I am, heh, heh, heh. Usually the guy with the best deal [for Wally] is the most happy guy. And the guy I bent over backwards for [Wally taking a beating] is usually the worst."

Philosophically, Wally is simply a man enjoying what he does best. "I'm happiest when I sell. Hard work and friends. I've always considered myself an easygoing person. I have an interest in people. I try not to misrepresent. I do bend over backwards at times. I'm a little easy at that. I try not to get soft to the point where I lose money. And I've sold to three generations in some families here.

"I have no special hobbies at home in the arts and crafts world. I'm a poor Mr. Fix-It. I get on my nerves and my wife's nerves when I'm at home. I enjoy telling a good story. I don't know where I got it. And I might be at the point where I got too many monikers for people. I don't know where it [nicknaming] comes from. I guess it all begins in grade school. You see a kid has ham in his lunch, and you call him Toe Jam, and other kids hear it, and it spreads like fire in a one-room school. It's funny as you get older, but at that time it isn't funny at all. Most kids got very angry. . . .

"Now Gust Klenke is always Gloomy Gus to me. Peter Nelson, Ball Bearing Pete. There was Eddie Fat Olson and Eddie Thin Olsen. Pete Oleson is always Pistol Pete the Pill Pusher to me. Al Johnson—Wild Man. And there's Mike, Madman Till. Willard Erickson is Carpenter Cook. Bill Bastian, Sweet William. And Earl Willems is Early Times.

"When I was a kid in school, I was Pickle for Mickelson. That's sour. I don't hear it anymore. 'Clean Piece'—that came from the first dealer I worked for. It meant units and cars. It got to be associated with me: 'This is a cleeeean piece,' heh, heh, heh."

Bruce Hanson is back after test-driving the stone-crusher, telling Wally through the opening in the wall that he's got a trade-in for him instead of a cash deal. (For Wally, this is not a good deal). The buyer for Hanson's 1970 Ford sedan backed out, and now he would like to trade the car on the pickup.

"So now you want to drop it on me, eh?" he tells Bruce. "Put it in the *Reminder*. They sell anything there."

"No, I don't want to do that."

"I just can't trade old for old," says Wally. "Just can't put another one on the lot. Christ, there's no room out there now."

"Well, come on out and take a look. Tell me what it's worth."

The world's greatest used car salesman laughs, fixes his hat, and moves out to home territory—the used car lot. He walks slowly around the Ford sedan, doing the appearance checkout. Hanson is in the background telling him just how good it looks, explaining his problem with the buyer who backed out. Wally concurs: it is in pretty good looking shape . . . he'll come up with some figures—for the *Reminder*.

The look on Hanson's face says he doesn't care to do the *Reminder* thing; he wants to dump this baby on Wally now. He needs that stone-crusher pickup heap for carrying wood, and he wants it now.

Wally keeps smiling, gets inside, starts it up, says, over his shoulder: "It's got some pedal [brakes] left." Then in the most serious Saturday-morning-used-car-sales face he can put on, Clean Piece Wally begins the bargain in that sing/song voice: "Well now, what were you thinking of trading this for?"

He means money, of course, but Hanson first reads him as "For the green pickup? I was thinking even."

Wally removes his hat, scratches his head, shakes his head. "Even?"

Hanson advances his part of the bargain by explaining his problem in getting the title clearance on a new car he's bought, and in the meantime he'd like to get rid of this car, which he was supposed to have sold to that buyer who backed out, and he really is in sore need of that pickup at the moment.

"Even?" (Wally is still trying to live with that word, which he dramatizes to the point of a personal affront to his dignity). "I can't trade old for old. There's no room [he returns to that ploy]. Where am I gonna put it?"

Hanson tells him that the car is in such good shape, it won't sit around very long in the lot anyway. And besides, "Kenny [Church] in your own garage said he could use it," explains Hanson, driving home the bargain.

"Yeah, he'll use it," says Wally. "But he won't *buy* it!" Hanson holds fire while Wally takes another waltz around the car. There's a feeling he's somewhat impressed with this clean piece, that already in the back of his mind he's dealing it to a local customer who is looking for just such a car, and most importantly, it's a deal where Wally "comes out smelling like a rose." But somehow he's got to impress upon Hanson how much he really doesn't want to be bothered with the burden of this sedan, though he damn well would like to come out ahead on both the stone-crusher and the car.

"Now I'm gonna make you fall over dead," he tells Hanson: "$300 and the car. Take the pickup."

Hanson's eyes enlarge to twice the size, his face shows evidence to a rise in blood pressure, and he repeats, "$300!" . . . and falls over dead.

Wally doesn't give an inch. Hanson regroups his force and begins citing a litany of all the things wrong with the pickup, which is quite easy. He can start anywhere. "The tires are all bad, it doesn't even have a spare, it needs a new muffler system, the hood, look at that hood! It damn near flew off while I was driving it!" All this may be true, but Wally has two aces up his sleeve: everybody wants an old hunk-a-junk pickup these days, and as sad as the stone-crusher looks, it runs.

"I'm talking even," says Hanson again.

"I got to have *something* for the paperwork," pleads Wally. (A softening?) Jeff Lundh walks by the scene, much to his later regret. Wally draws him in, explains all the details with relish, especially the even-trade deal Hanson is suggesting. Lundh seems like a straight shooter, listens carefully to his man (he admits to me later that Mickelson makes him laugh so hard at times that he has to lock the door), and honestly explains to Hanson that he would just as soon not have another used car sitting out there at this time of the year.

"That's what I been telling him," sings Wally. "Look at this place. It's like a bazaar around here." Still, Wally confesses that there might be a few people around who could use a cheap car like this for work. He just might be able to sell it. "I tell you what," he says to Hanson, "$100 for the paperwork."

"You throw in a new muffler system and a spare," counters Hanson.

"As is," says Wally. "That's how she came, that's how she is. LaReine hasn't got time to futz around in there with all his tractors and stuff to fix. $100. Come on, we'll write up the papers."

"You throw in a new muffler system," says Hanson.

"I'm sorry I got in this," laughs Lundh.

But Lundh has a new approach. If Hanson needs the truck, he should take it. When he's sold the car on his own, they'll complete the deal. That way the lot will be free of both car and truck, and everybody's happy—except maybe Wally.

"If you won't give me $100, what will you give me?" Wally asks Hanson.

Hanson isn't talking. He's mulling it over. He came hoping for even-Steven, but now with the Lundh proposition, plus the Wally $100 cash deal, which he seems willing to negotiate, Hanson bites his lip and says, "$50."

Both Wally and Lundh disappear for a quick test-drive of the car, while Hanson is left alone walking around the green stone-crusher, slamming the hood down in place (it won't stay), checking all the rust spots (it would be easier to check where the green paint is), musing over the broken tailgate, the hole in the bed, the torn upholstery, the tires that may or may not last to the edge of town . . . saying aloud to himself, "Maybe I shouldn't a said $50." But then reflecting, " 'Course, he's not getting any prize either."

The two men return. Lundh bows out, leaving it to Clean Piece Wally to seal the deal. Hanson still wants a muffler system or maybe a spare tire. "Even the floor boards are rusted through!" he argues with Wally.

"Oh just put a little sheet metal on that, throw a carpet over like the kids do, and it's real good," smiles Wally. "$50 for the paperwork."

"How long does it take for a title to clear?" asks Hanson.

"That's like saying how long before I die," says Wally.

"I wish I had your money," says Hanson.

"I'll tell you what," says Wally. "I'm gonna retire. How would you like to be a car salesman in Sister Bay? Can you eat on $50? How would you like my job, huh? "

"I'd like it," smiles Hanson. "But I don't have your line of b. s."

"Should we go in and write it up then?" smiles Wally.

And they do.

I recently reviewed a fine book, First Person America, *for one of the Chicago newspapers, and in that review spoke of how much this country has lost in the way of natural language among its people, its native humorists and born storytellers. I thought of Wally Mickelson when I wrote that review—Wally, and a handful of others in these parts, who are so totally and honestly themselves, you can't help but listen and enjoy.*

I don't believe anyone in the county ever called me more often than Wally to say how much he enjoyed something I had published in the Advocate. *(And there were times, if he didn't call, I figured the piece of writing must have failed.) Often, when he sold cars in Sturgeon Bay, he had access to the paper a day before I and had the jump on me, and I would have to recall very quickly just what I sent Chan and what Wally was so enthused about.*

Every story I wrote about someone reminded him of yet another story, and another (all of them funny), and he would regale me with his wonderful reminiscences, always ending the conversation with his latest slightly off, slightly on color joke: "Hey, did you hear the one about the Swede and. . . ."

I shall miss that immensely. And all his crazy nicknames for everyone. He was always going to take me to Kewaunee County sometime (last spring, last fall, this fall) where we would hit some of the small towns, local taverns, in search of my Slavic roots—which Wally was sure we would find in one of the local watering holes.

A Lundh Automotive memo/letter to me (and Wally was an inveterate letter writer too), dated 8/15/79, addressed to The Hour of the Sunshine Now Kid, included a Xerox copy of a review he did not like (and Wally was an avid reader too), plus his unprintable one-word review of that reviewer, and a final note: "Let's go to Kewaunee Co. next week—that will be more enlightening. Signed, Wally."

I regret never having made that trip with him, and all the stupid, though honest excuses which I/we wrap up in the words: "I'm too busy." No one should ever be too busy to share a good time with a friend. The time is always too damn short. And "regret" is the saddest word in the language.

The day Wally died I was, ironically enough, reading proofs of the chapter on "Clean-Piece Wally" in this book. And I was smiling at his words, reliving those times, and looking forward to next spring when he'd hold the whole book in his hand, then call me to tell me what he thought.

Regrets, regrets . . . there are more of them than anyone cares to admit. I don't regret the time spent with him last month, seriously exploring the possibilities of buying a used car from him in Sister Bay. All those stories he told me. His incredible sense of humor.

I don't regret meeting him at Al's occasionally for coffee, or standing outside of Al's one morning a few weeks ago to listen to what, for me, will be the last Wally Mickelson joke:

"You see, heh, heh, heh, there were these two old women, heh, heh, and one of 'em had moved to Florida, and the other called her one time to out how she was doing. 'Oh,' she says, 'I'm living with four men.' 'Four men!' the other old biddy says. 'Yes, I get up in the morning with Charley Horse,' she says, heh, heh, heh, 'Then I spend the morning with Arthur Itis, get through the rest of the day with Will Power, and at night I go to bed with Ben Gay' ! Heh, heh, heh."

I can't imagine anyone not liking Wally Mickelson or ever forgetting him. Few people I know could walk into Al's (or anywhere), and instantly turn all the sad faces into happy ones the way Wally did. The man had an infinite capacity to amuse, to change our feeling, and that is a rare and precious human quality.

I shall miss the voice, the stories, the laughter, the man, dearly.

Phil Austin: A Figure in the Landscape

He is often mistaken for a stranded motorist, his van hugging the shoulder of one of the county's back roads in all seasons, all kinds of weather.

"Can I help you?" says the passerby to the man seated inside, staring into a distant landscape. "No, I'm all right." "What are you doing?" "Painting." "Who are you?" "Phil Austin." "Oh, I should have known."

A permanent resident of Door since 1969, he is one of the handful of established painters here with national credentials and one of the few water-colorists in the area who work "on location," preferring, almost celebrating, the possibilities of capturing the meaning of an ever-changing landscape.

To see this man make a painting, to see what an artist sees, to recognize his attempt to hold in color, line, composition, and individuality some of the beauty, mystery, tradition of this place, of what was and is Door. To maybe even capture what isn't here, but to put it back in place because it belongs.

It's a cold afternoon near the very end of February. The depths of snow still hold down the fields, still cling to the trunks of trees. Ice on the back roads. Some wind. An overcast day, another gray day in Door, with an occasional glimpse of a very yellow, very bright sun. A hide-and-seek day. Austin is at it again.

He turns toward Sand Bay, and then into Little Sand Bay, where the local fishermen, Lee Peterson and Clyde Olson, have given him permission to come into the area to paint. He stops some distance before the snow-swept dock and surveys the scene. Two trucks face in opposite directions upon the dock, the figure of a man beyond them, fishing boats tied in tight. Snow, ice, a gun-metal gray sky, water to match, only darker, bluer . . . and the occasional suddenness of sun, changing everything in sight.

"Wow! This is kind of wild, painting against that sun. But I like that little boat *Shrimp* there, with the snow backed up against it. I'm going to work with that, I think."

He takes out a sketchbook, which looks like a hardback novel bound in black, turns to an empty page, and frames out in pencil a small rectangle, roughly 1½ x 2 inches.

"I start with a thumbnail. I've got to figure how much I can eliminate here and narrow down. First, though, I think I'll take a couple of camera shots here while the light's good. I always carry my camera with me. Once in a while I get some fantastic shots for reference material. I'm slowly building up a library of Door County scenes. I've got buildings and stone fences and animals in all seasons. The nice thing about this zoom lens is you can compose and include just what you want.

"I work on a thumbnail like this to start with; otherwise it's pretty difficult to visualize how you're going to use the space and how much you're going to use in the painting. One nice thing about this spot is you get all the little buildings on the other side of the bay that really make an interesting skyline over there." The sound of his pencil shading in the boat, the buildings, the sky, the sound of his fingers smearing the lead.

"I put the strongest dark and lights together in the most interesting spots. Now I'm picking up the distant light off the bay, the *Shrimp* here, coming into the foreground. I'll reduce the truck in size so it doesn't compete with the boat. This is where the pencil thumbnail pays off, because I don't have to commit myself. Where the sun shines on the water, I'll use pure white paper. Even where the snow comes in, it will have some tone to it. There's a nice repeat there, the second truck coming this way. Those little saplings grouped there make a nice vertical, a nice accent. Well, I guess that's what I want."

The thumbnail complete after an intense ten minutes or so of Austin's concentration, he reaches for his "stretch" of British handmade paper and begins a large drawing, his eyes moving from the thumbnail to the real scene beyond the window of the van, to the large sheet on his lap, putting things in place in line and mass.

"Boats are something else, a good deal more difficult. You've got to get them drawn right. A lot of people say these fishing boats are like old shoes, but I think they're beautiful old boats, beautiful lines." The foreground goes in, the horizon, the general land mass across the bay, then some buildings.

The real scene outside suddenly takes on dramatic life as a fisherman appears between the trucks and begins moving down the dock, walking, stepping into the very foreground that Phil is now delineating. A futile attempt to reach for the camera, but no time.

"I'll move quickly to capture him," says Phil, discovering at the same moment that one of the trucks is pulling away, and the man, the fisherman is almost directly in front of him, only seconds away from disappearing behind Phil's own van.

"I don't think I can use him—no time—but he would have been nice to include. That truck, too, I'll have to paint from memory. Oh, the light's going to change a lot. You know, another thing that's nice here, those goldenrod stalks—perfect for getting into the foreground."

Seeing. The satisfaction of awareness in a man, sixty-eight years into his living, so in love with his surroundings, his work that his whole being delights in it, seems to say, "Look, I'm painting! I'm most alive in what I do! I'm complete." The achievement of that point in life does not come easy for most men, artists especially. For some it may never come at all. "I should have started forty years ago," admits Phil.

What he was doing, though, before achieving his present state of peace, was growing up in Waukegan, Illinois, studying art at University of Michigan, marrying, raising a family, working for a commercial studio in Chicago for five years, quitting there during those five years to work for a local agency for eight months, only to quit again and return to his old job. "But you should never do that," cautions Phil. "I went back, stayed for about a year. Finally I did some moonlighting and began freelancing about 1950.

"I was forty years old. I said, 'Life begins at forty,' so I started to free-lance. It was pretty rough for a while, but later I began making better money than on my job, and I was feeling great about it."

The integrity of the man should not be overlooked. In a number of instances, in both his commercial studio period and freelancing years, Phil declined to do work which was against his moral principles.

"Because I was brought up not to drink, I felt I was a hypocrite working on ads for liquor all the time. I felt I had no right to promote it if I didn't believe in it myself. I told my boss about it, and from that time on I really got it. He thought it was pretty funny and ridiculed me all the time. I declared myself and was really persecuted about it." The Schlitz export account came up during his freelancing years, "but I had to say, I'm sorry, I can't. That's why I quit my other job. I got another guy from a fellow agency to do it, but he eventually took over the whole account, which I finally learned after three months of waiting and no work."

Bad times again. No accounts, no money left in the bank. "I borrowed all the money I could on my insurance policies. It took me over a year to get back on my feet. Then I started to build a business again, this time with more diversified accounts. I wasn't going to depend on one account like before. Then the best thing that happened: as I got more experienced, I began to upgrade what I was doing, because I was learning by doing all the work myself. From 1950 on, I never worked for anybody else again."

Home free? Not quite. "I must have been freelancing about ten years when calamity really hit. I went to have my eyes examined, and discovered I had scar tissue developing in the middle of my right eye. 'I have to tell you,' the Doctor said, 'it's not going to heal up. And if it gets in your other eye, you're through.' I was told to work only seven hours a day, no weekends. I had double vision. I couldn't gauge distance with a pen. I had to admit I couldn't do that kind of close work again.

"It's the same old thing. You have to be hit in the head sometimes to do the thing you want to do. Well, if I can't do that kind of work again, I'm going to have to do watercolor. Maybe I could find some way to do watercolor for commercial art. I had been painting, of course, showing once in a while, selling one occasionally. But nothing which would make me want to do it for a living.

"I thought maybe I could do some stuff on spec [speculation]. They were just putting up the Prudential Building in Chicago at that time, so I did a painting of it when the steel work was up ten floors and just starting. When I finished, I called up the rental agency and told them about it. And they bought it! That's the first thing I had ever done on spec. Other work of this sort followed, including a painting of the new Chicago *Sun-Times* Building with the first cargo boat of paper tied alongside the dock."

All this set off a series of related projects, from Chicago newspaper magazines to the *Ford Times*, and even book illustrations for Children's Press, where he ended up working six years, completing twenty books.

"The nice thing was I had a little more time to paint seriously on the side. All of a sudden, though, I realized there weren't any more books coming from Children's Press. 'Well,' I said, 'maybe this is the time I should start to paint full time.' And you know, the minute I left commercial art I began to do better. From that time it went on and on till now, when I'm doing great!"

Though he had known and painted Door County all through the '60s, a weekend in '69 brought him up here for good. "We came up and stayed at On the Rocks in one of the A-frames. I really liked it. One morning Edwina [his wife] said, 'If you like it so much up here, maybe we ought to just sell out in Chicago and move up here. I couldn't believe she'd be so enthusiastic about moving up! So I said, 'OK, let's look for some property.' We started building ["Skyledge" in Gills Rock] and moved up in December of '70."

So Phil Austin, ten years later—a survivor of sorts, having weathered moral and physical conflicts—is very much at home now in this countryside. "The right eye is still blurred vision, but it doesn't impair my color vision at all. I have good vision in the other eye. It's no problem. I've got used to it. You ask the lord to heal your eye, but he doesn't; he does something better. He lets you paint, lets you really enjoy what you're doing, and lets you make a living at it."

Phil continually works his pencil over the large areas of the painting to be: that sky, that light. "Well, it's starting to come to life now."

Most of the artists up here agree that light in Door is something special. Some compare it to the Mediterranean, others to Mexico and the Southwest. "I think the light's fantastic up here," says Phil. "Alaska was like that too. There was fantastic light there. But I think one of the things most remarkable are the skies we have here. I would guess it has something to do with the two bodies of water which sort of play off each other. From my place I frequently just watch the skies off Washington Island. I sit there and make quick sketches just to get the feeling of what goes on in the sky.

"I think everybody acknowledges the fact that Door County is pretty much like New England. The trees are about the same, but the rocks there are sharper, more angular. And the coastline: you got a lot more rock going out in the water.

"I like all the evidence of the past here—old houses, old log homes, fishing tugs. I find myself frequently doing old houses. I just finished a painting, "Remember Cap's House": a little section of house with just a few boards standing. Then I filled in all the empty spaces, sort of phantom-like, with phantom curtains, phantom wall paper, an old table and a kerosene lamp. Sort of a double image: what's left of an old house and what's remembered."

In the same way Phil, this moment, is both seeing and remembering the very Door County fishing scene before him. "The *Shrimp* here in the foreground will have the detail; a whole string of boats would be a little too much." He holds up the sketch in his lap. "Well, I think maybe that'll be all right."

At age sixty-eight, at least five hundred paintings of Door behind him in the past seven years, Phil readily admits to wanting to perfect his art even more. His only regret is "I should have started sooner." Sixty-eight years? Young in these parts. He smiles. "Come to Door and live five years longer." Artist, teacher, student . . . it all comes together.

"The Clearing-In-Winter does a real favor for me with Jim Ingwersen's life sketch classes. It keeps me in trim. I'm just beginning to get where I can really do some of the things I've always wanted to do. I want to do more successful paintings. I'd like to get the figures in to tell more of the story of Door County."

He begins sketching the figure of the elusive fisherman into painting before him, though the man walked quickly out of the scene some time ago. Austin, remembering the movement of his legs, the position of his arms: "He looks like he's going the wrong way, gettin' away from me instead of walking to me. There, now it's coming.

"Now if I can get that brilliant feeling of sun burst—glare—it's going to be fantastic." He begins pouring a jug of water into a plastic bucket, opens his box of paints in his right hand. "You can't emphasize that brilliant sun unless you emphasize the dark. I'll see what I can do here, build up the impression of that brilliant sun. It's so bright I can't do anything now. Wow!" His brush is wet, swirling around the color, laying in another cold gray.

"I work with a limited palette and use only seven colors: Alizarin Crimson, Vermilion, Cadmium Orange, Cadmium Yellow Pale, Viridian Green, Ultramarine Blue, and Cerulean. I teach this way because I think people learn to see color a lot faster. Basically, I paint for value. I think value is more important than color. I mix the value with Ultramarine Blue and Vermilion, and then I add color either in the box or on paper. Then you don't change the value, but you can change the hue. When you mix color you get in the habit of evaluating it to see what it really is. Now I'll mix some red in the lower part of the hull." The brush slaps around the tray again, the tip very deftly taking on water and a range of color guided, seemingly, more by sensation, intuition, than by any conscious movement of action or reason.

"Now some Cadmium Orange because this side of the hull is a little warmer. When I started to paint fulltime, it really made a lot of difference in my work. I really improved. When you paint all the time, you begin to do things unconsciously which before you had to remember to do." He goes over the lines of the boat now with a smaller brush. "I may have gone too dark, but you got to do something to emphasize that brilliant sun."

Time to a watercolorist on location? "You have to memorize things because they change so fast. Like that figure [the fisherman] is here and then gone. The trucks, gone. I have to remember what was happening so I can get the feel of it.

"I can leave white page for the sun, but I've got to build the contrast now. You work exactly opposite in watercolor than other mediums. You have to decide on your light and leave it, which is the opposite of oils. You know, it's a funny thing. I didn't even know watercolor existed before I got to college. Then I was so excited about it. I came from such a small town, but the kids in the art classes in college would whip the stuff out so easy. I was always behind, making up work. I was a C student. But I finally concluded it's the desire that counts, not the initial talent. I was an also-ran in art."

"Oh, boy, has that light changed. I better get something in here before it's gone . . . that shadow there on ice, off the hull. Now there's a nice shadow off the boat on the foreground that gives two depths."

Seeing, looking, observing in an artist's own way. "I look for unusual light, color. I find that there are places here at certain times of the day that are fantastic, and other days, nothing. Sometimes I even write notes to myself: 'Go to a certain place on a rainy day, or a foggy day, or when it's snowing. The quarry on Q, a great place I saw first one snowy day. I came back on a sunny day, and it wasn't great at all.

"Most people develop a way of working different from anybody else's. Pete [Steinmetz] does great things with a sponge. Other people use a lot of texture. Then there are the things we're inclined to paint, which interest us and we're inclined to look for. Probably some of everybody's nature turns up in what they see and the way they paint it.

"I kind of like trying to record things that someday would be gone, so people could see what things used to be like. Some people just don't see it. You learn to look for it when you paint. I can make people look and see, remembering the beauty that's there. It used to worry me when I was young and idealistic. I felt painting wasn't doing anybody any good, that I wasn't doing anything for anybody by painting. I was only pleasing myself. I feel compelled to paint now. When I see things that are interesting, like this fishing boat with snow piled up, it is something that I just have to record. Something that has to be done. I really don't know how to describe it or why you do it. The way some people who see mountains have to climb them, I see things and have to paint them.

"I feel there is an awful lot of beauty in our world that people miss, and someone has to point it out for them. I see a lot of beauty in things today, too, not only the past. These fishing boats for instance. I don't find any satisfaction in painting pleasure boats. These are working boats here, these fishing boats, and they're related to our life."

Past and present, and an artist very much aware of what's here, on the Door County scene: what's already gone and what's disappearing almost every day. "Oh, a lot of it just goes with time. There was an interesting old shed over there, on the other side, for example." This was on Sand Bay, where the *Islander*, the *Ramona* and the *Hope*, all working fishing tugs, once tied up in a natural scene of beauty so true the shed, the boats, the nets, the men, the water that there could be little doubt in anyone's mind that this was life, and this was art, and that this, somehow, all together, was Door.

"The shed was falling down, and the fisherman had to take it down. They felt it had outlived its usefulness. I hate to see that go, but I realize they have to be practical, they have to make a living. If a building outlives its usefulness, you have to tear it down. I've done it myself."

Still, Sand Bay is not quite Sand Bay any more, never will be again. And there is a conflict of sorts in this artist, Phil Austin, a man who must record the evidence of the past in today's light, yet a man who knows he must accept and understand the native's tendency toward practicality over preservation.

One wonders how much longer it will be before all the naturalness of the landscape is gone, and we have to rely on the artists, our own memories, our imaginations, to recall the way it was.

"I don't know if people here would preserve this stuff. Some of them are aware of it, but some of them aren't. I don't know if they look at something through new eyes and think, 'That was a beautiful building.' I've had several of the Weborgs over to see my paintings. It's amazing the sense of beauty many of the natives have. I have been amazed sometimes at the commercial fishermen, my experiences with them. I think they get a kick at the way the gulls come around their tugs when they feed them the fish guts. Things like that. They're very much aware of the beautiful things around them."

Yet Phil admits some do not see the picture at all. A painting of his titled "Network," for example—a Door County scene of fishermen drying and fixing their nets in a field—brought a native reaction of "You mean someone would pay you $500 for that old painting?"

"I see the futile struggle the ecology group goes through, keeping things good, not overcrowded. I guess I'm not much of a crusader. Some of it's going to remain, but the interesting areas are getting more and more crowded, and there are fewer and fewer of them. Time takes care of some of it—the scene over there at White Fish Bay, that old shed going down over there on Sand Bay."

As for the fishing boat scene right in front of him? The very painting-history he is now recording? Time and the very moment? How long does he suppose even this will remain? "I guess it depends on whether the DNR is going to put the fisherman out of business. Who's going to take care of them? Can they be preserved?"

And yet the preservation of the fisherman, the scene, is going on now in the eyes of Austin, in the hand that holds the brush, captures the color, the movement, the feeling.

"I'm painting from memory now," he says, working in the trucks, contemplating the figure of the disappearing fisherman. "One thing I've had to learn to do the longer I paint is keep things a little more fluid. I tend to be a documentation painter—putting down things I see rather than interpreting what I see. That's too bright; it gets too important that way, trying to control what's important.

"If you work wet, it all fuses together and doesn't get too specific, rather than creating an object. The things I'm trying to record now are all the things I won't be able to remember too well. Now I'm going to throw in the sky. It too will make the winter sun seem brighter. You see, I've got to force the dark sky in order to make the water stand out. I've got to lift the sun out now with a damp brush to make that soft image of the sun up there. Now, to put in the distant edge there while it's still soft, to retain the character.

"Probably one of the hardest things for a beginner to learn is timing— to do something before it gets too dry, or not dry enough. To know when you can do things, and when you can't.

"I have to remember to leave a rim of white on top of stuff for that light bouncing out of the water. Now, to get a few little trees that have some character here . . . and I have to put them in so they look like part of the wash. If you wait too long, they won't spread in. Now I've got to get that shoreline in there before it gets too dry, and I'll do it blue to get the feeling of snow. It's working. It looks like there's snow back there.

"The sun's gone again. I've got to do this from memory to get the feeling of light. If I'd have gone much darker, it would have looked like moonlight. I guess there's no chance of that sun coming out again. Well, here goes . . . I'll see if I can get the feel of it. I hate to lay a tone on this foreground, but I'm going to have to make that white sing back there. I'll put a little orange in it to warm it up, get the feeling of the sun on it. Then the cold shadows become colder by comparison. I have to kill all the lights everywhere else.

"The trees now, you see, will form a vertical axis where the main interest is. This should pull it all together. It'll give a second dimension now too, putting these branches in and pushing the boats back at the same time.

"I'll clear up some of my white snow by taking the pencil lines out with an eraser. You know, I started painting on location like this because I learned it in college. Now if you took a shot of this with a camera, it would never reflect the changing mood we've had. You get kind of a composite this way of what's going on. Look at that sky there! This is a very unusual day. A lot of times you just stumble on things like this."

The color of Door? Blue? Gold? Green? For some of us here it's gray on white. Winter is the only real and meaningful season for what we feel, see, and know inside ourselves. To Phil Austin? "We get a lot of blue-grays in the distance, portions of landscape. Then warmer on the foreground. A lot of chances to use blues and warmer grays, and cold grays. There are lots of beautiful grays here that are interesting to paint. The preponderance of evergreens gives us a lot of greens; they all have a lot to do with the overall color that you see. Sunrises, sunsets are fantastic around here. We have big skies, a lot of chance to see what is going on in the sky because of all the water. You can see such a great distance. We're seeing clouds now [over Lake Michigan] thirty-five, forty miles away. You don't get that opportunity in closed places.

"I've learned a lot here. I've learned there's a lot of color in snow, not just blue and white, but color from surrounding objects. It was pretty darn nice of Al Johnson to say, 'There's nobody who paints snow like Phil Austin.' "

He concentrates finally on the white, unpainted figure in the watercolor before him—the disappearing fisherman who must now come to life. "He was a strong silhouette. I don't want to do a portrait of him. I don't want him to become too important. I'm stalling about putting him in. I'm afraid to try it. I used to be afraid of foregrounds too, till I learned it just takes a little bit to say the whole thing. Leave enough so the viewer uses his imagination. Otherwise the painter spoils it for the people. I'm a very poor teacher, but I have almost unlimited enthusiasm for watercolor, and that's what I try to teach."

His own enthusiasm suddenly becomes evident as he begins splattering the entire painting with a water soaked brush. "This may seem kind of crazy," he laughs, "but it'll loosen it all up."

Then back to the figure again, who seems to be haunting the artist this fading afternoon. "Well, there's only one way to do it—just get in there and paint it!" He slaps the colors on the figure in colors best described as Phil Austin colors. "I've got to relate him a little more to his surroundings. This is important in a figure—to get the stress points in subtly where they belong, to give him action."

A sigh: the figure is not right. "I don't know how far I should go. I have his features a little too strong. I have to lift out some of that light. There, that's better. The figure has got to be convincing in its gesture for one thing. It can't be self-conscious, like he's aware he's there. He's got to be completely free of being in the picture. I don't want him to be aware that somebody's painting him. He's got to be going about his business. I'll pick up some light on his forehead and chin so you know that he's there and not just a blob. I'll give him some rope so his hand has a reason for being there. I really tackled a rough one today. I like that: to capture the emotion of the day."

Karen: A Dance to Door

Spring. The green dance, from the smallest roadside plant in a vertical upsurge, to trees bursting in leaf, swaying to morning skies woven in rainbows of returning birds, from the mystical white transformation of ice and snow in bays to the miracle and movement of water. I am stillness, I am dance; I am death, I am life. Know this for what you are. Everything moves.

Trillium twirl on the woodland floor. Here a deer ascending; there a bird tapping out an ancient rhythm. The world and spirit are renewed in a season, the county of Door comes alive again. And along the shore of Egg Harbor, a young woman, Karen Weis, dances.

She is the plant upsurging; she is the orchard turning toward blossom; in this moment, she is the water, the sunrise, the sunset in Door.

"I always loved to dance," she tells you. "I loved to move. I remember a class where we were to do these keep knee bends, like this, and the teacher, Margret Dietz, would come by and run her fingers along the back of your spine, and it felt like a magic touch. She didn't like to talk a lot. She always expressed herself through dancing. But that was an inspiring moment, her fingers along the back of my spine. I felt like leaping.

Born in Minnesota, Karen Weis came to dancing in her high school years upon the encouragement of friends. "When I was studying dance, I never thought I would be a professional dancer. I just loved to dance. When they asked me to join the company, I don't think I really understood what I was getting into."

She was first a student of dance at the College of St. Benedict in St. Joseph, Minnesota, and then became professionally associated with SPIRA, *A Company of Dancers*, also of St. Benedict, and later Portland, Oregon.

"At St. Benedict there was no degree as such in the dance program. You paid a lot of money for no credit. I'm just a high school graduate without a degree or anything. All I ever did there was study dance and then join the company as a professional for two years.

"The day would start at eight in the morning with a good hour's workout. Lots of times I would have three rehearsals, an hour and a half each with a fifteen-minute break in between. There would be a late lunch. Afternoons I would either teach a class or take classes. After that, you would work on your own choreography, mostly at night."

After five or six years she left the company. "I found out I had different goals, different things I wanted to do. They had been my teachers, but I needed to break away from them. I turned twenty-three. I wanted to change my life."

Parental reaction to a child wanting only to dance? "My mom loves my enthusiasm for dance. I remember her showing me how to fall, which she learned in a modern dance class in college. My family, generally, is not artistically oriented. I grew up hunting and fishing with my dad and three brothers. My dad's wish would be for me to become a secretary, settle down, raise a family."

Still unsettled, though, she finds herself a dancer at heart, somewhat adrift in Door this moment. She is no longer a member of a company, regenerating herself, perhaps, in this special setting, working as a waitress at Al's, sometimes pondering her next move. A dancer does not remain still very long. Nor can she explain what she is all about without suddenly resorting to movement.

"Modern Dance is the only dance I've ever done. It's not the disco scene, it's not ballet, it's not jazz. It's not Martha Graham either. What it's dealing with is the basic movement starting from a walk, taking off into a glide, into a run . . . and then you can take off into the air.

"What happens if I take off into the air and then go right into the ground? You fall, but leap. What happens when you leap and go into the ground? You have to rebound for even that. So you're playing with curves, circles.

"When you dance, you're totally giving of yourself. It's physical, but you're also revealing your whole self to the audience. The last solo piece I did, I was able to work with our composer, which was a good experience. You're both creating at the same time, the music and the dance. The name of the piece was *Newton's Law*: what goes up must come down. It was just playing with gravity, a lot of leaps involved."

There is no music in this springtime setting of Door. No music but the sound of waves conversing with the shore, a slight sigh of wind, a lone gull choreographing with the movement of sun and sky around his wings.

Karen sits momentarily, rises to explain something, always prefacing her moves with "okay," and inevitably, quite naturally, retreats to the silent movement of her body for the truest self-expression.

"Dance is natural, because you're doing it all the time. It's movement. If you're just going to the grocery store, you're dancing. When I'm performing, I have to have enough confidence that when I go on stage I don't have to think about what comes next. The music puts me in my place. It's all very ecstatic.

"I guess I think of dance as a love for life. You offer to people something that is very personal to you, and that you work very hard at. You're projecting your emotions with every type of movement you do. I guess it's just a real positive, powerful feeling, even if it's a dance of death."

The beauty of a place like Door is the beauty often found in those unsettled people, like Karen, who often touch down here ever so briefly. The dancer, in this instance, absorbs all the wonder of the natural landscape, transforming it, sharing it, expressing it, personally, for all those who don't quite experience it in the same way, or even bother to express it at all beyond Chamber of Commerce platitudes of "God's Country."

"When I was dancing, I had one month off a year. I would come here usually for about two weeks with a friend. I resigned from the company in January of '77, but I worked until April. I had to teach. I had to ease new people into my position. Then I came here. I danced at Birch Creek Farm last summer in that splendid summer music workshop, the Performing Arts Academy near Egg Harbor, directed by James Dutton. I'll dance there again this summer.

"I've done little dance classes along the way, but I haven't performed since. I guess I feel now like I'm doing things I'd always wanted to do when I was with the company—like travel. I work out here, experiment. I just go into a room and dance. I experiment, like what happens if you turn on a spot for five minutes and try to break out of that? Your first impulse—to dance!"

She likes to teach and might pursue that here for a while, if there is an interest. "It's best when you start a class that you have a workout first. Most people are pretty tight to begin with. So you start with something like just standing vertical—standing like this—while you're warming them up. Then moving across space, going through space with that movement, swinging, and maybe then move it even more, take it into the air. There has to be that initial impulse to get you to move."

What is to become of the dancer and the dance?

"I like it here. I love to be around water. It's continually flowing here, changing. When I think about what I'm going to do with dance, I think first of all whether it's worth it. But I find that when you do dance, and you have people watching you, for a time they can escape their lives. The dance just draws them in. People love to see me do it, I guess. I feel I am a good dancer with the knowledge of it I have, and the love. So I feel I have to continue, but where and how do I do it?

"I attended a performance of Annabelle Gamson at the Children's Theater in Minneapolis, the Walker Art Center, and then a class with her the next day. I knew she was going to be good. I had heard a lot about her, and she was . . . oh she was good! I guess what she did was reinforce modern dance for me. Like, there it is again, I see it. Not the avant-garde or anything else, just modern dance.

"I felt, watching her dance, that I just wanted to do it. I felt, 'I've got to meet this lady. I've got to work with her. I would like to study with her in a summer workshop.' But then I think, 'God, I don't want to live in New York, in that kind of an environment.' But, if I had the money, I probably wouldn't think twice about it. My dream would be to be an apprentice under her—to learn those dances.

"Winters up here are too fierce, and I love movies, theaters, concerts. It's like a retreat here for me. I don't think I could take it as a year-round thing. I thrive in the city, but if people here are interested, I'd be more than happy to teach dancing. I'd love to give a lecture-type demonstration. I'm waiting for the music now for Birch Creek in August. I'm waitressing at Al's. I'm listening to a lot of Mozart."

Karen danced professionally with SPIRA, studied with Margaret Dietz, did workshops with Paul Taylor/Ririe-Woodbury, Natraj L. Rajaram, Alwin Nikolais. She has taught, designed costumes, and even choreographed some dances of her own: Joy, Forces, Abstract Walking, Skirt Study, Anxiety, Air, Reflected Images, Appearing and Disappearing.

If she could dance Door at this moment, if she could choreograph what she sees and feels around her, what might that be?

No hesitation. A smile and an immediate release of the body. "Oh, all kinds of things here. The other day down here, I was watching the waves, that movement, that rolling [she, rising in place, stepping onto a stage of the shore, the waters of the bay for a natural backdrop] that rolling, rolling, like this [her back slightly bending, arms rising gracefully over her head, bringing it all forward, backward] . . . just that in itself is a very beautiful movement. In the landscape, a lot of the rock formations, the cliffs are gorgeous. And the deer [she laughs, she smiles, she raises her whole body] . . . if I can get my eyes on a deer, the trees, the fields . . . the fields with just that constant swaying motion, like the S curve in the body. Yes, orchards too . . . they have their own feeling, so short, bent down, but you know they'll come up again next year.

"Oh, I get into a lot of sunsets here. That diminishing point—how it all just closes in." Her arms envelope it all in a final homage to dance.

Freddie

He's a laughing, singing, dancing fool of a man, Freddie Kodanko, sixty-five, of Liberty Grove, the A.C. Tap, the Frontier Saloon, and any celebration within reasonable striking distance of his old Ford tractor and his dancing feet. The man's a wonder in this county that tries so hard at times to take itself oh so seriously, cashing in on peace and quiet, quaintness and charm for the tourist trade, at the expense of native life in the woodwork, a little zaniness and joy that might be a truer measure of some of the spirit still left in the people who worked this county as a way of life.

Not to say that Freddie is the pride and joy of all the local people either. For Freddie's dancing is like a mirror held up to those solemn spirits who suspect evil wherever there is music and dancing, not to mention drinking. And these people, I'm convinced, are hell bent in these parts to write an 11th Commandment for all the Freddies in the world: Thou Shalt Not Enjoy Thyself.

But may the gods, the true people, and the county sheriff protect Freddie on his long day's journey into night, plying the back roads, the dark roads on his tractor, lit-up, singing, and heading for home. God knows how a spirit such as his must be protected. Freddie, so close in touch with what most men spend a lifetime trying to grasp: happiness.

It's a rare thing, a happy man. They say only saints and fools ever come close. I've come across large doses of it in people at times: musicians making their music, singers singing their songs, artists discovering their images. Work, love, nature, children, play . . . it's all around, little pieces of it to pick up and hold for a while. Quite often, those with very little have more of it than most.

But happiness as a sustaining drive, as an energy, a force, is very rare. Freddie, I suspect, has a greater hold on it than just about anybody in these parts. He's got his work, he's got his music, he's got his drink, he's got his dancing, he's got his tractor to ride.

I've seen Freddie dance his way out of the Frontier Bar in Baileys Harbor, sit momentarily on the bench outside the Red Geranium, talk to the birds on the wire, then dance his way down the street.

One crowded night in the old Blue Ox (I believe the Birminghams were playing) Freddie began doing his dance alone at the doorway, turning round and round, laughing, shouting, his very dancing self just parting the sea of people, picking up a girl here and there to twirl around with him, dancing till he danced himself right out the back door . . . only to appear at the front door again in a matter of seconds. Last week at Old Ellison Bay Days, there was Freddie in his place, early, at least an hour before the parade was to start. Freddie sitting all alone in front of Clayton's, all decked out in a snappy sport coat, shirt and tie, a nifty little hat, waiting for the good times to roll. Music all around the man.

Freddie comes prepared to enjoy himself, and there's music with the man wherever he goes. He has his own battery-powered portable stereo phonograph set up alongside him, and a crate of record albums within reach.

"These batteries," he says. "I don't know if these batteries'll last, maybe two hours. There's no plug around, don't see no plug. He ain't open yet? I got all kinds of music, Hahaooooeeee! All kinds. I got polkas, I got bluegrass. Yesterday, I was hayin', hayin', phew it was work. Don't you see all these records? I'm gonna dance . . . polka, everything. Haaaooooeee! Hey, did you see me on TV? Channel 11? I was dancin'!"

There are stories and stories about Freddie. He's living literature in our landscape, a walking folktale.

A warm and quiet summer evening, some days later, driving the back roads of Door, I find Freddie on the farm, pitching a little hay. Cats all over. Kittens and cats perched on the railing and the steps of the small house. Cats inside, outside the screen door. Freddie's mother, eighty-nine, like a lace shadow behind the curtained window, her head waving gently. Concerned, perhaps, about her boy Freddie out there with the cats, with a pitchfork, near the garden, and the stranger come to call.

A furry cloud of cats scatters around my feet as I greet Freddie, a little shy in the setting summer sun, but moving the pitchfork around like a dance. "You know what's botherin' my garden?" he says. "Old Jackie Boy," he exclaims, dropping the pitchfork, moving into a patch of acorn squash, taking hold of a plant, pulling off a dead leaf, putting it to my face. "Old Jackie boy, the 14th of June—late frost. Know what this is? Poppies. When they come in bloom, the garden looks soooo nice with poppies in between. Red poppies!

"I've been farming ever since I was a kid. My Dad was truck gardening. He got me an early start on how to do it. I was born in that big white house there across the road. Fifth of March, 1913. Lived there. Then twenty-eight years in the state park. Fish Creek school for eight years. I didn't pass with a very good standing, but I got to go to Gibraltar for a few months anyway. Gracie Slaby, one of my teachers.

Ohooooo, I liked geography, so I learned wherever in the world things are. History, history I liked, and general science. English not so good."

Freddie running to the barn to get his hands on a scythe. He wants his picture taken. Freddie moving through the long grass with the scythe, swaying with it like a dancing partner.

"I wrote the *Door County Waltz*. I wrote four of them. Don't know where they are, gave them to my sisters. Lost them. Say them? No. I can sing one. I wrote four of them. Three of them with one stanza, one of them with three stanzas. I'll have to sing that one. I know most of it. I should know it. I sang it in the tavern last night. Got shined up a bit.

"See this grass here? I got to save this grass here for the parade [the 4th of July parade in Baileys Harbor]. The Frontier [Saloon], they want me to be their host driver for the parade. I'd like to be, I'd sure like to be. I'm not sure if I'll do it or not. The Piper String Band, that's it! That's what they're having at the Frontier. Haaaoooeee! A band! I had to walk every day to school, 2½ to 3 miles. Six in the family, I'm the oldest, the only boy."

Freddie on his knees now in still another garden. Freddie pulling weeds by the handful, while up and down the rows the cats follow and frolic. "Know what this stuff is? Foxtail. Know what this stuff is? Quack grass." Freddie fondles one of the kittens. "Ah, Sweetie, you want some peas? Here's some peas. Sweet, huh? April 14th I put those in. These are early, these are later. I sell my beans."

Following Freddie now, shelling peas, munching them. They are good, Freddie, they are real good, as good and real as the man who planted them, as good as this earth you keep working. "See this new fence? I made it myself. That barn there, that barn there is over 100 years old. My Dad built this barn here, this one in 1923. Sawmill over there. We didn't saw nothing now since over a year. Beckstrom? Yeah I sawed wood for him, used to."

Then into a small shed. Boxes. Wooden boxes. Yet another odd job for this hard-working, hard-drinking, hard-dancing old man. No, not *old* man. Gray-headed, yes; and a sporty little red mustache. But limber enough, loose enough in body and mind to reduce it all to dance. He's setting up a vise now, grabbing a plane. He wants another picture taken, Freddie working the wood.

"Apple crates these are—hundreds of 'em. I make them, make them all. Oh, pottery people buy them. They even come up from Milwaukee and get them. This here one goes for $3, these for $2.25. That's cedar, all cedar . . . some pine, some ash, some tamarack. Here's my saw. I didn't take one step in the swamp last year. I made 300 of these big ones since Labor Day, pretty close to 400 all told. Orchardmen buy them. They've even bought some for rabbit pens and stuff like that. Oh boy, do I make boxes. They use them for albums. For libraries. At the Frontier, they even got them for back bar, for liquor and everything."

Freddie planing away on a piece of wood, his yellow and white "Door County" cap slightly askew. Freddie out of the clear blue sky suddenly singing, "Thou art the only one . . . One most wonderful county under the sun . . . With your hills and lakes and islands where all your scenery commands . . . You're beautiful to see, the most precious to be . . . From shore to glimmering shore, and to the tip of Door . . . 'Tis here for everyone to enjoy, for all of us, girl and boy . . . Through all the townships we know and everywhere we go . . . You're the very best county to see . . . Even our homes in Liberty G. . . .

"Goes like that. Sang it last night at the Frontier. Got a little shined up.

Ah, the tales of Freddie. He threw a party once at the Frontier, the occasion being the dimes he was saving. When he had 10,000 dimes, he was going to throw a party. 10,000 dimes or not, the party began, with Freddie standing at the bar, singing, "My ship has come in, my ship has come in."

Freddie putting the plane away, moving out of the shed, down the field. "Hear that? A robin. I'll show you my potatoes. This is my corn.

"Birds . . . some are so nice. Wintertime you don't hear 'em much. Just the blue jays talk. Spring, there comes all those beautiful birds. Robins sing, cardinals, field sparrows. Bob-o-links. There's one pretty sound. Ever hear a bob-o-link? They got such beautiful songs. Hear that? Robins. I know quite a few birds around here.

"Door County—I guess this is about the best I know of, being around this place. I can go visit my friends at the bar, at ball games, do a little dancing.

"My Dad was a dancer. I inherited dancing, it was an inheritance from him. He did it different than I did. He did jigs. I do ballet and a little jig. I used to play the harmonica and the Jewish harp and dance at the same time. It's enjoyable. That's the best part for a person, to enjoy himself with the music and dancing. One time I danced in the school program, about a four-piece band. A home talent show. Oh maybe twenty years ago. It's like an inheritance from my dad. Oh, you should have seen my dad dance. He'd put his heel right up on the table!

"Yeah, you just have some refreshments, and away you go. Refreshments, yeah, something like that fermented malt beverage. Hahaoooweeee! Some wine . . . something to make me feel gay.

"See this here corn? They'll be a couple of them knee high by the 4th of July. Did you ever see tamarack? That's tamarack right there. Worms in the corn. Crows in there too. "

"I lost my driver's license about eighteen years ago. D. D. The sheriff's boys, they took me up for not attending to my driving. That was D. D., drunk driving. The sheriff's boys took fault in my driving. But the sheriff now, he's took a liking to my dancing, my ballet. You don't need no license for no tractor. I got lights on there and a couple of triangles, but I got to be careful so I don't get in trouble. Think the sheriff'll know about this?"

Freddie moving over into the potatoes now, picking up rocks, tossing them. The garden, all spread out, is all pretty much Freddie's business, Freddie's doing. "I do it myself. Get up around 6 o'clock. Bed? I don't know. Refreshments? Whenever I feel like it. Stop in maybe after hayin' or cultivatin'. The A.C. Tap, that's my fav-O-rite! Haaaooeeee! It's close by. And they got the ball park there.

"I been buying records for over forty years. Some 78's are forty years old. Altogether, must be three hundred I have. I like old time polkas and waltzes . . . and a little bluegrass mixed in. Oh boy, these potatoes took beautiful. No sign of no bugs or anything."

Freddie with his potatoes, his onion sets ("They go like hotcakes"), his apple crates, his sawmill. Freddie the truck farmer, Freddie the last of the hired men. Maybe the last of the native folk heroes, people like Freddie fast disappearing from the local history of this land, never to be replaced—certainly not by city folk. All the old Freddies of Door, people with little or nothing, nickel and diming their lives away. Scratching. I'm reminded of neighbor and friend old Charley Root, making fish boxes to hang on. Fishermen selling chubs door to door. Small orchardmen being beat continually by the market or the weather. Scratching. All of it going now with the price of land at a premium. The final disappearance of the native—bought out—if he has any land left to sell.

"Oh, I make a few dollars with my vegetables, my beans. I make some with my lumber and posts, and some working out. I can always use more, but I'm satisfied. Never overdo it when you want to sell something. I don't own anything, no. I got a thirty-year lease on the land. After that, I don't know. . . .

"Marriage? Well, no. Too many revocations! They take your driver's license away, and I just don't have no chance to go out. Had to stay home. Then I got the tractor. Lonesome. I believe I'm better off by being single. I can go off, don't have a wife to keep me home. Girls are nice, nice to visit. A little dancing—that's all right. I like my freedom. Freedom with my Ford tractor! Haaaaoeee!"

We're across the road now, over to another field. The sun is burning a deeper, final orange. There's a peace and a lush green warmth to the land at this time. Freddie picking strawberries, tasting them. "I got to go out hayin' so much, help load the wagon, fifty, seventy-five pounds. Here's more potatoes. There's your potato bug. I hill these with a garden plow, push, push. You know what that is? Onion seed. I sell that for sets in the spring. Those darn cut worms—see how they took that stuff, that row?"

Freddie on the road now, walking back home, jumping up at a tree. "Ever see this here? That's wild filbert. You know, you should take a picture of me sittin' up in the cedar tree! Haaaooooeee!"

"My Dad, he was the best violin player in Door County. He used to play tremolo fingers and tremolo bow. He was sooo good. Talent scouts from Chicago wanted to sign him up in the Stock Orchestra. He was a logger in Upper Michigan, 1903. He used to hew tamarack ties, thirty, forty below zero. I never got nowhere he did.

Freddie suddenly lunging toward a tree, trying to swing his leg over the first branch, laughing like hell at his own fun and foolishness. "I need a ladder. I need a ladder to get me going, then I'd be up there some!"

Finally back at the house, Freddie pats his tractor, a DOOR COUNTY USA sticker fixed to the front of it. "Runs like a top." He starts it up.

I open the door of my own car, reach down to the floor, and break open a 6-pack, buying Freddie a beer, not to egg him on, not to make a fool of the man, but to honor him in a way. To show thanks to a man for being no more than who and what he is. "Ah, Strohs! My fav-O-rite!" he laughs, rolling his eyes. "Kodanko is Austrian!" he says proudly, and then disappears into the house only to return the gesture of Strohs with a can of Tuborg. Freddie is a man with good taste in brew. The cats are at his feet, all around him.

Freddie and cats bring back a tale of some years ago. Seems Freddie, after a long night of drinking and dancing at the A.C. Tap, all of a sudden headed for home on his tractor—with no lights at that time. Friends at the bar, concerned for him, figured they'd better follow him to be sure he made it home safe. Once on the road, there was no Freddie in sight, and they feared the worst. They caught up to him near the house, though, the tractor pulled over and Freddie on a fence talking to his cats. Cats, strangely enough, he somehow managed to name after the alphabet. But with a typical Freddie touch, not just A, B, C, etc.; Freddie doubled the letters for the cats' names: AA, BB, CC, DD, EE.

Back inside the house again, Freddie's turned his music on: polka music, which neither rustles the image of the old mother behind the curtain nor startles the cats between his almost dancing feet coming through the door.

"My Dad," he says, his eyes starting to water up; "He got lost. We had a manhunt for him. He got lost in the swamp. Nobody knows if he got lost or somebody took him away. I just inherited dancing from him."

Some men, in self-righteousness, ignorance, or pity, might label Freddie a fool. Others, I suspect, understand who the real fools are.

Toby: The Kite Man

Tako-kichi.

It begins every year around this time, with the earth in its turning, the sun reawakening all living and dead spirits. There's a smell to the earth, to the air, a feeling to it, especially the silent invitation of the sky and the wind to come closer in a way, to be one with it all.

In the city, in my youth, the fever came upon us with the first warm winds of March and April. We did it in the streets, in alleys and playgrounds, finding only pieces and patches of sky to play around in. The smallest opening, between backyard trees or the grim geometry of telephone wires, was a challenge, a way in—or out, depending on how much your feet were on or off the ground. If you were really lost in it, you discovered you flew! And if you were really fortunate, there might still be a prairie at the end of your block where you had a whole field to fool around in with paper, sticks, rags, string, wind and sky.

Tako-kichi, the Japanese call it—"kite crazy."

And here in the county, around Fish Creek, lives a man who sells and flies and dreams kites, Toby Schlick, of the Fish Creek Kite Co. (adjacent to Doug Butchart's Thumb Fun).

Toby is definitely *tako-kichi,* a grown man, kite lover, kite flyer, kite seller, kite dreamer surely on the path to one day becoming an honorable kite-master, an artist of noted distinction. And possibly, like Hokusai (Old Man Crazy about Drawing), he will be Toby, Old Man Crazy about Kite Making.

But if you knew Steve Kastner's old Fish Creek Cycles on F, in the early '70s, or if you knew the early days of Kastner's first crusade to turn the whole country on to cross-country skiing (and biking), you may have seen Toby around.

You may not see this in him now, bearded, driving a van that seems held together by faith, doing a little carpentry here, a little welding there to make it through a long winter without kites. For Toby is yet another Door County mystery man of sorts. Not many of the natives know him, know about him. And Toby would probably prefer it that way.

He was the quiet man in the background totally absorbed in the intricacies of 10-speed bikes. He assembled them, repaired them, maintained them, moved himself and others into the wonder of such machinery, the Zen in the art of 10-speed bicycle maintenance. In winter, working for Steve, he turned all his energies into the inner/outer pleasure and pursuit of cross-country skiing.

He has always been, I suspect, a man very quietly on the move. A man, to this moment, still evolving—and open to that, aware of it. And in at least this one sense he is alone: an artist.

In another sense he remains a man with two feet planted firmly on the ground. He has both a history and appreciation of this place. "I came here when I was thirteen," he tells you. "Twenty-one years ago. I came here for diving. Doug [Butchart] had a place in Green Bay. Our whole family came up and we camped in the park. I've lived here year around now for about ten years."

His attachment, from early on, consciously/unconsciously, has been to nature. "I have a degree from Madison in Biological Aspects of Conservation, but I haven't made a nickel off that yet. Most of the people in my major are working for the DNR. And those who are competent are leaving in droves. It's become kind of like a police force."

The dual nature of Toby Schlick: love of the natural world, but a respect and fascination for machinery as well. A Honda mechanic, no less. "When I went to college I fixed motorcycles. Yeah, that's true." A contradiction? Seemingly so, but the essence of Zen.

He spent two years in the service in Korea—1968, 1969—as part of the Army Security Agency ("I saw zero kites when in Korea"), and came back to Door in 1970, where he worked for Steve Kastner from '72 to '75 or '76. "I guess Steve said, 'You want a job?' And I wasn't doing anything at the time, so I started repairing bikes, then got into cross-country skiing. I skied better than 300 miles this winter.

"I've always done things with my hands since I was a little kid. The bicycle—one of man's most efficient inventions. It still is. I still like bikes, but I don't fix them anymore commercially. I got out of the bike and ski business because I found out you just don't get any chances to do it yourself."

The move from motorcycles to 10-speed bikes in his Door days may seem like a backward motion to some, but to Toby and others of his insight and nature it's perfectly natural, certainly understandable.

"It was kind of an evolution for me. I was part of that '60s group—a consciousness-raising period in our lives, a hopeful time that actually changed many important things. Biking, cross-country skiing, running—I'm in better shape now than I ever was in my life.

"I like to think I've got a fairly simple lifestyle. I have been working on simplifying it for quite a while. Biking and cross-country skiing are perfect. I feel every year, hopefully, I'm refining it more."

In the process of evolving, of simplifying, kites unexpectedly flew into his life about three years ago and the focus, the spirit, has been there ever since.

"I think I was an average kid and flew kites in the spring a little bit. When I was ten or twelve I made a box kite which went up and then crashed, and that's the last time I flew a kite till three years ago. Around that time a friend said she never flew a kite before, and I thought, 'Well, that's not right.' So I went to Bunda's, bought a kite, and flew it.

"Then I got some books about kites, and. . . ." He's not quite sure how to describe what's come over him, and embarrassed to probe aloud the spiritual ramifications of such a "toy." "Well, it's almost cosmic how I got into it. And here I am—a kite junkie. I own just about every book on kites in English and Japanese. Whenever I get into something I get into it completely. I'm also a book junkie."

He lives in a small apartment just down the road from the Fish Creek Kite Co. where, in the spring, every noon now, you will see the sky alive and ablaze with kites of all sizes and shapes, all beauty and wonder. Rainbow kites, snake kites, hand-painted Japanese kites . . . the oldest, the latest, the best he can get his hands on. And put into yours.

Tako-kichi. No, you may not quite see it in his face, in his gestures (without a kite in tow) as he sits at a desk in his apartment, expressing a simple fascination with such toys, but there are kites, literally, flying everywhere about him, though they may hang on the walls like paintings, or rest in corners anxious for flight, or peek out of boxes. He is comforted with kites about him.   And it's a marvelous feeling, surrounded by such color, design, and poetry in a second floor apartment overlooking fields and sky, a feeling in itself of being airborne.

"There's a misconception in this country that kite flying is kid stuff. People come into my shop and I tell them that kids should be from eight to ten to get into it. Before that they need a lot of help."

Kite flying: how to define it? "I call it a science, a sport, or an art. A synthesis of all three. There's still a lot of science in it. Meteorology departments still use them, but kites are almost universal. Just about every continent, every culture has had kites, except I can't find a reference to Africa. Kites are somewhere between four and six thousand years old. It all started in China, but of course Japan will dispute this. It's the world's oldest toy next to the doll. They've been used in war for observation, for dropping things on the enemy. There's just a fascinating history to this business.

"For sport, there's this thing where you just go out and fly a kite by yourself and do what you want.   There's also something that's coming on strong now—kite fighting—which has been going on in India for a long time. The British have come up with a lot of two-string kites, for steering, and there are starting to be contests with these now. The most technique and skill comes in kite fighting, controlling your kite.

"The world's indoor record for kite flying was just broken in Seattle, the Kingdome, during the half time of a Sonics game on January 31st. They kept this glider kite up, a single string of silk thread, for nine hours and fifteen minutes.   That's real finesse—indoor flying.   It's pure technique. It's hard to b. s. under those conditions.

"They are getting into more and more kite competitions: the largest, smallest, fastest, etc. The American Kitefliers Association just last year had their first annual meeting in Ocean City, Maryland.   The Washington Kitefliers Association in Seattle is probably the most active group in the States now."

Yet given the science, the competition in the world of kites, their essence remains a beauty in themselves, akin to the bird. "The art of kites," says Toby, "is probably what I'm most interested in, the aero-dynamics of it, the aesthetics of it—what's on a kite, the art of just flying.

"I'm into the aesthetics as a collector, like the kites you see around you, behind you. This one next to me on the wall was made by a kitemaker, Yanase, who I visited in Japan. This particular kite is called a *tungari.* I like the brush work. The whole thing. It's a real tradition, kite making in Japan. Yanase is a fourth generation kite maker. There were 110 kite makers in Tokyo at one time. There's only one left, a man named Hashimoto, close to some eighty years old.

"I'm sure with a very large percentage of my business with kites, the kites are never flown. They just hang on the wall as art. I won't sell a kite unless it flies good, however."

The American form of kite that we all grew up with is not a particular favorite of Toby's. "Ours in the two-stick diamond, or Eddy kite. Designed by William A. Eddy on Feb. 4, 1891, when he built five of them to lift a self-recording thermometer, the first automatic record of temperature aloft. From that came the famed Eddy kite. I can't understand how we've been stuck with that kite for so long as the only choice of kite. It's hard to fly for beginners. A lot of adjustments have to be made, compared to this." He pulls out a small, beautiful orange polyethylene kite called a Scott Sled.

The Fish Creek Kite Co. is about to enter its third season. "Memorial Day to Labor Day, seven days a week from 1 to 5 p.m. are the official hours. Still, some of this depends on weather. On a good flying day I'll be there early in the morning. I'll begin doing weekends very soon now. In the fall it's weekends through Fall Festival, same hours."

You can often follow the kites in the sky to the Fish Creek Kite Co. "Organic advertising," he smiles. "They are the best form of advertising. If there's any wind at all I'll have four or five kites flying. I can stick them in the ground, and they'll fly all day.

"The first season was encouraging. I sold a lot of kites. I was really surprised. I had about a one third increase last year. This season may tell the tale whether I can afford to keep it going. I think if I could find a good location that would give me November, December business . . . well, that would take care of me financially for the year. I'm losing about half the income, half the season, by not having the Christmas business.

"I'm sure I could plot my daily business by the weather. If it's a beautiful, calm day, I won't sell any kites, but if it's windy, people will come in. Kite flying is a perfect thing for Door County with the beaches and the shoreline, to fly them over the water.

"I have one of the most complete shops in the county. I have more numbers of different kinds of stock than most kite stores I've been in. The first year I didn't even carry a 'diamond' [Eddy kite] deliberately. I have a complete selection of raw materials to make your own kites. And I have a few kits. Also, I have over 100 different kites (ready-mades) from China, Japan, Indian, Indonesia, Taiwan, Korea, Brazil, England, Germany, the United States and Canada. The ready-mades go from 29 cents to $80.

"Ninety-five percent of the people who walk into my shop buy a kite. Everyone feels he can fly a kite. There doesn't seem to be that much to it. The main thing is you don't have to run with a kite," says Toby. "That's an American myth: you have to be a kid, and you have to run with your kite in springtime."

On the wall of his shop there is a poster which states: HOW TO FLY A KITE. "Contrary to popular notion, it is definitely not necessary for you to run with your kite. If you follow these simple general hints, you will find launching and maneuvering your kite surprisingly simple. Let a helper carry your kite downwind about fifty feet, holding it overhead, nose pointed up and bridle side facing you. Pull in on the string as helper releases kite. The kite will climb upward. Let out string as wind begins to push kite. To gain altitude, jerk the string in when the kite nose is pointed upwards, letting out more string after each jerk. In general, when the kite is pulling against a taut string, it will continue in the same direction it is pointed until the string is relaxed. When the string is relaxed, the kite will begin to float. When the nose points in the direction you wish it to go, quickly pull in string hand over hand and the kite will move in this new direction. When the kite begins to dive or head for trouble, give it slack, and then send it safely off in a new direction. To bring your kite in, just pull on the string in a hand over hand motion and continue walking to avoid tangling the line. You are now ready to rewind the line onto its spool."

Last year, early in May, Toby traveled to Japan to attend the famous Hamamatsu Kite Festival, one of the oldest and largest sporting events with 60 neighborhood teams of 50 to 150 men each competing to cut down the opposing teams' kites—a 400-year-old tradition of celebrating the city's first-born sons.

He also spent a good part of his time visiting some of the great Japanese kite makers such as Yanase and Hashimoto, going into their shops, observing their artistry. "We dealt with techniques in making a kite: how to bridle a kite, stuff like that. I visited a lot of kite makers. Each area of Japan has its own kind of kite, between 100 to 200 different varieties throughout the whole area. I pretty well thoroughly did everything I could with kite making. There is nowhere in this country where you can learn this, or meet a fellow like Yanase, fourth generation kitemaker. Off the record, I would someday like to be a kite maker. It would be nice if I could."

The pure pleasure of kites is something our Western culture associates with child's play, a phase children must eventually work out of their system and get on with the business of becoming serious adults.

Still, as Toby reflects, "Kites have been part of religions around the world. There is a Central American culture where kites are flown over graves. It's a family project to make the kite. It's some sort of releasing of beneficial things for the spirit. The kite is then brought down and burned over the grave itself. The Polynesian culture uses kites to appease the wind gods. There are two wind gods: Tane and Rongo."

Kites: what a release of imaginative possibilities. An act of transcendence, man and the universe. Spiritual flights unending. Night kites in the light of the moon, singing kites with hummers attached, kites and lovers, the mystic kite man in communion with the cosmos.

Kites are so indicative of the mysterious East. A Buddhist monk once wrote, "My kite rises to celestial regions, / My soul caters the abode of bliss."

Basho, a famous Japanese poet, described it this way:

> A kite
> in the same place
> in yesterday's sky!

"There are, of course," says Tat Streeter in his book *The Art Of Japanese Kite*, "other activities that produce the same or a similar feeling of well-being. Children discover them without being told; adults have to be reminded. I often think it would be nice if children started out playing golf and going fishing and ended up as adults flying kites."

Toby, kite man, considers all the silence of the art, all the beauty and history and joy, and calls it, "a form of meditation. I'm not sure what's magic about kites, but it's been going on a long time. It's just magical."

Al Johnson

Coming into downtown Sister Bay on 42 from the top of the hill is not a particularly beautiful or memorable sight, especially after the quaintness of the white village of Ephraim, tucked along the bay, with its church steeples probing the heavens, and its history of Anderson's dock, Wilson's, the Moravian settlement.

Sister Bay means business. If the traveler glides, holding his breath, through the silence and serenity of Ephraim at sunset, he is abruptly hurled back to reality in a downhill run onto the main street of Sister Bay, one foot riding the brake pedal, eyes fixed for trouble at the sudden intersection awaiting the wanderer at the bottom of the hill.

Neither architecture nor natural wonder hold the traveler's immediate attention. But if you're looking for sidewalks, a drug store, a department store, a barbershop, a hardware, a bowling alley/restaurant, an honest-to-goodness local tavern, gift shops, pizza, a delicatessen, gas stations, a supermarket, a bakery, a furniture store, a funeral parlor, plus a number of motels, a hotel, and some good dining places . . . this is it. Sister Bay means business.

So does Al Johnson's Swedish Restaurant and Butik, the true center and soul of Sister Bay, and perhaps, in the long run, its conscience as well. Here the eye does rest and delight on a building of authentic Scandinavian design, goats on the grass roof and all. For Al and his wife Ingert, rare business people indeed, seem a bit beyond the average business operation and definitely set a tone for the way things might be.

No, Sister Bay will never be Ephraim. But what Al and Ingert are suggesting with their restaurant and butik is that it can be unique, both a successful and beautiful village in its own right without the clamor and cheapness of a tourist area like the Dells.

Sitting in the living room of his tastefully furnished, rustic Scandinavian log home—beautiful paintings, massive stone fireplace, honest wooden furniture, an arresting view of the bay just outside the glass doors—Al Johnson has come a long way from the old Chicago neighborhood, one of the toughest: 12th and Blue Island.

Swedish pancakes made the man. Pancakes and a love for people, business, Door County. And perhaps even more than all this, "Behind every good man there's . . ." someone like his Swedish wife, Ingert, with an instinct for fine taste and old world harmonies of nature, design, and people.

A rather subdued Al Johnson sits before me this morning. If you've seen him in action in the more natural habitat of his own restaurant, you would think the man possessed of a singular mood: high geared, volatile energy, especially in the summer season, where he is often observed bent over one table, wiping it with a cloth in one hand, setting up an adjacent table with a fistful of knives, forks, glasses, napkins, somehow clearing a third, and pouring coffee at a table behind . . . while a new waitress stands helplessly by, witnessing the act in terror and confusion as Al, totally in charge, keeps a clear head for quick conversation with customers, or directs orders (in English, Swedish, or Al Johnsonese) to whatever poor soul of an employee happens to be within his firing range: "A 4-top here . . . set up that 2-top by the window . . . they need a high-chair . . . Hello, how are you? . . . coffee for that table behind you . . . How many are you? . . . put two tables together over there . . . where's Ingert?"

Those of us who haunt his place after the season, long into the fall and winter, know a different Al entirely, a somewhat more relaxed Al. When he isn't hanging on the long cord of the kitchen phone, pulling it with him far into the dining room, when he isn't shouting-laughing-cackling into it, calling everyone from Baldy at the sheriff's office in Sturgeon Bay to Eddie Valentine, whiling the winter away in Florida, he sometimes finds time to sit at the table of regulars each morning (or afternoon, or evening) and air his views.

His obsessive energy for running a fine restaurant is then channeled into free swinging conversation (debates, arguments, fights) on politics (local, state, national), the Bears, the Packers, jogging, running, cross-country skiing (he does them all), education, world affairs, the *New York Times*, the *Wall Street Journal*, the *Door County Advocate*, and the *Chicago Tribune*—a constant source of irritation among the ex-Chicagoans hibernating at Al's, expecting the paper (their life line) to arrive every day on schedule, as it usually does during the tourist season, only to discover that once again, come fall and winter, delivery is chaotic at best. The Monday edition may arrive on Wednesday, or it may never arrive at all.

"Hey, Norb," yells Al one morning last fall. "*Trib's* in?" (Just how I became responsible for the lackadaisical distribution of the *Trib* in these parts, I'll never know.)

"No. The papers didn't come in."

"Again! What the hell's wrong with those people?" exclaims Al. "This is gettin' out of hand. Gimme a name. Gimme somebody down there and I'm gonna call and get some action, find out why the hell we can't get those papers up here every day. Who do I call?"

"I don't know. Call Jones," I tell him. I don't know Jones from the late Colonel McCormick, but I think he might be managing editor or something. Besides, I don't think Al's going to do anything about it anyway. But I should know Al by now.

He bursts into the kitchen, picks up the phone, and calls the *Chicago Tribune*. (I fully expect him to pick up the phone and call the White House someday.) A few minutes later he returns to the table and announces to one and all, "The *Trib*'ll be here tomorrow! You better believe it! [Bang! goes the fist on the table.] And the *Trib*'ll be here every day from now on! [Bang] I just talked to that guy Jones. Hey, you know what he said to me? 'Are you the guy up there with the goats on the roof?' " Bang. Laughter. Bang.

Notorious, that's Al. Spontaneous. A man of many interests, many dispositions. Mercurial. Indifferent. Hot and cold. One morning he may take a cup of coffee, sit down next to you, and seriously discuss the state of education in the county (or the country), and the next three mornings (or the next three weeks) he may barely recognize your existence. But he knows you're there. I've never met anyone who didn't like him, and for all the hell his help must take at times, in the height of the season, hardly a one of them would care to work for anyone else. "He's generous." "He's fair." On this everyone agrees.

By far his most constant conversational topic these days is Sister Bay, the state of Door County in general, as he views it from his vantage point of the busiest restaurant in Door.

"Basically, Sister Bay hasn't changed as far as the people in town," he says calmly. They're the same as when I started thirty years ago, the same stores, the same people. I don't think the people are any different here than anywhere else. You got your liberals here, your conservatives. In Ephraim you got your *real* conservatives. Sister Bay is basically the business hub of the north end. It's always been that. And I think Sister Bay people have moved a lot faster than Sturgeon Bay, but in a different way. I have found Sister Bay will band together behind something if they really believe in it: donations to the fire and ambulance service, the dock. The clinic, when it first started, was financed 100% by Sister Bay. We don't have the bickering here that they have in Sturgeon Bay.

"I would like to see Sister Bay and the Door County area not lose its charm, the charm it's noted for. I'm afraid all too often the business people here get carried away by their work, which in the long run gets them away from the direction they should move. I'd like to see the business places remodeled with Door County architecture, to retain its country flavor.

"But you've got to remember Sister Bay is the business end. Everybody comes here to shop. And I think people here have a tendency to place their values in different positions because they are a business area.

"If I'd ever be really wealthy, and had the time on my hands, I'd just like to take some of these business people to different places to see their charm, places like Vermont. I think it's important to make them see this. I don't think they grasp anything from what I say.

"I think we're getting far too many signs here hanging over the sidewalks. I think we made a mistake when sewer and water came in by not putting all the electrical lines in the same ditch. Now we've got all the wires, all the transformers, everything out in the open.

"People thought I was making a big mistake when I built my place [the imported Norwegian native log construction of the restaurant, outbuildings, and his own home], but we live in a predominantly Scandinavian area. I had a special reason for building such a place: what can I do to put something back into Sister Bay that will be basically Scandinavian, and relate to the whole area?

"It was not an overnight thing. My wife and I spent six years talking about it, looking at the possibilities in Scandinavia. When the building was finished, I will always remember the old carpenter we brought here to put it up. He sat across the street and said, 'It's kind of ironic. I come all the way from Valdres, Norway, where they are now putting up concrete buildings, where we are taking the culture away, to find what belongs in my country.' "

Al, a two-term member of the village board, presently a vital member of the local school board, remains very much the concerned citizen, very much aware of politics and power in the county. "I used to think there wasn't any politics in Door. Now I think maybe it's all politics with the way things are going on.

"Basically the county is Republican. I always think it's bad when a county goes too far one way or another—Republican or Democratic—when people just vote for party. But I think Door County is one place where you could put any name down for the Republican party—somebody who doesn't even exist!—and the person would win. I believe that seriously. I don't think people here are politically active as they should be. The younger people coming up aren't involved at all. You got to remember I come from the city of Chicago. Every ward is run by a committeeman. But there are people in this county who I don't think can be swayed by a committeeman. "

Al readily admits that conservatism in the county has no doubt contributed to the relative peace and security found here. "I never have to take the key out of my ignition. I'm not concerned if my kids don't come right home from school. You know your next door neighbor better than you do in Chicago." Those things are well and good, and certainly acknowledged.

"You know, there's never been a bigger controversy here than the park system. But when it comes right down to it, how many people would vote out the park system? Not a one of them! People won't come out *for* it, but the more parks you got in the long run, the more you're going to preserve for the people to enjoy. I do believe that people don't like to get involved. I found that out with the Gooney Bird Golf thing here. People are afraid to step on other people's toes.

"I myself, if I pick up the *Advocate*, you know the first place I look? I go right to the Legal Notices to find out what's going to affect the town I live in! I think we're getting some buildings that are being permitted to be built in the county, that are going to be problems that are not going to go away."

Al Johnson's Swedish Restaurant and Butik did not become the heart of Sister Bay overnight. His father, Axel Johnson, bought the building (once a grocery store) in 1948 while Al was attending Marquette University, where he majored in criminology. He dropped out of college in '49 to help set-up and open the restaurant, but eventually went back to Marquette to complete his degree. "I had a partner then, but I bought him out in 1951.

"The reason I opened the restaurant is that I used to work at the Cottage restaurant there for Johnny Vieth during summers. I always enjoyed cooking. I learned a lot about cooking when I was away at school. I always had a meal job. And I learned a lot from my mother. She taught me how to make the pancakes, make the fruit soup, how to pickle the beets, the herring, how to make Swedish meatballs. The restaurant is absolutely the main reason for all the Swedish products sold in all the stores here today. No question about it.

"When we opened [it was originally called Al's Restaurant] we sat 48 people. We served Swedish pancakes for 55¢ a plate, coffee was a nickel, no charge for the second cup, 20¢ for a hamburger, toast was a nickel, Swedish meatballs, a complete dinner, $1.25. I locked up the restaurant in winter. Got my degree in 1950."

Al was born in Chicago in 1925, went to Sweden when he was six years old, and attended grammar school there. In 1934 he returned to Chicago, lived on 12th and Blue Island, and attended both Holy Family Grammar School and St. Ignatius High School. To this day he is a firm believer in the Jesuits and their hard-line approach to the classics in education.

"In summertime, as soon as school was out, my dad would ship my sister and me to Door County. Primarily my folks wanted us off the streets of Chicago in the summer. He would always board us here at a farm and pick us up on Labor Day, which was always the saddest day of my life. We had no relations here, but our contact was the Field family around North Bay.

"I picked cherries up here in those days for 3½ cents a pail. The place to go then was Husby's—the Cherryland Restaurant, right on the corner where Husby's is today. The bar is basically the same. There was the soda bar on one side and the tavern on the other. I used to always go there for a black cow. A black cow at Husby's was a real treat.

"Emma Husby . . . she was some woman, let me tell you. She helped out a lot of people that folks don't even know about. She had a heart of gold. She could work with the best of them. She was in a wheelchair in her last years—in her 90's—and she ran that place till the day she left it. She was a huge woman. She seemed a very tough person, but underneath, a heart of gold. She had two shots of brandy every night, right up to the time she died and left the place. Nothing, absolutely nothing hypocritical about her."

Al will never quite forget the opening of his restaurant: Memorial Day weekend, 1949. "On the very first day the septic system broke down. The whole damn thing backed up, right into the restaurant! We were packed."

There was yet another memorable day: Mother's Day, 1950—perhaps the birth date of Al Johnson, entrepreneur (pre-Scandinavian architecture, pre-goats on the sod roof). "I flew in orchids from Honolulu for every mother. I was just packed from morning till 8 at night. I'd never seen so many people in my whole life. And no question about it: the orchids pulled them in.

"What I miss about those days is when I used to open the place at five a.m. in April, and the people would all be out there sitting on the docks, fishing at that time. The perch, jumbo perch, were tremendous then. I used to get all these people in my restaurant. There was no other place open at that time of the morning but mine. I think everybody in Sister Bay fished in those years, 1949 to 1953. Then it started to go downhill. But then you could almost say with certainty that from one year to the next the perch would be back in April. At that time too you could be sitting out on the bay in your boat, dip your cup and drink the water. That bay out there! The scene is basically the same out my window here, but it's a different story now."

Al frequently cites the influence of his father in those early years. (Axel Johnson died Easter Sunday, April, 1976.) "Without the help of my father, and the help of Sam Erickson, Willard's dad, I wouldn't be where I am today. Sam was always my builder at the time. Sometimes the money was lean, and he'd always carry me, never pressure me. Sam never missed a day in my restaurant till the day he died.

"My dad was a complete liberal. He had the distinction of working for the largest Catholic church in the city of Chicago. A seven-room flat went with the job, and he wasn't even Catholic! He had the combination to all the safes; he emptied all the poor boxes once a week. Trustworthy, that's what he was."

Al took and passed the test for the CIA in the early fifties and put the restaurant up for sale in 1951 for $22,000. "But I couldn't find a buyer. I decided then to stick it out, not go with the CIA or the FBI."

His style of running a restaurant in those days might be best described by an expression of our times: laid back. "Easy going. A sign on the restaurant read 'Help Yourself. Gone Fishing.' The coffee was going . . . help yourself. I wasn't open on Sundays. Once I even left the back door open for a friend, Joe Mohr, and told him to go in on Sunday and cook his own breakfast."

Those were the heydays, and the hell-raising days of Al in Door County. He looks back over those long years of bachelorhood in Door, and with a slight smile on his face. "Tremendous. Lock up the restaurant at eight, dead tired, take a shower, get a new life! Waterskiing in the middle of the night . . . parties . . . and back again at the restaurant at five the next morning. But you can only do that for so long. You got to start putting something away. My friends? Eddie Valentine, Louis Berns, Bob Boettcher, Baldy, Johnny Vieth, Bud Evenson, Dick Weisgerber. One time Eddie and I were down at a tavern league convention in Chicago, at the Palmer House, having a ball. It was ten below outside. We found this travel bureau open, and ended up in California.

"Both Eddie and I started out with Peterson on his world cruise. We went from November to April and got as far as the Panama Canal. We both had to come back and go to work. Terrific adventure, going down the Mississippi."

Al Johnson didn't find religion to mend his ways, settle him down, but he did find and take a wife, and that has made (and continues to make) all the difference in who he is and what he is all about today. "I think the major change in the restaurant took place after I met Ingert. Then the cultural aspect in me began to mature.

"I got married in 1960 when I was 34. Yeah, that was late. Maybe the war had something to do with it, WWII, paratroopers, 101st Airborne, England, Germany, France. I was in G-2, Intelligence. I was in the Battle of the Bulge, jumped over the Rhein. August, '44 till late 1946. I met Ingert in Sister Bay. She was working at Gordon's Lodge. She came to this country from Sweden in 1952, and I met her in 1959. She's the artist in the family. If she should ever decide to take up painting, she could. She's terrific at it. She's got a terrific memory, terrific perception. We can leave the county, come back three months later, and if there's a tree cut down, she'll tell you so. In that respect, she and I are different. She can walk into a house once and later tell you the color of the wallpaper. I might be able to tell you if there was any wallpaper or not.

"She believes everything should be coordinated, the back of the restaurant should look as good as the front, the washrooms should be spotless. The first year we got married we started a major rebuilding project in the restaurant. It was her pushing, her initiative. And there's no question that we doubled the business overnight.

"She put the hostess system in, she put the uniform system in. In those years, 1960's, we brought over eight or nine girls from Sweden to work as waitresses. We've gotten away from that now because of the laws today involving work permits. I had them immigrate in the country then, but the law changed. The big reason I brought them over was because on Labor Day I'd lose all my help. The Swedish girls could stay with me until November first. I hope to have two girls again this year. Let me tell you those eight girls could do more for diplomatic relations with our own girls and the public than anything I know."

Ingert's early attempt to initiate some change, put a little class in Al's Restaurant, was not exactly welcomed with hurrahs by Al. "When she wanted to put carpeting in the place for the first time, we had our first big argument. I was against it. I was afraid we would get too fancy. I was afraid I would lose people, my everyday customers who would not come in anymore once it was carpeted. But just the opposite happened. The second thing she did was to decide that all our dishes and silverware should be Scandinavian.

"But if I had not married Ingert, that building would not be there today. She was the driving force for that architecture in Sister Bay.

"This is a very independent girl. She's been on her own most of her life. If she makes up her mind, it's got to be. She's very persistent this way. I certainly wouldn't classify her as a liberal, though. She doesn't believe anybody should get something for nothing. She's anti-union. She tends to believe that unions have a role in destroying small businesses. She's never been out of a job herself, never on relief, and has always bought her own cars ever since she came to this country.

"She likes the old things to be carried on, the old traditions. She tends to pick her friends that way. She thinks there are places for guys like Ernie Anderson—wood craftsman—and she doesn't want to see that die out. Our building is a craft that is dying even over there.

"I think Ingert has done more to foster rosemaling in America than any person I've ever met. She's done so many things to keep this going, and for no personal, monetary gain. She feels that if you don't push these things, they have a tendency to die out."

Today the restaurant defines the man (and the woman) more than anything else. The butik, the variety and quality of items to be found there, speak for Ingert herself. The other Scandinavian outbuildings on the grounds, the benches, the flowers, trees, shrubs, the pond . . . all create the peace and presence of countryside.

"I don't think that the restaurant caters to any one person or another. The summer tourist . . . it used to be that 89% of our business was done in those six months or so. But that's beginning to change. One thing my operation has tried to foster is service with a smile. That's the Scandinavian way. And the place could not work if I did not work at it. That's the name of the game. I have never asked any of my help to do work that I wouldn't do myself. I got 92 people working for me now. I look over the years, I think out of the thirty years I've been in business, I think I lost three people out of direct conflict. And I've always taken back anyone who's wanted to come back. And I do believe sincerely that Al Johnson's Restaurant has been a definite help toward girls going through college.

"My kitchen knows when I move into the dining room. The tempo picks up immediately. It's bound to pick up. The tables get cleared up and set up faster. I don't want to take anything away from my help, it's just my natural tendency. I've always had super help.

"I hate job descriptions. Everybody's got to help everybody out. When the place opens at six in the morning, it's got to be ready. It can't be half-ass."

If there were definite growth stages in the rise of Al Johnson (the original free-and-easy style restaurant, orchids for Mother's Day, Ingert, Swedish waitresses, the new log building) his crowning moment has to be the decision to put live goats on the sod roof of the new restaurant July 15, 1974. Neither Sister Bay nor Al has ever been the same.

You can stand outside his restaurant on a summer's day and see and hear everything imaginable as tourists gape, drop their teeth, wave, smile, laugh, take thousands of photographs, back up into one another, into cars, into traffic, angling for the perfect shot to show all the folks back home. "Hello" "How are you?" "See the goat?" "How do they get them goats up there?" "Look, he's looking right at me." "Take a picture." Gypsy Rose Lee, in her finest hour, never commanded the attention of an old goat named Oscar.

"It was always my intention to put a goat on the roof once the building was finished," says Al. "You see it over there—Scandinavia. The goat is on the roof to keep the grass down. But before the building was completed, the first thing we built with grass on the roof was the sign. And my birthday is on December 9th. So on December 9th in comes Winky Larson right into the restaurant with a goat named Oscar! He had ribbons on the damn horns, a note on it: "Happy Birthday."

"Well, Winky got a little snozzled, and he was going to teach the goat how to get up on the roof of the sign. So he gets this plank . . . and the goat got up, but Winky didn't. Winky broke his damn collarbone!

"Then the restaurant got built, and Oscar went up there. I got some more goats, but the only problem was, Oscar taught all the other goats how to jump. One time I looked up there and all the goats were gone! Now what the hell happened? Oscar had them all down below eating the petunias.

"Well, Oscar's dead now. But he was a real ham. Time and time again, people taking his picture, that goat stood on top of the roof and never moved. People actually believed that goat was a statue up there. The goats—no question about it—created a sensation. It's the number one question asked in all the information booths in Door County: 'Where's the place with the goats on the roof?' They have been photographed more than the centerfold in *Playboy* magazine.

"Goats don't like lightning. There's been many times I've run up there in the middle of the night in my pajamas, chasing them damn goats. When a storm started, Oscar used to get way up there on the peak of the roof and look straight down the road, and wait for me coming in my truck. He hated the helicopter too during Fall Festival. I had to go up there and hold him when the helicopter went over. I'm going to get another goat with horns like Oscar. I'm going to have a pigmy goat up there too, and an Angora. I'll have four altogether."

There's no question that Al's love affair with Sister Bay and the county has been a long one and is far from over. And there's no question that his concern for the village and county is real.

"The quicker this county gets a master plan with some teeth in it, the better everyone is going to be. I had a fellow come up to me in the restaurant last Sunday and ask, 'What have they done to Ephraim?' You know where his favorite place is now? Jacksonport. The charm is gone from Ephraim.

"I'd like to see a forty-acre moratorium on building, but I'll settle for five or ten. I know that's selfish, but just because mistakes have been made long ago, we don't have to continue making them. I hate to see a house on every fifty-foot lot. The county now is getting so small that unless you zone it, it's the only thing that will save the place.

"Sewer and water should be set up throughout the county. I'm not against parks in Door, but I don't want to see all the parks turned into campgrounds. I'd like to see some code adopted as to what you can and can't build. I know that's radical, that it denies the right to build anything you want on your own property. The sign ordinance is good, but it still has a long way to go. Signs are not a real necessity. The Women's Beautification Board has done a hell of a lot of good for Door County.

"I think businessmen are in a position right now that they can alleviate some of the problems for their sons and grandsons. They've got to ask themselves, 'Why do people come to Door County?' And if they are honest with themselves, they've got to move forward in voicing an opinion as to what's best for the county. I had a kid come up to me in the restaurant and say, 'You don't need a Gooney Bird Golf here. We've got that back home.' Most realtors are cold, callous, and their one and only interest is the buck.

"We've got to get the business people together in the county and start talking about each place. 'What can I do to continue my success, and what can I do to make it more attractive?' I'd like to tell everybody in Sister Bay to stop taking business for granted. I can remember how on Labor Day at three in the afternoon you could fire a cannon down the street both ways and never hit a thing. The place was empty and it stayed empty till next Memorial Day.

"This year I've had the best winter I've ever had in business, and it was cross-country skiing. Bill Bastian will tell you that all the skiers he had all winter at his place [Village View Motel] were cross-country skiers. Winters are terrific. But I think Fall Festival has gotten out of hand. It's got to be an uncontrollable monster. Too many people in too small an area in too little time. Someone is going to get hurt. The same thing could happen here at Fall Festival that happened in Sheboygan with their Bratwurst Day. It's not there anymore. Out of hand. Fall Festival was originally designed for the home people to celebrate the end of the season. Now, with the advertising, it's drawing people from all over the Midwest."

Though the tourist trade remains the better part of business for him, it's the local people, the regulars, he still holds close to his heart. "My restaurant is full of them on Saturdays and Sundays, and many of them are there every morning. And if that would cease, I don't think I would want to run a restaurant.

"That coffee table of regulars: everyone from ultra conservative to ultra-liberal! Many problems have been discussed there, all kinds of discussions, political, athletic, intellectual. I just love to go down there and sit at that coffee table, morning, afternoon, night, especially when there's a controversy going on. Any time I want to start a controversy, all I have to do is sit down there with Wink Larson and tell him, 'Boy, I wish the state would take that land of yours already and turn it into a park!' And that'll do it." With so much on his mind, so much concern for his own business, plus the future, the peace and beauty of the entire county, one wonders if a man like Al Johnson has time to sleep, or any dreams left at all.

"I had a dream one night that I sold my restaurant," he confesses. "And the first thing the guy did was paint it black! I woke up in a cold sweat."

Doc Farmer

"Did you hear the one about . . . ?" There is no end to the stories of Doc Farmer. He's in his seventies now, more than 45 years of country doctoring in his bag, and suddenly faced with his own prescription of semi-retirement. There's a good deal of talk around the northern end of the county of how Old Doc Farmer's going to step aside soon for a younger doctor to try his hands at rural American medicine.

Rumors, of course, abound, and the clearing house for most talk and little truth is Al Johnson's Swedish Restaurant in Sister Bay, just a few healthy steps from the Nor Dor Clinic, where Old Doc Farmer reigns. Late mornings, though, and early afternoons you can often find him holding court at the talkingest table at Al's with Pete Oleson, his sidekick pharmacist friend in attendance, a revolving cast of local characters, and frequently Big Al himself maneuvering to wrest control of the daily topics of conversation (taxes, education, tourism, local, state, and national government) by sheer volume of voice. The topic at the moment is Doc Farmer's threatened retirement.

"Hey, Doc, when's that new doctor coming in?" barks Al, standing at the head of the table sipping coffee.

"Soon as they can find him a house big enough to live in," laughs Doc Farmer in his own, inimitable way, something like the way "The Shadow" used to laugh on radio. "He's got seven kids, you know, and one in the oven, heh, heh, heh."

"Well, I'll tell you one thing. When I'm sick at three o'clock in the morning, you know who I'm gonna call up, don't you! I don't know where I'd be if I didn't see you walking in with your pajamas on under your coat, carrying that bag."

The whole table gets a good laugh at this, though Doc claims he wears a robe over his pajamas for night calls. One joke, though, leads to another, and no man alive knows and tells more jokes than Old Doc Farmer. The only trouble is, most of them are unprintable. They do work wondrous cures for his patients and friends, and as for rural medicine, Doc Farmer style, there's really no difference between the two. That's just one of the things that will be sorely missed when Old Doc Farmer goes.

"That's like the one about the two old ladies . . ." and he's off again. I'm convinced some of his best patients fake an illness just to stop in the office and hear Doc tell a new story.

But Doc, you see, is both storyteller, and story. As much as you might hate to use the overworked description of a man being a legend in his own time, Doc Farmer is pretty much that way to many people in these parts. For as many ribald stories as he tells about people and life in general, twice as many sincere and sometimes humorous ones are told about him, by the day, by the week, by the year. It's incredible how many lives he's touched and just what a large role he plays in the imagination of the people.

"Well, Old Doc Farmer says a shot a brandy a day'll do my heart good. And what better excuse for a man to insure an extra healthy heart, than more than one shot of booze a day?"

Old Doc Farmer says this, and Old Doc Farmer says that. Some of the things he's really said, and many of the things have already been enlarged by folklore. The truth of the matter is Doc Farmer still lives and breathes and practices in these parts and is appreciated and respected by more people than he will ever realize. If you put it to the people why this is so, you barely get one half the story.

Doc Farmer was born in Canada 1903 or 1904, in December, "so close to the end of one year and the beginning of the next, I can never remember which one." This makes him 70 or 71. His father was English. "I was the seventh son," Doc explains. "King Edward was on the throne then, and I was named after him. I'm a direct descendant of a Lord Mayor of London," he also says. We won't go into that, though the Doc seems mighty proud of it.

As a young man, Doc was a machinist and studied to become a mechanical engineer. Then his father got hurt on the farm, threw his neck out of place, and was straightened out by a visiting osteopath from Chicago. For some reason, young Edward Farmer was rather impressed with the body mechanics performed by the osteopath, who in turn encouraged him. "Why don't you come down to Chicago and go to school?" he advised.

Which is exactly what Ed Farmer did in 1923, enrolling in the Chicago College of Osteology for five years. "I worked my way through school," he's proud to says, "mostly working as a waiter."

After his schooling, he began practice in Saskatchewan, Canada, for several years, and then went down to Escanaba, Michigan, for three years, where he ran into the heart of the Depression.

"I went to Washington Island, then, in 1933. They guaranteed me I would make $3,000 a year there," he laughs. There he stayed for twenty-five years (going back to Chicago for additional schooling till he was licensed to practice medicine and surgery as well) except for a stint in

Sturgeon Bay and in New Mexico, in 1938, where he and his first wife, a nurse, ran a mission hospital at Grants, New Mexico. "Treated Mexicans," he says. "Mostly delivered babies for $15, if we could get it. But the people were wonderful. I came back to the Island in '41."

The Island was something special. His two daughters were born there (a son was born in Chicago) and his second wife, Margaret, is a native Islander. Though Doc finally came to Sister Bay and helped establish the Nor Door Clinic in 1957, you have the feeling that the best years of his life were spent on the other side of Death's Door.

"I got $1.00 for an office call then, and $3.00 for a house call anywhere on the Island. Most of the time I even threw in the medicine. I was Town Chairman for a couple of years. I took up flying once, but it got too expensive. I liked living there.

"If you had a $50 bill, you never had to pay for anything. Nobody could make change. Everybody trusted everybody else. The Island was supposed to be dry, but you could buy bitters, and it wasn't against the law. But bitters, you see, is 45% alcohol. You drink two or three of those and you're set, heh, heh, heh.

"When I went fishing, the ferry would blow a special signal if they needed me on the Island. Or if I was going rabbit hunting, someone would blow a horn. I made lots of calls with a team of horses. There was an airplane on the Island for emergencies, which we used for the hospital in Escanaba.

"All the babies were delivered at home. We had one girl there who had a little training. Oh, we had a few accidents, but we handled them pretty good. I remember once we had to deliver a baby by flashlight, no electricity then. I delivered a premature baby there (2 lbs., 13 oz.) using a homemade incubator." When the thermometer on the incubator would not work, Doc had to resort to Mrs. Farmer's candy thermometer.

"One time I was out tracking deer," he laughs, "and a gal came into the house in labor. Well they sent a guy out to look for me, and I spotted him, but I kept trying to lose him because I thought he was trying to horn in on our deer. Oh, I got back in time. Everything was all right.

"There was a kid there who shot his arm off with a shotgun. We were going over to Escanaba with him in the plane. We got about a mile off the Island when the motor cut out and we had to land on the ice. This was almost spring when the ice was beginning to break up. We landed and pretty soon we were sitting in water up to here. We started carrying the kid back to the Island, taking turns. I'd have to go up ahead every so often to see that the ice was safe.

"The arm had to be taken off. I remember when the kid came to and I told him I had to remove his arm, the first thing he said to me was, 'Did you take the ring off my hand?' I didn't.

"I took very few of them to the hospital over there. You learned to handle everything yourself. We had oxygen, some antibiotics, not too many of them.

"You know, we had the Lutheran minister over there one day. I gave him a shot of booze after I had taken some blood from him for a transfusion. When I was done, he started rolling up his other sleeve. 'You want some more blood, Doc?' he said.

"I had a patient too who was dying of cancer. Oh, he knew it. There wasn't much we could do. He was all skin and bones. 'I'd jump out the window, Doc,' he told me, 'only it's not high enough.' Well, you'd like to be able to take them outside and shoot them like a lame horse when it's that bad. I left him some morphine to ease the pain. 'Don't take more than half of it, or you'll be dead," I told him. "He took it all."

Doe Farmer in the flesh, you see, is something else. He is what we used to mean by a "real person." He's a doctor besides, so none of this should be all that shocking. If he tends to take away some of the mystery and sacredness we've attached to medicine and surgery, it's probably all the better for our own health. And maybe when you've lived through all the stories he's experienced, his habitual laughter helps to ease the pain he never shows.

Payment on the Island in those days? "If they hadn't any money, you just treated them anyway. Once in a while you'd get some beef. We'd get eggs, home-smoked bacon and ham, and lots of fish. Practically every family on the Island had a still. I even drank it before it got cold. That's one thing they excelled in. It was no money, but it was fun. If I hadn't had a family, I'd a stayed there. What more does a man need than a place to live, enough to eat, and good friends?

"But I had kids in school, and they wanted to go someplace where they could get music. So that's one reason I left in 1957 and came here to get the clinic established. The population, too, was going down. From 1,000 people there were only 500 when I left."

Doc occupies the first office to the right at the Nor Dor Clinic, but you're just as likely to find him at his receptionist's desk, on the phone, or in the lobby. That's another thing that takes a little getting used to with Old Doc Farmer: there aren't very many secrets with him. When you live in a village, or on an island, how many real secrets are there anyway?

I exaggerate a bit, of course, but it's mighty hard at times to keep Doc from diagnosing, prescribing, and tossing a good joke or two, right in the lobby of his office. Women have been known at times to be a bit embarrassed by all this. "Yeah, I'll call Pete up and order some pills for that high blood pressure of yours." But, what the hell—what's so secret about being sick? Especially among friends?

Eight o'clock in the morning, and Doc's at the clinic, rummaging through his files, on hand before the customary nine o'clock opening just in case some early morning patients should need him. Appointments are not all that necessary with him.

He's a rather natty dresser (checkered pants, mod shirt, western bolo tie) with trim gray hair, a thin mustache, and a cracked Danish pipe. He's against cigarettes. "You keep smoking those," he tells one of his patients, "and you better make your reservations early next door [Casperson's Funeral Home], heh, heh, heh."

Wally Mickelson walks in now, a local school board member and car salesman. It's difficult to determine if Wally came in to seek Doc's services or if he just came in to shoot the bull. For the life of me, though, I neither hear nor see anything bordering on medical attention, aside from Doc's opening question, "Are you sick, heh, heh, heh?"

"Yeah. Of high taxes, ha, ha, ha." From that point on they diagnose and prescribe all sorts of cures for the school system (cut out the hot lunch program), what to do with Patrick Lucey (tar and feather him), how to protect the local drug store which is always being broken into (get so-and-so's mean dog to guard the place—"Yeah, he could bite the burglars; then I'd have some business, heh, heh, heh"), fixing leaky toilets ("Give it two aspirin and call me in the morning").

He's interrupted momentarily to answer a phone call from a woman with something in her eye, while simultaneously helping out another woman who has just stopped in to get some medicine for a child's earache.

Wally Mickelson is about to depart, but not until he calls the Doc to the side (so the receptionist, Helen Daubner, and Doc Farmer's medical technician, Andrea Tischler, won't hear) and lays on a "little Johnny" joke you won't ever hear in Sunday school—a joke that cracks up the old Doc completely. "Say, but did you hear the one about this old guy at the bar and these two young. . . ."

A couple of women walk in then, and a teenage girl. One of the women is just along for the ride, while the other wants a check-up for a daughter and then one for herself. The daughter goes in first. It seems she isn't eating properly.

A short while later, Doc returns the daughter to the mother with the verdict: "She's in pretty good shape. I told her she should eat a good breakfast every morning. So many of the kids today don't eat breakfast. I straightened out her neck, fixed up her lip a little."

"Then she's all right?" asks the concerned mother.

"She's in pretty good shape. If I were fifty years younger, I'd say she was in damn good shape." He laughs the famous Doc Farmer laugh.

The mother goes in next. "Oh, you're going to have a baby?" he says to her, while accompanying her into the office.

"Yes, after all this time . . . I don't know how it happened." (I can only imagine Doc Farmer's reply.)

The pregnant woman comes out about a half hour later. Doc shows her the room at the end of the hall where he will deliver the baby, along with the help of his wife, Margaret, and his medical technician, Andrea.

Doc Farmer and the babies he's delivered in the office make still another story. Most of the local mothers who have had the experience swear by him, and now, in a day and age when home delivery and the midwife are back in style, who's to say the Doc didn't know what he was doing all along?

"The trend is back to home deliveries," he says. "It's better if they're born at home. They've more or less built up a resistance to many bacteria they might come across in the hospital delivery."

Going over to Al's for a morning coffee break (hot chocolate for him) Doc explains about the pregnant woman. "I never saw her before. I delivered a baby for a friend of hers, though. She came all the way from Algoma, can you imagine that? She wants me to deliver her baby." Doc has delivered two babies so far this year. "1,500 in all, since I started."

Back in the homey confines of Al's, Doc maneuvers through tables full of friends and patients, stopping here and there to say hello, exchange opinions, and either pick up or deliver a good joke or two.

Doc expounds this morning on everything from malpractice suits and tourism to house calls and old age. "I've never had any malpractice suits," he says, but with the increase of tourists in the county each year, Doc admits, "I'm scared of them. I don't know them like the local people, and they're all malpractice conscious these days. So I try to hurry them on, send them back to their own doctors. I've run through as many as 100 patients a day during the summer.

"I charge $5.00 for an office call, $6.00 with a shot. House calls are $5.00 plus a dollar a mile one way. I put on an average of 25,000 miles a year making house calls. And when I told the Medicare people about that, they wouldn't pay me. They didn't believe anybody made house calls these days. Even the IRS came here to check on me."

He speaks, too, of the differences between rural doctoring and urban doctoring and the problems in finding anyone to replace him in the past two years. "We have more variety. We become pretty proficient in many areas. You get so you can almost sense what's wrong with your patients. But who wants to be a rural doctor when all the money is in the city?"

As for the aged, he's against most nursing homes. "Just another racket. In the past, we kept the old people around. There was always a grandma around the house to darn socks, take care of things. She was needed, and she felt she was needed. In the past, two people could take care of ten kids. And now not one of them can take care of one old person."

Old age. "How do you live to be 100?" Doc Farmer relates an old joke. "Well first you reach 99, and after that you have to be careful!"

I return to his office near the end of the day, and Doc shows me his Lion of the Year award in 1955, and the long poem written about him by L. A. Davison, one stanza in particular which still rings true:

> His diagnoses are correct
> from pregnancy to gout.
> And usually his treatments cure . . .
> He knows what he's about.

Patients continue to trickle in, though it's already 4:45. "Can I see the doctor?" "Sure, we're just talking here," he says. A mother comes in to have a child's throat checked. (The child screams 'OUCH' as most children do.) Another mother comes in with her son, who needs an examination for sports.

"Track, eh?" says Doc Farmer. "Those other guys are going to beat you. They got longer legs. You're going to run faster, though, eh? Heh, heh, heh."

At about five minutes to five, in comes the Town Chairman, Laurence Daubner. "Here comes the King of Liberty Grove," laughs Doc Farmer.

"Is the Doc in?" the King replies. "Yeah, but I have to get home soon to get that Manhattan that's waiting for me."

The Doc takes him in (behind unclosed doors) reads his blood pressure aloud, gives him a good report ("I'll give you a few pills to take along") and some sound medical advice ("Don't lay around worrying about it. And take a walk") plus a lot of argument about Bill 300, which is about as unhealthy in these parts as the DNR, Patrick Lucey, and the cherry business combined. They continue to talk and argue, till the receptionist finally announces, "I'm going home. You two guys will be here till 5:30. "

Thursday is Doc's day off. He lives in an impressive stone house on four acres of land two miles north of the clinic, a place that his patients are always proud of pointing out to strangers—"That's Doc Farmer's house"—a kind of a local landmark, in a way, where patients have been known to pound on the door for help in the middle of the night.

Margaret, his gracious wife, has set the garbage out near the door for the Doc to take out as I stop to visit with him on his day off. The Doc is in the dining room, one foot up on a chair, tying a shoelace. He had two house calls last night, including one around midnight. Does he ever get used to them?

"Never. Especially in winter when I have to get out of a warm bed." But the significant thing about the man is that he does. And in a day and age when dependability in a human being grows more and more rare, you begin to place a very special value on a country doctor who is always there.

Rough though he may be in spots, you slowly come to realize that he is precisely what the people may want in their doctor: not a man of few words, wrapped in himself, wrapped in white, methodically hustled from one cubicle to another cubicle by a host of grim nurses in some sterile, sacrosanct office set-up; not a specialist up to his ears in degrees and the latest equipment, especially computerized billing; but a man who lives amongst you, dresses like you, talks like you, shares many of the same interests, and has no pretense at being any better than you except for his particular skill.

"I was visiting an old couple the other day. He's 89 and she's in her 80's. Neither of them getting any Medicare. They can hardly make the taxes, and they can't afford to pay $6.50 a month off their Social Security for Medicare. The old guy should go to the hospital, but he said to me, 'No. I'll just stay here and die. We need that money to live on.' Most of their diet is potatoes and oatmeal."

It must be this common sense style of doctoring that the people take a liking to: a doctor who never charges them much, fixes them up just fine to keep going till the next time, and, most significantly for a professional, seems to be on their side. If you can't trust the politicians these days, at least you can trust Doc Farmer.

He's more than a bit anti-hospital and anti-technology at times. "It's purely for the doctor's convenience, not the patient's. Hell, I've sewed up a two-inch cut with a plain needle and thread in an emergency. In other words, you can make things do. You don't have to have a million-dollar operating room to make things work. Two to three out of four surgical operations are not necessary according to a survey made by a surgical group at one of the Eastern hospitals."

As for his bout with the Medicare people, who told him his patients should go to the hospital instead of his making house calls, "I could see them for six months for the price they'll have to pay one day in the hospital. National Health Insurance is coming, but it's got to be administered better than Medicare. Most of the doctors are hurting themselves. They're over-charging Medicare patients. And there's too much control on the top, especially by the FDA."

Doc Farmer has his critics among the professionals and among the people. Because he has a D.O. rather than an M.D., there is talk at times that he is not really qualified, though he is licensed in medicine and surgery. But if you've put in 47 years of service on the human body, you ought to know how it works. Even his detractors will always credit Doc Farmer for one thing: "If he can't handle it, he'll send you to somebody who can."

"Oh sure, I'm aware of my critics . . . people always shopping around from doctor to doctor. But if something happens to them, and they need me, they'll get just as good care as if they were friends of mine. I believe in giving everyone the kind of help I would like to get. Call me anything, heh, heh, heh, as long as you pay me."

He's interrupted by a phone call, which Margaret passes on to him. "Tell 'em it's my day off," he laughs. He takes the phone, listens, laughs, diagnoses, prescribes. Someone is calling about a woman in her 80's, who is getting dizzy spells. The caller is thinking about putting her in the hospital for a check-up. Doc thinks that would be alright, but probably unnecessary. "She's not getting enough oxygen up in her head. Tell her to take it easy, lie down a bit, and come in tomorrow. Hell, I get dizzy too, especially if I've had one too many. Sure, I'll make arrangements if you want to take her in. They'll give her a good check-up, and she'll come home and be dizzy again."

A lot of the troubles that Doc Farmer treats are related to old age. "Arthritis, heart trouble, hypertension." Middle age, as he sees it, is a time of adjustment. "Ma's afraid she's getting old and Pa is looking elsewhere. So Ma and Pa get mad at each other. She goes and gets a nervous breakdown while he goes and gets drunk.

"I get a lot of depressed people. They want some magic pill that will take care of it. You don't know if it's on account of the kids, or a fight with the old man, or what. A lot of them are women going through the change of life. A lot of them are fine if you put them on the right vitamins and estrogen. And you got to smile at the old man a little more, I tell them. Do things together."

As anyone who has gone to Doc Farmer knows, he was advocating vitamins and health foods long before the Earth People rediscovered their importance in man's daily diet.

"In the early days, growing up on the farm, we didn't use any poisons. There are over 3,000 additives in foods today that nobody's ever even examined. We don't know what the hell they could be doing to us. You know, a mouse or a rat will never eat baker's white bread?

"We need protein every day. It should be mostly farm-raised soybeans, cheese, yogurt. Lots of salads, fruits, vegetables. I've got peaches, plums, and walnuts here. None of them sprayed. Unpasturized milk if you like it, but you don't need it. And supplement this all with natural vitamins and minerals. No white flour, no white sugar. Use honey. "

Doc opens a kitchen cabinet and begins a litany of his own vitamin and mineral intake. "Vitamin E, good for circulatory problems. I take 1600 milligrams each day. I take a multiple vitamin that has everything in it. I take 5000 milligrams of vitamin C each day; 20,000 milligrams of vitamin A; four A&D capsules, that's cod liver oil. I take four manganese pills, two lecithin capsules, two vitamin B complex, two desiccated liver pills a day; four bone meal tablets; brewer's yeast on my cereal; one kelp tablet a day; one zinc tablet; vitamin B6, four a day; and two tablespoons of bran. I have two eggs for breakfast, but never hard boiled or fried. Only poached or soft boiled to keep the lecithin."

As for the greater problems of man in society, Doc doesn't have any revolutionary prescriptions. Youth drugs, alcohol, abortions all bring on only old-fashioned remedies in his book. "It's all a part of the break-down of the home and the lack of religious training. Schools nowadays are just a bunch of fun and not enough education. It's the whole damn thing from government on down, and I don't know how you're going to change it. Now we have important people in government who say it doesn't hurt to smoke marijuana. The trouble is, these kids aren't old enough to make any judgments. This country is getting overrun with tranquilizers and depressants, uppers and downers. They do just as much harm as overdrinking. I like a good drink myself. I'll have one a day, though.

"Like it says in the Bible, 'The sins of your father will be visited down upon your children, even into the fourth generation.' "

Doc Farmer and religion? I've always wondered about that. Do his stories ever get back to the local ministers, or his own prescription for a good drink now and then?

"Oh they're all my friends. No, they've never said anything to me. Listen, some of them like a snort once in a while themselves. I tell you one thing, though, if you entertain them, you don't have to get an extra bottle of booze, heh, heh, heh."

Doc Farmer's seen enough medical miracles, though, to give him a faith in God. "I'm not a non-believer. . . . Did you hear that honey?" he says to his wife who, it would seem, is more of a believer than Doc. "I just had too much of it shoved down my neck by my old man who was kind of a lay preacher." And as for humor, Sunday audience approved or not, "If you can get a patient to smile, they don't feel so depressed. So I always like to tell them a good joke. Maybe a Polish joke, or a Belgian joke. Like, do you know what the most dangerous job is in the Polish part of Milwaukee? Riding shotgun on the garbage truck. Or, did you hear about the big fight over in Brussels? Six seagulls and a Belgian were fighting over one dead fish!"

Find it, fix it, and leave it alone is Doc Farmer's real remedy. Osteopathy came in during the Civil War, says Doc Farmer. "A. T. Still began it. He was known as the bone doctor. His idea was that the rule of the artery was supreme. You free up the circulation, and you get health." But we're not going to miss the osteopath from the Nor Dor Clinic, when his time runs out. We're going to miss Doc Farmer.

Louie Smolak: Sculptor

The man smacks of style.

Always casually dressed but fashionably attired.

Pug, pugnacious, pugilistic, the man is a wonder with words. He stands 5' 6", weighing 177 pounds at this stage, his late sixties. A neatly trimmed gray beard, he looks more and more like the aging Hemingway of *The Old Man and the Sea* fame. A snarl crosses his face at times. His husky voice can deliver a quick, cutting remark (his opponents: politicians, dilettantes, Philistines, the Chicago Bears, the Green Bay Packers, Muhammad Ali, the modern art world, old friend suddenly a new foe, etc.) and a knockout punch honed from a razor-sharp mind. "Him? That cipher!" Bang goes the fist on something resounding, and that takes care of "him."

Instantaneous combustion. Fancy footwork and the arabesques of ideas. Ah, the opposing forces in this man. Temper tantamount to flash fires. Contrasts. Even contradictions.

He's a fighter, yet neither punch drunk nor cauliflower-eared; his hands can clench into a pair of devastating fists, or shape space sensuously in forms to make any passing observer gasp for breath .

Smolak—just the name sounds formidable. "It translates as *guts*," he'll tell you. This is a stance, a condition, that the man, the former boxer now an artist readily accepts.

If the face seems fierce at times, and the ideas, dialectics, superlatives precisely pronounced (often from the side of his mouth in rough-and-tough Chicago mobster style) appear intimidating, let it be known that there is often rollicking (sometimes ribald) laughter too, gentleness, and equal parts of concern as well as anger over the entire spectrum of the human condition.

I've known this man, artist, boxer, fisherman, golfer, sports enthusiast, sculptor, storyteller, iconoclast, Chicagoan, Door Countyite, lover of lox and bagels, good food, good drink, kindred Slavic soul for a good five years or more, sipping coffee with him at the counter at Al's, morning after morning, listening to his stories (often the same stories), sharing his moods, time and time again. A difficult friend at times, he remains one of the most fascinating individuals around.

Some people find it hard to talk to Louis Smolak, but those people haven't learned. You don't talk to Lou Smolak, you listen. You throw a word, a phrase, an idea at Louie, and then sit back and listen to the marvelous tales, anecdotes, jokes, personal experiences, little known facts, biographies of artists, fighters, politicians, musicians, historical, religious, and technical information pour forth.

Some people around these parts take night courses, read books, and watch PBS. I listen to Louis Smolak. When Bill Beckstrom was alive, if you were fortunate enough to find yourself seated between these guys at Al's, you could receive the equivalent of fifteen hours of college credit in one morning.

The other morning, Louie and I are talking about people promising to do something for you. The subject of promises instantly reminds Louie of a story about Ben Franklin.

"Did I tell you this one before?" he asks. (I always say no, though it's usually yes. But this time it's no.) "Well Ben at one point in his early life ran into a nobleman who gave the young Ben Franklin a load of promises. 'You just come to London,' he told Ben. 'I'll see that you do all right.' So Ben fell for that line of crap, went to London, and found himself stranded there! I learned very early in life to take promises with a grain of salt."

Lou Smolak's early life remains an intriguing story in itself. He was born in Russia ("Belorussia," he would say in sonorous tones, "White Russia, the western part of the country, one of the great flax growing areas") in a place called Dubashnik, "named after the oak and the aspen. An estate area. We owned practically a whole bloody town. My father's people were the overseers of one of the great horse farms in that part of Russia: the raising, the breeding, the training of horses. The owner of the stable was a Polish count. The existence was rural on both sides of the family. Landowners. Squires. I believe that grew to be important in my impatience with urbanity, my discomfort. I always felt my natural milieu was in the country, like the old Tolstoy fable. You heard this before, haven't you?"

I nod no, but the answer is yes, a thousand times. I love the story anyway.

Louie begins smiling at his own Russianness. "To anybody but a Russian, gold is the symbol of wealth. But to a Russian, it's land. Well, there was this Russian peasant who got in trouble with the Czar and had to beat it the hell out of Russia. Boundaries being what they were, he remained in the confines of the country, ending up in a remote area of Siberia. When he awoke, he found himself amidst a tribe of very generous and giving people. As he slowly came to his senses, the chief informed him he could settle there, and that he could have a piece of land. All he had to do was get up at sunrise and all the land he could encompass from sunrise to sunset would be his. He couldn't wait, of course, until the next morning. He got up at dawn and there was the chief and the people waiting for him at the appointed mark. He started out on his journey by walking. Soon he decided to trot because in this way he could cover more land. 'Now if I ran,' he thought, 'I could encompass an entire empire.' Well, he ran and ran, eventually ending up where he began, and promptly dropped dead from exhaustion.

"How much land does a man need?" Louie laughs heartily. "That's Russian."

So, too, are all of Louie's memories of his father. "He was a career cavalry man. He had his ears and head full of so many Cossack adventures, he couldn't wait to get into the cavalry at a very early age. He fought all through the Russo-Japanese War and was eventually wounded and incarcerated in Japan for a year. After the war was resolved, through Theodore Roosevelt, he was repatriated, and wound up with amoebic dysentery. My father survived all this, yet found out he was still in the army, much to his disenchantment. He married at this time, and then asked his father for his patrimony and went to America to establish himself. His destination was Chicago because there were family connections there. It took him a few years of nosing around, learning the language. He worked on Randolph Street with relatives who were in the produce business there. When he was officially established, he sent for my mother and me in Russia. He had never seen me prior to my arrival in America. My father eventually did well in this country and was successful in becoming a big commercial factor in the potato market on the wholesale level in Chicago."

Seated in a comfortable chair in his living room, surrounded by his wood and metal and bronze sculpture, Smolak appears a satisfied man, who has come to terms with himself, his private history, a touch of the Russian aristocracy about him, though a restlessness persists. ("The Commissar," I've heard him called in private. "The Little Czar.") Above him hangs a magnificent oil portrait by Jim Ingwersen, faithfully capturing the sculptor, Smolak, at work with a welding torch, resplendent in the kind of light one finds in the paintings of the old masters. The visage of the artist, his skillful hands, enforces the reality of the man himself once again.

"My early years were spent in the Humboldt Park area of Chicago. A mixed neighborhood—Polish, Russian, Jewish, some Irish. The area had been primarily Scandinavian. In fact, I went to the Hans Christian Andersen School. "I didn't work at the market with my father. My father had the European attitude that this kind of work was beneath his social status, so I was expected to devote myself to enterprises of a higher order like playing the fiddle, getting as much culture as possible. I was an avid reader. I'd go through five books a week from the library.

Thank God for the Chicago Public Library system! My interest in sports was as natural as a duck taking to water. At first it was softball. Then football.

"I went to Lane Tech, one of the most remarkable high schools in the country, rated, when I went there, as one of the three best high schools in the country. It was not a neighborhood school as such. You had to be in the upper third of your class to get in. It was a remarkable school for its extra-curricular activities—the only school that had a daily newspaper, a monthly magazine, and a yearbook all done by the students and printed in the school. The monthly magazine and the yearbook were outlets for the artistic. That's where I had the chance to illustrate—do pen and ink drawings for these periodicals.

"Lane had no music program, yet the Lane orchestra was banned from competing with other symphony orchestras in the Chicago area. In order to give other schools a chance, they banned Lane.

"I won the state poster contest in Urbana, Illinois, and Lane had no art program at the time. We did have an extracurricular sketch program. There were extracurricular programs that encompassed just about everything. The teachers just all volunteered."

Given Louie's almost natural intellectual bent, his old world background and a family which encouraged such endeavors, and the atmosphere of Lane Tech, all this seemed to come together in his early artistic leanings.

"The impulse was part of my nature. I drew. If I saw a blank piece of paper, I had to make a picture on it. I started whittling the first time I had a jackknife in my hand. Drawing was part of my interest . . . I just always drew. No outside agency provided that interest. I was always a hotshot in grammar school around Christmas time. My drawings always stood out at that time. I was better than anyone else in class. But the career orientation toward art did not happen till I got to Lane.

"One thing that fascinated me early on—in relation to my reading— was how so many books were so wonderfully illustrated; that this is what I thought I wanted to do. There was the fellow who taught N. C. Wyeth—the father of the present Wyeth. And N. C. Wyeth's own illustrations of *Treasure Island, Kidnapped* . . . they were magnificent. Very important. To paint like N. C. Wyeth, or draw like he could draw. It never occurred to me at the time that my real bent was sculpture, as much as I liked to draw. That came later, much later.

"While at Lane, by the way, I participated in track and football. I got my first boxing lesson at Lane." Smolak the boxer is still another story to this fascinating man: artistry of yet another kind, hands that make and hands that break, the creative and destructive force both flowing in the same human being. (Don't we all possess this and fail or refuse to look at it? Develop it?)

"Boxing was something that appealed to me to no end," confesses Louie, settling down into his chair, easing himself into this part of a personal narrative in the way of a refined gentleman in the confines of his private club might sip the smoothest of cognac, draw on the rarest of Havana cigars, and get on with his tale.

"I was a very pugnacious shrimp. I was the shrimp of the family, and being the shrimp, I had to prove something. My macho nature needed an outlet. I was always trying to prove myself physically as a result of that. Whenever I saw a man bigger than me, my natural instinct was, 'What would it take to knock him down?' I got into many fights in the schoolyard. Finally, when the opportunity to channel this into an enterprise which was a skill-related thing became possible, I did. I became a boxer.

"My first lessons were given to me by a remarkable little Prussian coach at Lane, a man by the name of Kahle. The guy was a fantastic gymnast. He also coached fencing and boxing. I found fencing intriguing, which eventually led to lessons in boxing from him. The art of boxing derived directly from fencing. Most people don't realize that. They're identical, the same balance and footwork. The delivery of a left jab is identical to a thrust in fencing. I got a very solid groundwork from Kahle who understood both sports. I learned the basics of boxing there.

"After I got out of high school, in my spare time, I used to haunt an incredible gym on Madison Street—Kid Howard's Arcade. This was the training facility of some of the greatest boxers who had ever lived. I saw Jack Dempsey there. I saw practically every champion during the era of the late '20s and '30s working out at one time or another. Late contemporaries of mine: Barney Ross and Tony Zale. This led me to take some lessons there from great trainers.

"It was just something that got my adrenalin going—not a career. It was a Saturday thing.

"I was going to the Art Institute at the time—my first two years of college. I worked very hard there. I did homework until two, three in the morning. Then the Depression hit and I could no longer continue. My Saturdays were spent at Kid Howard's."

There was only one scholarship offered at the Art Institute at that time, and Louie lost it by something similar to a technicality. "I had no facility for making a fancy notebook," he scoffs. "As a result of not being able to get that scholarship I matriculated at Illinois State Normal University, where I got a degree in art education. It cost $75 a term there in those days. Illinois State was a lead pipe snap compared to the Art Institute. I pulled off very good marks. And I put myself in a pretty good economic position," he smiles.

Enter the amazing ability of Smolak to integrate his talents, to put head and heart and hands to use.

"This was the heart of the Depression, you recall, but I handled the economics by getting some fights lined up while at school. I fought at 'smokers,' American Legion things in various tank towns in Illinois, Indiana, Paducah, Kentucky, Peoria, Illinois—one of the more sizable towns. I gradually fought my way up to the main events, which were six-rounders.

"It presented no great difficulty for me. I had the opportunity to develop a heck of a lot more skill at Kid Howard's than any of the opponents I faced. I won every gosh-dang fight with no trouble to speak of. I went by my regular name. Oh, sometimes they referred to me as 'that Polak.' It didn't bother me a bit as I collected my $25 or $30—which was a lot of money during the Depression. Sometimes there were two fights a week. Sixty bucks! I supported myself and a couple of room-mates who were on the borderline of indigence—pretty goddam poor."

It is ironic, considering this man's artistic talents—the fine mind, the concern for the downtrodden—that someone with all this should find satisfaction in his fists.

"It was just a natural, short temper that got me into a hell of a lot of fights. How else can I explain it? I was blessed with a very strong physique. I fought at 147 pounds. I was built along the lines of Rocky Graziano. I was never an amateur when it came to boxing. That was important. I should say that I never fought as an amateur. The only thing that got me into the ring was economics. There was no joy or satisfaction in getting into the ring. When the seconds leave, it's the loneliest place in the world. It's scary before the thing starts. Then, after you become used to it, the fear leaves you and you become engaged in whatever faces you in the ring.

"If I hated someone in a fist fight outside the ring, I could probably kill him. Inside the ring, that's different. I had no animosity toward my opponent. I just wanted to outbox him, beat him decisively."

After graduation from Illinois State Normal University, Louie went back to Chicago with his degree, back to the Depression with nothing to do, no teaching jobs available. Eventually he landed a job as a draftsman through a boyhood buddy who was working in a plant that manufactured surgical instruments and electronic equipment.

"I stayed at that for three years, but I used to fall asleep at the drawing board because it bored the hell out of me. As soon as I could, I got a job in the plant itself." There, working, apprenticing with some highly skilled German machinists Louie began to develop a talent for tool-and-die making. "Having been blessed with better-than-normal manual facilities, this was a natural milieu for me. I won the respect of these skilled machinists, and it was a mutual thing."

Louie and his buddy then joined forces, opening their own machine shop in a garage, moonlighting after the normal working day, and eventually turning the operation into a fulltime business during WWII.

"Toward the end of the war, although my partner was a natural genius in designing tools, he had not one wit of business sense, and so we got a divorce, and the plant went to hell. I told him I was quitting, I got my money out of it, and he ran the whole damn thing into the ground in eleven months.

Louie married in 1943. "When I had my first business, I got Edie out of Pennsylvania. I met her through relatives of hers who were living in an apartment building my father owned. We hit it off quite well. I did all my courting through the mail. When I was on an economic plane that could comfortably support a spouse, I visited her in Altoona, Pennsylvania, and proposed, and she accepted me—in September, in the beautiful Allegheny Mountains, and we were married in November. I brought her back to Chicago, where she went into teaching after about a year."

Working in the machine trade proved to be a good part of Louie's life in the years ahead, whether he worked for other companies, or once again began his own business—which he did, with the same partner.

"What I did this time was own all the tools. We shared the profits. He contributed extraordinary skill. We stayed together the second time for about five or six years, and then I dissolved it. I wanted no part of business anymore. My mother had gotten terminally ill at this point. It was a traumatic time. I nursed her for three months, 24 hours a day. The second business dissolved right after her death. I didn't know what I wanted to do exactly. I did know that I no longer wanted to work on a full-time basis."

The artist seemed to take hold of him again, although Louie readily admits "in all the time I had been working, I did a lot of woodcarving. My interest in whittling had, by this time, been channeled into wood sculpture. I found out that sculpture was really where I belonged. Back when I was working on my first job, I discovered Alexander Archipenko—whose work I had admired—had started a school of sculpture in Chicago. Just as soon as I could, I enrolled in some night courses. Although he was a pioneer in modern sculpture, he believed in a very solid, basic program. I derived a great deal from him. This was my entire formal education in the art of modern sculpture—only six months. All I could afford at the time. But just being in contact with him, getting the feel, verbalizing the direction to take in sculpture, was all I needed.

"I was a serious woodcarver prior to this time, from the time I got out of Illinois State. And when I bought my first house, I had a workshop where I could carve. The type of work I was doing then was very naturalistic, very realistic. Lots of details—the human figure, entirely. Figurative art. Never attaining what I set out to do, mostly frustration. Nevertheless, the urge kept you going. The attainment, never the fulfillment.

"Then, as time went on, my original prejudice against abstraction was gradually dissolving as a result of my reading, observing, thinking. I was finally realizing that many of the great qualities of art were abstract. It was a gradual moving toward abstraction for me. The first piece I did was when a friend brought me a piece of ebony. And that was only semi-abstract, where the design was paramount. This is it: a little ebony Madonna. The first one that was not naturalistically dominant.

"I liked it. To me, abstraction posed greater challenges. When you do something naturally, the elements are already defined. That's simplistic. When you're involved with attempting to give artistic expression in an abstract way, you are more related to what a composer of music is trying to do—expression through rhythm, space, balance, all the abstract elements that go into it.

"The other early piece of sculpture I did was a stylized figure of Job, where the dominant factors were space and rhythm.

"I exhibited at that time at the Chicago No-Jury Shows, and the prize winner one year was my Job, which was displayed at the Findlay Gallery in Chicago, where the No-Jury exhibit was held. The No-Jury Society was a forum for artists whose work was non-establishment in nature because modernism had not achieved great acceptance in Chicago at that time.

During the '50s and '60s Louie admits, "I made a commitment to sculpture, probably finally arriving at what I always wanted to do. At that time, too, I was becoming aware of other mediums—of welding, of building-up directly with bronze—and began to model directly with bronze on a steel armature. I also involved myself directly with progressive art movements in Chicago. I exhibited in a very prestigious art show in the Midwest—new Horizons in Sculpture—and managed to be exhibited there a couple of times. So I kept working, exhibiting, and selling occasionally during this period. And then we moved to Door County in 1970, '71."

And so, though Louie Smolak's move to Door does not relate precisely to Tolstoy's fable of the basic Russian need for land, an element of truth persists.

"I had always known my natural milieu was not one located in a congested area. I always wanted to live in an area that had space, where the scenic beauty was important to me. For years Edie and I were looking in Wisconsin. In the late '60s we bought land in Door County and moved here in the early '70s. I convinced Edie to take an early retirement from teaching, and we built our original place in Fish Creek."

My personal introduction to Louie came about four or five years ago through Bill Beckstrom, whom I often visited at his house and plant farm next to the Red Barn complex between Ephraim and Sister Bay. I remember sitting in Bill's beautiful hand-hewn home one morning, absorbed in Beckstrom's talk about a particular musical composition he had heard over the state FM station the previous night, or discussing a conversation he had recently had with his close friend, Doc Stevens, and moving from Stevens to a book he was reading, and from there possibly on to his interests in plants and the ice age, followed by a description of a very mystical artist, Escher, whom Bill had recently discovered and found fascinating, and then on to wood, one of his favorite subjects, all its variety and particular qualities which Beckstrom truly loved to work and explore with his own hands . . . and in so doing, reached toward a book-cluttered table to run his hands over a fluid, female torso carved in wood, partly abstract, partly figurative in the way of African sculpture.

"That's beautiful," I told him. "Did you do it?"

"No," he said. "A sculptor, he lives up here now, a guy by the name of Lou Smolak. Do you know him? Jesus, he's some character." Bill drew deeply on his cigarette, inhaling the smoke in that rattling laughter of his. "He was a boxer, can you image that? He's a hell of an artist. Russian. You've got to meet him."

Sitting here listening to Louie, I am once again reminded of Beckstrom. "My first exhibition here in the county," says Louie, "was at the Hardy Gallery. My early acquaintanceship here was Bill Beckstrom, who was very instrumental in introducing me into the mystique of Door County. Bill often provided me with wood for carving.

"However, in time, I began to assume a new direction once I settled in here. I thought that some of the designs I did would look good in cast bronze, and I proceeded to have some of these designs cast in that way. The 'Adagio,' the acrobats, was the first. The second was the head, 'La Blond.' And I've gone on with this now, right on up to the big one downstairs, 'Mother and Child.' Someone will have to come up with a more poetic name relating to maternity." He laughs.

The original home he built in Fish Creek was sold a few years ago because of the increasing traffic in that area and the distraction of a nearby amusement park. Louie, true to his Russian soul, has now buried himself far off a back road and deep into the woods south of Sister Bay.

"I can't explain the exact attraction to Door County," he says. "I derive no inspiration from the county itself other than the place and the opportunity to work—unlike a painter here who can draw from the county. My inspiration far predates anything here that could influence my work. Yet the county has been very good for me. It has afforded me some excellent shows. I later became acquainted with the painter Jim Ingwersen, and we managed a couple of exhibitions together that were harmonious, despite the fact that the approach to art was extremely different in conception for each of us.

"Because my work became exhibited in this area, I was able to do a one-man show at the Bergstrom Art Center in Neenah, which then purchased one of my pieces for their permanent collection."

Part of my friendship with Smolak can be attributed to the basic instinct of a writer to shut up and listen when others are talking, but beyond that, we share a certain "Slavic Soul," hard to identify exactly. It's made up of old Chicago neighborhoods, old language, ethnic food, "characters" (real or imaginary) out of the past, thick soup, dark rye bread, homemade bakery, not to mention a dark, morose moodiness at times (bordering on madness), a certain wintriness of the heart, heavily fatalistic, in which we know the world's all wrong and only we are right . . . in the country of the blind only the one-eyed man is King. And we are one-eyed. That sort of thing.

So much for self-indulgence, self-pity, and self-expression, Slavic style, except for this: Door County can be very beguiling, especially for the creative artist in search of peace and recognition—the Scylla and Charybdis of these parts, to be navigated through Porte des Morts. The isolation to create—yes. But there is also the gnawing need to break out, to show the world who and where we are. This often proves frustrating, because the movers and shakers in the powerful art and publishing centers of this country are far from Door County, far from the Midwest.

So either the artist (who does not draw directly from Door County) puts in a few years and then leaves, or he remains, pursuing his own way, finding much to bitch about along that way, over coffee at Al's, or at one of Smolak's Door County-renowned lox and bagel luncheons at his place where he (under the gracious hostessing and hard work of Edie) plies you with Bloody Mary's, fantastic lox, "Chicago" bagels, cream cheese, homegrown tomatoes and onions, imported beer, specially blended coffee, ethnic bakery, and rare brandy to settle the meal, the conversation, the moment. And you leave by late afternoon, looking for your legs, determined to set the world of art on fire once again.

Even without this stimulus, it is not uncommon for Louie to refer to himself as a genius, or to place himself in the company of the most heralded sculptors working in the world today. "Look at this," he told me a few weeks ago while in the process of putting the final touches to a magnificent bronze sculpture, tentatively titled "Mother and Child": "It's as good as anything around, anything Henry Moore has done! I'm just a goddam genius, but who knows? Who cares?"

"I feel my work needs a wider forum, a broader exposure. While the work of artists whose work is purchasable by the tourists, people who inhabit the area, the very nature of my work is so time consuming, so costly, it needs a wider forum such as the big art galleries. Much of my larger work would be more related to institutional purchasing: businesses, banks, churches. There is no outlet for institutional work in this area.

"I have to travel long distances to get my work cast. There's no foundry close enough to have it done here and shipped to me. And my work is costly. My present piece downstairs ("Mother and Child") is worth $15,000. Even smaller pieces, inevitably, have to cost a few thousand dollars."

Though he calls himself an abstract sculptor, he draws the line between his work and some of the wild work being done in the name of modern sculpture these days. "I believe with Epictetus that there is a design in nature, and that this primordial rhythm has inspired all of man's aesthetic expression. What more evidence of this truth than the unbelievable beauty of the paintings in the caves of Altamira, or the remarkable aboriginal art of America, Africa, Polynesia, and Micronesia that has been the inspiration of so much modern art? This surely must point up the absurdity of the requisite of a philosophic treatise to validate a work of art. I am referring to the convoluted sophistry to rationalize the packaging of a building or the snipping off of the garments of a female exhibitionist, as examples, on aesthetic grounds."

Moving downstairs to his studio, I am faced with yet another final achievement of Louie Smolak's incredible artistry — "Mother and Child," a bronze sculpture weighing 360 pounds, standing some 45 inches high, radiating an almost inner light, flowing in form, begging to be touched.

"Part of my basic tendency toward the eternal arabesque," he attempts to explain it, "the instinctive rhythm that seems to flow in all my work, from wood to bronze. I've always been affected by sensual rhythm. A lot of my work has no preconception. This one did. I don't consciously go about a drawing that will make itself into a piece of sculpture. Often it's subconscious doodling. I find myself doodling on the borders of a newspaper while I'm solving a crossword puzzle. It's almost subconsciously an interesting design, my affinity toward certain rhythms. That's basically how this began. Its design became a wood carving first, and then I tried to conceive of it as a bronze. That's the history of the thing."

The sensual? Louie? The size of him? The bulk of him? The hands that have pummeled other men silly in a boxing ring? Those same hands now touch the radiant form of his creation, then gently meet and follow the rhythm and flow of the bronze. "The sensual . . . that's part of my personality. The sensitivity to form, the tactile sensitivity. It's a case of hands and eyes. You make forms that you would like to feel as well as see. "

And when does he know the form is finished, is complete in his eyes?

"To paraphrase Renoir," he smiles, "when asked when he thought his paintings were finished: when he thought he could feel, run his hands over her."

Does Louie Smolak truly believe he's a genius?

A burst of hearty Russian laughter: "Sure! What the hell's the point of working if you don't? Like Frank Lloyd Wright, I've always preferred honest arrogance to phony humility."

James Ingwersen:
Portrait of the Artist as Environmentalist

The authenticity of a natural landscape is often expressed by the dwellings its people construct and inhabit. There are those things men build that fit perfectly in place, seem to rise from the earth like the adobes of the Southwest, the tea houses in the Far East, the weathered barns and farmhouses of the Midwest.

As time passes, especially here in Door, the old farmhouses, white, weathered, log, or abandoned; the weathered or red painted barns that glow especially warm in sunrises, sunsets, and storms of all seasons; windmills, corn cribs, silos, outbuildings gracing green fields and blue skies with a silver luster to the wood—these things lend character and life to the landscape, enhancing the setting with a richness found only in dream, or art . . . and finally, memory.

They tell, they show who the people were (or are). They are reminders of the completeness of man in a natural environment, in peace with what is. They quietly testify for the understanding to remain the way they were . . . in place. To be restored, if possible, preserved . . . or even to disintegrate slowly in the way of time and the elements.

Portrait artist James Ingwersen and his wife, Phyllis, chose to preserve, restore, authenticate the old Moegenburg homestead on Old Stage Road, South of Sister Bay. And though a living room ceiling was torn out to open the place up, though walls were stripped to get down to the basic log construction underneath, though cedar shingles were added to the outside . . . whatever was done, one way or another kept the truth of the entire house, including the barn, converted into a studio, and the granary, converted to a gallery.

There is the immediate effect of pastoral peace upon the scene. There is a reverence for farm and life, for what it was and what it should be. There are special touches in and about the Ingwersen place that quietly lift a person's feelings about art, in a sense, which is everywhere—house, barn, yard, fields. There is the total integration of place and person, something almost completely lost in the structures we put up these days and call home. When you become aware of how the Ingwersens have incorporated the past and present, you question again the desecration of the landscape going on throughout the county, and the country as well.

"I am interested in the total aesthetic environment that you live in," says Jim Ingwersen, "and this [his home, his buildings, his land] is what Door County was for years, and I just wanted to preserve this. We have always been interested in our environment. I think you have to be asleep if you're not aware of what's happening to the land around here. You just want to preserve what's left—especially after coming from a studio in a city where you don't even own twenty square feet."

About four years ago Ingwersen found himself involved in preserving a forty-acre parcel of land across the road from him which a developer had purchased primarily for the purpose of stripping the land for yet another project within the county: Pine Ledges, a golf course, condominiums, an entire complex to be erected upon one of the last natural areas of any size remaining in the county, Marshall Point.

"The guy was actually going to just strip that land and leave it. Just strip it down. I contacted some neighbors. We had a meeting. We got some petitions. I hired a lawyer. Rodney Kahr, another neighbor, hired a lawyer. We went down and put our case before the Resource and Planning Commission. We got the DNR interested.

"A local excavator said there were ten to sixteen inches of top soil; the DNR said zero to maybe ten inches. We called Mero [the developer] and said we don't want to see a gravel pit across the street. Eventually we defeated it. Actually, I think that this little thing stopped that whole Pine Ledges thing over there because we were opposed to the stripping of land around Door County." (Another positive outgrowth of this incident was the creation of the Door County Environmental Council, Inc., a non-profit organization which continues to play an effective, often brilliant role in educating the public, primarily through ads, of changes going on in the county that could affect the good of all. Jim Ingwersen eventually served as president of that council.)

He remembers first coming to Door County in 1936. "My folks used to bring us up when we were children in the summers. We rented a place in Ephraim, and I camped here in summer while in high school.

"I was really so busy with my art the next ten or fifteen years after high school that I never really gave Door County a thought. I did bring Phyllis up one year, the middle '60s, and we stayed at Anderson's Hotel. But Phyllis is strictly a city girt and she said, 'No way!' Then about 1970 she began to change her feelings a little. She saw the Key books (*The Key to the Door Peninsula* published annually as a guide to the many points of interest and services in the county) and she felt that at least she could put up with it here for four or five months a year. That was our contract, and I slowly conned her. We got animals, ducks, a goat . . . and it was difficult," he laughs.

After high school, Jim studied at the American Academy of Art for four years. Then came a two-year hitch in the Army. "Then I hung up my shingle as a portrait painter."

Ingwersen now enjoys a national reputation as a portrait painter, recently completing portraits of A. C. Nielsen, and Supreme Court Justice John Paul Stevens. Prints of two portraits of children, Gary and Gretchen, done sixteen years ago have very likely become the most popular selling children's portraits ever with the number of prints sold reaching the million mark. Both pastel and oil portraits of his hang in a number of homes in the county, including the Miller Art Center in the Sturgeon Bay library.

He "captures" people. He holds them dearly in his hand, his mind's eye, his whole being while slowly rendering them into art. He captures faces, feelings, gestures—a moment in a person's life—and holds it there, skillfully in line, in composition, in color, giving it a permanence, a reality of unquestionable beauty. In his classes at the Clearing-In-Winter (and the sketch classes he holds in his own studio) he is fondly referred to by his students as "the master."

Yet when he is questioned about his art, his drives, he does not come up with the usual answers. It is almost as if the romance of the artist's life has been reduced to practicality—but then honed to something else very different: more real and true, a continuing process as Ingwersen seems aware of the times, the fashions surrounding him, and even more aware of who he is and where he's at.

For he will honestly tell you he became a portrait painter "strictly to make a living. My father had been in the advertising end of commercial art for years. He really tried to dissuade me. Almost everyone in my class went into commercial art. I was basically a figure painter. When I went into the service, I began doing some portraits. Then I began to sell a few, and that's how I got interested in portrait painting."

Ingwersen himself, with his tiny round spectacles, appears to have stepped out of a portrait by one of the old European masters. He's a quiet man, more comfortable in the role of listener than talker. He's also a man who seems to relish laughter and companionship, if it develops; but he's more in tune with the peace of the Door countryside than any particular excitement. Still, his work, his art, his real love is people.

"I have an attitude of people are beautiful. They are more beautiful than they know they are. Some that I paint, commissions, are executives and everything, yet they're still human beings. But it's nice to be able to pick your own subject, people who have some character to them."

Are the people he has painted here, some of the local people, farmers and fishermen, in some way expressive of this very setting itself? Are faces here any different?

"No, no. I don't think so. I think they're just faces. I think they have
a different feeling about them, a different sense of humor. Everyone has
a character of his own above and beyond his environment. I think you
can find interesting people all over.

"But maybe they do have a character of their own here. There's so
many different types in Door County. I love to paint the farmer-type
individual because his face is weathered, his hands are big and beefy and
strong and lots of character to them. Some people love to paint the
beautiful people. These farmers up here never look like that kind to me,
whatever that means. But this is a very subjective feeling to me. These
things are interesting to me because I've never known people like this,
having been brought up in an area of Chicago—the North Shore— an
area of rather dilettante people which I couldn't wait to leave.

"When I came to Door County I wanted to get out of portrait
painting. All portrait painters get sick of it. It's a form of commercial
art—pleasing a client. For the past ten years I've painted people exactly
the way I see them. It's a much better arrangement, and actually, people
are more pleased. I do get a little tired of painting business suits and
ties. Still, it's a good living, and there are things I do for myself—any of
the local people who will sit for me. They usually walk off without a
comment, but it's a freeing sort of thing: painting what you want.

"If I could, I would just paint what I wanted to paint, anything that
just happened to appeal to me. I'm hooked on people, though. People
are the world. They've given the world what it is. People—the
challenge of being human, the human condition—are fascinating. I think

a tree is beautiful, but I can't get into painting trees. My statement of people is so inferior to the subject. And I don't care who it is— Michelangelo, Leonardo da Vinci—it's still a superficial image of this very complex thing."

When an artist as fine as Ingwersen seems somewhat divided in his work, inevitably the question arises: Why paint clients for a living when you should be painting this, all around you?

"Well, money is not my hang-up. I've never worried about it. There are other, personal reasons, I guess. I suppose painting is just not that important. Life is more important. Maybe that's it. I try not to lie. I try to understand myself in relation to the human condition. I try to be human.

"If I had to sacrifice a human being for art, I'd say the hell with it. I think to be a true artist you have to be very selfish. You have to say the hell with any relationship you have. It's a lonely, often brutal experience. I could let the world burn, but I think the world is more important than my painting."

Door attracts the painter in Ingwersen, "just for the natural beauty of the area. Light? Probably purer here, less filtered than the city. Yes, there are probably subtle differences in light, but I think all light is beautiful. Without light—nothing. Door County is just a beautiful environment to live in. If I had to stay in the city and paint portraits all my life, I'd probably jump out the window."

What disturbs Ingwersen is what disturbs many of us here: the diminishing landscape. "The buildings get torn down. Steel barns replace wooden barns. It's a sign of the times, our value systems. We've changed our values."

The architecture that now begins to overrun the countryside reflects a predominantly suburban culture which is alien to this place. Condominiums, slipshod remodeling jobs, trailers, ranch style homes, prefabricated buildings set in the midst of once beautiful acreage: one begins to suspect the natives are no longer home, the countryside has been surrendered to buildings that may look neat and trim in the suburbs of Chicago and Milwaukee, but cast a blight upon this landscape.

Gas lamps out front, paved driveways, immaculately trimmed lawns, even a few plastic pink flamingoes. City people, boxed-in minds carting all their crap and clutter of "home" with them. All their concepts of organized security. All the tiresome lines and forms which pacified their urban-suburban style, with the natural life held in check by power mowers, edge trimmers and perfect flower gardens. What is lost, destroyed, is all the character of a land once true in weeds and wildflowers, trees, brush, and dirt roads.

Inevitably to be lost along the wayside as more people and developments creep in: animal life of all sorts. Anything too natural, too real to upset the secure mentality. With these people will come sidewalks, streetlights, fireplugs, street addresses. Already they are out to name every damn road and lane in sight, pave every gravel stretch, since dust disturbs them.

Let it happen, if it must, in the towns and villages of Door. But please, leave the countryside alone. Leave the acreage in large tracts of 40, 60, 80, 100, what this county was.

Steel buildings are a pox upon the landscape. Granted they are more economical for the farmer, but they can never replace the true value of a wooden barn. Leave these, please . . . and the mystery, the pleasure, the surprise of unmarked roads. The pure discovery of a scene, something beautiful in the landscape, to which you can never quite direct anyone, or perhaps ever find yourself again. It's just as important, at times, not to be able to return to what it was, or where it happened, and leave the mystery of the image forever within you.

Leave the countryside wild. Leave it to the natives, the poor, the outsiders who wish things to be left as they are, undisturbed. If you dislike raccoons raiding your garbage and garden, if you dislike mice in your walls in winter, bats in your bedroom on summer nights, red and grey squirrels invading your birdfeeders, snakes slithering near the house . . . if whippoorwills disturb your peace at night, if rabbits and deer hassle your garden . . . if the wonder of all manner of weeds around the house and at the road's edge does not give you pleasure—then stay in the villages and towns of Door. Better yet, stay home. Do not build. Visit on vacations only.

(I await a renaissance of native architecture: log homes, white frame farmhouses two stories high, with front porches, gables, and tin roofs.)

"I want to keep Door County beautiful because it's beautiful," claims Jim Ingwersen. "Others may want to keep it for themselves. There are selfish natives. You can always say that beauty is lost on people who are too familiar with it, don't appreciate it.

"Us 'transplants' probably have a better knowledge of what true ugliness can be, and it seems Door County is hell bent on becoming as ugly as other places in the country. It's not a question of blaming anyone. It's just enlightening them—which is what the Door County Environmental Council does. Yes, I'm a member because I'm concerned. I want to support it as much as possible. I don't do enough. None of us do. The idea is to enlighten people, to make people think what might happen. To convince these people that what they want, what they think they want, isn't all cracked up to be. Again, it may be just economics. It's very discouraging. You think you win one after losing ten; then you discover a year later you lost that one too."

Jim, perhaps more so than many of us, has tried working directly with the natives. He realizes for the county to be somehow held in check, some understanding must be reached between environmentalists and natives.

"A young farmer was here one time. We went around and around on these things. He doesn't want to sell out, but these people are forced out of their property. It's happening all over the U.S. The small farmer is being taxed right out of his land.

"Yet try to get them to do something about it. I asked this young farmer to bring another young man to one of our meetings on it; he never came. He's very intelligent, very aware this young farmer, yet he knows it's hopeless, like he's a victim."

The role of business? "I feel they are just riding on the crest. They don't give it much thought. They seem to be for everything that brings money into the county.

"I think what bothers me more than anything else is the transplanted people who came up here. They love Door County, yet there seems to be this great feeling on the part of the local people that they resent these people. If the local people would truly be concerned, they wouldn't feel that they were being closed in. We want to try to help them maintain a quality of life.

"Realtors are in business, and that's the way they look at it. And they will fight for every square inch to put a house on it. This thing on the Hotz property [between Europe Lake and Lake Michigan]—the prime motivation on that was we were going to be out $ 10,000 in taxes every year if the state took it over. But what of the real value of the land? The DNR did buy it, preserving the land from development.

"I think there is an element of outside people coming in to do in the county. They see gold and want to grab it. I don't think they give a damn about the county. A whole, new outside breed coming in, and the county is throwing itself wide open. Even Mr. Lucey [former governor of Wisconsin, Patrick Lucey] said it'll be one big recreational area, if projections are right.

"There are very few native-type people making a living here. First of all, they can't pay taxes. They're appalling. So, I think, eventually, the locals are going to lose control. They're going to become the minority. And when that happens, you're going to hope like crazy that the environmentalists take over and not the business people, the outside business people. That's the last hope."

The Death of a Country Road

It was the kind of road you came upon unexpectedly, and because there was a quietness to it, a beauty, a mystery, you followed it wherever it led.

Dirt roads of this sort seldom lead to anywhere special. Their direction, for the most part, is an inner route, a self-exploratory tour guided by nature and the season.

Distance does not matter. Ten footsteps could lead you past wild-flowers, under the sheltering, swaying branches of old trees, into a personal landscape you were quite unfamiliar with, but welcomed.

But a dirt road can die too, just as an animal, a plant, a tree. And the more this county seems to come to life with buildings and people, the more it seems to die.

This once-quiet country road ran east and west for about a half-mile and could be picked up either off a back road "they" newly named and marked Timberline (it always used to be called Daubner Road, which was good enough, since this was Daubner territory), or off highway 42 just beyond Weborg's "Smoked Fish" sign on the way to Gills Rock.

I don't know what they called the road when they first cut through, but for some years now our sign-happy people marked it and called it Isle View. If you follow it on east beyond Timberline/Daubner, you'll find a modern, two-lane, paved road that lost all of its former beauty as a gravel lane when the road had to be widened because the land was selling, people were building, and the County couldn't get a snowplow in there, etc. etc. (Spare us the reasoning of reasonable men, Oh Lord.)

Anyway, forget that stretch of Isle View. It's gone.

And the half-mile piece of scenic wonder that's left is about to meet the same fate.

To some people the beauty of a country road is merely its convenience to a major highway. It's just a bothersome little stretch of bumps and dust and narrowness, something to get done and off of when the smooth singing surface of the real highway begins, and the destination can be reached with ease. Hell, I'm for better roads through higher taxes too. But there are some roads, like this half-mile piece of pleasure and contentment, that might for the good of us all be better left alone.

There is a privacy to country roads. Just you and the trees and the weeds and the flowers and the wind, and maybe the sun, the sound of birds, of insects, pieces and patches of sky . . . and a little dust clouding your heels. Try parking the car and walking a stretch like this for a change, biking it, cross-country skiing it. That's the way to learn a country road.

I placed my faith in this piece of gravel road, hoping nobody would ever build there, hoping the chain reaction of new people, proximity, road widening and paving would never happen.

It's a road that runs mostly straight, with a few gentle dips—that I'm sure our highways engineers will love to fill in and level.

It's a road where in summer, with trees in full leaf, you entered a sort of long cathedral of branches, of dancing light. You were not only on the road, but in it. It both carried you aloft and carried you quietly from side to side, like the movement of a river.

It was a most extraordinary experience, this road. It had a life of its own and spoke in summer green, autumn gold, and winter white.

It was a road that took you past a few old cottages that nobody seemed to inhabit. They seemed small, and natural, and in place; not the intrusive suburban-type dwelling that calls your attention to it, and makes you lose sight of the road.

It was a road I wish had remained unmarked, for some of the best things in life are those we know nothing about and just happen to come upon. You're driving along and come across an unmarked gravel road and you take it, just for the hell of it. And you discover a whole new experience in a place you thought you knew.

Maybe you never find the road again, if it remains unmarked, but that's all right too. The good memory of just one brief journey, lost forever, could last a lifetime.

I've been on roads like that many times in the Midwest, the Southwest, Mexico, England, Yugoslavia, Greece—old dirt roads and lanes I know I'll never find again. But I'll remember them, the good feelings about them, their texture, their field of vision, their character, their sense of secrecy and silence. I remember everything about them but where I was going, probably because I wasn't going anywhere. That, too, is a comfort in country roads.

I'm reminded of all this because when I turned onto this country road nearby the other day, I witnessed something, I guess, akin to vandalism, rape, and the first signs of death.

The cathedral of trees had been destroyed. Trees that had once lifted and cradled had been chain-sawed down to ragged and smooth stumps. They have torn open the entire roof, as it were, and destroyed the privacy and soft light of the road. Dead branches lay like funeral boughs covering an ever-widening roadside.

There are reasons, of course: new homes, and people wanting access to them in winter, the county plow unable to get down the old narrow country road. Trees must come down; the road must be widened, the gravel must eventually be paved.

Privacy, the peace, the poetry of a road, is gone, lost, dying, dead.

It doesn't really matter to most people.

It won't be missed, certainly not by the new home owners, or the drivers who prefer paved roads, or the tourists who can explore this country only by maps and road signs.

As soon as we get this whole county cleared of dirt roads, as soon as we make the whole place easily accessible to all with solid pavement and street signs, then we'll know for certain where we're at—and how to get out, fast.

A famous poem by Robert Frost, "The Road Not Taken," ends,

> Two roads diverged in a wood, and I—
> I took the one less traveled by,
> And that has made all the difference.

Our differences keep disappearing in the Door countryside.
Our similarities grow like an urban plague.

Dave Etter: A Poet of the Midwest Visits Door

"I like birch trees," he says, pipe smoke drifting around him, studying a Door landscape of woods and fields. "I like birches and maples. I just like trees."

The Tree Chopper

chopped down
a scrawny tree
yesterday

peach
dead
and more fun

I need
a whole forest
to fool in

For the record, David Pearson Etter, poet, visited Door county for the first time on June 30, 1979, and stayed for two weeks at Wills' Cottages in Ellison Bay. With him were his wife Peggy and his two children Emily and George. All of them are fine, warm, and very real people.

I just didn't want any of this to slip by. A lot of known and unknown people pass through Door, and occasionally, as in the case of Dave Etter, one should take note of this.

There's some speculation that the great American poet Vachel Lindsay once visited his friend Jens Jensen at the Clearing in Ellison Bay. Sherwood Anderson, the story goes, once spent a night in Ephraim with a female traveling companion and, when his mode of making it through the night was discovered, was run out of town the next day. There is rumor, too, that Carl Sandburg once wandered around Fish Creek.

So who in Sam Hill is Dave Etter? Well, you should know, although poets spend most of their days (especially in the Midwest) about as recognizable as that tree in the forest. I've frequently taught Dave Etter's work in my classes, especially a little poem of his called "Snow Country," one of his first, finest, and most anthologized poems:

Snow Country

only
a little
yellow

school bus
creeping along
a thin

ribbon
of snow road
splashed color

on the white
winter canvas
that was

Wyoming
from the train
yesterday

Etter likes school buses, likes snow, likes yellow. I don't know about Wyoming, but he sure loves the Midwest, though he was born in California and didn't settle down here till later. "I was always very much interested in the Midwest, because my mother came from here, born in Rockford, Illinois. My parents met and married in St. Louis."

He saw it for the first time at the age of eighteen. "Really what I noticed was the trees and the green grass . . . it was just different. I really got excited about it. I was *never* a Californian."

Etter likes cows, cornfields, crows, and country courthouse squares. Illinois, Wisconsin, Missouri, the whole Midwest. Front porches, back porches, baseball, picnics, marbles, bicycles, kids, hollyhocks, beer, school-houses, Grandmas, trees, prairies, rivers, first loves, dogs, sunsets, dandelions, small town characters, railroads, graveyards, booze, cicadas, apples, tomatoes, zinnias, scarecrows, girls in April, willows and water-melons, birds and barns.

Barn Dreams

Barns.
So many dreams of barns
blazing in the prairie sun.
Red barns, stone barns, round barns,
barns empty or falling down,
barns with cupolas,

hay-eating barns,
barns smelling of horses and old leather.
And winter barns, too,
crusted with ice and snow,
open to the winds.
Dreams, the dreams come on.
Me, all ages of me
entering barns,
sometimes in a daze or remembrance,
either corn or cattle outside,
maybe a goat inside,
or perhaps the girl I lost
ages and ages ago
at the Illinois State Fair
sitting quietly on a bale of hay,
saying, "I've missed you so very much."
Oh, may the green winds of chance
blow me always toward
barns.

Etter's first book, *Go Read The River* (University of Nebraska Press, 1966) was praised far and near, won awards, and brought him a quiet kind of Midwestern fame. It was filled with a lot of just perfect stuff — short lines, wild images, small town talk, and sometimes laughter of a sort that builds unbeknownst in the gut of a man till it bursts from the mouth in mirth:

Two Beers in Argyle, Wisconsin

Birds fly in the broken windows
of the hotel in Argyle.
Their wings are the cobwebs
of abandoned lead mines.

Across the street at Skelly's
the screen door bangs against the bricks
and the card games last all day.

Another beer truck comes to town,
chased by a dog on three legs.

Batman lies drunk in the weeds.

His second book, *The Last Train to Prophetstown* — also well received, also published by the University of Nebraska in 1968 — was followed by a steady stream of other books from various small presses: *Strawberries,*

Crabtree's Woman, Well You Needn't, Bright Mississippi, Central Standard Time, and his most recent, *Alliance, Illinois.*

To date he's published more than five hundred poems in over 130 publications, appeared in forty-some anthologies, has eleven books to his name. He reads frequently on many college campuses, and once shared an engagement with famed poet Stephen Spender. There's much history to this man. Tradition. Suffice to say he's the best thing to happen to poetry in the Midwest since Lindsay, Masters and Sandburg. Suffice to say he's taking in Door County with a fresh look at the moment, though he's a man at peace in the past, where his memories linger, and he feels most comfortable.

Why I Don't Go to Parties Anymore

They don't dance to Glenn Miller's orchestra anymore
or ask to hear Tex Beneke's "Don't Sit Under the Apple Tree."

No one wants to talk about France in World War Two,
or listen to what FDR said to Charles de Gaulle in 1941.

All my boozing is done alone on the kitchen floor
or in a rocking chair that scars the attic boards.

None of the old gang calls me on the telephone anymore
or sends those cute snapshots of the wife and kids.

I haven't seen Doreen Mitchell since the seventh grade
or had a heavy date with Nancy Huddleston since high school.

I must have died years ago in an overcrowded candy store
or in a subway train, screaming "Let me out of here!"

Introducing Dave Etter to Door, bouncing around the back roads, side roads, major and minor byways of this particular Midwestern setting, the summer of '79. "I sure like this place," he says.

How do you show a friend who's never been here what this place is all about? Especially a poet who sees, and then sees through? With a poet, you don't tell him anything. You show it. You feed him fields and wildflowers, birds, barns, windmills, woods, water, abandoned farms. You point to page three of the *Door Reminder*: "REWARD!! For Return of Lost Siberian Husky. Blue Left Eye." And you smile. "Too much," says the man who renders images into art. "Blue left eye . . . too much."

Mostly you leave it to his own eyes, his own ears. You let it work, let it settle. Let him make the meaning himself. Poets are slow cookers. Their nature is to let it all simmer for days, weeks, years.

Wills' Cottages? "It couldn't be better. It's perfect. If I come again

I'd like the same cottage, number six. There's just one thing . . . what's that guy's name over there? Gus Klenke? Well someone there in the morning keeps revving up a motorcycle, just revving and revving it up, you know? And if that thing ever falls in gear, they'll be picking him out of a tree."

Wilson's? Emily trying to maneuver the biggest double-dip ice cream cone in her life. "I like mint chip," says Etter. "I *love* anything mint."

We share an evening at my place drinking Sour Beers, eating tacos, salad and refried beans. "You couldn't have picked a better meal," says his wife, Peg; "Dave loves tacos." "Just about my favorite dish," says Dave. "And I love, I mean I really *love* refried beans."

In another part of the kitchen his son George is querying my kids as to why only a Mexican could come up with refried beans. "Only a Mexican wouldn't get them right the first time," he says.

Then we walk, Etter and I—a quiet walk in the fading light of the countryside, talking Chicago and other places, other writers, poets, mutual friends. Other lives. His eyes, take in everything in the landscape. He pauses near neighbor Matt Daubner's white farmhouse, the lights in the window going on for evening. "I like that," says Dave Etter. This kind of quiet scene sings to him. "This is the Midwest."

Night, back at the house now. More talk, drink, music, recordings of poets. We talk of Langston Hughes, Dylan Thomas, poetry and jazz, and listen to the old Brooklyn voice of Henry Miller. The beat goes on.

Days and nights do a summery tumble, while time neither stands nor sits, just floats with no numbers, no names. . . .

More places: The Clearing, Gills Rock, Northport, Newport, Uncle Tom's, houses, farms, people, stories . . . maybe someday, poems. Writers absorb everything. My friend Lou Smolak once said, "Writers? They never say anything. They're just like a sponge. They take in everything."

A night on the town—Baileys Harbor (Sin City, some say) and a spot at the bar of the Common House. "Paffrath and Dykhuis" do the entertainment. Good, real good. Drinking Johnny Courage, listening, listening. "This is some place," says Etter. "We don't have anything like this where I'm at." (Elburn, Illinois, is a place only small town guy Dave Etter could find.)

"I'm from a town so small that both the entering and leaving signs are nailed to the same post," Etter's been known to say at his poetry readings. "For excitement we usually go down to the bakery and smell the fresh rolls. For excitement we head out west of town and watch the front move in."

"I wish I could say those were original," he remarks. "But they're not."

Pub crawl, from the Common House to the Blue Ox (he's talking Nebraska now), to the Frontier Saloon, where we're entertained by Mary and her tales of a parrot named Banana, while pool halls click behind us and we have a final brandy.

Then a morning meeting and talking with Hal Grutzmacher, fine poet in his own right, teacher, bookseller, bookman. Etter and Grutzmacher trade hard-time tales of life along the poetry trail. Later, at Grutzmacher's book-store, Passtimes, Etter discovers five copies of an anthology he's in: *Pictures That Storm Inside My Head*. The title is taken from the last line of his poem, "From a Nineteenth-Century Kansas Painter's Notebook."

We visit Wilson's, to peruse the magazine rack—"I love magazines"—and then the back streets of Ephraim. In Chick Peterson's Gallery, Etter stares, studying a magnificent painting of "Grandpa's Barn," with the haunting presence of the old farmer, specter-like: just the feel and tone for a Dave Etter poem. A talk with Sue Peterson on the deck. A sharing of the clear view and the breeze from the harbor. Etter, checking out a typewriter nearby. "I love typewriters," he says, his fingers drawn to the keys, tapping soundless, invisible images.

We look for Freddie Kodanko, somebody Etter should meet. We try the farm, the A. C. Tap. Etter scratching out notes (he is an obsessive journal keeper) on bits of paper, matchbooks, the margin of a newspaper. "What's the name of that road? Old Stage? ZZ?"

We say hello to Sydney J. Harris at Al Johnson's, meet Wally "Clean Piece" Mickelson at Lundh Ford, trading stories and jokes. "What was his last name again? Mickelson?"

We spend a morning at Richard Nelson's in Ephraim. Nelson, ironically enough, is Dave Etter's former boss at Northern Illinois University, where Etter continues to work as a manuscript editor for the press.

"What do I call him?" he asks quite seriously. "I mean, he's always been President Nelson to me."

"He's just another Door Countyite now," I tell him: open, personable, a very nice guy. Just call him, Dick. He's an Illinois, a Midwestern buff. He knows your work and has collected it.

"Just 'Dick Nelson,' huh?"

There's an afternoon of fishing with Etter and his son George on Europe Lake. "I haven't fished in a long time," says Etter, fumbling with a rod and reel. I cast a red and white daredevil for him, explaining the motion of reeling in. George is trying worms. Etter retreats to his own strange world, puffing a cigar, sipping a Pabst, letting the daredevil sink to the bottom of the lake. I'm ashamed to tell him he's not doing it right. You give a poet a bucket of worms, he'll probably put the whole bucket on the end of the hook.

The beer's cold gold, the water's blue-green clear, the daredevil's dead at the end of his line: Etter's gone fishin'. I'm talking New Mexico, desert country, mountains, and getting mostly silence.

"The trees," he says. "All this green . . . I'll probably never leave. I'm gonna milk the Midwest till I die."

> There are green worlds in the grass,
> gatherings of laughing men.
>
> There is hope in the grass.
> And I found innocence there.

Near the end of his stay we start in late morning toward the interior of Door, looking for farm country. Recalling his first contact with the Midwest, Etter says, "One thing that really impressed me was the farms. I'd always liked good farm country, where the country people were as healthy as the people in town. To me, the Midwest is interchangeable with America. It's the heartland. It's where it's at. Everything else is just a fringe area."

He wanders around a deserted farm for a while, weathered barns and buildings, old machinery, everything that speaks beautifully, naturally of another time. It's everything he likes to give voice to in his poems. He's home again.

From Maple Grove Road to County F. In the distance, the white framed Zion United Methodist Church stands stark and Midwestern true amidst maples and fields and a country graveyard. It's a Grant Wood painting come to life. We walk this scene too, quietly reading the gravestones—Johnson, Sohn, Franke—while the wind rustles the maples and the sun burns a warm and steady peace upon the earth.

"I've written a lot about country graveyards," muses Etter. "You do too many graveyard poems and pretty soon some guy comes along . . . 'Etter? Oh yeah, he's the graveyard poet.' "

Country Graveyard

> Cows with eyes of buttered moons
> doze along the barbed wire.
>
> Weeds grow to impossible heights.
>
> I call out my family names
> across the campsites of stones:
> Etter, Wakefield, McFee, Goodenow.
>
> Cedar trees shake fat crows
> from their ragged beards.

In the farmhouse back from the road
shades are drawn against noon sun
and grace is said before the meat.

I stand among the gravestones
where a wet-nosed wind coughs
gray dust on my pinching shoes.

The rusty bells of the brick church.

Goodenow, McFee, Wakefield, Etter.

We pause at Paul's Glass Bar next—a place for everything, everything in its place. It's a still-life, a period piece in small town bars, circa 1940. A couple of cold glasses of brew feel good in the afternoon's hands of July. "I've written a lot of bar poems," says Etter.

The afternoon slides into Kangaroo Lake, Jacksonport, Cave Point Park. "What impresses me about this place is all the water, the fact you can go from Green Bay to Lake Michigan in no time. I like water. I like lakes. I like rivers."

Final scenes. Final names and people and places. At the Common House, the Birch Creek musicians, a jazz group, show up late to jam. We're working on a foamy pitcher of margaritas with salty rimmed glasses because it's that kind of night: laid-back deep in jazz in Door County. Etter, who likes the jazz rhythm, likes the jazz sound, frequently composes his poems to the accompaniment of jazz music late at night, back in Elburn, Illinois.

We're talking poetry amongst friends, including the poet A. Ubbink. We're talking jazz. "If I could be anything, I'd be a musician—drums," says Etter. "The piano is my instrument. I'd play a blues piano," muses Ubbink. I can't think of anything else I'd rather be, though another pitcher of margaritas might lift me to the sun-drenched streets of afternoon guitars in Santa Fe, or carry me alive and well into Southwestern nights, with rhythms quiet enough to tell about.

More final scenes: Etter at Jim and Phyllis Ingwersen's one morning, taking in the calm beauty of house and barn, studio and gallery, fields and trees. It's a painter's way in Door, a setting one could hold forever in memory and always find meaning and peace.

Both Etter and Ingwersen see/feel the poetry of landscape. Both revere the past, the countryside, the people: old barns, log buildings, local people, cupolas, farm animals. Etter in the log barn picking up a handful of hay: "I love hay." Jim, staring into the top of his cupola: "I'm going to put a ladder up there someday."

Driving away down County ZZ, Etter scratching down some "Ingwersen" notes on the back of a *Door Reminder*. "Now *that's* an

American painter," he says. I glance briefly at his notes and catch but one item: "Slim Jim."

What has the poet really seen? It's perhaps too early to tell. "The trees," he says again. "The unspoiled beauty. The somewhat New England type flavor of general stores. The harbors. It's good to see apples. I used to have some apple trees. . . . The peace and quiet. Birch trees, one of my favorite trees — what you don't get in Illinois. I'm very big on trees and farm country. I like water. I think that is really it: the fact that you have so much farm country and water. And it's all so close, like a miniature.

Much of the real feeling he keeps to himself, to sort out privately. Of such stuff is poetry made, when the time is right. Maybe a poem or two from this someday?

"Oh, yeah, sure. More than one, probably. It will if I want it to. There might be a quartet of certain things. Sure, yeah. But I always proceed cautiously. With new material I just kind of, you know, go slowly on it."

We will know then, for sure, by the poetry, that David Pearson Etter, Midwesterner, poet, was once in Door County.

> But I know now I know now
> it is first love of this place
> I want to hang on to

A year later I pick up a copy of Dave Etter's new book, *Cornfields*, (Spoon River Poetry Press) and find this poem:

> *Yale Brocklander:*
> > *Tractor on Main Street*
>
> Pay attention while I tell you this:
> That beat-up, manure-stained Farmall tractor
> you see parked in front of Jake's Tap
> is the same Farmall tractor
> that was parked in front of the bank yesterday.
> Get used to seeing it all over town,
> because Tom T. Cassedy won't be put off
> just because some lady judge up at the Courthouse
> took away his driver's license
> for driving drunk into a tree.
> Now, a Farmall tractor is not a Lincoln
> or even an International pickup,
> but as Tom T. says, "it's transportation."
> He's a persistent cuss, that old coot is.
> His face may say "ignorant,"
> but his eyes say "devious."
> He knows more than one way to get in to town
> for a snort or two, or three, or four.

Emma Toft

I can't really say I know Emma Toft. I'm not sure many people can.

At this point in her life—eighty-seven years old, living for the most part in the Dorchester Nursing Home in Sturgeon Bay—I'm not sure there are many of us she knows, much she remembers, except for the immediacy of the moments spent next to her, visiting, holding her rough, calloused hands, sharing her thoughts and laughter.

She is still the gentle but firm lady, still Miss Emma, still a quiet force to be reckoned with in this county. She is legend, bordering on myth, and has been so for many years.

Emma comes back to me in images, snatches of conversation.

Perhaps the majority of us who feel we know something about her understand her really in that way, for the essence of Miss Emma was the privacy of her personal environment in Door County: Toft's Point. Miss Emma sought those three hundred acres or so of virgin timber, plants and animals left to the privacy and magnificence of their own splendor, Mud Bay and its quiet inlets of nesting ducks, the rocky Lake Michigan shoreline shaped to hold the dreamer, be it water, sun, moon, or the mere perfectness of it all. Much of this we'll never know, for all of this was Emma's secret, though she shared the common earth basics of her vision with us all.

I remember visiting Toft's Point recently with Frank Pechman, hiking the area, absorbing the magnificence of the view from Mud Bay, reflecting on man-made "magic kingdoms," yet marveling at what an absolute private, personal, natural kingdom of her own Miss Emma possessed and bequeathed, in a sense, to us all. I remember images of Emma standing on this very rocky, rugged shoreline holding a gentle hand to her face to hold back the wind in her white hair.

"She had everything here," I thought aloud. "She needed nothing more to give life meaning. She was content."

"That's what bothers me," said Frank. "Why am *I* so unsatisfied? Why isn't this enough for me? Or you? Why are we always looking for something else?"

I retreated to my customary silence, the secrecy of self, the only answer I have when I don't know.

Images. Before I ever knew her name, I recall sitting in a snack shop in Baileys Harbor and observing a white-haired woman come in and take a table. No fuss was made over her. No one did much or said anything. Yet she instantly conveyed a sense of presence, as if she was there and suddenly the atmosphere had changed.

What captured my heart about her was her dress. For though she smiled, spoke softly, possessed refinement enough to be a member of any Door County social set, here was this lovely woman dressed to the teeth in blue denim, work shoes, and a red bandana. Even before the blue denim craze in American society, Miss Emma dressed for comfort, to please no one but herself. There was always this sense of self and youth about her. And even very recently, having been invited to dine at the Baileys Harbor Yacht Club, she entered the room dressed in her own inimitable fashion: blue denim and a red bandana.

Though I had no idea who she was at the time, I knew she was unique, the most striking old woman I had ever seen. I loved her for that.

She took on more meaning for me once I began teaching at the Clearing. She was revered there, and still is today. The then resident managers, Claire and Dorothy Johnson, sang her praises. There was a beautiful photo portrait of her on the piano in the main lodge. Former students of the Clearing constantly passed the lore and love of Miss Emma to new students: stories of her lying down to stop bulldozers, linking her arms with others to form a human chain to protect the trees from loggers and more bulldozers. Legends of a feisty old lady were shared and told again and again.

And each Thursday afternoon, students at the Clearing for that week would more than likely get the chance to meet Miss Emma at the traditional picnic held at Toft's Point, just past the Ridges. (The Clearing, the Ridges, and Toft's Point—three almost sacred landscapes in the county—are synonymous with Emma Toft and Jens Jensen, synonymous with the sanity of preserving our natural environment. Early environmentalists, they were called "conservationists" at that time . . . a man and a woman who lived what they believed.)

But I have always had some difficulty with this woman, Emma Toft. The more I knew her, the more she tended to fade away from me. I would talk to her occasionally at the Clearing. I would listen to her, observe her being badgered to death by questioning students during the picnics at Toft's Point. Everyone wanted a piece of her.

What is it in human nature, I would often wonder, that almost compels us to create a legend out of someone's life? I would find myself holding back, making the perfunctory handshake and greeting, then disappearing into the serenity of Toft's Point where I suspected the real Emma could be found.

She has received countless honors and awards. Endless stories have been written about her from local newspaper people on up to writers of the stature of Edwin Way Teale. On October 2, 1974, Representative Harold V. Froehlich read a tribute to her ("Emma Toft: Queen of the Peninsula" by George Anastaplo) in the *Congressional Record*, testifying to her gentleness and strength of character. She has made her mark. How many times, I wonder, has the poor woman been asked the same questions over and over again? "Jesus!" I wanted to scream at some people. "Lay off! Let the poor woman enjoy the day. Don't trespass on her graciousness."

But the singular question remains: just who was (is) Emma Toft? I would venture to guess that most of the people in this county couldn't tell you for sure. And perhaps only a handful of outsiders could.

The particulars of her achievements remain somewhat over-shadowed by images of a gentle but firm woman, respecting and delighting in the naturalness of the earth. Emma herself would probably take you to task for calling her important. Then she would smile and laugh a little. Then she might modestly reply, "Oh, I don't know; I just tried to leave everything where it belonged."

Anastaplo, in his tribute, recalls certain vignettes "revealing the freshness of Miss Emma. The day she invited Mertha Fulkerson and Jens Jensen over to see the arethusa blooming in her front yard, and it turned out that the "front yard" was a swamp which ruined Miss Fulkerson's dress-up shoes. The day she brought a baby skunk to The Clearing to lighten Mr. Jensen's deathbed. The days she had gone out on snowshoe from her winter quarters in Baileys Harbor to feed the deer on her side of the peninsula."

She was born in 1891. I know that for a fact because she showed me the entry the other day in her family bible: Emma, born Feb. 9, 1891.

Her father, Thomas Toft, born in Denmark, was a strong force in molding Emma's character. He loved the land. "He loved the trees," says Emma. "You can still see them standing there [Toft's Point]. Never been cut."

He worked the limestone quarry at Mud Bay and eventually bought the property which came to be known as Toft's Point—presently over three hundred acres, much of it virgin timber which her father refused to cut, refused to cash in on, and which instilled in Emma's mind an early and abiding sense of the preservation of nature.

Local battles were fought there over land ownership, and the right of a property owner to preserve his land. But the vision of Tom Toft remained. Developers were beginning to take over the other side of Mud Bay in the late 1960's (which they renamed 'Moonlight Bay', much to Emma's disgust), but the Toft tradition of preservation prevailed— Tom Toft's legacy to Emma, her brothers and sisters, and Door County itself—a legacy of simply leaving things where they were, where they belonged.

So thanks to the Toft family. Thanks to Emma, and her nephew, Thor, who kept the property, who kept the faith. Today, all of Toft's Point is preserved, having been sold in 1968 to The Nature Conservancy, a twenty-seven-year-old national conservation organization with over fifty thousand members devoted to preserving ecological diversity through the acquisition of natural lands. The Nature Conservancy then deeded Toft's Point to the University of Wisconsin for supervision.

So the land remains untouched and forever out of the reach of hungry realtors and developers. Tom Toft's virgin timber still stands. Classes from the Clearing continue to hold their picnics there, with Emma sometimes in attendance.

If she inherited a certain strength of character and pioneering spirit from her father, from her mother came the gentleness of spirit, the knowledge, the caring for plants and all living things. "Mother taught me the flowers and the berries," she says with a sigh, with a lilt in her voice.

What did Emma Toft do that was so important? Well, if the vision and preservation of Toft's Point were not enough to gladden the hearts of old-time conservationists and modern-day environmentalists (and anyone who cares about the future of the County at this time), certainly her role in the preservation of the Ridges, that invaluable area of old, old shorelines (geology in the making) with plants and flowers of glacial period origin, was the one particular act which brought her attention and began the legend. At this point truth and fiction meet, and *the* Emma Toft was born.

There was a movement in the 1930's by the Door County Park Commission to literally destroy what is known as the Ridges today. "Holand [author of *Old Peninsula Days*] on the County Park Board wanted to make a trailer park out of it," explains Emma. (To this day she holds no great love for either Holand or his book.) "The Ridges had always been a treasure. And here Holand and his gang had already cut a road partway."

Although Emma herself claims that the real value of the Ridges was not completely understood or known by her and some of her people at the time, she knew it "belonged there" untouched; and she was instrumental, the catalyst (along with others such as Jens Jensen and Albert Fuller, botanist of the Milwaukee Public Museum), in educating others on the reasons for preserving this invaluable piece of land and history.

The story goes that Emma Toft literally stopped the bulldozer in its tracks by lying down in front of it, thus saving the Ridges. For this singular, heroic act, she is long remembered and celebrated.

"That's not true," laughs Emma. "Mertha [Fulkerson, Jensen's secretary] made that up. I can't stop them [the people who spread this story about her]. If they're happy, let them enjoy it," she laughs again. "That wasn't Emma Toft. Well, if they're gullible, let them believe it— perhaps, if it was necessary, I would have done it."

What did eventually happen was the purchase and preservation of the land in 1937 by a small group of conservation-minded individuals who came to call it The Ridges Sanctuary, Inc., a non-profit corporation that exists on annual membership dues and private contributions. The first significant donation of $1,200 came from The National Garden Club. "Mr. Jensen said it should be called a *sanctuary*," adds Miss Emma.

A charter member of the governing board, Miss Emma has her differences with the Ridges these days. And though, because of her years, she may not grasp all of the problems concerning the organization and maintenance of such a unique piece of landscape in these days, she is entitled to her feelings: "I get fed up with this begging all the time [money the Ridges must seek patrons for survival]. I never begged from anybody. I'm too damn independent. I have no time for these beggars.

"If we'd let the bulldozer go in, the Ridges would have been killed quickly. There'd have been a sudden death. Now, we're slowly killing her with thousands of people tramping, tramping, tramping. Which would be better?

"I just don't like to see big buses coming in [this has been stopped]. We should eliminate it entirely. It needs to be controlled. It hurts me to see it going.

"I don't know who said it, but London said he would give I don't know how many millions if they could make a replica of the Ridges. Nobody can. No man can. It's a master plan. And we shouldn't destroy it."

In the early 1960's, both Emma Toft and Bill Beckstrom participated in a radio program devoted to the Ridges. Bill, professorial in his explanations, related some fascinating scientific phenomena on the geology and plant life of the area. Emma, when questioned about picking wildflowers, simply said, "I don't think we even think of picking them, they are so lovely there. And if you pick any wildflower, you almost have to take a tree, or the creek, or the sky, or something else into the room with it. You don't get anything unless you do. So you better leave it there for the many, many people to enjoy."

Emma has grown to represent the conscience of the entire county. Before anything else in the landscape is disturbed, men should be reminded of Emma Toft.

What else matters about her? She taught for many years in various parts of Wisconsin and as far away as North Dakota. (She remains a teacher to this very day.) She began to teach immediately after high school, "in Rowleys Bay," she explains. "Thirty-two dollars a month. I was eighteen at the time. When it was Thanksgiving, I walked home [Baileys Harbor] from Rowleys Bay. I was independent, you bet!"

She taught also in Jacksonport on County A. "I had seventy-five . . . a snag of kids there. I don't think I sat down all day while I was there. I had to do my own janitor work. I got $50 a month. There was a hell of a lot to do."

At one point in her younger years, for reasons not entirely explained, she gave up teaching to become a nurse. "I worked at the Presbyterian Hospital in Chicago. I came home, though, with father's death. I came back here, and I never went back to the hospital."

There was one love in her life, a "friend" she calls him, and just the slightest remembrance of that time past brings tears and a broken voice to Miss Emma.

"I had a friend . . . I knew him from Rowleys Bay. Yes, that was my boyfriend. We were engaged [Emma crying]. He was killed in the First World War, in France. I still had my people . . . you carry on."

And there was one other man, a visitor, a friend who came later. A widower wrote Miss Emma, explaining his interest, his intentions. But romance has a way of slipping away when day-to-day survival occupies most of your attention.

"I was at Mud Bay, trying to make things go," recalls Emma. "So, that was gone. I never answered the letter. It was very unkind of me."

Emma and her mother then opened the house to guests at Mud Bay (Toft's Point). And this was to be her life, running a very comfortable, old-fashioned kind of resort, up to the time of her mother's death, and afterwards as well, on her own.

She Milked cows, grew vegetables, prepared meals, fed and killed and dressed her own chickens. "I was happy. I wonder myself sometimes how I did all these things. The outdoors was my life. I did no advertising. If you give people a good bed and excellent meals, they'll come back. And they'll bring their friends."

Frank Pechman and I recently visited her at the Dorchester just to say hello, just to rehash some of these things. With her cane in hand, a sharpness and sensitivity in her eyes, she seemed physically capable of living out her life at the house in Baileys Harbor, and the summer place at Toft's Point. But her memory fails her at eighty-seven, and there is a danger with that in living alone. "Five minutes after we leave she won't even recall we were here," said Frank. And that was true.

She talked about her family again, about her mother and father, her favorite brother, Will. About her nephew, Thor, in whom she has absolute confidence and love. She reminisced a little about Jens Jensen. "He was capable," she said. "He built those buildings [at the Clearing]. He tried to do good. One winter I took painting there with Gerhard

Miller. Jens—I liked him some, but he was kind of boastful. He was just a human being like you are. My dad would have put Jens in his place."

She laughed when we reminded her of how many people looked up to her and loved her. There is little boastfulness to Miss Emma, too. "Oh, there are a lot of people I am not loved by. I chased them out of Toft's Point!" And often she did, at the point of a gun—hunters, especially, on the track of her deer which she loved and fed.

Sitting on the edge of her bed, dressed in a navy blue pantsuit, her head crowned in white hair, Emma still loves to laugh. All the wrinkles form naturally there, around her mouth, along her eyes. Tears, too, come quickly.

I mention Bill Beckstrom.

"Yes," replies Emma. "How is Bill?"

"Bill is dead," I tell her. She raises a calloused hand to her mouth like a child who said something she was not supposed to. "Oh," she sighs softly. "I didn't know Bill was gone. I didn't know he was dead." And then the tears.

What does she think she will be remembered for? Silence for a while; then she says, "Trying to keep the home place. Making people enjoy the out of doors. If you can't make people love the out of doors, then they're ignorant. Make them enjoy it. It's the little things. That's, I suppose, why so many people don't see it."

She rubs her calloused hands together, studies them, rubs them some more. She's been known to take sandpaper to smooth them down. "I rub them together, work them off," she sighs.

She isn't optimistic about the county's future. "I'm afraid it won't be what it is today. Well, I suppose there'll be richer people get in here. I hope Mud Bay isn't disturbed. Ephraim is still holy?" she asks as an afterthought and laughs. "Try to keep it natural. They don't need to bring in all these new-fangled ideas. It will lose all its charm and beauty. I don't know; I think there are different people coming into the county. Not like the pioneers.

"Greed is the main problem, don't you think? One of the biggest problems. It's all money, money, money, the root of all evil. Cutting the trees. If there's a tree, make it a log! They'll cut it down, just like that. That's greed. Father had to pay extra taxes just to *save* the trees."

Eighty-seven years old, and she still measures a man by the strength of her father's character. She sees weakness, I fear, in too many of us, men and women alike.

"A man has his own mind. He's a sissy if he's influenced by anyone. He knows what's right. He knows the difference. Sincerity, that's right in with it. My brothers were *men*. My father was a *man*! Greed, greed, greed—I wasn't raised in a family of greed."

She rubs her knobby hands together again, then smoothes the flowered bedspread in small circles with her fingertips.

"I am religious," she says, "but I'm not a fanatic." As she digs down in a drawer and pulls out an old family Bible to recall her birth date, I am reminded of her words a few years ago: "I don't know what you mean by religion. I read my scripture every morning. I'm never alone. I'm never afraid, except of man. Some of these people that are so religious, well, I shouldn't criticize them, but I just question how much their religion really means, because they don't live it. It's better to live it and not pretend you're something that you aren't."

Death? "I'm close to it. You wonder as you get older, you wonder about it. I hope when I go, I go out like a light. That's what my hope is.

"I would like to be with my people again, but I never have felt that way. I think that after you get older, you question a little more. You question things, you know? It's been quite a long road. . . ."

The Clearing

There is this place, The Clearing, in Ellison Bay, Wisconsin, just outside the village where I now live, some 125 acres of mostly woods, a few fields, high on the limestone bluffs overlooking the sunset, and the waters of Green Bay. (The rural and the wilderness side by side, and a view of the setting sun to afford hope for tomorrow.)

There are these buildings of stone and log, in complete harmony with the place: the main lodge, the schoolhouse, the dormitories, the pioneer cabin, the cliff house, a private place of retreat, to write and consider the clarity of water and setting suns.

There was this man, Jens Jensen, a landscape architect who studied the structure of earth—oil, stone, water, plants, flowers, trees—and arranged, adapted, planted and planned landscapes for others who were not so sensitive to the poetry of natural settings.

Jensen—a Danish-born but uniquely American artist who came to Ellison Bay from Chicago in 1935, at the age of seventy-five, to build his school, The Clearing—would leave Chicago a heritage as significant as that of Frank Lloyd Wright, his contemporary and friend, only not as obvious, perhaps; more practical, more natural, more for the common good. Jensen would leave the entire Westside Park System which he designed: Union Park, Humboldt Park, Douglas Park, and his masterpiece, Columbus Park.

Forest preserves, too. He had the insight and inspiration to preserve large tracts of land for future man . . . sanctuaries of natural peace, for those in the city who would come to need such solace.

But his real dream was to build a school, The Clearing, for both urban and rural man to experience the quiet teachings of the green world—roots, rocks, water, wind, birds, sky, stars, sun, soil—beginning with soil, most significantly.

> The ages have proven that a feeling of the soil is fundamental thinking, but we have never taken time to ask ourselves why this is true, why people and nations go to sleep, follow false trails, and decay, when they lose sight of the soil.

> —Jens Jensen, *The Clearing*, "A Way of Life"

There is this Clearing, then, almost forty years later, sponsored now by the Wisconsin Farm Bureau (thanks to the foresight of Sid Telfer, Sr.) after the death of Jensen, age ninety-one, on October 1, 1951.

Above all, there is the spirit of the goodness of man in a natural environment, which Jensen understood almost mystically and envisioned for others, and which affects and transforms all those who discover their private clearings here for a week or more, perhaps year after year at this unique school for soul in Door County, Wisconsin.

There is, too, an interesting and involved history about this man and place, the original concept, how it grew; the building, the land, the fire, the problems of financing such a private dream, the students and teachers and visitors who came; the difficulties Jensen's secretary, Mertha Fulkerson, faced upon his death when the preservation of The Clearing was much in doubt.

One must experience The Clearing first, then delve into the significance of its history afterwards.

I speak now as one who came upon this place quite accidentally; knew immediately and almost intuitively what Jensen was after; studied, privately, his life and works; and stayed on for the many years to teach. For The Clearing is first of all a school—it's a rather unorthodox school, but nonetheless a structure does exist. It's not a "closed" school in the style of what Frank Lloyd Wright established, but a "folk" school, in the tradition of the Danish concept of communal living and common craftsmanship. A place where one can open oneself to all sorts of possibilities in a natural setting.

The courses run by the week from mid-May to mid-October. Usually two courses are offered each week, seldom to more than thirty students total, for The Clearing, as Jensen envisioned it, should be a place for men to deal quietly with themselves and their surroundings in small numbers.

It is a "total" experience, communal to an extent that each week a group of people share three meals a day, a class, and many of their personal feelings and experiences. There are private rooms and dormitories—though "dormitory" calls to mind a type of building totally alien to the Jensen landscape. Even the "dorms" are completely natural, made of log and native stone, and so very humanly habitable.

The cost for all this—room, board and tuition for the week—is by any standard reasonable, bordering on a bargain. (Shades of Jens Jensen, the dreamer, the artist, who never knew just what money was all about, how much to charge, and frequently offered his services for nothing. When asked to design the Lincoln Memorial Garden in Springfield, Illinois, he replied, "I will give my best and there will be no fee.") To Jensen, value had something to do with what went on inside a man, what he wrought, and how carefully he looked, listened, learned from the natural things.

The "Clearing" begins, in a way, the moment you arrive at the front gate on a Sunday afternoon and follow the twisting road through the woods into a sudden opening, a very real clearing indeed, and finally on to the very buildings themselves, the flowers everywhere, the birds performing in and out of season, the warm welcome and honest hospitality offered by resident managers like Claire and Dorothy Johnson, who succeeded Jensen's secretary, Mertha Fulkerson, upon her retirement in 1969. Don and Louise Buchholz followed the Johnsons in 1976 and continued to carry on the direction of The Clearing with insight, concern, and dedication. Mertha Fulkerson, who died in 1971, and all the resident managers reflect the almost indefinable spirit of The Clearing that takes hold of one so quickly, something similar to the atmosphere of a religious retreat, I would imagine. With the sunlight filtering down upon you through the trees, the waters of Green Bay working their ice-age ways along the limestone bluffs, you realize that Jensen, whatever his private history, knew what he was up to, and understood how such a place must be passed down to others, intact. He possessed this responsibility toward the earth.

He would tell students of landscape architecture, "First grow cabbages. After that, plant a flower. When you have successfully grown a flower, then you can start to think about growing a tree. After watching a tree grow for several years, observing how its character develops from year to year, then you can begin to think of a composition of living plants—a composition of life itself. Then you will know what landscape architecture is."

But how do courses in photography fit into the Jensen concept of man and nature? Or French, weaving, health, early American quilt making, the New Testament, woodcarving, retirement, chamber music, writing? They do. Everything fits. Pure composition. One way or another, amidst the natural wonder of such a setting, the composition develops in a week's time, the clearings within a man are felt deeply, and one becomes whole again.

"Thank you, Jens Jensen," I recall a student of mine writing near the end of our session.

I must be personal now, for The Clearing encourages such revelations of one's self amongst others. I will tell you a little bit about how it goes with me, how I teach, what I learn, how we all grow from the Jensen encounter.

I begin with questions, of course, spoken and unspoken. Who are you? What kind of writer do you wish to become? How much can you reveal? How do you want to be? These are palpable questions for writers, perhaps, but a place to begin. Certain clearings to be established.

> In all our endeavors we must start from where we stand,
> and from there grow. The song that bursts into being must
> come from the heart. . . . The poem that has come from the
> depth of awakening has the unfathomed tempo of sounding
> waters. Only then can our work be of any value.
>
> —Jens Jensen

I seldom mention Jensen in our sessions (what, after all, does a landscape artist have to do with the fine art of writing? Everything, everything), yet I discover that much of what I teach, much of what I know, was already there, in Jensen's book, in The Clearing itself, nature as the great open classroom. So I endeavor to preserve this harmony. In the midst of the teaching I am always experiencing certain lucid moments, certain clearings, and a sense of self-renewal.

I remain open to their desires. Which way do they care to go? I'm willing to learn. Where should we begin? Poetry? Or should we chart the inner and outer landscapes of story? Tell me, and we'll move together (too quickly, I warn) toward a number of possible endings. (One week is never enough time.)

So probably we begin and end with philosophy. From there we move to words, simple words, and then feelings, structures. My "lesson plan" depends upon whatever energy we manage to generate each session. One good thought, one fine poem, one personal revelation can call to mind a thousand directions of self-discovery within me. "I never know what I'm doing from one day to the next," is the only prerequisite for inspired teaching. Teachers who know exactly what they're doing don't know a damn thing.

Give me a roomful of dolts for the day, and I become a dolt for the day. Give me at least one exciting person sending out energy, and I will respond in full for the entire class. Give me two or three, and teaching becomes art.

A Philosophy for Writing—I want them to think about this first, to feel it. "The way to do is to be," said Lao-Tzu; I throw that out for openers. "The way to write is to write," I paraphrase. "You've got to see where you're at and envision what kind of a writer you intend to become.

And you've got to have wild visions for a full sense of life. You've got to grow and take chances.

"But if you have no other desire in life than to write cook books, I'll still expect you to write the best damn cook book around. Or if you're in the Local Paper Syndrome and wish to remain in those comfortable confines of Letters to the Editor, Hospital Reports, Church Functions, etc., okay, but I'm going to expect you to put a little more hell in your community reports, have a little more fun with yourself. God knows we need all the humor we can find in small town living. And I hope all the while that you would think of outdoing yourself, writing beyond this.

"Writing is self-discovery or it's not writing." We begin with that because I just happened to say it, because that is what I have learned and believe. I tend to be as dictatorial about this as Jensen is about landscape architecture:

> Quite naturally, since I have spent almost a lifetime in the field of landscaping, my understanding of this art is greater than of all others. Landscaping is a composition of life that unfolds a mysterious beauty from time to time until mature age. All other arts are founded on dead materials.

I move into words and associations, if that's how I feel, if that's where I think the students are leading me. What does WIND make you feel? Or, how BLUE is the BLUE within you? (I must move into metaphor first—only a week's time—and I must probe for empathy even faster.) How are you going to tell me what a MAN, WOMAN, OBJECT *feels* if you can't transcend the confines of your own self? How are you ever going to write anything but obituaries?

So pretend you're a plant (a prairie rose), an insect (a spider), an animal (a loving cat with a KILL pattern of 'bird' in its eyes) or, for laughs, a tough man caught crying, a fragile farm woman, mother of five, caught fleeing the pastoral life.

This moves us (from poetry unexamined for the moment) into an open structure for STORY. Where do you begin? Anywhere. Where are stories? Everywhere, everywhere. This here, right now, is a story. . . .

"Once upon a time" stories began there. They still do, though the times are always a changin', and a writer must keep himself open to infinite possibilities.

> This is the story of the prairie rose that is an unalterable part of the land of which you and I are a part. . . . The Clearing is a story of the infinite message of this lovely flower.
>
> —Jens Jensen, *The Clearing*

STORY, then: putting yourself on the line, easing yourself into others, predicaments, places, imponderables to tell about, to share by showing.

ASSIGNMENT: Something I came across this morning: a stunning red fox killed on the highway. The tragic beauty of it, an animal you seldom see slaughtered in such a way. Raccoons, skunks, squirrels, birds, yes—they are frequently at the mercy of cars. But never a fox. What was it attempting in its motion, its hunger? Why did it miss, so handsomely gleaming in its fur? But no, no . . . that's perhaps a poem, not a STORY at all. Scratch that. Begin again. . . .

ASSIGNMENT: Story projection. Project yourself into a character at a specific time, in a specific place, who wishes to possess something (idea, object) that he has been denied all his life. Yes, and somehow resolve this. If you're a man, be a woman. If you're a woman, be a man. Make this felt. Reflect on your own life, the things you've never possessed or even considered, till now, how terrible the sense of loss must feel.

Enough. That is the way the teaching goes with me at The Clearing, two sessions a day, individual conferences in the evening, Monday through Friday. What we discover about ourselves, about writing, goes far beyond this, affecting thoughts, actions, conversations throughout the week, at meals, morning, noon, and night, and hopefully long after the week at The Clearing. This is the way, I feel, Jensen expected ideas to be planted in his setting and sooner or later to come to flower.

As for the students, they are as varied as the plant life in any landscape. Men and women; young and old; professionals and blue collar workers; self-righteous and self-conscious; loud and soft; happy and sad. Somehow or other they all find The Clearing.

They come mainly from Wisconsin and Illinois, but they also come from places like Croswell, Minnesota; Valparaiso, Indiana; Brooksville, Kentucky; Aberdeen, South Dakota. Jensen's word, each year, reaching out like waves far beyond Ellison Bay, Wisconsin.

Friendships are formed within class sessions, around the dinner tables, where excellent food and constant conversation mix so well (this, too, Jensen believed in, the fellowship and learning to be discovered at the dining table) and in and about the natural setting.

I must protect the privacy of the students, but how I wish I could detail their lives and feelings for others. Conversations, revelations strung out from fear and anxiety to intense self-discovery, laughter, naturalness, mystical convergences and love.

For me, living too much in the woods, too far from Chicago too much of the year, in the dire absence of such human stimulation and contact, my week at The Clearing comes on as a big high, where I remain and take great comfort for weeks after. For many students, I am told, the feeling is identical.

More and more this Clearing, which Jensen established in 1935, seems to reflect the air of NOW: the NOW of Esalen in California, the NOW of Encounter Groups, the NOW of Open Education and Ecology, the NOW of altered consciousness. This is, perhaps, precisely where Jensen was more than thirty-five years ago. We keep changing the name of Natural Living, but basically it was/is simply this . . . a clearing of the mind, a place for us to discover the peace and possibilities within ourselves.

That assignment in story I gave. . . . I recall now this tremendous woman I had in class: the privacy about her, how she made herself felt that morning she read her impelling story, how she made herself known and loved by so many in so short a span of time—such compassion, she could bring a man to tears through gestures, voice, words, her very sense of being so alive, so involved in the world.

"I seek clarity," her character reiterated in a hopeless, boxed-in setting of the mind. "I want clarity, clarity, that's all."

You took around the urban, suburban landscapes, and it's so hard to find it there in the terrible things people are doing to themselves in the dwindling absence of the natural landscape so conducive to the welfare of the whole man. And you read Jensen's words again:

> In my travels I have visited many cities, cities that were planned and cities with no guidance, and I have found no city where man has not enslaved man. For thousands of years man has enslaved man in cities and for a little while longer man will continue to enslave man, but faith is breaking the fetters. A little while longer and our cities will ring with man's inheritance, and the open door and the living green will follow man and be an unalterable part of his home . . .

And you try to measure his hope in his time against the desecration of the landscape today, and you realize that the hope for tomorrow in setting suns rests almost entirely in these small green islands of sanity, these clearings for soil, growth, and human awareness. And so you return, begin again with people and place . . . and seek clarity . . . and trust, this time, the story will be understood.

Sid Telfer Sr.: Orchardman

Sid Telfer Sr.: Driftwood Farms . . . fruit grower . . . orchardman. . . .

I revere the old ones, especially those often more alive than the young. I hold them to my consciousness whenever, wherever in the world I find them: Greece, Yugoslavia, Hungary, Italy, Chicago, Door County. I'm certain there are small truths to their lives that must be passed on.

I first crossed paths with Sid Telfer Sr. five or six years ago at the old Ellison Bay post office when Walter Severson was in charge. The post office, I discovered, was the true social center of rural America.

There, every morning, was Sid, getting in or out of his car with his faithful Dalmatian, Pansy, occupying the back seat. Frequently beside Sid sat a beautiful, almost regal gray-haired lady, whom I was to learn later was his wife, Inez. By his looks, his dapper manner of dress, I figured Sid Telfer to be a man in his sixties, but he must have been in his late seventies at that time.

Either Walter Severson or Claire Johnson (then resident manager of the Clearing) must have introduced us one morning. Aside from trading names and the usual weather reports, the relationship did not develop much further than that for many years.

Each of us, no doubt, learned more about the other in the usual manner of small town "character development": plain old gossip, the ritualistic passing of information sometimes true, but usually false. Though it's the false, we'd rather believe it, for it's usually a hell of a lot more interesting than the truth.

I heard both good and bad stories about old Telfer from that point on, but very few, if any, unkind tales about Sid. At worst he'd been accused of being a bit standoffish at times. He no doubt appeared that way to me in the beginning, but I learned later, when he became a student of mine at The Clearing-In-Winter, that that Sid's initial demeanor only signified that the old man was sharpening his wit. I was to discover that there was more than just a touch of Twain to Telfer.

"What do you want to write about me for when you've got all those other fine people, Phil Austin and them?" he asked me in an absolutely serious tone of voice the other day. "You want the bad along with the good . . . that's what you've come to me for, huh?" And then a slight trace of a grin on his face followed by sudden laughter when he knows he's got you. Eighty-four years old, and he's still pulling your leg.

Telfer and orchards. You can tell a lot about a man, some say, by the way he prunes his orchard, and Telfer's trees were said to be the most carefully pruned in his time, truly beautiful to behold.

Then there was Sid Telfer and Jens Jensen and The Clearing. Legend had it that it was Sid who helped preserve Jensen's dream by convincing the Farm Bureau to sponsor The Clearing after Jensen's death so that the association, the values to be found in men and nature, can continue. That was a fruitful planting, too, for the old orchardman, with the yield (basically spiritual) increasing each year.

Sid was born in 1894 in Ft. Atkinson, Wisconsin, one of the largest dairy areas in the state. His father was a Guernsey breeder, purebreds, and Sid was well acquainted with the usual farming chores.

"Dairying ties a person down," he tells me as we sit in the comfortable living room of his Driftwood Farms home in Ellison Bay. The Navajo rugs covering the floor lend a Southwest touch to the room, contrasting to the stone fireplace designed by Jens Jensen. Sid gets up occasionally to poke some fire in the hearth. Pansy, the Dalmatian, is fast asleep. "That's the thing that's always been wrong with dairying. But my brother married one of the daughters of one of the owners of a nursery business back home, Coe, Converse & Edwards, and I started to work there on summer vacations."

He studied agriculture at the University of Wisconsin, Madison, for two years, majoring in dairy husbandry. "At that time they had a course called 'the middle course' in agriculture. The only thing you didn't take was advanced algebra and chemistry. Otherwise it was all the same."

Sid completed his studies there and continued working for the nursery each summer. "Then Mr. Coe asked me one day, would I be interested in going up to Ellison Bay? I never heard of Ellison Bay, but two fellows up in Sturgeon Bay, Bingham and Lawrence, were promoting the orchard business in Door County [the area known as Roen Orchards and now largely in the hands of Wink Larson]. Mr. Coe had stock in the Ellison Bay Orchard Company. I was hired to take care of the dairy end, since they were going to put cattle on part of the land.

"I was twenty-two when I married and came right up here. Inez lived in Chicago and came up to Ft. Atkinson to visit relatives. We came up here in March of 1917. We came by train and shipped our car, a Model T, by rail. We came to Sturgeon Bay and stayed about a month. I pruned orchards there with Bingham.

"The first year I was up here at the Ellison Bay Orchard Company, the fellow who was running it quit, and I took over the orchard end of it. The cattle were forgotten. We had 200 acres of cherries and apples and then farm land, over 450 acres in all. Of course, I had worked in the nursery, so I knew something about pruning and planting apples and cherries. I had done a lot of that. I stayed with the Ellison Bay Orchard Company for twenty years; then it was sold to J. Arthur Friedlund. I was with Friedlund for five years, and then I came down here and got into orchard work on my own land.

"That first year with the Ellison Bay Orchard Company we lived in a canvas house, 16 x 32 feet, made of canvas with a wooden frame. We set it up on the highest place, and every time the wind blew, I had to hold onto the house so it wouldn't blow away. There were five rooms to it, four 8 x 8's and a 16 x 16 in the center. It stood right up there where the water tower is on the hill in back of Wink's."

Sid smiles and then laughs as he recalls another scene from those days. "My wife wasn't too great a cook, and these fellows, they were going to have a Board of Directors meeting up at our canvas house one time. We brought some boxes to sit on . . . we didn't have much there. Mitchell Joannes from Green Bay was there. He had money in this thing. So my wife said it looks like they're going to stay, and I'd better get some stuff for lunch. I went down to Ellison Bay, down to Ed Evenson's store. He had everything there. The cat slept in the bag with the coffee beans. What a place. I bought some pork sausage in brine and she cooked it. She didn't freshen it or anything, and it was so salty a person could hardly eat it, but Joannes said, 'This is the best meal I ever ate.'

"We built the house in the first year [where Jeanne and Dave Aurelius operate Clay Bay Pottery]. Then we built those other places around there. We used horses and mules the first year for working in the orchard. We didn't have tractors. During those years Bingham and Lawrence were planting orchards all over the county here . . . the north end, that is, north of Sturgeon Bay. They had all the faith in the world in this business. In fact, they were right in believing in it. It was good.

"Cherry orchards—we believe in them. When they get into production, they'll go fourteen, fifteen years. We always worked the soil good, real well for a new orchard. One place we planted forty acres of potatoes the first year. This loosened the soil, made it better for planting. At that time we planted two varieties. Early Richmond and Montmorency. Early Richmond ripened first; this way your harvest extended over a longer period of time.

"We were planting twenty feet apart, square, which would give you just about a hundred trees per acre. The trees were planted in April or May, as soon as the soil was workable. We always tried to bury the root stock in a couple of inches of ground cover.

"You cut off the branches to four to six inches immediately. Try to even them up so that a real strong branch would be cut to encourage the weaker one to grow, to dwarf the bigger one. To establish the new tree, you always cut off more of its top to give the roots a better chance to grow.

"Pruning! God I used to get in trouble with the people when I pruned an orchard and started cutting all the tops off. 'Windshield farmers' I called them—people who sat in their cars and told you how to do it."

As there was a pattern to an orchard, there were patterns, including seasonal ones, to orchard work as well. The preparation of the soil, the planting, the first pruning.

"Next they had to be sprayed. You spray against fungus which attacks the leaves. Then you use an insecticide against the insects which attack the fruit. Then we'd cultivate to keep the weeds down, the grass from growing until fall. We'd do this whenever we could get around to it. In the late summer we used to plant a cover crop which we would disc down the next year to give the soil humus. We used to put in rye. We sowed yellow blossom sweet clover and buckwheat too. Buckwheat grows fast and makes a good cover crop.

"In the fall we used to shovel dirt to make a mound around the trunk of the smaller trees. It steadied them against the wind and also kept the mice from girdling the trunk.

"Nothing more to do then except pruning before spring. That wasn't much of a job the second year or the first. But after your trees get size, then pruning gets to be a big job. We used to spend all winter out there. Damn cold. Lots of clothes on you. We wore mittens. We used a long-handled pruning saw."

Sid gets up for a moment to tend to the fire. For a man in his eighties, he moves with a sure step and keeps his mind active and always alert. He has a bit of a hearing problem at times; once in a while he forgets. As for old age: "I just don't think about it. Say, a funny thing one night in your class last winter: after class I was talking to Uncle Tom Collis and this hearing aid of mine started making those funny noises because I still had it turned up all the way so as I could hear you. Well, it was beeping away and Tom was wondering what that noise was. I didn't say a thing. Finally I just pointed to my head and said, 'Electronic brain,' and walked away. I'll bet he's still wondering about that!"

Sid's not finished talking about pruning yet. "All the way through, from the time you plant, you have to watch for a bad crotch—the branch will split off when you get a load on it. The center of the tree should have a modified leader instead of letting it get way up. Keep it even with the rest. Keep the whole tree in balance, that's the main thing.

"I guess we were pretty particular about the type of tree we had. A lot of people in the business are in it only to get all the fruit they can get.

But we were interested in the tree itself, to get a good, sturdy tree. I guess a man could trim between ten or fifteen trees a day my way. We didn't usually go out if it got very much below ten above. Sometimes, with drifts, we had to shovel snow away from the trees to keep the branches from going with the melted snow. We always pruned in the dormant stage, from after the leaves go till spring. April is a good time, one of the best times.

"You get cherries after six years. Then you watch the insects more."

How do you "read" a cherry tree?

"You can tell right now, by looking at the buds, if there's been injury up to this time. There would be a little black spot in the center, right in the base of the bud. Chances are it's the cold weather, or it could have been a dry season previously.

"At blossom time, if there isn't a pistil in the center of the blossom, then there'll be no cherry. But a person often gets fooled in looking at a blossom and thinking it's dead. There are just so many of them. It's called June drop. A tree can carry just so many cherries; the excess fall off. You can tell before your June drop; if the cherry sets, the fruit develops very fast. If you've got a good long stem on the cherry, and the cherry is there, you can be pretty sure it's going to develop a good fruit."

Weather is always the most crucial factor in the history of man and the soil. Weather can make or break a Door County fruit grower and farmer. Good seasons, bad seasons. "You need sunshine and nice weather . . . moisture, that's all. The only trouble with Door County is you get a late frost that they don't get as often in Michigan. And that can do a lot of damage.

"You can get brown rot from too much moisture. High humidity or rain. Lack of sunshine is another thing. And also there can be wind damage which will bruise the cherries.

"Art Friedlund once said, 'I thought I knew what gambling was, but I don't know anything.' It's probably as big a gamble you can get into as anything. It seems funny that back in those years we never thought about all the problems you have today. If you had blossoms, you had cherries. That was all. One year, there was a lot of snow, and all the branches that were buried under snow produced blossoms and fruit. And those above the snow, nothing. Just a skirt of cherries all along the bottom. You know, they talk about tough winters, but I don't think we have them anymore."

There are also man-made problems, as Sid sees it. "I would blame everything under government control. That's what fixed me. I'm not willing to put up with all the demands they make in running a cherry camp or anything else. Apples, you see, have to be harvested by hand. You need pickers.

"Oh, it's nothing today compared to what it was then. They're about

out of the cherry business here, and apples is pretty much the same. Over time, the prices were so poor that a lot of people got out then. Then there's the problem of competing with Michigan. I don't think we can. They don't have the winter we do. Their trees grow taller, produce more than we do.

"This here business of shaking cherries has changed the whole business entirely, even in the pruning and shaping of trees. Now it don't matter how tall a tree grows. Before, when you picked it by hand, it did. We tried to grow our trees so as they could be picked by hand from the ground or with a ladder. Now you prune them up higher to get your equipment under."

Sid left J. Arthur Friedlund in 1942, and moved "down here," as he calls it, to Driftwood Farms. "I had this land before, and we bought more of it. I came here because of the wind. The wind ruined everything over there. I wanted to get away from that, and that's why I came down here. We had cherry trees that were producing by the time we got here, and we had apples almost ready. I suppose we had fifty acres in apples and cherries. We're down to nine acres around the house now, and barely an acre and a half of orchard right behind us. We had cattle once too. In later years we had beef. But I always liked apples. Apples better than cherries. "

Three years ago Sid Telfer and his wife, Inez, walked into my writing class at The Clearing. I t was the first year of an attempt by some of the people in these parts to open The Clearing in winter for those who didn't get a chance to attend in summer (both natives and outsiders), for all those who find the winter just a little too long.

In my time I had taught writing from the grade school through the university level. I had taught kids from "below average" to gifted. I had taught dropouts, drug abusers, runaways, housewives, factory workers, ministers, executives, Vietnam vets, a nun, a couple of ex-cons, and plenty of just plain folk. I had taught at The Clearing for five straight summers. But in all these experiences I had never taught a student eighty years old. Now all of a sudden there was Sid plus his wife, Inez, who was eighty-one (and a pretty fair poet in her own right, I was to discover).

I decided I would not try to make it any easier for anyone because of age, though I was very conscious of both Sid and Inez. I merely assumed, as always, that we were all in the same boat: people with a desire to communicate as best we could, regardless of age, background, or education. We all, at least, had our own stories to tell, and with eighty years of them under your belt, there had to be something to say. Aside from age, my only other reaction to Sid's presence (unexpressed) was a good feeling that the philosophy of The Clearing was still working. For here now sat Sid Telfer, a personal friend and neighbor of Jens Jensen, still involved with learning, still a true believer in the essence and spirit of The Clearing. Trite as it sounds, I was honored to have the Telfers, though I was afraid my teaching techniques might scare them away. (Inez, to this day, still won't accept poetry that doesn't rhyme, while Sid is game for just about anything.)

I'm not entirely sure what Sid learned in any of my classes (he's been with me every winter since and once during the summer on a scholarship). But as anyone who calls himself a true teacher will tell you, you always learn more than you teach. I merely suggest ways of doing things, and Sid goes and writes it the way he sees it anyway. Which is all right, the way it should be, because the man has his own style.

I gave an "association" assignment early in that first writing session: write about an object, an article, a thing. Define it as personally, as specifically, as you can. You and it. Write, always, about what you know.

I had no idea what went on in the mind of Sid Telfer. I wasn't certain he could write at all. When I called on him, he prefaced the reading of his work with the usual student reaction: "Well, after hearing all these other good things people wrote, mine isn't much." Yet here, in part, is what he wrote:

> What are you going to describe. An article or thing, for that is the assignment for today. But what thing? I am lying in bed supposed to be asleep, but that assignment, describe an article. It gets me.
>
> There is one thing I might know a little more about than any other as I have lived all my life with it. And worried about it more, I presume, than was necessary. The apple. There are three varieties in the refrigerator downstairs, and they are all good, but one is especially worth considering. McIntosh, Delicious and Cortland are the three kinds.
>
> The McIntosh is a solid red, beautiful apple with a tender skin, white flesh and very choice for eating "out of hand" as the old time horticulturist would say. The Delicious with a long pear shape and of good color with five very distinct points on the lower end has great eye appeal and is desired for eating by a great number of people. The Cortland is the largest of the three, not as striking in color, flattened on top and bottom and would not be chosen for appearance, but is desired by many for all around use.
>
> The apple is probably consumed in more ways than any other single fruit in the world and is the oldest too. The Bible tells that when the earth was formed and the Garden of Eden was planted to beautiful trees and trees of the choicest fruit, it was from the apple Eve made a selection. It is also said a bowl

of apples appears on the table in the painting of the last supper
. . . There is no fruit, to my knowledge, used in a greater
number of ways than the apple. It is eaten fresh, baked, fried,
made into delicious apple pie, apple butter, sauce and all the
other culinary delights found in cook books . . . and then in the
fall when the fragrant odor of ripe apples permeates the
orchard the time has come to gather up a few bushels, grind
and press them, making that delicious apple cider. Better keep
some for later use, as hard cider adds cheerfulness to an
otherwise dull occasion, and later the cook might want some
vinegar for making pickles. On that note this treatise must
close or we will have a rotten apple.

We continue the discussion of apples in Sid's living room this afternoon. He likes apples because "You get plenty of time for harvest. You
use the varieties that will extend over a longer period of time. You can
store and keep your apples. We had a cooler . . . we could store 20,000
bushels of apples. This way we could pack them out in winter time on
order, so that the buyer got fresh-packed apples.

"I think Cortland is the best all-around apple there is. They're a large
apple and can be used so many different ways. They keep well. They're
good for baking pies, for salads. You can cut a Cortland in two and it'll
be white tomorrow."

Sid gets up, goes into the kitchen, and comes back holding a large red
apple, which he hands to me. It's cold and firm and quite beautiful to
behold all by itself. "Now there's an apple that's just been in common
storage up to now," he tells me. "It's been in storage since September.

"If anything is good, it's picking apples in the fall. No big rush. It's
nice, clean work. With cherries you're up to your elbows in juice.

"I always like trees and plants. I enjoyed pruning, shaping up a
young tree. I thought you accomplished something by that. I think I
enjoyed apples on the trees and packing maybe the best. I'm kind of
fussy about things. I was always pleased when we put up a good pack."

Telfer and Jens Jensen. "He gave me a lot of confidence to meet
people. I'm no good at it, even now. A fellow like Frank [Pechman] can
walk into a room and make friends just like that. When I get in with a
group, I don't know what to do next. I guess I'm not so easy to get
acquainted with. I sometimes wonder about that. Jensen made me feel I
could go anywhere and meet people and to apologize for anything.

"We rode around together a lot. He'd point things out to me. He
always felt that little plants and certain trees had a certain affinity that
was important. He'd take a stick and clear a space on the ground and
take half an hour explaining all the things he saw. I never realized there
was such a thing.

"He was always a gentleman. When you went to his place for dinner, you wore a jacket and a tie. You didn't go in shirt sleeves or a sweater. A woman would walk into the room, and he was always on his feet.

"You know, he didn't have classes as such at The Clearing. He just got a bunch of people together and talked. Jensen's philosophy is what they got. He was always for the underdog, the common man, the farmer, people who worked in the dirt and used their hands. He didn't have much respect for people with money, but when he needed it, he knew how to get it from them.

"In nature, he felt that all the parks, the beaches, all of it was for the common man to appreciate and enjoy. We probably knew each other as well as anybody. Hardly a day went by when we didn't get together.

"The future of this area? It was going down the drain. He knew that. From Chicago to Milwaukee would be one big city, he could see that. He didn't like the tourist that came up here. He had no use for them. They didn't see anything or appreciate it once they got here.

"Today, he'd be pretty disgusted with the whole thing. He would be opposed to building the bridge, building more roads, bringing more people in. He would be absolutely opposed to that. But then . . . they got to go somewhere. He would respect anyone who came here who would favor setting tracts aside for the future. That is what he did. That is what he believed in.

"That get-together at the old Ellison Bay Schoolhouse we had this year, that party at the end of The Clearing-In-Winter: the food, the music, Jensen would have loved that. He liked getting all the townspeople together. He liked dancing, having a good time.

"He would visit me in the orchard. He was interested only in the fact that I was growing something. And he was interested in the workers. People around here were afraid of him. He was never accepted. The barber told me one day, Jensen was a communist! Well, he wasn't. I wonder what I would have been today had I not met Jensen. Outside of my own parents, my immediate family, he was the most important person in my life. He influenced me most, more than anybody.

"Yes, I too feel the county is going down the drain. I feel bad about it. *For Sale* signs, *Sold* signs, *Keep Out* signs. There isn't the freedom. What do you do about it? Nothing. I'll let the next generation worry about it. There isn't anything anyone can do. How can you do anything? The only thing you can hope for that there is enough of the beauty left in Door County for my grandchildren to enjoy it. Encourage the neighbors to keep their trees so there is something of beauty left."

Recently Sid has channeled his writing energy into putting down on yellow legal pads, in long hand, in old-fashioned pen and ink, the story of Jens Jensen. Recalling Jensen's appreciation of aquavit, Sid disappears into the kitchen, returning with two glasses and a bottle of white wine.

"It's hard. I never realized writing was so damn hard. And I imagine it's harder for me than most people. I don't have nearly the command of the English language I had when I came up here. I suppose because I don't use it here with most people.

"I know I made a mistake. Instead of learning how to write, I should have learned how to type. The only thing wrong with a typewriter is that they don't spell right all the time. I write at night, like two o'clock. I think, 'I bet with morning it'll look terrible.' But it doesn't look so bad.

"I wish I could explain what Jensen was, and I can't. I read his stuff, and it's all way over my head. It's too far out for me. So I write about him as I knew him. The experiences we had."

Inez enters the room. She's been away to a meeting most of the afternoon. Her eyes sparkle. She is a lovely woman at age eighty-four. They have been married for sixty-one years, and the two of them together is a very special thing. She is pleased he has made a fire and happy there is a visitor. Sid looks at her with a straight face. "I suppose you'd like a glass of wine now?"

"Oh, I would."

"After all, you've just come back from a church meeting," he kids her.

Sid has been doing much of the cooking and baking lately, though they often go at it together as a team. "I'm not only a great writer," he'll tell you. "I'm also a great pie maker." He is especially proud of his apple pies, his blueberry muffins, his Spanish chicken. They often kid each other about how their memory sometimes slips.

"Gee, I saw Ruth Jones today," smiles Inez, "and asked her who she was." They both break into laughter.

"That's how to make friends," kids Sid. "Someday you'll go around asking people who you are!" he tells her, the laughter continuing.

Inez, so refined, so much a part of Sid's life, so much a part of the community, sits back in her favorite chair, a glass of wine in her hand, stares into the fire and recalls a few of her own accomplishments.

"I started the 4-H here," she says. "And I started the Farm Bureau's Women's organization."

"Yeah," Sid interrupts, "and she started welfare too." More laughter.

"No, old age doesn't bother me a bit," he says. "I don't pay any attention to it. I enjoy life just as much now, more than ever. I'm glad I can remember all these things. It's just too bad people can't live long enough to appreciate all they been through.

Kash: A Potter's Way in Door

Takashi Yamada is not a household name in this county, though his work appears here and there in private homes, hovering on shelves and tables, inviting the eyes to pause and see. There's not a bit of Scandinavian to Kash, as he's called. Still, what he forms and extends with his hands, what he draws from both body and spirit . . . much of his pottery remains a quiet celebration of Door County: trees, water, sun/moon, sky.

A touch of the Oriental? Perhaps. More importantly, he's a Japanese-American potter redefining, expressing a love affair with landscape, calling it his, making it ours to hold in two hands, to feel, or to move gently into with repeated images that delight the eyes.

Though you may purchase it, though you may own it, you never quite possess one of Kash's pots, especially the Door Landscape series. The motif of trees, or water, or sun/moon turns you in, takes you out, lifts you to some other realm entirely. Objects of peace and meditation, beauty and the inner source: Kash may be the only artist up here who has touched this so closely. And he himself might be unaware of it, or prefer the silence of the art to speak for itself.

In my journeys outside the County, I once found myself partaking in the ritual of a Japanese Tea Ceremony at the Buddhist Temple in Chicago. One part of the absorbing experience I shall never forget was the Tea Master holding the empty piece of pottery before the green tea was poured, holding the cup in both hands, feeling it, absorbing all the beauty it contained, then bowing to it, and explaining to me that in Cha-no-yu (tea ceremony) you honor the potter as well. I am reminded of that in viewing the pottery of Kash.

He keeps a low profile, Takashi Yamada. There's a privacy of person and place about him that should also be honored. You will not see his pots at any of the local art shows. You will not see an ad for his work in the Door *Reminder* or the *Door Advocate*, or find him fanning his public image in any way. In fact, one is never quite certain Kash is here. Only one shop in the entire county (state, country) carries his work: artist Charlie Lyons' unique and very special Paint Box Gallery in the Red Barn complex on 42 between Ephraim and Sister Bay. And though Kash himself maintains a studio at Madeline Tourtelot's The Studios (formerly the Peninsula School of Arts) in Fish Creek, he does not particularly care to be disturbed by visitors.

Yet he is a good man, full of surprises, stories, laughter, thought . . . and all kinds of great conversation. He is perhaps Door County's best and only link with the East, though he might deny this himself, having been born in Los Angeles.

"I grew up there. I have good memories of the big city life. Yes, we talked art at home, always Japanese art. My older sister was a painter, went into art. My dad was a mechanic. He came from a wealthy family in Japan, came here to study electrical engineering. But then my grandfather went bankrupt, and my father ended up fixing cars, a body and fender man. There's a sad story."

World War II brought out a lot of hatred in this country, hatred particularly directed toward people of German and Japanese blood. Kash recalls his father: "He was attacked every day. People beat him up, spit on him." The family, though, did not experience the concentration camps that the American government set up. "Anyway, the concentration camps were really a protection for the Japanese-Americans," claims Kash.

His mother, too, maintained her ties with the East. "She was born in Oakland, but in my mother's day, the thing to do was send the child back to Japan for schooling. She was married there too."

Kash's own schooling? "The twelve most miserable years of my life were spent in the public school system. You talk about delinquents. I was one. I don't have any pleasant memories of grade school. Lots of fights.

"In a sixth grade art course, I starting painting. I remember getting into my own little world. I got my first painting praise there. I remember that vividly.

"Also in the sixth grade I was in the school choir. One time a scout from the Mitchell Choir Boys of Hollywood came to the school, and I went with them. I made a record with Bing Crosby, Ella Fitzgerald, Gene Autry. I was on the Bell Telephone Hour. I even sang in the movie *White Christmas* with Bing Crosby. I sang first soprano; as I grew older, second, then third.

"But I went to private school then, seventh, eighth, ninth. From our earnings we had to pay for the tutor. I was with the choir from about the age of twelve to fifteen, about three years."

Kash was brought up in the Buddhist faith, but in high school converted to Catholicism. "I spent tenth and eleventh grade at St. Agnes High School in L. A. In high school I started doubting things, even Buddhism. Religion, period. And now? Nothing. Zero. Atheist. I do not believe in God in any shape or form. People, yeah, people: bad or good. Basically people created God after their own image, not vice versa, which I guess goes along humanist lines. Nature? If you want to label that 'God,' fine. But Buddha, J. C.? I don't believe in any of them being the ultimate. Religion tends to separate mankind more than unify it."

Kash came to Milwaukee in 1956. "My father slipped a disc, and he asked my sister and her husband, in Milwaukee, if they would take care of the kids—two brothers and three sisters. I went first. Then, little by little, my younger sister, older brother. I finished high school in Milwaukee and then went to the Layton School of Art there for four years, majoring in sculpture."

Sculpture and the Layton School of Art, however, did not determine Kash's direction in life/art so much as his introduction to master potter Abraham Cohn of Milwaukee and Door County—the Potter's Wheel in Fish Creek. (Both Kash and potter John Dietrich of Ellison Bay apprenticed with him.)

"I started with Abe in his Milwaukee shop in 1958. My sister was taking lessons from him. It was through her I got to know him. I'd go into his place and look around, being interested in form and whatnot. It was my sister who said, 'You should take lessons. It would help you in your concept of form.' Then Abe said, 'Well, if you'll stay in the shop and clean up for me, I'll give you the lessons free.' So, being hard up for cash, I agreed. I was his apprentice for about four years. In between I went into the army for two years active duty: thirteen months in Korea."

Abe as teacher? "He's a great potter to watch; you learn through osmosis. Just to watch him throw. No talking, which is very Japanese. I'd just sit and watch him throw by the hour. He never pushed himself on me. Never said, 'This is good; this is bad.' Always something very positive to say about me. I always felt I was getting somewhere. If I wanted to sum it up in one word: he taught 'craftsmanship.'

"Abe is still that way. His pots are very clean, very presentable. Slop pots never got by Abe at all. Craftsmanship is a technique in itself. I don't think you can teach anyone art, but you can certainly give him the tools. And Abe certainly did this: understanding the clay, the tools, what certain materials will do. If you don't know this, you're lost."

"After centering," explains Kash, "believe it or not, it's the height of the pot. You always seem to get about four inches, and if I used a larger hunk of clay, it would just get out of hand. Then, all of a sudden: seven inches. It just suddenly one day comes: the finger pressure was just right, the clay was just right, the speed of the wheel. It's like swimming. All of a sudden it comes. Once you learn to throw inches, you never forget it. I remember all the things necessary to get them.

Other plateaus? "Finishing the pots. Trimming the foot. Then learning to pull handles, attaching handles on to shapes. And glazing. Finally, glazing.

"I hated it. I always thought, 'Wouldn't it be great to be an Italian potter somewhere and have someone else glaze the pots?' I dreaded it. I was lost till I went to Japan, 1972. I had no concept of what to put on the pot. All I was interested in was shape, making the pot, form."

He traveled to Japan with Madeline Tourtelot to work as her assistant in producing a film on the porcelain potter master, Manji Inoue. The experience, ironically enough, brought Kash closer to his own art and closer to the Door County landscape.

"What I learned in Japan, and Mexico, was how the people looked at their environment. What I learned was what to take from environment. I learned to look at Door County, the Door County landscape. When I began to do it, I felt like a watercolorist. It seemed so natural, having lived here for so long.

"The thing that always intrigued me here was nature's repeated patterns. I would go to Peninsula State Park, and there was a view where you could see tree tops. That whole tree thing has always intrigued me. The repetition and the serenity."

Kash does not look upon his work as Oriental. "I think what most people see in my work are certain delicate things going on, and immediately it's Oriental, an Oriental feeling. My sister, the artist, even tells me that. But I don't see that. I think it's stereotyping."

Aside from the tree motifs, Kash describes other elements of the local landscape which have influenced his art. "Also a contrast of textures, other trees, the calm waters. Big open areas, sky. I've done quite a few with a moon or a sun. The circle is such a beautiful shape.

"The Door County Landscape series started when I returned from Japan. I started coming to Door in 1958. I'm not interested in reproducing the county, by the way. It's more sort of an impression, the feeling for Door County I put in my pots. People ask me, 'What kind of trees are these?' Basically, they're sort of stylized.

"And this is a continuing series, sort of a stepping stone. You might say I'm on a plateau right now. Where I'll go next, or when I want to go, I have no idea. Right now I feel very good, very comfortable doing it."

It would seem that once the techniques are mastered by an artist (provided he doesn't get too comfortable) the plateaus that follow are plateaus of self-revelation: a constant growing and coming to terms with just who one is now, and where he is headed. Kash, in his very sensitive probing of Door, reflects, again, the true essence of the artist in search.

"You know, there is one thing about Door County as opposed to the desert for example. This isn't original with me, but I've thought a lot about it. The desert is very masculine. It's always on the defensive. There are things in that landscape that bite and scratch and kill and hurt.

"Then you have Door County where there's this feminine attitude . . . very soft, very protective. But the people are the opposite. What I try to do with my pots is make them very feminine, nice and round, to get away from sharp edges."

Kash settled in Door in 1965 when Abe Cohn recommended that Kash teach art for Madeline at her Peninsula School of Art, which she directed. "I was just out of the army, back in L. A., working for the telephone company at the time. I bought this motorcycle, a Honda 305, and rode it all the way here. I've been here, more or less, ever since. I've spent three winters here. The others, usually traveling, primarily to Mexico, and that one time to Japan."

His work pattern is true to his feelings. "I try to work as intensely as I can while I'm working. For a while I got in this trap: always wishing I was doing something other than what I was doing. Now, if I'm sailing, I'm just going to sail. If I'm in the garden, I'm going to garden. This saves a lot of energy.

"As for doing fifty pots a day? No. I'm living. I'm making enough to get by. Actually, if it wasn't for Madeline, her patronage, her giving me a studio, a place to work, I don't think I could make a living at it. In that way I feel very lucky to have Madeline's belief in my work.

"When I went to art school, I always said I would never make a living at my art. I'm not a production potter. I have the luxury of being able to delve into art, aesthetics, self-expression or whatever. All I know is I can afford to spend more time on my pottery, individual pieces. Again, Madeline comes into this: 'Don't do production. There are enough production potters up here. Where I'm at right now, I don't have to think about technique anymore. I can think about ideas."

Because he is Takashi Yamada, one of the ideas he must live with in these parts is what some of the others, the majority, might feel about his presence. The Spanish-Americans, who came here originally to pick cherries, must also live with this. So must "Black John" Henderson. "Hey, Chinaman, go home," Kash is occasionally told by some of the young people. Among some of the older natives, he admits, "there is a redneck feeling."

"I see John [Henderson] at the lumber yard, and I hate the way they call him 'nigger' there. And you know, I see Roberto there [Bob Cuellar, alias "Loco"] and he looks at me, and I sense that I almost remind him of who he is, that he is Mexican. One time I was in there talking to John, and Roberto says, 'Hey, you two guys look like brothers.' Everybody started laughing. So I said to Roberto, 'You know something. You're starting to look more Swedish every day.' Nobody laughed."

If he finds no solace in many of the people up here, he does find it in other ways. "As far as I can see, clearly it's the land I draw upon . . . my interpretation, my feelings." Neither books nor friends influence his art a great deal. "But my friends, with friends it's like having a drink. I can really relax. I have a handful of close friends. It takes me away from my pots. I tend to pick people who don't talk about art.

"Another thing about Door and the Midwest in general is that it's really a fine place to get to know yourself. Less distractions here, more space. The East Coast, the West Coast . . . all the talent leaves the Midwest because they feel they can't survive here. But it's a good place to really find yourself. On the other hand, once you find yourself, it's deadly to stay here. The landscape is more closed in, more secretive. The natives are like that. You know, when the birds migrate here, you don't see the local birds. As soon as they leave, the locals return. I think, my God, it's just like the natives."

That final link to the Far East, is Kash—from Door County, from Milwaukee, from L. A.—meeting Manji Inoue, master porcelain potter, in Japan. This was certainly a significant milestone in the way of a Japanese-American potter. But just *what* did he bring back with him?

"Manji Inoue was in training to become a kamikaze pilot near the end of the Second World War. And just before he was to board a plane, and they were ready to seal him in, the war was over. But the important thing was, he was ready to die for Japan. He brought this up with such *pride*, such *determination*! The hard, hard thinking he went into. 'But you know,' he said, 'I do everything with that spirit and dedication of a kamikaze pilot!' He went into *Kendo* then [the martial art of sword fighting], and with the kamikaze spirit, he became a champion. His biggest criticism of the youth of today is that they lack that spirit. Even if it's the wrong thing, at least you have dedicated yourself!

"You know, that old Taoist saying: One way to know yourself is to find all the paths that lead away from you."

Ignacio Gonzales: Migrant

Ignacio Gonzales is a poor man amidst this land of plenty, but he is not to be so easily dismissed.

"I just a Mexican," he smiles at you, dressed in hand-me-down clothes, unshaven, earthy brown skin, missing teeth. "Mexican-Indian."

A small man, prone to joking and laughter, driving a battered red station wagon, he is identified by most of us as one of the Mexican migrant workers who move in and out of Door in cherry and apple season. Ignacio and his family came through that way in 1969. Only Ignacio stayed on and has been odd-jobing his life here ever since. What Ignacio Gonzales seems to know most about life is being alone, working hard, and surviving on the barest margin, the thinnest dream. For now, all he wants is to get his teeth fixed. For a seventy-two-year-old hired man, that may not be the grandest dream, but for Ignacio, that will be a good thing. And after that, maybe a friend will help him see if he can get his Social Security back, though Ignacio Gonzales fully expects to continue working till he returns to the earth.

"The Mrs. [Mrs. Ahiquist, who has been looking after him lately] she take me to get my teeth fixed. I got no money. I gonna maybe get some new teeth, though. See, they pull 'em out here, and here. . . ."

I recall seeing this man in a cherry orchard nearby at least eight or nine years ago. I had spent some time in Mexico a few years before that. Something about the migrant life had always fascinated me, people on the move, following the crops, wresting a living from the land as best they could. All very romantic, but with a touch of dignity in their labor. This was the closest source of *The Grapes of Wrath*, for me, a book I taught and loved. And here was this small Mexican picker, always smiling, always laughing, enmeshed in branches, buckets hanging from him, bending, stretching, climbing ladders, circling the trees in a dance, his nutty brown hands in constant touch with the ripe red cherries. His woman was in a tree close by. The children were scattered in still other trees. A family of pickers, they swept through an orchard like the wind.

Here was a touch of old Mexico in Door County, I felt, a culture of old myths, hot sun, memorable food, mountains, jungle, simple people, peasants possessed with such a real sense of life. I had lived and studied and traveled among them in Mexico for one summer; it was good to be around them and their language again.

I don't recall what I said to the cherry picker, but some of the language erupted. He had a fine sense of humor, a native wit. "Hey," he said. "You think they got some beer here for a old Mexican?" Bright eyes, the smile. Then the laughter.

For many of us who recognize Ignacio (and call him by his nickname, Charlie), he remains part of the migrant mystique: poor, uneducated, different, no sense of place or property—no real value but common labor, in cherry and apple season. And so, though Ignacio has been among us for ten years, good times and bad times, much of his friendship with us remains a very momentary thing—a "Hello" and a "How are you?" in passing—but never really knowing or caring who Ignacio Gonzales is, how he is, where he came from, or how he survives. In fact, some of us are even startled to see the old Mexican suddenly appear among us in the middle of winter.

Ignacio Gonzales lives here, is part of this place, whether anyone cares or not, though he owns not a piece of the land he has worked and never will. "My wife," he told me last winter, "she left me. I all alone. She don't talk to me. Kids don't talk to me. I don't talk to them. Nobody talk. I alone, living in the trailer now. They in the house. They don't say nothin' to me."

Family conflicts are private matters and should remain just that. No man is all good, even Ignacio Gonzales, who has been through some strange times. He had been a step-father to the woman's children for some years, but now finds himself back to where he has been most of his life: alone, abandoned.

He lives on an old farm outside Sister Bay. For the past few years, he and the woman and children occupied the house and maintained the property. All is as it was, except that Ignacio has moved to a small trailer near the barn. Here, in the tiniest of living spaces, he maintains himself and whatever is left of his life. He has no contact with the woman and children in the house.

A wooden shed serves as a storage place and entranceway to the trailer, where inside everything is reduced to tininess, even Ignacio himself, standing near a small sink, lighting up an old fashioned gas burner to warm up the place a bit.

Late afternoon sun filters through the small window on the west side of the trailer, filling the space with a comfortable light. The walls are decorated with everything from calendar scenes of nature to religious mementos. Although Mrs. Ahlquist is guiding his spiritual life these days, Ignacio privately confesses, "Religion is all the same, you can say."

There is one chair in the trailer. Three clean shirts on hangers occupy a space just above that chair, where Ignacio now sits. Between us, on the floor, is an electric heater. I sit on a built-in bed, layered and layered in blankets, where, along the other side, the curving end of the wall and back of the trailer, freshly laundered pants, shirts, and underwear are stacked. We are separated by a distance of perhaps two feet. It's a late afternoon in spring, but there is still a sharp edge of coolness in the air. Ignacio keeps his jacket and hat on, and lights the other burner with a match.

Such living conditions may seem alien to many people, especially in these condominium-conscious days in Door County. But let it be understood that there is an undeniable coziness to Ignacio's solitary domain, a lot of creature comfort. And before social workers and good Christians everywhere, well intentioned though they may be, toss up their hands in shock over the living conditions of this man, let it also be understood that he retains a certain sense of pride in the way he exists and the freedom he possesses to live his time as he chooses.

"I was born in Texas," he says, digging in his pants pockets for a wallet to show me the name of the town he cannot quite pronounce: Runge, Texas, October 23, 1907. "Was raised in Chicago, other places. "No father, no mother, I raised myself in Chicago since I was nine years old. My home was the dump; that's where I was raised. My stepfather left me in Chicago, he run away with some woman and leave me there. No brothers, no sisters.

"Was a kid in Chicago, just goin' 'round askin' for something to eat. I sell papers and rags for a penny a pound. That's where I get a little money to buy a little groceries. Never went to school. Oh, yeah, sure I miss that. If I was in school, I wouldn't be working like a black bull, still working like a bull . . . all hard jobs. In Chicago, later, I work in company, factory. I was interpreter for the rest of the Mexicans. Then I work for Piggly Wiggly Company, rolling barrels of meat."

In 1969 he came to Door via Chicago, not the usual route of the migrant wave, starting in Texas and fanning out across the country. And though Ignacio and his family were instantly absorbed in the Mexican migrant population, they always worked alone.

"I come here to pick apples in 1969. Then I do some pruning. That's what I do here since, picking cherries and apples and pruning. Now some different jobs too—shovel snow, rake leaves, clean up. I do my garden here, sell raspberries, strawberries. That's the way I do my living. Just making a living, that's all. That's how I living. Don't make no money but pay the bills. I owe some yet. Always owe some yet. You want a smoke?" He pulls a crumbled pack of Marlboros from his coat pocket, offering me a cigarette.

"The lady [Mrs. Ahlquist] she don't want me to smoke no more," he says in a sing-song voice. "No good for me. I don't smoke in her place, only here once in a while. Only drink maybe a beer once in a while."

Sitting in the chair, drawing deeply from his cigarette, the sun resting gently upon his chin, he pauses long between his periodic bursts of talking. No one has ever been too interested in him before, his story. This is strange territory to him, remembering, talking somewhat seriously. He is used to, more comfortable with, quick greetings instead, a handshake, a pat on the back, a funny remark. He likes to laugh. It comes easier to him than this business of thinking about himself. He tends to drift away from me, silently staring at the gas flames or the cigarette between his fingers.

"I was always on my own," he continues. "With the family, there was nine. Now I'm alone. I used to pick 175, 180 pails cherries a day, all alone. That's what I do, from 6:30 in morning till seven, later, as long as I could see. I used to it. Work hard that way.

"Pruning, yes pruning too. You do it from the top: cut the suckers first, then you go down, cutting the big branches that are supposed to be cut off."

He stares out the little window above the sink, looks down at his hands again. I ask him about the rest of his life, what he thinks is still out there for him at the age of seventy-two. He doesn't seem to comprehend time in the way of future. Instead, time appears to work for him in a primitive way of seasons and past memories. A day-to-day existence has sharpened that sense of perspective.

"Just work and work," he smiles. "I don't know till when. No Social Security. I had it for a while, but then they told me it was in the wrong name. It was somebody else with the same name, and they took it off of me. I told them I don't think we can be twins. I told them I don't know very much 'cause I don't know how to read or write or nothing. But I tell you something, look, how can we have the same mother? It can be the same name, but how be the same mother? Something wrong. The Mrs. is seeing she can maybe get it back for me. We waitin' now to see. Why do they do that to me, huh? Just because I'm alone, don't know how to read?

"I just have to be livin' and tryin' to do the best I can. I don't know till when. I had some good luck, but when I was little, I sure try to make my livin'. Hard life when I was a kid. I don't even play the marbles when I was little kid. No dice, no marbles, no pool . . . don't hang around with nobody, just sell my rags. Now, almost the same way. I gettin' older and older. I don't know what's gonna happen to me when I ain't got no health. The most money I ever have was $700. But I just give it to the people I owe, and I left with $25 to get some groceries."

As for the good times: "Oh yeah, I did have happy times too. Pretty good life I had couple of years, back in Chicago. To have money, to go any place you like, to spend money, have a good job. Was a good time for me. And now it's gone. Those days are left.

"I don't think to go nowhere now. Just work on, that's all. I'm making my living all right anyway. From now it will be working, cleaning, raking. And my garden. Then picking. I can still pick 170 pails a day, that's for sure.

Winter nights in Door are difficult enough for most people to handle even in the midst of friends and family, but for Ignacio Gonzales, alone in his tiny trailer, they are impossible to imagine.

"I just stay in here, put on my heater, two gas burners, wait for the place to warm. Stay awake till sometime twelve o'clock, then turn the burners off and go to sleep. I watch some TV, that's all. I get lonesome. In the day I go right away outside. I help the lady help the old people, deliver groceries, meals, help the needy people. Sometimes, working hard shoveling snow off roofs for people. And sometimes, by seven o'clock, I'm sleeping."

He is not unaware of the beauty of the countryside which has become home to him, so far from Texas. He seems to even prefer this northern climate. "It's a nice and pretty place for me. I'm satisfied here. All the people know me, like me. They all help me. What more do I want?

"Good friends, they all like me. I know that. They say to me, "Hello, Charlie, how you been? What you know? Well, take it easy, Charlie.' "

Of his many friends, only a few seem concerned. "Frank [Charney] always gives me some eggs and bread, and sometimes to eat at the house when I work for him, help him clean the chicken coop and picking stones. Sam Subin gives me groceries, too. Day before yesterday he give me $10. 'You need some money, Charlie?' I say, no. 'Well, here's $10 anyway. Buy some gas or something.' When I go to his house, always it's the table first. 'Come on, Charlie, let's eat.' I say, yeah, good."

Ignacio Gonzales does not know Cesar Chavez, a hero to many of his people, and it is difficult to imagine just what he sees on the old TV set propped up a few feet away from his chair.

I try to imagine him at night, just as he is now, eating his food from a dish in his lap, trying to decipher those strange images coming across the screen. He recalls seeing the migrant people on television once: "I think, what are they doing there? They are in the story. That's what I think about myself here. Well, how can they be, such poor people. I think, I'm just like those people. I'm awful poor too."

Ignacio gets up and begins boiling some water. What's for supper tonight? "Some coffee, and eat them Twinkies," he smiles, pulling out a package of them from a brown bag.

"Yesterday I killed a rabbit. I had that last night for supper . . . and for breakfast today. I still got him hanging there. I raise rabbits to eat. I like them. At least I know what I'm eating," he laughs. "I kill a rabbit, I know it's a rabbit. Fresh meat. You buy some meat in the stores, you don't know what you eating."

Ignacio's recipe for rabbit: "Make pieces of it, put it in a pot, put some garlic, onions, one potato, and hot peppers. Let 'em boil till they get nice and tender."

He moves into the darkness of the wooden shack entranceway to show me what's left of the rabbit he killed yesterday. Half of a pink, fleshy body hangs by a piece of baling twine beside the doorway.

"I got here for two meals or more. It's five meals for a rabbit . . . this is only for me, though."

I follow him outside, still trying to comprehend just what a life like his adds up to. A small Mexican child under the hot Texas sun. An abandoned child, living in the dump in Chicago, begging, selling rags. A man, interpreting for his countrymen in a big city factory. A migrant cherry picker, destined to work out his life in Door County, Wisconsin.

Few of us can comprehend the days and nights of a life that seems so meaningless. Yet there is an excitement in his voice outside the trailer now, once again in the sun, as I follow the old Mexican to the barn where he raises his rabbits.

There are cages of them everywhere, their furry heads bobbing, a light coming from their eyes. He points to the old rabbits first. They are fat and beautiful in their cages, healthy looking and bright-eyed. Serene.

Briskly, Ignacio climbs into a large pen where the younger ones scamper about his feet. "They hide the babies," he says, getting down on his hands and knees, crawling on the straw floor, burying his arm in an overturned box and gently retrieving a baby bunny which nestles and floats in his hand like a ball of milkweed seed.

"Yeah, the kids they come to me sometimes to buy the bunnies. I sell a few of them, but not to kids. Mostly I give them to kids. 'How much you want, Charlie?' they say. I tell them, 'What? I don't hear you. Go.'"

The rabbit man, I smile to myself. Ignacio, the rabbit man, living off the good earth. In these "back-to-the-land times," in these games gentlemen farmers from the cities play in our midst, with their "farmettes," their manicured lawns and gardens, their token farm animals, one should pause and take note that among us lives Ignacio Gonzales, the rabbit man, who is nothing but the earth, knows it, works it, respects it for the wonder of all the dark secrets that speak to mind and body.

From rabbits we move to raspberries, a beautiful patch which he has been pruning and caring for all morning. "My raspberries. These I sell."

Along a stone fence he has set a long row of new plants from what he has pruned of the old. Nearby are onions from last year, which he says are still good. Onions for Ignacio's rabbit stew.

I joke about his Mexican heritage as the beautiful afternoon sun conjures memories of Mexico and New Mexico. "You've got it all, Ignacio," I tell him. "All except bright red chili peppers. Can you grow chili peppers too?"

"You can grow here everything," he tells me. "Even pinto beans."

The pinto bean—of course. A staple crop among Spanish-speaking people and Indians for years and years, one of the most nourishing foods to be eaten. Ignacio may not know the why or way of the pinto bean, only that it is good and a necessary part of his diet. He leads me to yet another part of the barn, opens the door: pinto beans, burlap bags of them, some still in the dry pods. "When my wife left me," he says, "I left her that field there and a hundred-pound sack of pinto beans."

He grabs a handful and begins playing with them from hand to hand. "I got so many pinto beans . . . yeah, you jus' soak them in water overnight or boil them for three hours till they're soft. Yeah, in a frying pan then, you push them down . . . refried beans.

"I got so much I give them Mexicans in Baileys Harbor some. I give them thirty, forty pounds and say I got too much pinto beans."

Ignacio and the magic pinto bean. After picking them, drying the pods in the storage shed, "I go after them," he laughs. "I put them over there in the corner and hit them with a stick . . . and they start jumpin'!"

In these times of a chaotic economy, where peopleare fat in their ways, intent upon possessing all they can grasp, securing everything for only themselves, it is a comfort to know that an Ignacio Gonzales still walks the earth, relatively free, proud, but with an instinct for preservation that oddly enough includes others as well as himself.

I take comfort in knowing that when and if the time comes when securities of all sorts fade away, it will be the Ignacio Gonzaleses who will inherit the earth, for they have best understood and lived an old Eastern principle of nothingness:

> The man of Tao
> Remains unknown
> Perfect virtue
> 'No-self'
> Is 'True-Self.'
> And the greatest man
> Is Nobody.

Once again I take heart in knowing that it is always the people who have nothing, who are willing to share everything: "Whenever you want," he tells me, "You just come and take some pinto beans. If I'm not here, just walk in with your bag and fill it up."

Chet: The Man Who Loved to Fish

He was one of a breed of men found in much of the Upper Midwest: a man who needs to live close to water, a man who simply loves to fish. He shared that love with many. Yet there was so much more to the man than that.

I would be hard pressed to say I had ever found a better man than Chet Elquist. He was an uncomplicated man, yet I'm not sure I ever really understood him. Others might ask what there was to understand.

We never discussed books, art, music, movies, how to live our lives, or any of the things that usually interest me, ideas upon which I base a friendship. Our conversations, many of them on water, in his boat, fish poles in hand, were mostly small talk. Still, I found great peace in the man who loved to fish, and his quiet mystery and simple goodness is something I often reflect upon and find harder and harder to express.

I think I now know what he was all about. And I think he, more than anyone, taught me what there was about this county, this natural environment, that sustained a man's presence and brought him closer to who he was. He did it with fishing, with gardening, with tending a small orchard, with fixing things, with helping people, with loving his home and family (and a dog named Sam), with leading a life mostly unnoticed and, in the end, with refusing to let go of that life without a fight. There was dignity to his dying.

His was not exactly an Eight Fold Path to base a religion upon. It was an unexamined life in many ways, but still a proper way to handle the days and nights as Chet Elquist lived them.

He was tall, he was gaunt, his strength was both inner and outer. He knew how to laugh, how to tell and enjoy stories about others as well as himself. He liked a shot of brandy occasionally, a beer, a glass of homemade cherry wine. Friday afternoons, after work at the Peterson Shipyards in Sturgeon Bay, a stop for a snort at the Red Room was obligatory. In a matter of hours, though, he would be back home on his small farm in Ephraim, spraying the cherries, working in the garden, fixing all manner of things both mechanical and natural. Somehow he managed to bridge the inherent differences of the two, giving them equal attention and understanding.

Observing Chet over the past ten years, I have discovered there is a "mechanics" to gardening, to raising grapes, to digging potatoes, to tapping maple trees for syrup, to making apple cider, to smoking fish, to making cherry wine, to keeping coons out of the corn, to catching fish on the inland lakes or far out on the waters of Lake Michigan, just as there was a natural way to rototillers, lawn mowers, all manner of engines. Chet would sooner make the piece, the part that was needed, than buy it. He handled the cold machinery of technology as adeptly as the soft machinery of earth. And somehow he had raised this and his whole life to a quiet art—no doubt unaware of it himself. For believers of reincarnation, this had to be his last time around: there was no karma left to him.

He was a mild man. He lived and understood the depth of silence, both water and earth.

In 1941 he married a good, hard-working, kind woman, Florence Moegenburg. They had two children: Kay, who became a teacher, left the county, and is now married and living in California; and Roy, who returned home after completing college, married, and is a young man very much like his father, with a love of fishing, hunting, and carrying on his father's way.

Much of what Chet was all about is remembered and carried on in the words of his widow, whom he fondly called "Flossie."

A widow alone in a rural landscape is quite a different thing than a widow in a large city. Her life was this man and this place. With his death, a little dying has taken hold of her. Her story moves in fragments, bits and pieces, impressions. Time stands still, it jumps, it sometimes doesn't move at all as she remembers Chet and the life they led.

"I was fourteen when I met him. He was working for our neighbor, plowing the fields for John Grasse. I was scared even to talk to him or speak to him then. But I was going to catechism class, and I was told to take some lunch to the hired man. I set it on the stone fence and ran. He was sixteen.

"We were acquainted with each other some years before we got married. Our romance was really a 3¢ stamp romance, letters back and forth. I got married when I was twenty-seven. I was doing housework in Milwaukee from the age of twenty-one to twenty-seven. I would come home in the summer and work twelve weeks in the resorts in Ephraim. The rest of the year here there was really nothing for a young woman to do. You had to get out of here. Then the Depression—you couldn't afford to get married. Those that did had to live with their parents."

Chet's life during all those years in between? Flossie shakes her head. "I really can't recall. Hazel, his sister, would know. Hazel would remember. His early life, he would always sneak away to Mink River.

He would be sent out to do some work, but then with his fishing pole he would always take off for Mink River. All I recall is he talked about one summer when he shoveled stones into a stone crusher. He farmed some. He went away to Chicago then, a machine shop, some place where he learned his skill: the machine trade. He also worked at International Harvester there.

"We were married in 1941, in Liberty Grove at the Christ Evangelical Lutheran Church. He was working at International Harvester in Chicago. I guess he thought he could swing it then."

Her parents were Adolph and Cora Moegenburg who owned and worked a beautiful old farm, a log barn and a log house, now owned and restored by artist Jim Ingwersen and his wife, Phyllis.

"It was the homestead. My grandpa came from Germany, and homesteaded it. My grandparents always lived with us. We were a hardworking family. I picked stones as a child. Picked the bug off potato plants. We got a penny for every one hundred we picked off. We had about eight milking cows. That kept us going with our eighty acres. That's what you tried to live on. You got your income and paid your taxes with the milking and the few things you could sell off the place.

"I left home early, about fifteen. I went to school for two years in Green Bay—business college. I lived with my aunt and uncle. It was during the Depression . . . not a job came from it.

"The first orchard I worked in was the Seaquist's. Oh, I guess I was nine years old. They came to get us in a truck. We had to pick all the cherries with stems. You could make 25¢ a pail if you picked with the stem. You could pick about four or five pails a day, so that was a money-maker then."

The early years of their marriage were spent in Chicago, ironically enough. Two native Door County people, unable to survive on the home front. "We lived near Logan Square first, then the Oak Park area—about six years. After that, we moved to Kenosha, Wisconsin."

The reason? "Fish," says Flossie, making a face, wrinkling her nose, a touch of disdain in her voice. "Fish got into his blood. What went through his mind? The fish. But it was nothing at the time, in Kenosha. Nothing. All that lamprey eel business. We made nothing. He bought an old rickety boat that wasn't safe to go out with. He started off with his brother Harold [married to Flossie's sister, Evie]. The boat was called the *Mary G*. It sure wasn't very solid. There were a few trout at the time, but it was just getting that there weren't any. We must have stayed in Kenosha about seven years. Kay was born in 1943.

"We were always just losing. One night they never came back. I thought they had drowned. I sat on the shore waiting for them. But that was one time he had a big catch, a big haul, and he just stayed out: he wanted to lift all his nets, get it all in. They sent boats out for him, everything.   He finally got in around nine or 9:30 instead of noon or right after, like they usually did. I wish he were here to tell these stories himself.

"For dinner we always ate trout. But the fishermen there told us to try the lawyers; they're better tasting. So that's how we began eating them. Some people call it the poor man's lobster.

"But during the seven years with the fishing, we were losing, losing. There was no money in it, and Chet finally went to work for American Motors. We moved back here in 1951. Roy was born in August, 1950.

"We bought this place in Ephraim before we actually moved up here. We bought it from Owen. Clyde Brown had it before. We moved above the garage. The rooms were there, but we had to redo it."

Their return to Door was not so much a dramatic decision as a man's plain desire to return home. Door County has done that to its native run-aways time and time again. Sooner or later they come back.

"The place we had in Kenosha was sold. The new owner raised the rent, and that ticked Chet off. He thought it was too much of a jump, and he was getting out of there and moving back to Door County.

"We were both born here, both liked it. But I don't think we set our goals on anything. When we came back here, it was back to work as a fisherman. I think he had that in his blood more than anything. He fished with Stanley Voight then; fishing was poor. He went to Kewanee then, expecting to work as a machinist. He lived there; we lived here. He came home on weekends. Then that became kind of a hassle too, and he finally got into the shipyards at Sturgeon Bay, and eventually worked for Petersons there. He stayed with Petersons till he took his retirement. The first operation, he went back there, after they took his stomach out. With the colostomy, he was forced to retire.

"He ice fished in the winter. He fished anytime he could spare. We had the cherry orchard, five hundred trees, for a sideline. Our life was all hard work and no pay. When there was a good year, then they wouldn't let you pick it. But I can never say there was ever really a good year, anything to give you a boost. We weren't born with a golden spoon in our mouth, just poor pay and hard work. No, we never got in on the breaks."

Chet: photographs, journal entries, images of the man recalled. A pack of old photographs from Flossie sits on my desk: Chet standing in his boat, both hands on the rod, working the line in the waters around Sand Bay; Chet still-fishing a river, maybe a creek, no one remembers where or how many years ago; numerous shots of Chet in the classic fisherman's pose: a smiling, contented man, eyes staring straight into the camera while the weight of a large fish pulls down on his arm. Oh what a beautiful burden, oh what a catch! A shot of the fishing shanty on ice; one "man with the hoe" photograph of Chet dressed in his usual green machinist work clothes, hoeing a row of potatoes, his dog Sammy lying down in the middle of the row, my son, Christopher, three or four years old at the time, trailing behind the quiet man with the hoe, out to get Sammy no doubt; and finally a shot I witnessed so many times myself, seated in the bow of the boat, but staring face to face at him . . . Chet in the back, one arm behind him controlling the speed of the motor, the direction of the boat, a furrow of water rolling away in a V, the eyes of the fisherman already plummeting the mystery and depth of water, sky, earth, heading out, both into and away from it all.

My memories of the man go back to the summers of 1967, 1968, when my wife and I spent our summers at his place in Ephraim, renting the apartment above the garage, the very place where he and Flossie lived upon first moving back to Door from Kenosha.

This was my first introduction to Door and its natives. It proved to be a friendship that would endure, though I am mystified to this day as to what my contribution was. The balance sheet of give and receive remains forever in his favor.

Going through an old journal, I notice my entry for May, 1969, the year we moved to Door County permanently:

> The Elquists came over last night . . . two fine people. For two summers we lived next to them and learned to understand and accept their gentle faith and hard life at times. Chet remains in my mind a good and natural man who takes his every breath for the freedom he finds in the countryside.

> Although he puts in his full day at the shipyards in S.B., it's back to his small farm, his cherry orchard in the late afternoon. I can't recall ever watching a man so solitary and sure of himself and the way of his life, as seeing Chet astride his tractor going down row upon row of cherry trees, spraying them, touching them, keeping them all in line. Sammy, the dog, trailing after.

> Mrs. Elquist, a hard working woman who has known the best of times, the worst of times. Seeing the condition of our house here in Ellison Bay, after just moving in, she recalled how she and Chet moved to Kenosha, how she feared the worst. Chet had decided to go into commercial fishing. "He said I would be sitting on silk pillows," she always recalled. They moved all their furniture in a trailer. It poured. Boxes and rugs and furniture were soaked by the time they found the apartment Chet had picked out for her. They lugged all their things up, and she hated the sight of the place. Years went by. Lamprey eel invaded the waters of Lake Michigan, and commercial fisherman like Chet were the great losers.

Yet fishing (and the orchard and garden) remain the subtle life force in this man. There is very little he would rather do than fish. He can tell by the shift of the wind if the time is right and the fish are biting. He will abandon his tractor in the middle of the field, hook the boat onto his old truck, and take off for the water, whenever he gets the call.

"Even if we don't get no fish," he would often tell me alone out there on the bay, just him and Sammy on the boat . . . "even if we don't get no fish, it's good to be out here"

Another entry, perhaps considering the man as a character in a story:

Chester Elquist is a free man, although bound to a shipyard, a farm, a wife and children. Chester Elquist has a cherry orchard. A tractor. Earth yielding tomatoes, corn, cabbage, potatoes, grapes, plums, cherries and apricots. What's more, he has a boat. Fishing gear. Hooks, lines, nets. His real art is water . . . fish, and singleness of journey. (That's better. That's all the fact and feeling I need to sometime come back and either embellish or strip the entry to fit the form it tries to be.)

So I fished with the man, summer after summer, mornings, afternoon, evenings; year after year, all seasons, even winter, when I sat in his shanty out on Garret Bay and watched him pull fish from beneath the ice. We fished on Europe Lake for perch, bass and northern, on Mink River for bass and jumbo perch, out of Ephraim for whatever was there, and on Lake Michigan for lake and brown trout.

He would call the night before or early morning and simply say, "Well, do you want to see if the fish are biting today?"

He fished in good health, and he fished as long as he could in his final days. He wanted the whole world to fish with him. He was known to invite even strangers. It was as if his was a religious calling: to convert all men into fishermen. After an extensive cancer operation at the Marshfield Clinic, he even invited the doctor who operated on him to come back to Door and fish with him. And he came. And they fished. And the catch was memorable.

I may have taken my son fishing for the first time very early in his life, but it was Chet who broke him in on the boat at an early age, Chet who patiently taught him to cast and bait a hook, Chet who always looked after him. He was his Door County grandpa, I always felt. "Well, it looks like we got another fisherman here," he would say.

If the truth be known, I was never a very avid fisherman; it was not in my Chicago blood, except occasionally at the Columbus Park lagoon. My father was not a fisherman. But I always wanted my son to be, and I still go out there a few times a year to seek whatever it was Chet found upon the water. It was always just good to be with him out there. Good to have a lunch along, some fruit from his trees, a few cans of cold beer. It was good to be just doing nothing. I never gave a damn if we ever caught a fish. I wanted him to catch one, though, just as he wanted whoever was along with him to catch plenty. He always placed great value in coming back with something, showing it to Flossie. It was a primitive instinct, perhaps, a man still wanting, needing to prove himself to his woman. He hunted deer this way too. Most of the natives still do in these parts. Bring home a trophy.

He did not like to get "skunked" as he called it, coming home to Flossie and admitting, "We got skunked." (He would sometimes go out again, alone, only an hour later, just to prove himself.) And he almost always "had a bite," though his summation for the whole experience that day might be "poor fishing," accenting the double *o* with a long, drawn out sound, like a wait.

The next day (or hours later) would find him revitalized, a new man, certain that things would be better. Water had to be a mood for him, an ever changing, ever new landscape. Maybe it was a better bait this time: "I've got some soft shell crabs," he'd say, or "some fresh minnows. That's the ticket!"

The freezer was always full of frozen fish. The man could exist on fish three meals a day: baked, boiled, fried, smoked, what have you. "Just a fish-head," he would smile and make fun of his appetites.

But what compelled him so? The basic economics of food provided so freely by nature no doubt played some part. The sport and art of wanting to excel, to be better than he was the day before, or maybe the competition of doing better than a friend or neighbor. All that plus whatever it was that made it so good to be out there.

"Good to be out there"—during those last few years of his life, I know that is why I accompanied him. Though I have learned to turn to quiet, to nature surrounding me in time of need—the woods, the fields, the shore—the utter tranquility of a fisherman upon water almost defies description or explanation. Perhaps only a Japanese painting comes close to capturing this, something like Ma Yuan's "Man Alone in an Open Boat," a man taking it all in, a man simply a part of it all.

Something like this morning, the mist over Europe Lake, the sun slightly held back in wisps of early morning haze, the floating world, the silent world, a fisherman drifting into it, in a small blue rowboat, a man loosely tied into this all by a line attached to the mirror of water . . . or is it the sky reaching down, holding us all? What is being fished?

Frustrations, troubles, complications. I gladly went fishing with Chet to be absorbed by what it was that was waiting for us out there. But this was nothing either of us tried to express.

There was one strange trip, however, one of the last he was to make

before he no longer had the strength to sit, to handle a downrigger, a
rod, or certainly the boat. One fishing trip I've never quite forgotten.

It was early fall. We went in on North Bay, just the two of us. He had
been losing considerable weight, was thin to the point of starvation.
Wrinkles took an old man's hold on his face. He no longer smiled as
much as he used to. He had very little to say.

He had suffered considerably the previous years: two serious operations, chemotherapy, even a desperate grasp at the latest supposed
cancer cure, Laetrile, banned in this country at the time, but available in
Mexico. He didn't give up—ever. He had always been able to fix everything, and no doubt he had all the intentions in the world of repairing
his own body as well. It seemed sensible to him, a natural man, that a
cure could be found in the apricot pit; it was something worth trying.

Upon visiting his daughter in California, this law-abiding citizen of
Door County would visit the clinic in Mexico where Laetrile was
available, and then smuggle into the States the supply that he needed.
He was impressed with the doctors down there. He had a feeling that
they might be on to something. "There's a lot of stuff about plants we
don't know," he said.

Bringing back the vials of Laetrile to Door County, he needed
someone to give him the injections. He turned, as so many of the natives
have always done in time of need, to the one, down-to-earth country
doctor who might share a dying man's hope for life: Doc Farmer. And
Doc Farmer, a natural health food and vitamin believer from way back,
simply said, "Laetrile, huh? Interesting stuff. I've been reading about it.
Made from apricot pits, huh? And you've got some, do you?" So Chet's
journey continued, claiming at times the Laetrile was working, admitting
at other times that he may have turned to it too late. Still, the pain
continued . . . to the very moment when we both found ourselves fishing
on North Bay one gray October day.

Chet was dying, and I was fighting some shadows of my own at the
time. We had to be the two darkest fishermen on the waters that
morning. We fished much of the interior of the bay for a few hours,
bringing in two or three small bass which we threw back. We said very
little. I recall feeling cold as a northeast wind began to stir the relative
placidness of the bay.

"Mighty poor fishing," Chet would say, as if to define our being
there. "Seems a fella ought to have more luck than this." He was fishing
with two rods: a night crawler on one; casting the other, using an
incredible collection of tackle: spoons, spinners, what-have-you. He
could never pass up whatever lure seemed to be successful for someone
else. Buying new lures was like buying candy. "This one's supposed to
be the ticket," he would say, truly believing it would change his luck.

And sometimes it did.

He reeled in the line with the night crawler on it, tried one more cast with a cleo, and then decided, "I think it best we head out some and see if there are any trout around." He prepared the downrigger for some deep fishing, and set up another rod as well.

"I'll watch," I said, pulling my line in, laying the rod across the seats in front of me. I disliked fishing at such depths. I was never quite certain if I had something on the line, or if it was just the drag that seemed to pull like dead weight.

I positioned myself in the center of the boat, and he began heading out of the bay under full power. The seas became choppier. Waves began breaking over and into the boat before long. The whole side of me was wet. Chet would ease up on the power at times, riding the troughs, trying to minimize the spray.

We were past Gordon's Lodge and heading directly out into the lake. The last thing I recall Chet saying was, "There's a buoy out there." I trusted him. He no doubt had a fishing spot somewhere near it. He seldom took a chance with a boat. Once, out of Ephraim, we had raced a line of squalls into the harbor just in time. He knew the waters as well as any commercial fisherman around here.

There were times, I swear, he could find an exact spot in an immense body of water where he had had great success days, weeks, months, years before. He knew how to line up the bow of his boat with some point on land, and that, plus instinct, his own inner source of orientation, told him just where everything was above and below water. He could point to land and show where eagles once nested.

There were now whitecaps on the lake water, and no buoy in sight. The water began pounding the aluminum boat, but Chet did not let up, even though we seemed to be headed nowhere, the water holding us to a standstill at times. When the whitecaps hit with full force, twisting us, lifting us almost out of the water, I looked at his drawn, determined face, unable to reveal the fear that had suddenly taken hold of me.

It was at that moment too, looking beyond his shoulder, that I first realized we were beyond the sight of land. North Bay was gone. The entire shoreline was gone, lost to distance and haze. Chet continued to adjust his downrigger and shouted something into the wind about one more final pass.

He may have been smiling; it may have been the last careless and happy moment in his life. He did not let up. I knew he was not afraid.

Nor was I at that instant. Whatever quiet force drove that man inside him, I suddenly picked up on. He was dying: he was diminishing physically, but not spiritually. I was down, headed nowhere. What the hell was I doing out here with him anyway? I hate this kind of fishing. It was all very crazy. We weren't catching anything. How could he possibly know where he is? There was no goddam buoy in sight. But

Chet was still going after it! And I loved his courage in the face of all of it out there. I relaxed. I took the cold wind and let the waters roll over me. Either Chet or something beyond him was in command. I didn't give a damn if we ever saw land. This was a celebration of sorts.

Much later that afternoon, cold, wet, "skunked," we would draw the boat out of the water onto the trailer, head for home, and never mention or try to understand what happened out there.

Flossie, thinking back over her years married to a man who loved to fish describes him simply as "unusual." "Oh dear, he and his little dog Sammy. He'd hurry up and do the work here, then take off and fish. No, he never tried to explain why he did it. His sister Hazel always said he went out there so much because there was so much peace out there. That's where he communed with God."

When cancer had finally gotten hold of the man for good, taking him forever away from his peace in fishing, confining him to bed in his own home and the extraordinary care of his wife, Chet's sister Hazel, and Flossie's sister Evelyn (three remarkable women), Flossie explains, "he really was not a complaining man. With all the illness he had, he accepted it and fought it like a trooper. He was always pleasant, patient with it, and did not make anybody else's life miserable because of it. He always had faith that he was going to get well."

Seeing the garden the other day, less than half of what it used to be, I can recall walking with Chet between the rows of corn, potatoes, tomatoes, sharing the pride the man had in what he and his wife and the earth had produced. And always sharing whatever harvest was at hand.

"Well, should we dig some potatoes for you?" he'd ask, and begin filling a basket. "The plums should be ripe. What do you say we fill a few buckets of plums for Barbara and the kids? The apricots are sparse this year. Winter is rough on them."

He especially loved his fruit trees and often experimented with a variety of graftings—apples, pears, apricots. He liked those mysteries too, and would patiently await the seasons to see and taste what new kind of fruit he had somehow created with his own hands.

Part of the widow's sadness these days is the realization that much of what she and Chet did and shared has to be let go. She is tired. She is alone. The man of the house is gone. She cannot keep up with either the machinery which Chet kept humming, or the manual labor which he spent so generously on plants and trees, from gardening to maple syrup making. Cherry wine? Apple cider? What do you want to try? He could do it all.

"It has to be team work," says Flossie. "Without him there's just so many things a woman can do. You need a man's work. You bet I miss him. I just think it gets worse as time goes by, being alone. You lose your strength and health. You wonder what's going to happen to you. I think a person goes into deeper thought as this goes on. In the beginning, I think you don't really realize it's true yet. Afterwards you find out you really are alone.

"A little bit of getting out helps. It's a change. If you have some of the children here, if you get in a bind, you feel you can call on them. But you wouldn't want to move in on them. You shouldn't expect that of them.

"No, if Chet were still alive—the raspberries, the fruit trees—he'd a kept on with all that. He'd a probably put in strawberries. You have to have something to do. With the fruit and his fishing, he felt he had it made.

"He had such a will to live. I think he'd a bought a little lathe too, to fix things for people who needed work done. He was always fixing things for people. He'd a kept himself busy. He was out scouting for a windmill before he died. He was interested in all kinds of things, like solar energy. He had a lot of things to live for yet, but it wasn't in the books I guess.

"Every morning, when he was dying, we would say our prayers. We said the Lord's Prayer, and then that little children's, 'Now I lay me down to sleep.' And we held hands together. He believed. . . .

"When he was dying, he knew that everything he knew was going to be undone. 'Well,' I said, 'we got the pleasure out of it. It wasn't all in vain.' In the end, he was more worried about his raspberries. He started them new.

"Now I have to let the apple trees go. They have to be sprayed every ten days. The plums and the raspberries and a few apricot trees I can hold onto. But the raspberries will probably be next to go—all the dead canes to be cut, the new growth. Then to weed them, spray them, pick them, try to sell them. That's too much work for one.

"The fishing . . . in the end, when he was under heavy medication, 'Throw that line out further!' he'd yell. He'd be giving instructions for pulling up the nets. 'Don't put that line there!' He was fishing all night. I don't know what he all said, but everything was fish, fish, fish."

This is just to set the record straight. A man died in his home in Ephraim last week after an extraordinary battle against pain and suffering and under the equally extraordinary love and care of his wife and family. He was a simple man. He was a brave man. He was, by anyone's standards, an incredibly good man; better than any of us could hope to be.

The man was buried yesterday afternoon, a cold, clear day, beneath a bluff, near a birch tree in Sister Bay. The visiting minister who delivered the eulogy at the church and spoke the final words at the graveside obviously did not know the man, not having once even mentioned his name or acknowledged the character of a man those of us there knew and loved and came to honor.

The minister spoke a good deal of sin, suffering, judgment, Saint Paul, and all that it amounted to (to me personally) was another dour delivery of dogma, another commercial for Christianity. "Our brother in faith" was the closest he came to naming the man. I forgive the minister for his uncomforting words of standard operational procedure which fell deaf upon my ears. I trust he will forgive me.

To set the record straight: the man's name was Chet Elquist. And his life was not marked by sin or most of the things the minister expressed which equate a good life with suffering for eternal glory. Chet's life was marked by an overwhelming sense of caring, each day of his life. He was the rarest of individuals—a giving human being.

Chet's life was the earth, the water, friends, the here and now.

Of the many times I fished with him, ate with him, drank with him, talked with him, depended upon him (forever depended upon his natural know-how to fix things or plant something) the subject of religion or morality—just how a man should act—never came up. He just knew goodness.

If you had an excess of produce in season (cherries, raspberries, plums, tomatoes, potatoes, whatever), you gave some to your friends. You gave even when you didn't have an excess. And there were times you gave when you had nothing at all. Then you "promised" your friends good apricots or fish or venison next year, when it would be better.

Fishing was his pastime, his passion, his sense of peace and oneness with the world around him. If the minister will excuse me, it was probably his religion. He laughed and joked about it, called himself a "fish-head," and left a legacy of fishing souls behind him—my own son included. Thank God both my children had a Chet Elquist in their life. "Well, I guess he'll be a fish-head just like me." I can hear him saying in that high voice. "A fella could do worse."

The man's life, so simply expressed, so harmoniously shared, could fill a book. But even then I'm not sure we would all understand it or have what it takes to live it, especially the final years, months and days.

In the end one might call Chet a "true" Christian after all, though no one needs to take credit for him. He was all his own doing. I prefer to remember him as a friend, incredibly human.

This is just to set the record straight, Chet. Some of us who received so much from you felt you deserved a more personal goodbye. I have written about all manner of men in my time, but the best of them will always remain mere reflections of you.

Evie: Native Woman

The native women of Door . . . who are they? What are they all about? Perhaps their lives are not meant to be shared, only quietly lived. They're unquestioning lives based on family, tradition, religion and hard work. There's an industriousness to their daily living quite different from their counterparts in the cities. Though the native women of Door may share the usual experiences of childhood, womanhood, marriage, making a life in this landscape has a uniqueness about it that a woman from Chicago, New York City, or Los Angeles will never know.

Evie (formerly Evelyn Elquist, now Evelyn Olson) is married, divorced, recently remarried. This is not quite the normal pattern of the native housewifes in these parts, who tend to settle in, perhaps, and make a life like Evie's sister, Florence Elquist. Flossie and Evie are as different as two sisters can be. The two sisters married two brothers, Chet and Harold Elquist. Evie, though, was a bit of the maverick right from the start, and in many ways, out of place here compared to many of the native women. She loves a good time, laughter, a social drink, down to earth humor, gossip, language so earthy at times it's a pleasure for a man to listen to a woman handling it so well. She is probably the most intensely alive native lady I met here. Seeing her, bent over, picking parsley in the garden the other day, I commented aloud on how much her back must be killing her.

"My ass has been sticking up in the air so much these days. . . ."

And as for strawberries: "Christ, take some. I've eaten so goddam many strawberries the past week that if somebody asked me to barf strawberries, I could do it in a second."

She's fun to listen to, fun to be with—an attractive woman with a precious sense of self, a zest for life rather rare in this countryside. An unsinkable Molly Brown.

When she was fourteen, she made her first attempt to seek a life elsewhere. "I lied about my age. I was just fourteen, and I went to Milwaukee to an employment agency and applied for a 'Mother's Helper' job. I got the job for $5 a week. It was mostly babysitting, peeling potatoes for a mother and father, grandma and grampa and two girls. This was just a summer job. The next year I did the same thing. I went back to Milwaukee and lied about my age. This time I had two little kids, really little, to take care of. Only $2.50 a week. I didn't like it. When cherry season came, I went back home and picked cherries, 4¢ a pail, which was better. Those were the days when you put a heap on, and if the heap wasn't big enough, they sent you back. I picked eleven or twelve pails a day. At the end of the day we went over to the house and had cake and ice cream, and we got paid."

She's an intelligent woman, Evie. If she were growing up today, given the potential for women in our time, there is a good possibility she would have gone far beyond Door. She might have become the nurse she thought of becoming. She could have very well succeeded at anything she set her mind to. (Would she have been any happier? Possibly not.) She likes people. She has a genuine sense of caring for their welfare. I'll never forget the time and care she gave her brother-in-law, Chet Elquist, in his final days.

"I went to school at Appleport," she says. "Then Gibraltar for four years. That was it. I was in high school when I worked at Wilson's, helped in the kitchen, in the back for Mrs. Wilson. That was when I got my first lesson on how to set a table. At home on the farm we never put a spoon at every place. My God, we were never fancy!

"Other summers? I worked part of one summer at the tea shop in Fish Creek: room work, kitchen work. You ate everything. Nothing was wasted. She would serve me chicken skin, put through a grinder. Old potatoes were put through a ricer and then paprika on top, put in the oven and warmed. The chicken skin was like a salad or sandwich spread with mayonnaise." She recalls her anger when the woman paid her only $2 after promising $5. "I wouldn't work for her when she wouldn't pay me the $5 she promised. 'You just take it and shove it,' I told her.

"Then in high school they started in with some of the work projects where you could earn money. I remember I got to sit in the principal's office the hour before school lunch. We were given apples and oranges and candy bars. I got so much a month, maybe $2. It wasn't much, but that was the only kind of school job available, and only a few of us were lucky to get it. So, I had some money. I could buy a candy bar on Sunday and when I went to Emma's [Husby's], our folks didn't have to give us money. Cherry money was used for clothes and school books."

As for the ambitions of a young girl then, "There was not much. There was cherries, some resort work. I hated school. The only class I enjoyed was Home Ec. I was not studious, and I was not obedient like the rest. Flossie was straight A, and I mostly got by. She was always obedient, very studious. Not rebellious like me.

"I'm interested in things done by hand, the home crafts. I still am. It probably came from Grandpa. He did the wool raising, the spinning and knitting. He was also a basket maker. He gathered all the willow bark, and all these things he worked on upstairs. What is now Ingwersen's kitchen was our pantry. It had big glass doors where we had all our good dishes and all the beautifully knitted doilies which my grandmother made. That always stayed in my mind as a child: God, that was beautiful, I thought. A whole cover for the couch, which was just beautiful. And it was beautiful to me then, before anybody here talked about handmade things like these days. When I think about it now, I can still feel the way I felt about those knitted doilies . . . nothing's more beautiful than that."

The hopes of a young Door County native girl after high school? "No, I didn't want to stay here. I really wanted to get away. Too gol' darned confined here. You wanted a little more excitement, like hitching to Baileys Harbor for a movie. To get out! To leave here. To just get away! It was just really confining. If you couldn't walk to it, you couldn't go to it. People would come here from outside somewhere, and there was really something exciting about them, what they saw, what they did. And what the hell could you say? You raked the hay?"

She graduated from Gibraltar High School in 1941. "The war began, and there were jobs everywhere in the city. I went to Chicago. Florence and Chet were living there, and I went to live with them. I got a job in a Greek restaurant, my first waitress job: $11 a week and meals and tips."

And what does an innocent Door County country girl confront in the classic and traditional business of a Greek restaurant in the big city? An old Greek, of course.

"A dirty old man," she laughs. "And let me tell you, the other two old guys he had working for him weren't much better! And there was no way out of that damn kitchen except them two doors! Oh, golly, I'll tell you. . . . Then I went to Sears, which was kind of interesting and fun. Moved around a lot from department to department. I was never bored at the job. I worked there from September to December. Then I went to work in a sewing factory which was converting over to making military things. I discovered I didn't like that kind of work. No place to sit down and eat. We had to stand up and eat in the washrooms. I went back to the Greek. By that time I had learned how to handle the old man. But that wasn't the best deal. It took a while to get all these wheels in operation. Better wages were being made in other places. So I went to International Harvester . . . better money. Inspection work. Then I got married, 1942.

"He [Harold Elquist] was in the service. I got married in Chicago. I stayed there about a year and then went to Detroit where he was stationed. I worked in an ammunition factory in Detroit. There I was on inspection right off the bat. I stayed for two years and then back to Chicago when he was discharged. We went to Melrose Park to live. The first daughter, Joyce, was born, and I didn't work after that. Then we moved to Kenosha. Harold went into fishing there with his brother Chet. Florence, Chet and I always stayed very close together it seems. We were never separated too long."

So Evie's life too was inevitably drawn to the Chet Elquist passion for fishing. "I didn't work in the sheds," explains Evie. "Florence and Chet lived by the water. We lived in a third floor flat. Harold was up and gone before I turned around. He was not a fisherman; that I know. Harold was not a man of long patience. Chet was a man of long patience, detailed work. If Harold couldn't do it in five minutes, forget it. He was not an ambitious man. He was a good eight-to-four worker, and that was it. No, he was not a fisherman where you had to go back and slug nets, hours and hours of work. He was not a fisherman. And it just went from bad to worse.

"I just wanted to stay in the city. I had no desire to come up here. I never was an outdoor person. City life was pretty fine with me. Yeah, I might have been a suburbanite.

"In Kenosha I learned knitting for the first time. I'd buy books. That trunk there is full of books on knitting. I just thought it was so pretty, so beautiful. Then I got into tatting when we moved back here. I learned from Florence Charney. She's still living: a beautiful, old woman who always made stuff, done stuff. A very simple life. Never had much.

"While we were in Kenosha, a farm up here was for sale, and Harold came back up and bought it before I knew what happened. I had no desire to come back here whatsoever, but he wanted a farm. There were ten acres of cherries, eighty acres all told. Cherries were up. But I was unhappy coming back. I just never felt happy or satisfied here.

"We were just always so damn poor. Then he [Harold] got sick with that lung business. He was sent to a veteran's hospital in Milwaukee. Christ, that was the year the cows got the bangs disease. They couldn't keep their calf. They'd throw them. We had seven damn cows left. Then about the night before Roen's was going to pick the cherry crop, a damn storm broke. I think we got $200 for the whole goddam crop. Then we had to get rid of them cows, couldn't keep them. We had such a big mortgage on the place. The cattle were mortgaged. The loan company took the mortgage on the cattle.

"I couldn't work. We had three kids by then. We couldn't get money from the V.A. because the farm was considered a business. So . . . shit! He came home. Had the lung operation. He was really sick after that. He got a little better in time, but the bad throat never did leave.

"When the kids went to school, I used to pelt mink at the mink ranch in November, when it was quite cold. I could walk there from the farm. Floyd Lettie's mink farm, just down the road from where we lived. I flushed them, scraping them off with a drawbar, taking the bulk of the fat off the skins. The pelt would be on a post in a freezer. That way the flesh, the fat was nice and firm. You didn't have it too warm in there. After a couple of breaths in there in the morning, you got so you didn't mind the smell so much. But you never got the smell out of your clothes. After a while they got them electric machines for pelting. Then they didn't need nobody to do the pelts.

"I don't know what the hell we were living on. Not much. I remember our church took one offering for us. We had a little over $200, and that was our income. Christmas time came, and there was money in envelopes . . . food, clothing, gifts from all the churches. They came with food and donations. Everybody came and gave us something. I remember Kay [Chet and Flossie's daughter] visiting one time, seeing all these gifts and things and saying, 'Oh, Mommy, I wish we were poor!'

"That's really when I fell in love with Door County. There was no way I could leave after that. You never get over what people did for you. After that, Harold never got well, never stayed well. He got back to work. He drove a truck for Jake [Kodanko]. But it was always a little here, a little there. You put a checker board in front of you, all your money, all the different places it had to go. Nothing lasted.

"One winter we went to Florida and he worked in a filling station, and that was pretty good for him, for his health. My daughter got a job. Then he figured a warm climate, that's what we would have to head for, once the kids were out of school. So we always went to Florida for the winter. My brother down there was good to me, generous to us. I did a lot of the housework.

"And that's about the time I started to go to my craft classes at the community center, in Boca Raton. I worked in a store there too. I worked part of one winter as a waitress, but I just hate waiting on people. I hate that about as much as I hate reading."

The marriage began to fall apart around that time. The divorce rate in rural America does not compare to the astronomical statistics of our cities. You did—you do—marry once, for life. You make the best of it. For a rural woman to decide to break up a household, destroy a belief the people of this county were taught to respect and accept, took a kind of courage seldom found among her God-fearing neighbors.

"The sickness, the poverty, the whole thing put such a taboo on being married. I wanted out, period! If we had a halfway decent life, we might not have gone the way we did. We left the farm in '68. We had a house built in Florida. We lived together in that house, but not together for one year. We were separated for four years before we got a divorce.

I would come back up here and stay with Florence during spring and summer. Eventually I got the cottage in Sister Bay from Godfrey Logerquist, the summer of '69. I started working for Al [Johnson] the same time, cooking in the kitchen. Then I went back to my brother's to live the winter of '70. I always figured I was alone from '69 on. It's kind of a separate drifting till you get the divorce, not sure what to do. You're really alone. When I got my divorce, I was very happy. I was forty-eight at the time. It was just such a big relief. I didn't have all the grief like beforehand. I just felt like I was out from down under. I had a job, a car, family. My kids were all grown. I was just happy for the years ahead. I didn't worry about 'My, someday I'm going to be old!'

"I was determined I was not going to be married again. I wasn't depressed being alone, really. I don't know what I hated about it [marriage], but it wasn't for me. If someone works with you, that's different. If someone appreciates you. Like Chet and Flossie. Even with him gone now, she won't think of selling the place. 'I can't leave Chet yet,' she tells me. 'I've got to stay here in the berry patch.' Chet is still there for her."

Returning to Door alone, however, as a woman alone introduced a whole new set of circumstances. "Immediately you do not fit in," says Evie. "You're dropped. Who do you entertain? If you have a couple in, what does the man do? You're not invited out, either. As soon as you're alone, even if you're a widow, you're just not invited out anymore. You almost wait to go to the store, because there you'll find someone who'll talk to you. Faye [her youngest daughter] was the one who really got me out. Faye would say to me, 'Hey, Ma, you're not going to lay in that bed and rot! Get dressed. We're going for a drink, we're going dancing!'

"Even in church there is no honest-to-God social life, someone to converse with. I always found that at a bar. That's where the people are. That's where all your nights go. A lot of them are there for conversation, to find someone to talk to. I know I spent a lot of time there. These people in the bars around here, they're really there to take down their hair, to say what they really feel. I don't think you have as many gossips in a bar as you do in a church. At a bar you could be a people watcher. Or you can listen.

"Kids were my best company. They're not interested in money, prestige. They were my best company, the young people. 'Hey, we're going to do this or that, come on.' You didn't get that from an adult."

Living as a divorced woman in these parts for almost eight years, Evie remained a rare breed and seemed to gain even more strength in her role as an outspoken woman. She would say things at times that good Christian men might think but be afraid to verbalize. She could undoubtedly make them blush. She had been through enough hell in her own life to realize her sense of womanhood and act and speak accordingly, knowing the tendency of most people to practice hypocrisy rather than honesty.

"I never cared what anybody thought about me from the time I was a child. They can form their own opinion. Because I *knew* what I was doing. In a small area like this you get a lot of that. Sometimes I feel almost sorry for them that they can't be more broad-minded than that. I never thought divorce was a disgrace. I think it's more of a disgrace for two people to live together who can't stand it.

"As for the country or the city, each has its drawbacks. I know Faye says it's much easier living alone in the country than the city. I think in a small community there's always someone who's going to befriend you. If you can take the gossip, and shed it like a duck does water, it's easier. You've got to be bigger than what they are. Before you *did* it, they knew it! That's the whole damn thing.

"Faye had the biggest influence in my life after my divorce. Joyce was married. Donny [her son] was off to service. Faye and her friends just plain took me in. 'Ma, I don't care what they say about you. If you're lonesome and want to go to town and have a beer, you go ahead.'

"Men all think they're wonderful. Nobody's good enough for them. Some of the men in these bars, they really have a problem, and really can't talk about it. There are some men who are nothing but chauvinistic pigs, but there are others who are really learning from you as you learn from them. I think the way you go into a bar makes a difference. With some people you think, 'Jesus, what a waste of life.' But others may come in there only after their day's work and just want to relax. I think a lot of people in bars are just plain unhappy with themselves, but don't know what to do about it. 'Hey, I got a problem,' and they go to a bar instead of a psychiatrist. I think a lot of them do that.

"And a lot of times I thought, 'Gee, I was glad I talked to that person. That was a new thought.' I think you can do good no matter where you're stationed in this world. Not to go to a bar just to drown your sorrows. You can't stay at this low point. You've got to come up. Sometimes it just takes someone to put a good thought in someone's head. Before you can plant, you got to put a seed there. And the seed is the beginning of the deed."

There is a weariness to bar life too, as Evie knows. The regulars become just that; the names and faces take on a tired history of frustration and defeat. "Through all this I could see I was not made for a bar life. I was not meant for being alone. I've got to have somebody. And once you get that feeling, that this is not for you, you want a different life, then you begin to see all the bad aspects of going to a bar. You begin hoping someone is going to come along. But the day you quit looking, that's the day it comes right to your door. And I don't want to go out with the idea I was man hunting."

Evie remarried in 1977 to a widower, a native, a hard working farmer, orchard man, Harvey Olson, seventy-one, a man she had seen around these parts most of her life. "He was always the pallbearer to me," she laughs; "Whenever there was a death, there was Harvey, the pallbearer. I met him at Earl's [the Sister Bay Bowl]. I was sitting at the bar having a drink. He asked me to dance. The Birminghams were playing. A friendship developed . . . bad days, good days, blues. He'd lost his wife. I'd fix him a cup of coffee. He'd ask me out to dinner. It just started out of two people in need. I'm very content now, the most content I've been all my life. We've really got a good relationship. It's a good life. We both work hard. We're good for each other. And it all happened by accident . . . going barring."

Friends and family continue to mean a lot to her. The care she and Faye extended to her late brother-in-law, Chet Elquist, might seem uncommon to some, but it's the natural way to act for a woman of Evie's character. "He was always willing to do something for you. Even when he was real, real sick, he always had time to fix something for you. He always had the time to take you along. Fishing, that was his life. That was like oxygen to his bloodstream. He just had to have it. There's a poster I saw of a man in a boat in mist with the caption, 'Take the Time.' That's how he was.

"He wasn't going to die. He was definitely going to make it. He fought. No, he was not afraid of dying. One day he talked to me when he was supposed to be sleeping. 'You know,' he said, 'My wife doesn't know I'm this sick, that I'm really bad off. You better go check on Flossie, she's been gone a long time. You better go check on her.' As sick as he was, he was still concerned about her, where she was, how she was feeling."

For a native lady, growing up with the traditional religious beliefs all around her, Evie continues to show personal growth. "Reincarnation—I don't even mention it to Harvey. He thinks I'm nuts. If they're not prepared for it, you can't explain a lot of this stuff to people. They just can't comprehend it. When you talk about the spirit world, they think you're talking witchcraft. You just have to have your own thoughts, your own feelings. I certainly feel these things.

"I've been reading *Siddharta*, Gibran. A lot of people would say this is all hogwash. I like the idea of reincarnation. I think it's kind of nice. I think there's too much at stake here . . . there must be something else. There's no religion that is perfect. They've all got a point. If they could really get it together, maybe they could come up with something great. But this little bit of my life . . . there's got to be more than that.

"When you deal with people, you've just got to make an influence. And it's got to be for the better, even if it's only little. If he hasn't got a smile, give him yours. What you are, what you present, is what you get back."

Phil Sweet: Minister to Ministers

They call it God's Country, Door County, and it may very well be. But I often wonder how the rest of the world, the rest of American society, came under someone else's dominion. Given the way people are hustling God's Door County these days, He may be out of place Himself in these parts before long.

I discovered early in life that the ministers and priests of organized religion are usually the last people to turn to for answers. Either they promise you heaven, consign you to hell, or tell you everything in between is all suffering. Almost no one will encourage you to question the possibilities of enjoying life for the Eden it is.

But there are exceptions, like Phil Sweet of the Hope United Church of Christ in Sturgeon Bay. The God-saving thing about Phil is that he doesn't have any answers either. Only more questions. And that in itself may be the only kind of honest faith worth pursuing in a man's brief life . . . at least this time around.

It's no life to be stifled to death with other men's answers, other men's virtues. Find your own. I don't want any man to tell me the directions to heaven who hasn't visited hell himself occasionally.

One of the things I admire about Phil Sweet is that he admits there are times he doesn't feel like preaching the Sunday sermon. What's more, he admits this openly to his congregation, and maybe this in itself becomes the sermon. "When I put on the robe, I feel it will protect me, especially when I am unsure of myself," he says.

A man carries his religion with him wherever he goes. Even if he has none, that is his religion.

And if it's a static, a settled, or even an inherited faith, that is the easiest of faiths to live with, isn't it? All the answers have been given to you; you attend the church of your choice each Sunday to be reminded of the answers; and you go back to living your daily life, mostly unconcerned about that fine line between right and wrong—till next Sunday.

The self-righteousness of many Christians often turns to missionary zeal—the worst kind of religious bigotry. I find that quite amusing, like the converting of "savages" to Christianity.

It is difficult to move into or exist in this county without a label—
Baptist, Lutheran, Catholic, etc.—and not be approached, or reproached,
to be *something*! (Chalk up another point for Phil Sweet, non-missionary,
who would probably ask of you no more than that you be yourself.) It is
difficult to raise kids free to choose a church of their choice (should they
ever care to) when the social fabric all around them is primarily based
upon who belongs to what church.

The Devil, too, is alive and well in Door County. Not long ago sitting
in a local restaurant, I heard a grown man attribute most of the world's
troubles (especially those on the home front: drinking, drugs, rock music,
hippies) to the Devil. Eliminate the Devil, and all would be milk and
honey again in God's Country.

"Yeah, let's catch that dirty old Devil and dump him across the line in
Kewaunee or Brown County," a stranger was heard to say in passing.

Phil Sweet calls the Hope Church "a center for religious pilgrimage in
human potential." A nice touch. It seems to leave it open for all of us,
with the potential worth seeking—"human."

The first time I saw Phil Sweet was years ago in a Mad Hatter
performance (a group of adults from Sturgeon Bay who read/act out
stories for children) in the village hall of Sister Bay. About fifteen kids
sat around the floor watching the Mad Hatters make stories come alive.
All the people were exceptionally good, but one man, with a beard,
seemed quite an actor, holding everyone's attention as he went through
the life and hard times of a storybook kid named Alexander (from the
book by Judith Viorst):

> I went to sleep with gum in my mouth and now there's
> gum in my hair and when I got out of bed this morning I trip-
> ped on the skateboard and by mistake I dropped my sweater in
> the sink while the water was running and I could tell it was
> going to be a terrible, horrible, no good, very bad day.

On and on it goes—disaster after personal disaster. Kids, even
adults, could identify with the lousy feelings of Alexander. Everyone
has days when everything goes wrong. And Phil Sweet, the man with
the beard, made it all very visible, very real, very human.

Sometime later I learned that Sweet was a minister, which both
surprised and delighted me. For a man of the cloth to resort to childish
antics in attempt to approach the complexities of daily life—for even the
very young—was highly unusual in God's Country, where we take our
religion seriously (on Sundays), and the Bible is the boss in books.

Young ministers/new ideas have short lives in these parts. There was
one who played "Jesus Christ Superstar" to his congregation. Another
was a bit too intellectual. Another was "just too young." None remain.

Sweet's survival is a remarkable achievement in itself. For surely here is a radical set loose upon God's home turf. True, his Sturgeon Bay domain is a confined one, and probably a bit more urban than the rest of Door. True, too, he lacks the evangelical energy to attempt tent-meeting conversions around the county, let alone personal visits or Bible class pressures from the congregation. Nor can one picture Phil Sweet and his family in a bus with SWEET SINGERS OF JESUS painted on the side, making the local Christian concert circuit, hymning their way into heaven and into our hearts. One is left with the feeling that when people are ready to ask questions about themselves and their beliefs, Phil Sweet will be around to listen and possibly explain his own feelings concerning the potential for being human. He needs no bandwagon.

Born in Franklin, New Hampshire, Phil would be the first to admit that his call to the ministry was no heaven-shattering thing. "Oh, I was raised in the church, but my parents were not fanatics about it. I got an A in public speaking in college, and that was probably a very important thing. I was never able to stand up before a group of people. I lacked the confidence."

He attended Andover Newton Theological Seminary, near Boston, for three years plus one year's internship. He went into the ministry partly because he wanted "to somehow confront the kind of established conservative religion grounded on nonsensical dogmas and formulated long before man was aware of any physical laws," and partly because "you have some sort of automatic in, some sense of stature in society."

Fresh out of the seminary, he answered the call of two churches in Campbell, Minnesota. "Many rural churches are very hard up for ministers," he kids. "I was not particularly wanting to go there. It was flat country, and the terrain made me uneasy. I was used to New England. Also, these were farm people, their lives all talk about the weather and the price of grain.

"But the church was still the center of their lives. The minister was a very important figure. I had two churches, and they were marvelous people."

The young minister with his first congregation "was scared stiff and green. Fear . . . for me it was not trusting my own thinking capacities, the people finding out how dumb I really was, not knowing how to operate a church.

"I've been plagued all my life with feelings of inferiority. It's been a terrible burden for me, not trusting my own feelings, partly because I've always been a rebel in my own church. If you're not going with the crowd, there is always a tremendous feeling of guilt."

For a man, a minister, to admit his own vulnerability, is a very rare thing. Phil Sweet, one soon learns, is far removed from Hawthorne's Minister and the Black Veil.

The first funeral, first death a man must minister to is never quite forgotten. "It was a young man," explains Phil, "thirty-eight years old, a heart attack. I did not believe in heaven or hell. I remember how difficult it was to say anything. I tried to talk about what happens after death. I said something like, 'The sun goes down in the evening, but the sun comes up again the next day. Life goes on.' I still have difficulties with funerals, meeting people's expectations of an afterlife.

"I like weddings. Weddings are family things. There's the sense of hope, the visions and dreams. I almost always say to them, 'You're not going to be able to live your dreams. It's not our shame. It's our nobility that we can reach so far and can't possibly grasp.'

"Christenings are also a favorite service of mine. The hope people have for their own children. I usually quote Gibran:

> Your children are not your children.
> They are the sons and daughters of Life's longing for itself.
> They come through you but not from you.
> And though they are with you yet they belong not to you.
> You may give them your love but not your thoughts,
> For they have their own thoughts.
> You may house their bodies but not their souls,
> For their souls dwell in the house of tomorrow, which you
>   cannot visit, not even in your dreams.
> You may strive to be like them, but seek not to make them like you,
> For life goes not backward nor tarries with yesterday.
> You are the bows from which your children as living arrows
>   are sent forth. . . .
> Let your bending in the archer's hand be for gladness.

Occasionally a minister here in God's Country has been known to refuse to marry a couple for one reason or another—church law, perhaps, or family or social pressure. Phil Sweet says he will marry anybody. "I've been embarrassed at times by that. I had a wedding once at the ski slope [Omnibus], a service that blared over the loud speakers!" he laughs. "Then the couple took off on a snowmobile, in white snowmobile suits!"

Trusting one's own feelings is not an easy way to go, especially in the ministry. Sweet, though, seems to gain strength, confidence, in openly displaying his personal feelings, and in expressing them. "I'm the kind of restless guy," he tells you, "who feels everything is questionable and needs to be overturned from time to time. It's just my nature. I was in trouble often there [in Minnesota]. When I stated that I did not believe in heaven or hell, that was a very misunderstood statement."

He was involved, too, with protest movements of the '60s. And there was a point when "the people were really, really upset. The town policeman was ready to fire me. Then about three years later, someone did an article on small churches, mine was included, and they said about me: 'He hurled bombshells at our truths, but we love him anyway.'

"And that was very important: that I could attack and get away with it. That I could honestly question beliefs. I mean, people ask, 'Do you believe in God?' What's more important is, what do your beliefs have to do *practically* with your life? I don't know if I believe in only one God. I don't know if it's important to go to church. I go back to A. S. Neill's book, *Summerhill*:

> A recent woman visitor said to me, "Why don't you teach your pupils about the life of Jesus, so that they will be inspired to follow in his steps?" I answered that one learns to live, not by *learning* of other lives, but by *living*; for words are infinitely less important than acts. Many have called Summerhill a religious place because it gives out love to children. . . . I personally have nothing against the man who believes in a God—no matter what God. What I object to is the man who claims that his God is the authority for his imposing restrictions on human growth and happiness. The battle is . . . between believers in human freedom and believers in the suppression of human freedom. . . . The new religion will refuse the antithesis of body and spirit. It will recognize that the flesh is not sinful. It will know that a Sunday morning spent in swimming is more holy than a Sunday morning spent in singing hymns—as if God needs hymns to keep Him contented. . . . Just imagine all that would be accomplished if only ten percent of all the hours spent in prayer and churchgoing were devoted to good deeds and acts of charity and helpfulness.

Without the freedom to honestly question beliefs, Phil Sweet claims, "I may have left the ministry if I didn't feel that. Carl Rogers in *On Becoming a Person* is the classic example. He thought seriously about going into the ministry and soon discovered that the seminary was not asking the right questions. "Almost all of us worked ourselves right out of religion," he says. It's been my experience that a person can be honest, and it can be done lovingly . . . not to change religious beliefs as much as to clarify what people believe."

After 3½ years in Campbell, Minnesota, he came to Sturgeon Bay in 1970, he says laughingly, because "after I put in my name, it was the only call I got. We came here, and it seemed like such an ideal place . . . the church itself, the congregation. The church had been known for its radicalism."

Phil describes his congregation as "most diverse. Not many traditional Christians could come here and feel very comfortable. Somebody said to me the other day that we sort of just gather in here. Awfully intellectual. Great readers. They really keep me informed. It's very much a seeking congregation. We're not in any way perfect. A lot of people here are people who have left traditional religion and have never found a faith where they could honestly be a part of it. Actually, to belong to this church all you have to do is say, "I want to be a member."

"When people do wish to join, all we do is say this covenant together: 'We are here because there is no refuge finally from ourselves. Until a person confronts himself in the eyes and hearts of his fellow person, he is running. Until he shares his secrets with them, he will have no safety from them. Where else but in our common ground can we find such a mirror? Here at last we can appear clearly to ourselves. Not as the giant of our dreams nor the dwarf of our fears, but as a person, part of a whole. And in this ground we can each take root and grow. Not alone anymore as in death but alive, a person among persons.'

"There ought to be some way to let our theological position known," Phil continues, "yet we can't truthfully handle any more than we have. We're hovering at just about three hundred in the congregation, yet I personally can't handle any more emotional problems. If you believe in a personal ministry as I do, that takes an enormous amount of time. There are a lot of ministers today who won't make a personal call."

It is clear from his conversation and actions that Phil Sweet has a great love and respect for the members of his congregation. "These people are very sophisticated," he explains. "They have that quality of intelligence that is sometimes scary. These people will do a lot of confronting. They might even disagree with me openly. (He has been known to leave the lectern at times during a service, and move to the center of the church, amidst the people, to read a children's story. 'What Can Make a Hippopotamus Smile?' cost him two members a few weeks ago.) It's a wonderful congregation here. They tolerate a lot of goofiness, but they allow me to have my opinions, and they're not sacred and we exist, testing our own experiences . . . and there isn't any sacred cow about what you believe and must not believe—everything is in a state of flux."

A good deal of what Phil Sweet believes is contained in: "An Eschatological Laundry List: A Partial Register of the 927 (or was it 928?) Eternal Truths" found in a book by Sheldon B. Kopp, *If You Meet the Buddha on the Road, Kill Him*. The list reads like this:

1. This is it! 2. There are no hidden meanings. 3. You can't get there from here, and besides there's no place else to go. 4. We are all already dying, and we will be dead for a long time. 5. Nothing lasts. 6. There is no way of getting all you want. 7. You can't have anything unless you let go of it. 8. You only get to keep what you give away. 9. There is no particular reason why you lost out on some things. 10. The world is not necessarily just. Being good often does not pay off and there is no compensation for misfortune. 11. You have a responsibility to do your best nonetheless. 12. It is a random universe to which we bring meaning. 13. You don't really control anything. 14. You can't make anyone love you. 15. No one is any stronger or any weaker than anyone else. 16. Everyone is, in his own way, vulnerable. 17. There are no great men. 18. If you have a hero, look again: you have diminished yourself in some way. 19. Everyone lies, cheats, pretends (yes, you too, and most certainly I myself). 20. All evil is potential vitality in need of transformation. 21. All of you is worth something, if you will only own it. 22. Progress is an illusion. 23. Evil can be displaced but never eradicated, as all solutions breed new problems. 24. Yet it is necessary to keep on struggling toward solution. 25. Childhood is a nightmare. 26. But it is so very hard to be an on-your-own, take-care-of- yourself-'cause-there-is-no-one-else-to-do-it-for-you grown-up. 27. Each of us is ultimately alone. 28. The most important things, each man must do for himself. 29. Love is not enough, but it sure helps. 30. We have only ourselves, and one another. That may not be much, but that's all there is. 31. How strange, that so often, it all seems worth it. 32. We must live within the ambiguity of partial freedom, partial power, and partial knowledge. 33. All important decisions must be made on the basis of insufficient data. 34. Yet we are responsible for everything we do. 35. No excuses will be accepted. 36. You can run, but you can't hide. 37. It is most important to run out of scapegoats. 38. We must learn the power of living with our helplessness. 39. The only victory lies in surrender to oneself. 40. All of the significant battles are waged within the self. 41. You are free to do whatever you like. You need only face the consequences. 42. What do you know . . . for sure . . . anyway? 43. Learn to forgive yourself, again and again and again and again. . . .

With all the movements these days toward greater self-awareness, with encounter groups, TM, TA, the move toward Eastern religions (movements, ironically enough, that have barely touched upon the small, isolated world of Door) are any of us really getting any better? Is there any less hate, envy, greed, anywhere?

"Go back to the list," smiles Phil Sweet. "Progress is an illusion.' But I'm the eternal optimist. I think there is more caring today. Some of the perennial 'shoulds' have begun to be shed. People are questioning old values, but then that backfires. I think there is a growing movement toward a more significant lifestyle, a communal one perhaps, a sacredness for all life. But money . . . money still tends to be what motivates everybody."

Religion and the rural life? The United Church of Christ states that many members of its church "still have close ties to the land; they either farm or engaged in work relating to farming . . . the church often lends its support to legislation which favors the small family farm operation." Phil Sweet admits, "My own fantasy is to be somebody self-sufficient on my own land. I'm a firm believer in Scott Nearing's ideas (*Living the Good Life*). We've lost touch with the earth. Scott Nearing's 4-4 idea: if one's bread labor was performed in the morning, the afternoon automatically became personally directed. One might read, write, sit in the sun, walk in the woods, play music, go to town. We earned our four hours of leisure by our four hours of labor. A non-profit economy," explains Phil. "You charge what you think is a fair return."

Some hours after I first met and talked with Phil Sweet recently in Sturgeon Bay, I happened to think that not once in over two hours of conversation did Christ enter our discussion. When I reminded him of this days later, Phil laughed and explained, "We are a Christian church. I'm a kind of post-Christian. We've begun to amalgamate all kinds of faith, together. Christ for me is divine, but we are all divine, all sons of God, not he alone. Who knows who he was? That was a great mystery."

A "minister to ministers" he calls himself. Just what is that? "Everybody's a minister here," he explains. "Everybody's a priest to each other. I'm just kind of a teacher to ministers . . . to counsel one another . . . to be listeners . . . to perform sacraments. A sacrament? A visible sign of something invisible. A grace and goodness of life. I really feel that everything is sacred in a sense. That everything is divine . . . that nothing exists outside religion."

I have never heard Phil Sweet or anyone else preach a sermon here in God's Country. I am not particularly proud of that. What I am is finally *free* of that, and Phil Sweet, I trust, will understand since it is the freeing process that interests him these days, and may be the truest religious act for all of us: "Freeing everyone," Phil speculates, "so that ultimately a minister will come to a service and discover there is no one there."

Emery "Dynamite" Oldenburg: Horse Trader

You see him sometimes down along his range on Highway 57, tattered Levis, boots, grayed galluses, silver belt buckle, a barn-type jacket with the pockets perhaps nibbled away by mice, a battered cowboy hat with one tall feather. You see him coming through the leaning weathered barns, through the corral, ambling out there near the cattailed pond often filled with ducks, moving out there amongst the quiet of his horses, patting a rump, smoothing a wide belly, chucking a chin, talkin' to 'em all.

"There's not a mean bone in your body, is there?" he asks, looking into the deep pool of an Appaloosa's eye.

In a county's natural landscape noted for its fishermen, orchardmen, and just plain rock-picking, hard-working farmers, Emery Oldenburg, sixty-seven, is perhaps Door County's first and last cowboy, horseman, horse trader. One of a kind.

"They call me Dynamite," he says. "I've had that name ever since I was a kid. My brother-in-law gave me that. He was always hanging some kind of name on somebody."

As a child, I would often question my father's departure by asking, "Where you going?" And inevitably he would reply, "I'm going to see a man about a horse." I never met that man or saw the horse—till now.

But I dreamed of horses through much of my boyhood, then traded in those dreams for other desires as I grew older.

Some men, however, never shake the dream their whole life long.

"You wanna hear about the time I caught the wild horses in Wyoming?" asks Dynamite.

Yeah. But not yet.

"My folks were both born in Germany," he tells me. "My dad was ten when he came. He started a business as a harness maker in Baileys Harbor, right across from the Frontier Bar. I was always horse crazy. My folks thought they could cure me when I was around ten. They bought me a mean Shetland pony, but it only made it worse. I really learned to ride on him. I guess it kind of came from my mother, too. My mother was really a horse woman. She could really drive horses.

"I used to exercise the stage horses when they came in with teams in winter. Those I could ride, I rode. And those I could drive, I drove with a sleigh. The stage ran from Baileys Harbor to Sturgeon Bay and back . . . oh, 1927, 1928, I'd say. I was born in Baileys Harbor in 1913.

"There were a lot of horses in the county at that time. Everybody worked with a horse. There were a lot of horse and buggies. I finished three years of high school. I guess I was just too damn horse crazy to know what I wanted to do. I ran away to Chambers Island to drive team, build a golf course. Lasted just one summer, though. Then I came back here and worked in the canning factory in Sturgeon.

"Then about 1935 I went to work in the shipyards there, and I stayed in the shipyards forty-one years. I was a steel cutter. Retired four years ago at the age of sixty-three. I've got enough to do now with the horses."

His house is small—rural Door County native, if there is such a style. Practical. Plain and simple. Everything in its place. But he does not appear to be a man as comfortable indoors as out. There is a Carter Brown paperback mystery novel with a sexy lady on the cover on the kitchen table. And a cribbage board and a soft worn deck of cards left over from a long night of playing cribbage with his wife, Irene. A small plaque on the wall reads, "If a man has enough sense to treat his wife like a thoroughbred, she'll never grow into an old nag."

We sit down at the kitchen table, and Oldenburg lights a Camel cigarette.

"You wanna beer?"

"No. Too early in the morning. You?"

"Naw. Not no more."

"How did you get started with the horses?"

"At one time I raised Arabians. Then I sold out of horses and went into cattle. About eight years of that. But the only guy who made any money was the trucker. I got all the work. Then I went into buckskin quarter horses. Maybe four or five years of them. That was thirteen years ago. The same year I caught the wild horses out there. . . ."

There's that wild horse gleam in his eye again—a time of his life like no other. But I want to hear more of the horse business first.

"Hell, I was buying, selling, trading horses in 1940. 1 just started fooling around that way with the horses. Those years a guy did anything to make money. The first horse I sold was that Shetland pony my folks gave me. I made a few bucks, I guess. Horse trading just came naturally to me. Once I traded a horse and a colt for a cow and a pony, and on the way home I traded the pony for an angus steer. That winter I had meat anyway."

You can sense a certain pride in this old horse trader, and though he's willing to tell all he knows about horses, he holds onto a horse sense privacy when it comes to sharing some of the real deals he's made.

"Can't say about that," he smiles. "Hell, my customers are out there. The people may still be around here! Oh, I traded Moonbeam off once 'cause she got the colic all the time. But my cousin, now my cousin really made a deal once. Maybe you shouldn't write this either. He once traded a horse for a heifer, a pig, three chickens and a dollar!" laughs Dynamite. "I always like that part about the dollar. A heifer, a pig, three chickens, and a dollar. For a horse! Now there's a deal!

"I got rid of those buckskins that time because I had a chance to sell 'em and make a little money. And that's when I went into Appaloosas. They were a rare breed at one time. They came from the Nez Perce Indians. The Nez Perce were the first Indians that ever practiced selective breeding. I picked up a nice stallion in Wyoming about 1966. Then I bought registered Appaloosa mares, and I've been breeding them ever since. That's the same year we caught the wild horses."

Buying, selling, trading in horses. What is a person to look for? If you're dealing in used cars or battered pickups with Clean Piece Wally Mickelson, there are certain "buyer beware" signs in the mechanics of the thing to watch for when you're trying to figure out how bad Wally's trying to beat you, or how anxious you are to stick him. How does this go with horses?

"I buy, sell and trade," says Dynamite. "Buying . . . the first thing you look at is his feet. If the horse can't walk, he's no good. Then he goes either to Japan, France, or in the can for dog food. The French eat them and pay good money for a nice fat gelding.

"Then you look at their teeth for age. You can tell an old horse: their teeth get longer, long and curved. After about eleven years, though, you can't be too accurate. The best years of a horse are from three to twelve.

"This is the main thing—feet, legs and age. The color of a horse don't mean nothing. You can have one of the homeliest horses in the world, and he can still be one of the best horses.

"The cost of keeping 'em is something else. Figure it out this way: forty bales of hay to a ton, and like in winter, a horse will eat close to a bale of hay a day. You're feeding him at least seven months out of the year cause up in this country we get nine months winter and three months poor sledding. I raise all my own feed. If I didn't raise my own, I wouldn't keep horses. Couldn't. I always have enough hay for two years, in case of a bad season. You have to have at least three ton a hay a year per horse. And that ain't too much. The winter's pretty long.

"I've picked up maybe forty horses in the County in the last few years because people just didn't want to feed them anymore. It got so damn expensive. If my barn had a higher ceiling, I'd be raising draft horses. You can raise your own fuel on the farm and get fertilizer in return, plus the work."

Horse fever. If ever a man had it, certainly Emery "Dynamite" Oldenburg seems obsessed by the sight, sound, smell, feel, love of horses. "I bought this place twenty-five years ago. I been married to Irene—she's got the beauty shop in Sister Bay—twenty-eight years. My second marriage. When I started in the shipyard I made $40 a week, and by the time I left I was makin' $40 a day. Horses is a disease, about as bad as having TB. It's an incurable disease, that's what it is. It's as bad as being an alcoholic, I guess. I had horses. I went into cattle raising and everything else, but I still went back to horses. A disease is what it is.

"Maybe it's just because I like animals. It's the same thing like with that cat that followed me from the barn. I get 'em as barn cats and pretty soon they're just living in the house. Just the love of animals, I guess. You saw how that horse Pepsi was pushing up to me. If I got out there now, they'll pretty soon all flock around me. They're jealous. They want to show their affection, too. Some people have said if my horses were any gentler, they'd be dangerous. They'd walk all over you. I can walk up to anyone of 'em, do anything with 'em. Any horse I got gets that way."

Is the horse trader still a horse rider? Does he saddle up at times and ride the old Oldenburg range? Has he worked the fields with horses?

"I'd like to have a nice team to work with someday, because it does something to you when you work with horses. It gives you a feeling right here," and Dynamite presses somewhere close to his heart and gut. "It's no fun riding alone. You have to have someone along help you enjoy the scenery. Irene don't ride. She's afraid of horses."

Dynamite's horse farm consists of thirteen at present. And he is a man who knows his own horses. "I've got one Arab and one Morab— half Arabian and half Morgan. They make a darn good saddle horse. They're gentle and tough. They have endurance and appearance. A small head, a little bit heavier body. The other eleven are all registered Apps.

My old foundation mare is sixteen, a well-bred registered mare: Chico's Apache Doll. She is the daughter of Chico Apache, the head sire of Walt Disney's Appaloosas. Then I have her daughter and her great granddaughter for brood mares.

"Now Pepsi [Pepsi Kota] I bought from a guy in Casco. Pepsi's the family pet, or nuisance. You open his door and he's always in the way. I ride him and I drive him. Hell, I've had so many chances to sell him! I had a real good deal to sell him once, but Irene said nothing doing, we have to keep him for the grandchildren. The grandchildren love to ride him. I tell you, if I leave it up to Irene, I'll have so damn many horses here, I'll be horse poor.

"My stud has got a name a mile long. I don't know who the hell ever named that horse. You don't ever call him by his registered name, it's just too long. You call him anything you want to. . . ."

Dynamite looks for his file box and starts going through all the registration papers on his horses. "Here it is, the stud's name: Swingin M Holy Smoke's Top Gun. That's his name. A helluva name.

"There are blanket Apps and leopard Apps. I don't have any leopard Apps. I think the blanket Apps bring a little better price."

I recall from my boyhood days, books I read, movies I saw, the challenge of breaking in a colt. There was always something magical about it, a rite-of-passage for a youngster.

"A colt should be a good two years old before you ride them. Otherwise they get tired, leg weary. Out West they don't break them till they're four or five years old, but here you can't afford to feed a horse that long if you don't get any use out of them.

"Colts, they're gentle from the time they're born. There's no trouble. First you halter break them so they can be tied and led. Then you just fool around with them, and then put the saddle on and let 'em stand till they get accustomed to it. Then you get on, and there's nothing to it. They don't care.

"When I wean 'em, I immediately halter break 'em. Then I can handle 'em in the stalls. I start puttin the saddle on 'em about 1½ years old. Start riding 'em around two years old for a short distance. They're weaned about seven months old. The whole process takes about two years."

Emery Oldenburg. Dynamite. A rare breed indeed in these parts. Door County is not the Wild West, but I read that gleam in old Dynamite's eyes . . . the time he went West and caught the wild horses.

"I started going West during my vacations from the shipyard in 1945. I rode roundup for a guy on the Shoshone Indian reservation in Wyoming for eleven years. We'd go up the mountains and bring the cattle down so they wouldn't get caught in the snow. Stay up there for a week.

"Then the one year they was just wanting me to come out and ride and round up wild horses. They had the trap all built. There were seven of us. All Indians but me, up on what they call the Sweetwater in Wyoming. It only took a day. I had my saddle and everything ready by four o'clock. Jesus, we drove and drove through antelope country, rocks, bush. Jim, the Indian I knew, wouldn't tell me anything, where we was going. Goddam Indians, you know, they won't ever tell you anything!

"We came to some ranch house to get the horses we were gonna ride. I immediately took the best and fastest horse. Those Indians looked at me. They knew I took the best horse. Then we loaded them horses on the truck. They already had the trap built along the BLM [Bureau of Land Management] fence. Them Indians had cut the fence, opened it up in a V. Then we started bringing up these wild horses, bringing them into there. We ran these wild horses for about thirty miles, and they just followed the fence and were in the trap, right into that V trap, before they knew it. We rounded up thirty-four of them. Boy, that was fun."

We move out of the house, into the back pasture where all his horses calmly feed, a scene of quiet contentment on a gray October day. Can old Dynamite see himself chucking it all in Door County someday, maybe heading for the West and the wild horses for good?

"I'm too old to start all over again," says Dynamite. "I figure I'll just stay here. Hell, you move away from your friends. . . . You get old and you don't circulate around as much and make new friends."

The horses look up, and one comes to him. "This was a mare so wild they were gonna kill her," he says, chucking her under the chin. "She was on her way to the killers when I got ahold of her. I call her Gypsy. Yeah, she's sure a wild and mean one now, ain't she? She follows me just like a kitten."

And Dynamite Oldenburg, Door County cowboy, roams through his herd, patting rumps, rubbing necks, his horses trailing after him. "Hell, I'll deal with anybody who wants to deal, as long as I can make a deal," he says, mumbling a real horse trader's creed.

Notes from an Exile in Dairyland

Sometimes I feel exiled in Dairyland.

Sometimes I feel it's all a natural process of conditioning.

Born and bred in Chicago's neighborhoods and alleys, coming of age in the backyards and backstreets of Bohemia (Cicero and Berwyn), discovering form and energy in the downtown streets of the Loop, what's a guy like me still doing on a northern Wisconsin peninsula, stuck in the woods (as I am this moment, waiting for a snowplow to clear a path for me), transplanted into a naturally landscaped country-side of unobstructed horizons, wild birds, shorelines, and tasty air?

Mornings like this, some eight years ago in beautiful bungalowed Berwyn, would find me in my "studio" (a storage room in the basement of an apartment building) working on stories and watercolors, preparing for my coffee break on Cermak Road. In the afternoons I would teach or go down to Chicago to visit the bookstores. Just walking the city was a poem to me.

But mornings I would hike it down the alleys to the corner of Oak Park Ave. and Cermak, pick up a newspaper at the stand, slip into the Seneca Restaurant for coffee and perhaps conversation, and pick up some groceries and a carton of milk on the way home. Good morning, Chicago.

I'm a creature of habits and rituals. I find meaning and, often, too much comfort in them. Giving up Chicago was not an easy thing to do. I tend to go about living the same way for years, moving things around, perhaps, only in my head. Oh, I make occasional moves to distant places, foreign countries, but always I come back to Chicago.

Some particulars. There was a full moon last night white to even imagine. There was no night last night.

This hour before sunrise in Door County, the snow is blue.

The foghorn casts a spell from Death's Door.

A rooster crows from a nearby farm.

I can understand horses moving off in a field in the distance.

Chickadees, juncos, sparrows and blue jays break from the trees outside my window in a frenzied, freezing search for sustenance. Blue jays actually call for me to fill their world with sunflower seeds. Small pleasures, indeed.

Down the road, Nelson's cows are munching hay in the barn, priming their own marvelous machinery, swishing and mooing big-boned black and white beasts with an eternity of summer pastures locked in their eyes. (I once saw a cow perform the milk act behind glass to a standing ovation at the Lincoln Park Zoo. Bravo! Bravo!)

As soon as the road is plowed, I've got to go down to Gordie's with my two-gallon jars and get some fresh milk. A strange satisfaction for a city boy on a cold winter's morning in the country: the warmth and smell of a red Wisconsin barn packed to the walls with black and white cows making their contribution to the daily scheme of things. (Jesus, Blei, you've come a long way from Chicago. And you're still a long way from home.)

More specifics. I mentioned some of the scenery, some of the sounds. But it takes a heap of boondock living to become attuned to such things. Back in Berwyn there was the jet stream of O'Hare overhead, doors banging in the many apartments all night long, street traffic, radiators hissing, the nightly stink of the sanitation district, a depth of soot gathering each day on the white window sills, and the occasional drama of a neighbor bouncing his wife off the walls across the gangway. ("Gangway"—what a delightful word. You lose such a vocabulary up here in time.)

Not one sound of a bird. It was all very glorious, and I miss it monstrously in those moments when I long to hear and understand that I am till part of the human condition. Nightmares are necessary too.

Crime, though not nonexistent, is pretty hard to come by in the Chicago style. I can't imagine anyone finding a body in a Door County trunk. There are no sewers to speak of. I can't imagine ever getting mugged while walking down my road, though a stray dog may hold me at bay for a time. I can't conceive of any danger lurking in a downtown district where two stores, a restaurant, a gas station, and a church vie for attention, and "nightlife" is untranslatable. There ain't no sidewalks to walk upon. All strangers are suspect, and everybody knows more about me than I know about myself.

What I mean, I guess, is a fellow breathes a little easier with Chicago gone—except in deer season, or late Saturday nights, early Sunday mornings, when it's best to stay confined to quarters and leave the country roads to the natives who have stayed perhaps a bit too long at the local tap and have been known to reroute the landscape in their search for home.

MORNING REPORT on local radio: "John Doe, 33, ran off of County ZZ last night, bent the old buggy around a tree to avoid hitting a deer."

I tell you, you just have to listen to local radio to be a believer, if you don't think deer are dangerous in these parts—especially on weekends. By God, whole herds of them must line up at the roadsides in the darkness, just waiting to hurl themselves on unsuspecting motorists.

I never saw a deer cross a Chicago street, though I do recall elephants in my time. I remember once witnessing a hit-and-run on those mean streets and experiencing the helplessness of it all.

But I did honest-to-God see four real live deer cross in front of me, in my woods, at dusk last week! And the feeling is something like Eden, snow covered or not. Which, I guess, does say something about where a man finds himself, given the proper conditions.

I won't mention "The Little Church in the Wild Wood," another one of my favorite local radio shows. But you can just imagine the comfort I find in the Daily Death Report as I tune in each morning to be sure they don't mention my name.

More un-Chicago conditioning: I don't ever lock my car or even take the key out of the ignition. (A 1968 Volvo with 148,000 miles ain't going nowhere anyway.) Homes are rarely locked. I trust my neighbors.

It's damn difficult to get away with anything in these parts when everybody's sort of a watchdog committee of one. And damn near impossible to steal away with anything day or night when the landscape, a peninsula, is actually an island, and there is only a bridge (which goes up), and the local sheriff has been known to call upon the services of his friend, the bridge tender, when a dastardly crime has been committed (a pickup truck or a wife, perhaps, mislaid) in another part of the county.

I don't follow Chicago's hit parade these days. Who's the Mayor of Chicago these days, anyway?

Consider this all just a growing bill of particulars, ruminations of a Chicagoan *in absentia*.

So you hear different; you see different; you feel safer, knowing some of the rules of life and death and survival in these parts. But a man begins to act and look different too. I don't know what a Chicagoan looks like, but it's a cinch he doesn't look like me anymore.

There's something very wily about the back-to-earth movement. I came out here with the intention of writing in peace. What the hell did I know or care about the good earth? Pearl Buck aside, the earth, as such, good or bad, never seemed as effective to me as concrete. Concrete made a definite statement upon the landscape: "Here, walk on me, run on me, mar me, stomp me, even break me. I remaineth forever, more or less. I endure."

So does the earth, of course, but in a more mysterious fashion. And one way or another, a man gets lured into it around here. Near Cave Point at night, the mist and the moon off the breakwater become one, like those floating Oriental paintings. The way toward Mud Lake keeps calling one's attention to the natural setting. Or else it's spring mud, summer dust, fall freeze, winter snow and ice—any and all combinations sure to do a man in.

I never promised myself or anybody else a rose garden—or even worse, a vegetable garden. Or still worse, an organic garden. But the poverty of a writer's life in Dairyland has sucked me into it (just as I never expected to go to the source of moo for milk). I don't know where I thought all that produce came from at the Jewel store back in Berwyn, but I sure as hell didn't suspect that a man like me would have to learn to grow it. What did I know about carrots? Or peas, beans, lettuce, cabbage, beets, potatoes, corn, squash, strawberries, raspberries? Some of that stuff you bought in plastic packages, dumped it into boiling water, and ate it in a few minutes with salt and pepper. And even if you weren't nourished, you believed it to be true.

I eat and farm organically now. *Boy* do I feel different! Each new year finds me pouring over seed catalogs from all over the country, nickel and diming my potential spring order to death. "Let's see, this outfit offers a package of bush beans for 39¢, and this other joint for 49¢ (I still talk a little like a Chicagoan), but I think you get more and better beans for 49¢, but what the hell, I'll save a dime and go for the 39-centers, especially since I've conditioned the soil so with cow manure from Gordie's barn, oh so ecologically me, upon the earth." Abundance everywhere.

My problem is not the ozone level in Chicago. My problem is how to keep the bugs from decimating the garden when it is ecologically a sin to resort to chemical killers. In Chicago, I could conceivably resort to a hand-gun. Here, I despair and swear a lot.

But ordering the seeds is nothing like getting the good earth turned over in May (standing knee-deep in gold from Gordie's cows), planting the good seeds into the good earth in June, cultivating the good earth in July, harvesting the good earth in August and September, preparing the good earth for winter (another spring) come October.

Fortunately, I have a good woman to handle much of the good earth when it comes to sowing, reaping, and preserving. Unfortunately, it's only me and a broken down rototiller, "*usted bastardo*," to turn and turn and turn the good earth between mechanical and human breakdowns.

Inevitably, three times a year *usted bastardo* will gasp once and die—spring planting, summer cultivating, fall mulching. Thus the name calling begins: "You bastard!" And at any one of these times I am subject to what I have begun to call my "annual organic hernia," since I must lift the heavy motha of a machine into the trunk of my car, haul it to a mechanic in the next town, and inform him once again, "This SOB will not work." Sometimes I change names for my machine.

I am not a very pleasant person under these countryside occurrences. I have been known to stand in the field and scream the birds out of the sky: "I AM MOVING BACK TO CHICAGO IMMEDIATELY! I HATE MY GODDAM ORGANIC LIFE!"

Once, in Chicago as a child, I raised a sweet potato plant in a jar. After it came to full foliage and began to rot and stink, my mother hurled it into the alley.

Once, in Berwyn, I bought a potted red geranium and watched it flower on the window sill outside the kitchen. I wanted to remember what it was like in Mexico, but the plant stole away one night.

That was the extent of my gardening experience in the City of the Big Shoulders. Yet here in Door County, I have settled in to see my own harvest. I have been known to ravish the good earth, literally pulling plump potatoes from the ground with both hands; ripping globs of sweet onions in ecstasy; snipping beans and peas from the vines with my fingers, swallowing them breathlessly; gorging myself with ripe tomatoes; biting into tough white kohlrabi till my teeth tire.

It's all a very sensuous thing, a garden in the raw. I revert to part animal in the midst of it.

Part Pan I am, having gotten "into it" so far as to plant my own vineyard, place an old bench off to the side of it under a spreading birch tree, and muse over the coming wonders of the grape. "Bacchus," I say, smiling sweetly on my vines. "*In vino veritas.*" (Though I have seen neither the wine nor the truth yet, and am beginning to suspect that Bacchus is bad news this close to the Arctic Circle.)

Still, I hear the music and even succumb to writing bad poetry from the bench:

> Counted cabbages this morning,
> felt their creaky heads.
> Checked my grapevines
> but the color of wine
> still wasn't there.
> Something seems out of place
> up here . . .
> too cold
> too wet
> for tender ambitions in grapes,
> though my trellises trill
> in the wind
> and sometimes
> I sing.

I have been known to transcend myself in such a garden of earthly delights. Just me, Thoreau, and Voltaire. Even so, no man knows my hungers at night, rocking here in the wilderness with visions of Big Macs, Coney Islands, and thick crust pizzas dancing in my head. Sometimes, in my condition, I see Chicago's skyline in the distant woods. Dancing women and neon lights.

The specifies of melancholia Chicago set in.

How do I look these days? Strange, strange. That's one of the last changes to take effect, though Door worked on the dress of the former Chicagoan from the very beginning. Back-to-earth can play havoc with a man's manner of dress—a whole wardrobe goes to seed.

I hardly recognize myself these days.

Once I was a fashion hound. I was taught that it *paid* to look good: you had to look like money to make real money. But now that I no longer make real money, I can afford to look like something the wind blew in. This was my father's favorite expression when I was not dressed sharp enough to suit him in my gentlemanly growing up mannerly days of the Chicago hustle. "Son," he used to say, "you look like something the wind blew in." Then I would put on a white shirt, a tie, and a sharkskin suit. "You have to look neat," he'd say, "to get any place in this world."

Figuring I've been no place since I left Chicago, I'm afraid I've reverted to what my father always suspected. I keep looking like something the wind just blew in, and I can't seem to do a damn thing about it.

A man's got to live his life, and right now, for the time being, this looks like mine and what I'm suited for. "You made your bed, now go lie in it," was another thing somebody else used to say to me. My mother, probably.

Well, the plow just came through, the road is clear, and I'm going to head out for the milk.

Fashions, for me, are old hat. Clothes kind of last forever under these conditions. I put on my same old pair of beat-up work boots, my same old pair of less-than-clean blue jeans, my same old torn flannel shirt, my same old denim jacket with a button missing, and my same old crazy green hat. Just so no one mistakes me for being anybody else.

Just look at what's become of him, I say to myself in the mirror. Just who could that be?

I was going to say something, too, about the sexual energy of a city and the contemplative aspects of a country life, contrasting them. Expound, perhaps, upon the source of power, positive and negative forces for a man of my means in this clime. How it's hard to keep the fires going here. How desire dwindles in the absence of temptation. How that is no way for a man to live . . . or die. How, in the stark absence of Michigan Avenue lovelies, even cows begin to look good to me at times. But no. Not now. That just might make me cry. Though there's still a touch of the old Chicago about me, mainly around those shifty eyes.

I was going to say something about distance and home. How no place is ever the answer.

I was going to say something about the Japanese word *yugen* for which there is no English equivalent. "To watch the sun sink behind a flower-clad hill, to wander on and on in a huge forest without thought of return, to stand upon the shore and gaze after a boat that disappears behind distant islands, to contemplate the flight of wild geese seen and lost among the clouds" means *yugen*.

To walk in the warmth of a barn of cows this clear morning, fill two-gallon jars with fresh milk, realize that home and being away are one.

And I am here.

Going to Gordy's for Milk

> I punch delicate holes in it, in my steps in the dark, moving now toward neighbor Gordy Nelson's barn where the cows, in their straw-smelling animal warmth, dream green pastures in such obsidian eyes. I fill two one-gallon glass jars with sweet milk, extinguishing the light, feel the darkness of the barn move with the swaying cows, and whisper-walk through the glass-white world once more, a gallon of milk gripped in each hand, hanging from me like lanterns of cold winter light.
>
> —journal entry

March, 1991. He's standing on the wide front porch of the farm where he was born, looking over a chair he's thinking of caning. Thinking about a lot of things he'll have more time for now—redoing old furniture, turning the old pig shed into a workshop, maybe raising some chickens. It's a typical "first-day-of-spring" day in Door—a little sun, a little gray sky, a little cold, a little snow in the air and still on the ground—but the fields around him, still far from green, seem noticeably more empty than I've ever seen them before. Gordy Nelson, fifty-three, of Ellison Bay/Newport—friend, neighbor, and dairy farmer—has sold his cows. There'll be no more marking off "milk days" on the kitchen calendar for me. There'll be no more "going to Gordy's for milk." That will be a sad loss for me and his other customers. But for Gordy it comes as sort of a relief.

Scarcely a week into his new life, he even looks different. Gone are the barn clothes and the cap. He is neatly dressed, already the air of the "gentleman farmer" about him, though he still buries the burnt bowl of his old corned cob pipe deep in the palm of his hand. We sit at the kitchen table now where his wife Donna fills our coffee mugs and tempts me with a plateful of homemade cookies. "Yeah, it sure is quiet in the barn," he says, smiling that shy boyish smile of his. Gordy always appeared like a grown-up Huckleberry Finn—not the hellish ways of Huck, so much as a very natural person, peacefully in place. The fields are his river of adventure and meaning. The tractor is his raft.

"My refrigerator went into a state of shock," says Donna, standing by the door of the fridge, holding up one of those ugly store-bought plastic gallon jugs of milk that look and taste like cloudy water. Homogenized,

2%, 1% . . . blue milk I call it. Not the rich, sweet-tasting raw milk of Gordy's cows, which I already miss. And the thick cream on the top of my sparkling glass gallon jugs, which lie empty now, already gathering dust on my back porch. What's a man to do for Gordy's cream come red raspberry time? I don't want to think about it.

"I was born in this house," he says. "The same spread. It's been in the Nelson family . . . oh, my dad moved here when he was a year old, 1895. He grew up here, went to Chicago where he was a milkman for a few years, then decided to go sailing—saltwater. He made eleven trips to China. He was a chief engineer. About 1922 he decided to come back to the farm. He was lying idle in Seattle. The longshoremen were on strike. He just decided to come back. I started milking cows when I was six years old, 1933, the year my grandparents died.

"It was milk by hand, not machine. We always had to do chores, six o'clock, before we went to school in the morning. I went to Newport school [Uncle Tom's new alma mater] at nine in the morning. It was a two-room school when I was there. After school we had to clean the barn, milk the cows . . . by 7:30, time for *The Lone Ranger*. We had Guernseys then, nine of them, red and white.

"When the barn was built [1928] it was built for twelve cows and three horses. Twelve was a good sized herd at that time. By the late '30s, 1940's, we began expanding. By 1941 we had almost twenty cows, still milking by hand. In 1942 we went to the milk machine. I was all excited. I remember the machine was delivered here on my mother's birthday. We had a party at the same time—after we got through with the milking. There were plenty of spectators in the barn.

"It was a double unit. It cut our labor force down from four to two. To me, it was a great invention. We did have problems, because we didn't know how to care for the machine at first. Milking a cow by hand took from five to ten minutes. A machine could cut that in half when you had an easy milker."

Machinery has always been one of Gordy's loves. "That was my main interest on the farm . . . running it, repairing it. I always liked tractors and all the farm equipment. The cattle were just an income."

"He always bought machinery in parts," adds Donna, "and assembled it."

"That's because it was cheaper that way," smiles Gordy, "and when it broke down, I'd know how to fix it."

"For three days he'd be reading the instruction books, and he'd block me out," says Donna. In the 1940's, with the milking machine and a larger herd of cows, the Nelson dairy farm began to take shape. "We got our first tractor in 1942. We were working with three horses before that. When we got the tractor, we still had to have horses because all our machinery was geared to that, planting corn, raking hay. The tractor was for plowing, harrowing, cultivating. Horses were just much more practical for them other jobs."

Gordy graduated from the tenth grade in Ellison Bay and entered the Air Force in 1946, finishing his last two years of high school while in the service. "When I got out in 1947, I went in company with my dad, a farm partnership. But in 1955 I went to Oshkosh [University] for a year and a half. That's where I met Donna. I was in secondary education, thinking I might teach. My two brothers are both teachers, but I really wasn't a studious person. That's when I bought the farm, the first of January, 1957."

Any regrets he did not complete college? "Sometimes. During the course of farming I felt there would be a lot easier ways of making a living. I got married around this same time, 1957."

As for some particulars of a dairy farm: "Oh, a hundred-acre farm of average land takes care of twenty-five cows. You need about sixty acres of hay land, twenty acres of pasture, twenty acres of grain, usually corn, but here it's been oats. I haven't raised corn for over twenty years. I just didn't have the equipment." Cows were "a gradual switch. When artificial breeding took over, 1947, we started breeding Holsteins. A Holstein is a hardier cow than the Guernsey, and it has better resale when you're culling them, if you're selling them for meal. Their calves are a little larger. You get more for the calves. The Guernsey would have a higher butterfat test in their milk, but there is more volume in a Holstein. I gradually worked up to a herd of thirty cows plus young stock."

One thinks in terms of a seasonal time clock to rural life, but for Gordy time mostly divided into two times each day: when a man was milking and when he wasn't. "We had our cows freshening all year around, so our flow of milk was pretty much the same all year around. In the summer and fall the cows are out all the time except for milking. The end of May, the first of June, when they get all the green grass, you do get a more grassy flavor to the milk. In winter they're pretty much in the barn all the time, out an hour a day for exercise. If they've adjusted to the cold, they can take twenty below—if that's their environment, if that's the way they been kept."

Through the '50s, '60s, '70s Gordy spent "almost twenty-five years a dairy farmer. Since I owned it, we just changed equipment. We put in a barn cleaner in 1958. We went from bulk milk to pipeline in 1973. Timewise, I couldn't say the pipe line saved too much time as far as milking. It's in the automatic cleaning where we saved. It works like a dishwasher."

As Gordy is concerned, the tough times in dairy farming came with the calving. "Calving problems? Sometimes you can work a long time to get a calf out, any time of the day or night. One time in the fall of the year I had the cows way south. When they came in, I noticed one was missing. I went out to look for her, and here she had the calf half delivered. I had to use tackle blocks to get her out. The cow, of course, was paralyzed. I went out there with a tractor loader to lift her up, change her position every so often. It took twenty-one days and she came home by herself. It was a pinched nerve in the hip.

"Another time, a couple of years ago, there was a cow heavy with calf. She was on her back, choking. I helped her that time, but a couple of days later I came out there, and she was dead."

What do you do with a dead cow? "A 1,200-pound cow is kind of hard to move. Before LaViolette [who picks up dead animals] we used to just drag them to the woods. The fox and the wild animals would take care of them. They'd be gone in a short time. Just a pile of bones left."

A dairy farmering day for Gordy was "up at six. Get the milking done for the truck to pick it up at 7:45. Then breakfast. Leave the cows out for their exercise. Clean the barn. Maybe some repairs around the barn you could do while the animals were out. Feed them. About noon I'd be through with the   morning chores. Lunch, and a little relaxing. Errands. I still went with the old grain sacks to the feed mill. Cut wood. About four o'clock you start thinking about the evening chores. Feed the animals again. Around 5, 5:30, you start milking again. Milking done about 6:30. Then supper. About eight o'clock, I'd check the animals again before I retired for the night. That last check would run anywhere from eight o'clock to midnight."

All of this may sound fairly routine, a fairly full day and night . . . and then you multiply that times seven days a week, and then you multiply that times twenty-five years. And then you begin to see why maybe a dairy farmer figures it's time to put his cows up for sale. It wasn't Carter or Reagan or inflation or milk price supports, or anything as simple as that. It was simply, "I just didn't want to be tied down anymore, seven days a week. That's it. If it was a five-day week I'd stay in it. There are just a lot of things you'd like to do, and you just don't find the time. When you do have an hour or two, you're too tired to do other things. I thought about this for the last two years."

"And last Easter," explains Donna, "he said, 'I'm going to go to sunrise service with you next year."

"You miss a lot of things," Gordy muses, "especially around six o'clock. Christmas. Potluck suppers. . . ."

"Our daughter's graduation," Donna adds. "We got there too late to get a seat to hear her deliver the salutatorian speech."

"If we went to town, Sturgeon Bay, and if it got around four in the afternoon, I'd start getting antsy," says Gordy. "People ask me if we're going to take a trip. Donna says she wants to go to Kewaunee—she's never been there." He laughs.

The loss of one dairy farm on the north end of the county may be no big thing to the Wisconsin dairy industry as a whole, yet it's one more indication of the county going through a change. I personally hate to see any of the rural go, while developers and condo-builders lie in wait in the woods, smacking their lips. I'd just as soon turn the whole damn place back to pasture and cows.

With Gordy giving up the cows, only two dairy farmers are left north of Ellison Bay: John Fitzgerald and Doug Sedig. In 1953 there were over forty members in the Lake to Lake Dairy Cooperative in Liberty Grove alone. "There are just thirteen members left now. Without me, twelve."

As for Gordy's future—"just crop farming. The farm will still be here. And the equipment is here. I try to talk Jim [the oldest son] into a line of agriculture other than milking, but he's interested mostly in milking cows. The farm isn't big enough to support us both, and I'm too young to leave it yet. I had thoughts about maybe going back to ten or fifteen cows, but I'd still be tied down to seven days a week. I've got to quit it entirely, to find out how other people live, to finally watch the six o'clock news."

Walking into the emptiness of the barn evokes more milk memories for me. It takes me back to my grandmother's farm in Michigan, where she sat on a stool, her tired old head resting in the big-bodied comfort of the cow, Flora, and aimed a warm stream of milk in my face. Where she sat me down beside her, my childish hands in hers, teaching me the marvelous soft machinery of a milking cow. And grandma working the miracle of milk into butter, whipping cream, sourmilk pancakes, and the taste of freshly picked blueberries in a chipped china bowl swimming in the thickest cream. Chicago milk was nothing special, though it too once came delivered to the door in a beautiful one-quart glass bottle with a thick neck of cream. Milk these days seems bluer and more tasteless. The processers seem determined to take the life out of everything, labeling it "non-" this or non-" that, telling us how much better off we are, now that we've lost our taste. A sad diminishment of the senses.

I shall miss those trips to Gordy's barn in all seasons, all kinds of weather, all times of the day and night. Going for milk was not an inconvenience; it was a pleasure. I shall miss the radio music that seemed to serenade his cows. The red weathered barn, the frosted windows in winter, turning the cold metal latch, the noise and smell of the cows with the mournful look in their huge liquid eyes, the straw, the hay, the newborn calves in the pen, the nameless, numberless barn cats-and their endless kittens. And the milk, of course. The stainless steel cooler that held a real treasure: the richness of fresh, sweet-tasting milk that gushed forth into pails and glass gallon jugs. And Gordy's home-style cash register: a beat-up, faded old Velvet pipe tobacco tin that almost always held just the right change.

Cows. How close to liking them can a man get? "Some were more likable than others . . . their disposition, more of a pet. I had one heifer, if I just called, it would come to me, want to be scratched. Then there'd be others that would have nothing to do with me. It's just myself. I never got attached to the animals like some farmers do."

Gordy describes "The Day the Cows Disappeared" (March 13, 1991) with a slight grin. "The day we shipped all our cows, there were five strangers in the barn and the cows were so nervous they got the diarrhea. It got so slippery you couldn't stand up. Cows spread-eagled. It was a regular rodeo."

"People come up to me and say, 'Didn't you cry after they left?' No. I felt pretty good. . . .

"But it was kind of lonesome to come out here the first time. It sure is silent."

Dar: The Woman Alone

She lives her seasons in an old frame white house perched upon a hill overlooking the highway and fields. The house is always getting away from her: the paint has begun to peel once again, the windows need fixing, the pipes are frozen again come winter, a family of skunks has taken up residence in the crawl space below, the wind has gotten hold of the storm door and broken the glass, the car, over 100,000 miles on it, won't start at ten below or above, cutworms have decimated the garden, the upstairs is cold for the kids all winter, there's not enough hot water left for the last kid to take a shower, the septic system isn't working, wood must be cut for the living room stove, bales of straw must be packed all around the foundation for winter. Someone on the phone wants her to attend the next school board meeting to continue her fight against centralization, someone else wants to know if she will have time to clean a cottage by Saturday, others continually seek her advice on child rearing, marriage, divorce, emotional problems, men, husbands, lovers, illness, recipes, and how to tune a guitar . . . demands, demands, demands on this woman's time. Everything, everybody seems to need some of Darlene Cooper's attention.

Inside the house there are clothes to be washed, six loaves of bread to be baked, four kids to be loved, listened to, taken care of. Someone has to get the milk, someone has to go to the store, someone should see if they can find Gust Klenke to look at the pump. It's acting up again.

"I need an electrician!" she seems to cry out at times. "I need a plumber; I need a mechanic; I need someone to clean the chimney . . . I need, I need, I need. The hell with it. I can't afford it. I'll do it myself."

The house is constantly alive with kids, animals, visitors, friends and strangers. The round wooden table in the kitchen, made especially for her by Ernie Anderson, is the very center of her world. Food is prepared and eaten there, gallons of tea are consumed there, messages and notes of all sorts are exchanged there, homework is done (from the youngest kid to Dar herself presently taking a correspondence course in English from the University of Wisconsin), books read, letters written, jokes, problems, confessions, idle conversations exchanged across it. A weary head, bent down and nestled in arms, can sometimes be seen asleep upon it.

I recall dropping by one time with a friend from the city, introducing him to Dar while she handled three boiling pots on the stove, put up jars of tomatoes, braided huge yellow onions to dry, settled an argument between two of her children, all the while anxiously maintaining the conversation among us, trading stories and good feelings. She talked loud and laughed hard. She wore her usual bib overalls and a turtleneck shirt. Her long hair hung freely over her shoulders. She was loose, she was open, she was fun. She was as good a listener as a talker. She said exactly what she thought and used the kind of language that comes naturally to most men, and lately to some women.

"Moses, move your ass," she said to the dog, lying near the table. "Give these guys some room to sit down."

Later I heard my friend Ralph Rausch say to his wife, "I just met Mother Earth." I had to smile to myself because she always seemed that way to me in the bearing and raising and loving of her children, in her desperate attempts at times to wrest enough food for her family, in her crazy quilt manners of earning a living by whatever form of menial labor was to be found.

She's the Walton Family minus the husband, the grandfolks, and the saccharine religion. "Family" (herself and four kids) is her faith, her way of continually finding and keeping herself together.

She's a woman who has gone through a total transformation, from a Chicago suburban housewife and mother (married to a druggist) and living a comfortable life, to a divorced woman, burdened to the breaking point at times, who has sacrificed damn near everything yet somehow gained herself in this environment. An environment she sort of suddenly found herself in one day because she was . . .

"Running . . . running away . . . running away from ticky-tacky suburbia, a place I didn't fit into . . . running from a bad marriage. No, I wasn't divorced at the time. I came up here on a trial separation. I came up here in June, 1970, and I lived on money I was going to spend on contact lenses. I always refer to my summer up here as my contact lenses that I never did get.

"I moved four times that summer. I had to move because I could never get a rental long enough. I was in Gills Rock. I moved from pillar to post in Gills Rock with all the kids. Why Door County? Well, I had been here on a vacation before. Chicago? I would never have stayed. I'm not a city person. It had to be some place more like a vacation, because this is what it started out as. I needed a break, and we thought maybe if I got off by myself it might help. I had been here before with my husband and the kids. I came up here in May with Terrie [the oldest daughter] and kind of looked things over and made a rental for myself. I had been married ten years at that point . . . married at eighteen. Amy, the youngest, was four. Terrie was nine.

"In the summer it was fine, because I still had the option to go back. So I really didn't think about it except as a vacation. We spent every day at the beach, and it was a beautiful summer. It was the last beautiful summer I had up here.

"I worked on Saturdays. I was doing cleaning for Wilson-Shaffer, and it brought in just enough money so that, with what I had already, we managed to buy groceries. But we didn't eat very well. We ate a lot of macaroni and cheese.

"No, I was not really trained to do anything else. Oh, I could type. I used to be a switchboard operator, a typist, after I got out of high school. But there isn't too much call for that up here."

And marriage, of course, was supposed to answer all her problems?

"Oh, it did. It did for all the girls in the fifties. Of course, of course, that was the answer!"

That first summer in Door was almost a fantasy, the perfect place to be. But the real world out there, the life back in suburbia — when did that enter into the picture again?

"Well, when my husband wrote and said [Dar breaking into sudden laughter], 'You're going to have to shit or get off the pot. You make up your mind what you're going to do, because I am not hanging loose anymore.' That was in August. And I thought about it all of about ten minutes. I was still renting up in Gills Rock. I thought about it. I thought, 'Can I go back? Can I start over again? Is that marriage worth working on?' We had already been going to a marriage counselor for about nine months previous to this. And I thought about it really hard, and I knew I couldn't go back and start over again. I probably could have gone back and started over in another way, but I couldn't go back and start over in a marriage. I just had to find out who I was. I had completely lost my identity in the marriage.

"And the months up here started me realizing that I did have the where-withal to take care of myself. I *was* a lot smarter than my husband thought I was. And I *could* do it, and it was a good feeling. So I said no. I'm not coming back. I had to go back to pack things up, and I turned around and came back up here and rented a house in Fish Creek just before school started.

"Once I made the decision, I was scared shitless. But one of my big, big points is stubbornness. And I would not say I can't do it on my own. I thought, 'Goddamn it, I'm gonna do it! '

"I rented that house in Fish Creek for nine months, late August till June. And that whole time I really had the option to go back. Well, not the whole time really, because in February, my ex decided to sell the house. And he wrote and said, 'Do you want to come back with the kids, and you can have the house? I'm moving out of it. I'm sick of it.' By that time he was sick of suburbia and all that crap. And he had found another woman anyhow. I thought about that for a while, and I thought, no, I've established a little bit of life for myself up here. I've found some independence. If I go back, I'll step right into all the family bullshit. You know, everybody's gonna mean well and help you to death. I had to be on my own. I had to do it myself.

"Oh, sure, my reason for leaving was more than my dislike of suburbia. It was my own lack of identity in the fact that I had completely lost myself in a marriage. I didn't even know where or who I was.

"And it was my ex. One time he screamed at me, in the fall previous to the summer I came up here. He said—and I think he's regretted his words ever since—'You can't be happy! You can't be happy in this life! You just do the same thing day after day, taking care of the kids, taking care of the house, being the model mother, being the model wife! What the hell . . . how can you be happy?'

"He's the one that brought it up. It really is weird. But you know, he was right. He had to kick me in the ass before I started to wake up and say, 'Hey, for ten years I have been living in a little suburban dream, the good wife role.' I was nothing, *nothing*! Oh, yeah, I was a good mother. I always was that. He wanted a wife, and he didn't have one. I'll admit that right now. He didn't have a wife. Oh, I don't know . . . he had a mannequin. I didn't love him. I don't think I loved him when I married him. In fact, I remember thinking when I was pregnant with Terrie, 'God, I've made the biggest mistake in my life! But I'm afraid to leave him now I'm going to have a baby.' So I waited until I had *four*, and then I left him! Sure . . . sure."

Her feelings pour forth very sincerely, with great strength, in a very matter-of-fact way. There is no remorse. There are no tears. It's just the way it is, what happened to her, what she's discovered in the way she's lived her life up till now. "I knew my ex and I never fit together. We're better friends now than we ever were before, because we don't threaten one another now, but I still don't agree with him in an awful lot of things. He's still very dictatorial, which just drives me nuts. He has absolutes. There is never shades with him."

For any woman making the final decision to go it alone, one wonders, in the case of Dar, a mother of four, no formal training for any kind of financial survival, just what it was it, what it is, that makes a woman like her so sure she can survive?

"Will power . . . and I knew he would continue sending child support money. I knew he was responsible and reliable in that sense. I knew I didn't have anything to worry about there. And the first winter that I lived with the kids in Fish Creek, truthfully, we lived just about strictly on that child support. I worked the fall at a motel doing motel work seven days a week. For three months I worked there.

"Our friends could have been knocked over with a feather when we separated. We looked like the perfect couple. We really put on the best front. We really did. The divorce was official in 1971, and he remarried that same year, if I'm not mistaken. My feelings about that? Relief in a way. Because he had tried before the divorce was final—oh, maybe even before the house was sold—to get me to reconsider. And by that time I really knew I was right. We didn't belong together. I was much better on my own. I don't know how he was. I'm sure I was being very selfish. He was probably going through a world of shit. In fact, I've been told that by my friends that he really was. He was very hurt. It was an ego thing."

The first year up here alone? Adjustments for the kids? How does a young, divorced mother handle all that?

"For me it was a hassle. I cried an awful lot that first year, and I'm not a crier by nature. I was scared, and I was lonesome, and I knew nobody up here. That took time. The Weborgs . . . yes. Wallace helped me a lot. He let me lean on him once in a while. I'm not a leaner either, so I didn't do it too much. Practical help he gave me. I rented from the Weborgs that first summer in Gills Rock, that's how I got to know Wallace. He advised me on things I didn't know about.

"N, the artist from Fish Creek . . . he wasn't all bad for me. He helped me grow up. He gave me another kick in the ass. I had lots of growing up to do when I came up here. I have no, idea what happened to him. He was an interesting person. He made me think about who I was and what I was. He taught me a lot of cultural things. He had me listening to classical music. Yes, he just made me think. He introduced me to some deep ideas. He was too old for me, though. Too dictatorial. He was fifty and I was twenty-eight. Maybe the age difference wouldn't have meant anything if I really fell for him, but I didn't."

A question, once again, of geography. Why this part of the world for a woman to find herself alone? There is a small but growing number of women, coming out of bad marriages, coming out of urban areas, and settling, starting again here, in Door County. What did she see here?

"Oh, I was just drinking in the beauty of the area. It really was a balm to me. I would go to the water, and I just realized last night that that water was such a comfort to me. I would go down by the shore, and I went there for comfort. Just listening to that water, watching it, watching the clouds somehow soothed me. And I needed that again last night. I found that out. And I remembered all I had forgotten about that. Last night I was in need of it too."

With money from the sale of the house back in suburbia, Dar was able to buy the home she presently lives in. "By the winter of '71 I had moved to the house up north in Ellison Bay, which I had bought in June. By that time I had made up my mind to stay up here and try to make a go of it, as long as I had got my foot part way in and made a little adjustment for myself and the kids. It was worth it for me to try to do it the rest of the way. And I really loved the area. I always have and always will."

Aside from the psychological adjustment outsiders from urban areas must constantly face upon moving into a rural area such as Door, the real facts of life are measured in dollars and cents. Unless you have an angle on the tourist trade, like owning a business, it's a very delicate survival for anyone without assets, and even more so for a woman alone.

"The first winter we were up here we lived on $4,000 a year, counting everything . . . $4,200 exactly. One adult and four kids. My ex was making sixteen or eighteen thousand a year when I left. I could hardly afford hamburger after that. We did a lot of scrounging. I mean a lot of people gave us deer meat and things like that, and I took whatever anybody gave me. We had moose meat one time."

Did she sometimes question the excessive generosity on the part of some people . . . men, in particular?

Dar bursts into laughter: "Ulterior motives . . . sure . . . there was a lot of that, a lot of that. But I didn't worry about their ulterior motives. I just took the meat. I didn't care. And no, I can't say anybody's ever pitied me because I came off as being too capable. Even when I was scared shitless, I was fine. I mean I *looked* fine anyhow."

For a woman alone, was there the companionship up here of other women, perhaps other divorced women?

"I didn't know of one. I didn't know one. Other women here approached me only to go to the Bible class, which I declined politely. Several of them tried to convince me many times. I found myself in an odd position. I was a threat to a lot of the women. I was aware of that immediately. When they grabbed their husband's arm when I walked by, I knew that.

"I took the kids to the Moravian Church in Ephraim, to Sunday School, the first fall we were here simply because I worked on Sundays at the Village Green Motel, and it was convenient for me to have some place to leave them. They had been going to church all along in suburbia. I'm sure it didn't do them any harm. I've never felt that way about church. In fact, I've felt with the kids, if they want to go, they can go. Nobody's ever expressed a desire to go. I taught Sunday School for fourteen years back home, so I've been the whole route."

The whole route includes her present status: no longer a member of any church. That too she seemed to shed once she established herself here. "Why? If I said 'growing up,' everybody'll jump into my shit, but I really feel that was it. I suddenly realized just how hypocritical it all was. No, I never questioned it back there. I never questioned anything! I never questioned a thing till I got off on my own . . . nothing, nothing, nothing. I'm embarrassed when I think of it.

"I think my friend, the artist in Fish Creek, probably was instrumental in this. He was an out-an-out atheist. I still don't consider myself an atheist. I'd say agnostic, if I was going to put a name on myself.

"So, for the most part, I'd say most people ignored me. Some were trying to help. I mean Wallace was truly trying to be good to me."

The details of survival on an everyday basis: "We had no telephone. No television. There were times when I didn't have enough money to put gas in the car, and I hitchhiked back and forth to town, to Sister Bay to do the laundry at the Laundromat. I had to call my ex that winter long distance and say, 'The kids have got to have snowsuits. They don't have the proper clothes for up here. Please let me charge it to your charge account, and I'll pay you back.' And I did. I paid him back. My own left foot got frostbitten that winter because I didn't have the right boots, but I wasn't about to ask him to let me charge my boots to his account. That would be like salt on the wound. So I didn't. I frostbit my left foot instead, and I've suffered with it ever since.

"I didn't know how I was going to survive in the way of a job, but I've always been very confident in myself, in my ability. I'm a survivor. I'm definitely a survivor. I know that I can make it no matter what I do. I just know it because I'm determined. I never thought of what I would do. I just lived from day to day. I knew I was very limited.

"I did cleaning that first year. Then I took on the job at the bowling alley [Sister Bay Bowl] the fall of '71. I cleaned there. I bartended a little bit in the morning . . . cleaning the kitchen, the bar, the johns, the bowling alley, the restaurant. It was a big job. It was a half day, six days a week, and I got $30 a week for that. But Earl was good to me. He really was. He was very nice to me. He was good to the kids. Then after that, the next year, I waitressed. I waitressed at the bowling alley for a year, and then I waitressed at Clayton's for a year."

Dar, too, found that the quality of employment around here leaves much to be desired. Jobs for a woman alone? "Ha! None. You know, just Mickey Mouse jobs. Nothing. Clerking, or working in a gift shop. $2-an-hour jobs. There isn't even much as far as typing and that sort of thing . . . office work. The Door *Reminder* is the only one that uses people like that. Waitressing is probably the most lucrative, and then you can collect unemployment in the winter. I couldn't say just what you could make a week by waitressing. But I figured out one time at Clayton's I was making about $5 an hour, figuring on your pay plus your tips. You averaged it out and it came out to about $5 an hour. And you're never going to make any more than that around here. Once, one night I made $55. Once. An average night, the busy season, was about $30, $35 maybe. You went in at four p.m. and worked until you were done. Maybe eleven o'clock, maybe midnight. It depended upon whether you got a late table and you were stuck.

"It's worse now with inflation. Prices have increased so much, people are going to cut somewhere, and that's where they cut: the tip. So I understand from girls that they're hurting even more now than they used to be and they're working just as hard. Waitressing is damn hard work. You take a lot of bullshit from people.

"I got out of it for that reason. I can't handle the bullshit. That's not my nature. I would come home so burned out that I couldn't sleep at night. My stomach would just be in a knot, I was so upset. And I'd think, you know, 'Why? Why are people so shitty? Why do they go out to eat if they're in a bad mood? Why don't they stay home and look in the mirror!' Yeah, sure, they take it out on you. They like to lord it over you. They have the money to go out and eat, and you go to wait on them and have to put up with their shit."

One has to wonder if a woman alone isn't better off in the city. Certainly the financial aspect of survival would be in one's favor in the urban areas.

"I really think, probably, I have a better chance of controlling my lifestyle here than in the city. I've thought about going back, and I've thought, 'Well, wages would be higher. There would be more job opportunities.' But then I thought the kids would be running loose, and I wouldn't have the control over them that I have here. And I would have to get back into the kind of lifestyle that I really don't like. But when the well went dry, I almost did give up."

Her income now is still derived from cleaning houses and cottages. It's still, primarily summer (tourist season) employment, with a handful of customers requiring her services on a full-year basis. The service, however, she has slowly developed into a small business of her own, employing one or two high school girls to help her during the height of the season (one of the girls being her daughter, Terrie). Does she see classes of people here, especially as she may run across this in her work?

"I never think about it that way. Oh, there are the very wealthy. Yeah, there's a definite class of wealthy people who hire others I guess. But I work for some people who definitely don't fall into that class — people like me who are working and would rather pay for somebody else to do their house than to try and hassle that thing out along with their jobs. I've met some really neat people, and a few asses. But some really neat people, both wealthy and non-wealthy."

She continues to be hounded by the cost of living. "As inflation increased, I had to work more, and harder, and it got to be a real drag. I am constantly struggling to keep my head above water. I haven't been making much headway, just managing to stay above."

And through it all, she continued to pursue some form of self-education, beginning, in the early '70s, with just the pure joy of reading, via correspondence. "I did a lot of reading when I first came up. I always have. I don't mean novels. I mean delving into psychology and that, finding out what makes me tick. No, I didn't do this in Chicago. It came here, in a growing awareness of myself, awareness of the fact that I had a lot more potential than I was using or had ever used. Oh, I was reading Fromm, Ashley Montagu . . . I can't even think of them all. There was a year I went through I read a lot of religious things. For the most part, I was on my own. I just went to the library and started looking through the sections to see what I like. I like novels. I always have. But I like to read something that tells me a little bit more about myself, or about human nature."

The "back-to-the-land" movement of the late '60s and '70s is in evidence even in so touristy an area such as Door County. The movement continues to grow to this day, though the increase in land values has held the "back to nature" people somewhat in check. Did she see herself becoming more and more involved with the Mother Earth image?

"Yeah. Definitely, definitely. The interest in nutrition that I got from Bea [Bea Lapp, a friend], because she was taking classes in college and she would come home and share all that. I had never become interested in that back in Chicago. Adelle Davis . . . that was up here. I began baking my own bread, growing and eating natural foods. Economics started playing a role too. Definitely it made a big difference living this way."

Other friends who began influencing her lifestyle? "Ernie [Anderson] came first, even before Bea. He introduced me to Bea. Yeah, I guess he may have introduced me to this lifestyle, but not nutrition and that. I'm the one who taught him about that. But he was definitely into a much more rural lifestyle. And Steve Kastner [owner of Omnibus] influenced me a little bit when I lived back in Fish Creek and got to know him. I was interested in what was going on in his head, and we talked a lot. He was interested pretty much in a natural lifestyle."

She reduces the social opportunities of a divorced woman in Door to two areas: "either the church or the bar, neither of which appeals to me. So I stay home. Oh, I went to the bars a couple of times. A lot of lonesome people there . . . no interests other than hanging around bars, no depth to them. But there really isn't anything else. And again, it's not my thing. I have no positive feelings about those places whatsoever. Anything that's said in a bar is horseshit, not the truth for the most part."

The dangers and frustrations of a woman alone in a rural area are real, though they may appear less visible. "It's easy to get into some really sticky situations," she claims. "You're lonely, you only want somebody to talk to, and you end up with somebody wanting to climb into bed with you, and that's not really what you had in mind in the first place.

"Also, people 'worry' a lot about me," she laughs. On more than one occasion her house, the car or cars parked there, her total living and being habits have been the object of a concerned kind of surveillance by some of the local ministers, and a few natives as well.

"Their lives must be so goddam boring that they worry about mine. A car is parked overnight: 'Oh, I see you had company last night!' It's unbelievable, the entanglements that you don't want to get into. But it's no different than anywhere else, except that in a small area, somebody's always looking over your shoulder. Things are misunderstood a lot. And there is always the negative interpretation put on something.

"I've never had too much trouble with telephone calls [obscene callers or the heavy breathers], and when I did, I knew who it was and I was able to say, 'Hey, bug off. Quit it or I'll tell your wife!' "

As far as the local community tolerating her lifestyle: "Through living with someone for a few years—Jesus, has it been five or six—I can say I've been accepted. Probably because of the kids more than anything. I really do think that makes a difference, that I have centered my attention on my family rather than running around.

"Oh, I've had static from a few ministers. I had a few very funny conversations with some of them who were going to save me. And one very *loud* argument. The rest were just discussions. Only that one was an out-and-out argument.

"They just wanted me to come to church and send my kids to Sunday School. They are good kids. I leave it up to them. My kids did go when Virginia [Olsen] was there [Trinity Lutheran Church, Ellison Bay]. They liked her. She's a good person. In some sense, my own standards for kids are a lot stricter than any the church could set up. I remember being so bummed out by some Baptist Sunday School propaganda—a picture of a kid flying a paper airplane, and the caption: 'God Does Not Love Children Who Misbehave Like This.' That was one time I pulled Amy out of Sunday School. That was horrible."

Her one loud argument with a local minister involved a common disagreement: "He argued about all the good Christians had done in this world, and I pointed out all the wars that were caused by religion, all the horrible things that were done in the name of Christianity, all the good people who go to church on Sunday and do just the opposite all week.

" 'What about your children?' he said. 'What kind of people are they going to grow up to be?' I told him I would hold my kids up to anyone of his Sunday School kids, any day. He huffed out of the house. It's one of the few times I ever got really loud."

And as for living with someone as opposed to marriage, "You've got all the disadvantages of marriage and none of the advantages. That's the negative. But then, at least there's somebody to teach the boys to do all the things that boys are supposed to do: use tools, something mothers aren't supposed to know. It's hard to relate to a boy when you've never been anything but a woman yourself. I think women are cautious, careful about things they do.

"The problems in just handling a house by yourself . . . Christ, I've learned to do things here I never thought I'd do, never even wanted to know about them: pipes that freeze, crawling under the house in winter and wrapping all the pipes after the plumber has thawed them, insulating the crawl space . . . all the goddarn things that go wrong and you never wanted to fix but you have to because you can't afford to have anyone do it for you. It seems to me that it's one nightmare after another: cars falling apart that I've tried to fix with bubble gum and Scotch tape. I took a course in auto mechanics at the high school just to keep an old car running. Lawn mowers that don't work, furnaces that poop out at five in the morning, pipes that flow in the wrong direction. Jesus!

"Gust [Klenke, fix-it man, friend, keeper of the honey bee] has helped me with all of it. He's the only honest-to-God Christian that I know. He's the best guy I've ever met. No, you can never pay him back. You never seem to. So you pay him back with some homemade bread, some apple butter, or some date bars—his favorite.

"A few months ago the well went. Oh, that was a bitch. And Gust came to help me with that too. But I had to have a new well dug. It cost me $3,000. Everything I netted in the previous year, cleaning houses and cottages, everything went into that goddam well—which put me all the way back to where I was eight years ago when I first moved up here. A financial disaster that almost sent me back to Chicago. I really thought seriously about it."

When you're feeding a family of four kids, gardening becomes a necessity rather than a hobby. And somehow, in the midst of all the other work, come spring, concentration on the garden becomes uppermost.

"It's very important, the garden. I use everything I can . . . I put up a hundred quarts of tomatoes, a hundred quarts of apple sauce. I freeze as much as we can get out of the garden as well as scrounge from anyone else.

"We eat lots of brown rice, lots of ground beef. We have never had a steak. We have chicken maybe twice a year because it's too expensive. We eat lots of casseroles. And I keep after the nutrition. I usually bake six loaves of bread every week instead of eating that store-bought crap. I belong to the food co-op and get a lot of whole food that way and save a lot of money. You put some work in it, but it's worth it."

As for raising kids single-handedly, "I think they've turned out real well myself. They did better here than they might have back there. They've learned that a family has to pull together. I believe very strongly in family. They've learned that the world doesn't owe them a living. You have to go out and work for it. And they're all working. They've learned their mother is a very human person who has to lean on them sometimes. That's reality.

"Terrie is the oldest. She's become a whole different person since she left for Australia [an AFS student from the local high school]. She seems to have matured, a sense of what she's like inside. She could never express herself before, openly with me, tell me she loves me. God, I hope she keeps it! It took me twenty-eight years to get where she is today. She's my dependable one. I can rely on her.

"David . . . selfish, perhaps, but really a neat kid. A beautiful sense of humor, beautiful wit. Dale is serene. That's what I like about Dale. We communicate without even words. We think alike, feel alike.

"Amy is absolutely unshakable. She's the kind of kid who could take the world by the tail. Anything in stride, new experiences. She's not the least bit timid; if only she would gain the wisdom to go along with it.

"I have very strong ideas on raising kids. I'm a great believer in discipline. Not beating them or anything, but kids have to respect your rights as much as you respect theirs. I think you should *like* your kids. You can't if they're constantly infringing on your rights. Most everybody *loves* his kids, but not everybody *likes* his kids. I believe very much in family, keeping them close to you, functioning as a family. Kids have to contribute to the family. For us it's a necessity.

"Education should be the opportunity to explore what they're interested in. It should be what we don't have here, a more open system. For the most part education is very boring here, but it doesn't have to be.

"I suppose I'd be sort of a low-key feminist. I definitely believe in all the opportunities for women, but I have a strong feeling for men. They have a very big place in our life. But a woman being, doing anything she wants . . . that's an idea whose time has come. No, I don't belong to N.O.W. The only thing I went to up here was a thing for working women. Trying to get better wages for women in Door County is like beating a dead horse. The men up here for crissake, are barely getting a minimum wage! I don't know what the answer is, probably unions. Certainly most business people up here aren't about to give their help any fair wages. I pay my girls [who clean with her during the summer] more than the big businesses here pay their help. Minimum wage they pay, and not one penny over. Who the hell can live on that?"

It seems obvious that because she is who she is, because of what she's said and done, both men and women enjoy her company and seek her advice, just like to talk with her. "I must be a good listener," she says. "And I've heard just about everything up here, everything from marital problems to new mothers with kids who are driving them crazy, to people feeling that they just can't cope with their lives.

"Bad times for myself? I'm super resilient, I guess. I always come back to the fact that I don't have any other real choice but to keep going . . . for the kids, to hold onto them. The fact is that I have to keep putting one foot in front of the other. Lots of times I spend days crying, but I always make supper.

"Sure, marriage again . . . but only for love. No other reason. I'm still a romantic. I'd like to remarry someday, but not in the near future. My ultimate goal is to have a close relationship with somebody. More than anything, that's what I want out of life. Feminists will scream 'cop out!,' but that means a lot to me.

"Door . . . just the beauty of it keeps me here, the tranquility of it. It's good for me. I find I need that. Terrie said something in one of her letters: she isn't sure she wants me to sell the house and move away from Door County. She feels she needs the openness, the woods, the water . . . to come back to that. I think I'd miss that too.

"But I've got to make a change. I feel like I'm going nowhere. I'm unfulfilled. I've got to do something important with my life, to get started in a different direction. I'm bored where I am now, earning a living the way I am. It's beginning to wear me out. I want to start using my brains.

"Right now I'm thinking about psychology, physical therapy, something in the medical field but not nursing. I do have a real feeling for people, even though I may say I don't like them. Yes, I'd be real surprised if I found myself here ten years from now. Shocked would be more like it. With the changes that are happening in the county, I doubt if I'd ever come back once I went away.

"The walk last night . . . yes, I needed that again. To go through the woods, down to the water, just to be alone, just to collect myself once again. I have so many demands on me. If I could close the door to my room and be by myself, that would be good too.

"Sometimes when I walk, I don't even think. Sometimes I suspend thinking. I feel. I listen to the water, to the woods. I feel really alone. Not lonely alone, but *good* alone. Something I've never really had.

Gust Klenke: Honey and Carburetors

He is a quiet man in tune with his work, equally at peace in the fields buzzing in sweet white clover, or hunched over the disharmony of a small engine misfiring in the cluttered darkness of his garage. Gust, the honeyman, will make it hum again.

A man of few words. Silence . . . then a long, drawn out 'Yeeeeep!" that rises in tone like a bee in flight.

A good year for honey, Gust?

(Silence) "Yeeeeep!" His fondest expression. That and silence: a positive acknowledgement of questions and statements concerning weather, local politics, mechanical problems, or the mystery of the honey bee.

And sometimes, a "yep" for no reason at all, just Gust moving through the midnight oil and grease of his garage (a dog usually at his heels) perhaps in search of a nut, a spring, a screwdriver . . . often a friend or total stranger standing in the shadows, depending completely upon the mechanical genius of this old man to fix what can't be fixed, to set things running right. And suddenly, out of an even darker recess of the old garage, out of nowhere, "Yeeeeep." Gust has found it. And it will be done.

Privacy personified, Gust Klenke is eighty years old, quick on his feet, quick in his thinking. He's the artful dodger in some respects, a man who is seen everywhere (even late at night along the highway, a lantern in hand, out on a walk with his dog) and more often than not can never be found.

Where's Gust? Has anybody seen Gust around? Don't ever expect to buy gasoline at Gust's unless Gust just happens to be there.

For more than six years I've been after him to talk, to get him down on paper . . . once I find him. I've hunted him in old orchards in his pursuit of bees. I've caught him a number of times, unawares, bent over a fender, buried in the depths of somebody's uncooperative engine.

Always he offers the excuse of work, or "I don't have nothing to say," followed by a little laugh, a shake of the head, and silence—perhaps better interpreted as shyness. He'll engage easily enough in small talk.

He'll crack a thin smile. He'll even let in an unexpected glimmer of light. But tell him he's lived a life that should be shared, and he'll look away, concentrate even harder on the work at hand, walk off in his cap and bib overalls, disappear into the hive of his garage, thinking, pondering the imponderables of a power mower someone has dropped off.

People are always doing this, dropping things off, leaving things up to him. Mechanical problems just dumped on his doorstep, only to be claimed days or weeks later.

"Did you fix it, Gust?"

"Fix what?"

"The snowblower."

"Oh, that thing. Yeah, take it."

"How much I owe you, Gust?"

"I don't know. Go try it first. See if it works." And Gust turns his back, disappears down that narrow path of a garage floor strewn with mechanical parts and all the paraphernalia of beehives.

Inside and out, Gust Klenke's Garage is a landmark in Ellison Bay. The place is nothing but an eyesore to some. You have to reach way out, or way in, to see the beauty of it all. It's a monument to a man who is what he does.

It is a graveyard of old automobiles and trucks, even a yellow school bus swaying in the weeds. Two gas pumps that sometimes work, when Gust is sometimes around to attend to them. A couple of ancient gas pumps, broken, just standing there in color and rust because there's nowhere else for them to be, and they appear perfect enough, in place, at Gust's corner. Clusters of silver containers of bottled gas, which he delivers from the trunk or back seat of his car—whatever car happens to be serviceable enough for his use these days. He goes through old clunkers by the month, by the year, then retires them to the weeds behind the house, finds another one there (frequently just dropped off, or junked at Gust's by a friend) and fixes it well enough to make his sojourns to the beehives nearby. (You've got to love the old man's style of make-do. He's refined it to a way of life.)

Old stoves, rusting pieces of farm machinery—all objects of art in a rural sort of way—round out his landscape of repair and disrepair, to remind him of things to be done, things to be cast aside for future conjecture or willful abandonment, left to the peace of quiet dereliction on Gust's premises, and always, no doubt, within range of his caring eyes.

"GUS KLENKE GARAGE" reads the peeling red and white sign, which is what his special corner is all about. A once-white, frame garage building that will probably never see another coat of paint, not by Gust. Signs advertising Quaker State, Atlas Tires, Standard American Oil Motor Club, none of which Gust pays much attention to, let alone provides. But HONEY FOR SALE . . . he can come up with that easily enough. There are jars of it on a table cluttered with old auto parts.

Yep. The place may be an eyesore to some, but I can no more imagine Ellison Bay without Gust and his corner garage than Ephraim without its white buildings and church steeples, or Sister Bay without Al Johnson's.

When Gust and his garage go, replaced by self-service pumps with digital numbers (or merely leveled for yet another unneeded gift shop), much of the soul of Ellison Bay will disappear, leaving only the spectacular view from Hanson's hill, the Pioneer Store, and the Galleries. (Progress, even in Ellison Bay, means destroying a beautiful old country church—Trinity Lutheran Church—and replacing it with a modern structure that would make a great bank or McDonald's in Sturgeon Bay.)

For Gust is a faith unto himself, to all of us, a simple, kind-hearted man who can no more turn away anyone in need of his know-how than he can stop a bee from making honey. His life is a life sacrificed (glorified) in serving the needs of others: farmers, fishermen, friends and strangers. Gust just *knows* how all things work on heaven and earth.

But getting him to talk, to tell about it all is something else. He'd sooner take apart a tractor with one hand and put it back together again blindfolded. He'd sooner converse with the bees.

Gust, about the bees. You, bees, honeymaking—how did it all start?

(Silence) "Got no time today. Got to open up some cottages. Fellow wants that lawn mower fixed right away . . . yeeeeeep. No time." And he goes into his famous walk-away act, leaving the writer buried in silence.

I meet the silence with more words, easing him back into small talk, maneuvering him as gently as possible into his own story.

What was the name of that old dog of yours? "Nellie? Nellie's gone. Before her there was Buckshot. He's gone too. [Silence] Yeeeeep. There was Tragedy. I don't know what happened to Tragedy. This one here? This one's called Sheba. My granddaughter gave him to me."

He disappears to the back of the garage, rummages through a drawer, gets down on his hands and knees, rubs the greasy floor, tries to retrieve a tiny screw he has misplaced.

I bend down to help him. "Jesus Christ," I say, faced with the improbability of ever finding anything so tiny under such conditions.

"That's what I say," exclaims Gust. "But that don't help either." Yet he does find it, walks back to the lawn mower he is repairing, and in his attempt to make some minor adjustment, accidentally drops the little screw somewhere in the engine. I attempt to find it for him, but Gust cautions, "Just leave it. That way I'll know where it is." He retreats to the safety of silence once again as I attempt to probe him a little more about the bees. His body, his scraped and soiled hands, his utter stillness is telling me, "I'm a busy man. Can't you see I don't want to be bothered? I have no need to be known to others. Leave me be."

But other voices tell me, 'Don't let this rare man go. Protect his innocence, but celebrate it too.'

"Gust, how about some kind of appointment? You're busy now, okay. What about tomorrow morning? Say ten o'clock? Or tomorrow afternoon—whatever's good for you."

"Appointments?" he laughs. "I can't do anything about appointments, don't you see?"

"Tell me what you know about the bees. Maybe I can just follow along when you check the hives. What do bees do in winter?

"Might set a few bees after you," he smiles. "Get you hikin' down the field." His eyes come alive like a small boy hoping to play a trick on someone.

"Gust," I want to say, "I'll even get stung to make you happy, if only you'll talk."

Then, miraculously, he leaves the lawn mower fixing for another time, and begins telling of the bees. "In winter you have to see that the bees are protected, that the mice don't get in the hives, that the entrances are open so they can get in and out and get air. In the wintertime they keep warm. It's all they do in winter, till the middle of February.

"They start to raise young bees then. They build brood before February. They raise the temperature in the hive. You got to see they got food when they cluster, otherwise they starve. Food is either honey or sugar water. Put a pail on top of the inner cover of the hole, upside down so they can get the feed out of the hole.

"They go by the sun, bees. After the sun crosses the line, when it starts crossing behind and goes north, they got to prepare. When the flowers come out, they're ready. They raise the temperature up there in wintertime, forty-five to fifty degrees in the clusters. But in spring when they start raising brood, they raise that up to ninety degrees.

"Like I say, they go by time, by the sun. That's how they find their way around too. Back and forth from their hives . . . they can tell by the sun, see by it. They guide themselves by ultraviolet rays. They don't need no compass."

Gust opening up is a wonder in itself, comparable to the secret navigation of bees. His own direction is free-spirited. I mention a season and he takes off. I hold up part of a hive and he moves back and off into another direction. It's like the old man has been storing this stuff within him for years, but nobody asked. Or he was too shy to tell.

"They raise brood all summer, till fall. After the honey season is over, they stop. They cut it back. When the fall season is on, the drones that are in there push out, so they don't eat any more honey than they got for themselves. The drone's a male bee; he's bigger. He don't get any honey. All he does, if there's a queen, a new queen, he fertilizes the queen and that's the end of it."

"Not much of a life for a drone," I kid him.

"You mate with a queen, and then you die. That's the end of him. I don't know if that's a good life or not," he laughs, then turns silent. "Yeeeeeep."

"Honey season begins when?"

"Early April, or about the middle. When the flowers start to bloom in the swamp. From then it lasts till first frost, November sometime. Usually when the full moon comes on, the sky gets clearer and the temperature drops down to freezing point."

"And then what are the priorities of the bee man?"

"Clean up the frames, repair, paint. In the winter, when you're not doing anything else, you scrape the wax off, get the comb honey box assembled. You got to have them all set. When the honey flows, you got to be ready."

He moves to another part of the garage, picking up a box. "This is a comb honey super. The bottom, that's called the brood box. We usually have three of these boxes for brood boxes. The ones on top we have for surplus, and that we call 'super.' "

Just why Gust has slipped into "we" is not entirely clear, since it is always he, alone, out there in the fields with the bees, doing all the work. It must be the brotherhood of beekeepers he identifies with. "Here's a frame that goes in the brood nest. That's where they raise young bees."

How many angels dancing on a head of a pin? How many bees building a hive?

"They start off in spring with three, four, five pounds. They end up with sixteen, seventeen pounds by fall if they get strong. Middle of June, July, that's when honey flow starts. It takes that time to build them up.

"If we buy package bees, that goes by the pound. It all goes by the pound. Bees, they get their stomachs full of honey, they weigh more. May, June, you got to check them. Got to go through them hives in April, May. We usually check every ten days. You go through them, tip them over, see if any queen cells have started on the bottom.

"From then on, they work their way up from the bottom box to the top. Then in spring, after we start examining, we usually put them down in the bottom. We have to reverse them, top to bottom. By putting them down below, the queen has room to work her way up. If they get crowded, they prepare for swarming. If they swarm, your bees are gone, so then you won't get no honey. You control the swarming by reversing them. You do this by the middle of July or so, then they're over the swarming instinct and you can forget about them. But that's nature. If they feel they're crowded, that brings it on.

"I usually leave enough honey in there so they got enough to feed on. Lots of times it gets cold in spring, and they'd starve to death if they can't get out for a week. Swarming . . . you got to keep the young queen in the hive. The young queen don't usually want to swarm the first year or so. The old queen does."

I ask him what he thinks about this business of the old queen and the young queen. I ask him if he thinks much about the way of nature. "The young queen is satisfied, I guess," he smiles. "The older queen, she's just getting older and wants to swarm out, start all over again . . . the way I figure it. They kill her, though. They put her out. She dies, then they drag her out. They replace her. That's nature. If it has to keep on, it has to keep strong. "

I backtrack, trying to give shape to an old man's life with bees. He moves too quickly in describing the work he loves. He is all over the subject at the same time.

"Let's go back to summer. Tell me about July. You and the bees in July."

"I'm reversing the supers then, seeing that they have enough supers on top. If there are queen cells started on the bottom, I cut them out, see that they're not started. If they aren't started, you know they aren't going to swarm. You give them ten days to see what they're going to do . . . they're starting queen cells every ten days. Then, all summer, just more supers. You got to have enough room there. Some people do it in different ways.

"Honey begins the middle of June, sometimes before. If you got a good strong crop of dandelions, you get some good honey from that. It's the first plant as far as honey surplus starts.

"But in the swamps—bushes, trees that bloom—the bees get pollen and stuff off that. That's the main thing in spring. If they can get pollen and get to work, raise them bees.

"You start taking it [honey] when they got it capped. It's ripe. Anytime after it's capped, you can take it.

"When cherry, apple trees start blossoming, it's all good for the bees. I don't know, but there were different kinds of weeds this spring, plus clover, sweet clover, choke cherries, wild cherries, when haying begins. If you got a moist year, with strawberries, raspberries, blackberries, it all produces good honey. July, basswood trees starts to bloom, some elms . . . they all produce good honey. Some years, farmers plant buckwheat. It's got a lot of honey in it. Other times, though, nothing."

"What makes a bad honey year, Gust?"

"Don't ask me. I don't know why. The plants grow, the blossoms bloom, but some years it don't produce no honey."(Silence) "Yeeeeeep!" He wanders away a bit, making a motion to pick up a wrench, returning to the comfort of his own silence. Maybe he's talked himself out, I think. He stands near the area of the old fashioned cash register where an old fiddle with broken strings once hung from above.

"What happened to the fiddle, Gust?"

"Oh, my son-in-law took it to be fixed."

A car stops out front. A man peers through the door, happy to see Gust inside. "Got any honey?" he asks.

"Sure, sure. Lots of it. How much you want?"

"Oh, you know. One of those big bottles."

Gust reaches around in the darkness of the garage and magically produces a glowing jar of honey. Holding it in both hands, the purest and brightest object in the entire garage, Gust appears to be passing the man a talisman of sorts, a golden afternoon in fall, bottled especially in Door by a native who moves quietly in the landscape, sharing some of the secrets of the fields, the plants and insects.

"Honey making, Gust. What about the business of honey making?"

He rummages under the lift for parts of a hive.

"After the honey flow is over—when they got a frame like this full, capped—we take that off. Honey ain't ripe, ain't good till it's capped up. A thin capping of wax is when we get ready to extract. We take a knife and take that thin cap of wax off and then extract. Sometimes I don't start extracting till after the honey flow is over, after the first frost. You got to get the bees out of there, take the whole box and go."

"What do you say to them? How do you get them out of your way?"

"Oh, several ways. Some people have a blower, blow them out. Some people shake them off. We have a bee excluder. They can get out through that excluder, but they can't get in again. If I'm in a hurry, I take the frames out, brush them off, and they go—where's that brush?—looks exactly like the one they have on those snow sweeping jobs. It's a regular bee brush.

"Stung? Not then . . . that don't mean nothing. The most dangerous time is now, when you're reversing the hives and you got twenty-five pounds of bees in there. But you can get bit anytime. In spring, when the weather ain't right, is one time. But now, good weather, they're out getting honey. They don't bother. They got other things on their mind."

"How many times you been stung, Gust?"

"Times! Times?" he laughs, sweeping me away with his hand as if I'm joking with him. "Thousands. I don't even count 'em. I don't even pay attention. How many times I got bit? Some days not at all. Some days maybe ten, fifteen times at once. Don't mean nothing. Some days bees crawl more, right up your leg. They really crawl. They don't fly in the dark. If you got any holes in your clothes, they like to crawl. No, as far as gettin' bit, I don't think about it. I never did swell up from it like most people."

Clearing the bees from the hive is one thing, but extracting the honey is yet another project which occupies much of Gust's time. I follow him now from the garage to one of the small cabins near his house. He's going to show me where he extracts the honey.

"After I cap it or extract it, I set the boxes on the hives and let the bees clean it all up nice. Then I take them off and store them in the shed over winter. In winter you scrape off old wax and clean them up for next summer. The brood boxes are left in the field. That stays there, either 2, 2½ or 3 boxes. They stay there all the time. That stays over winter . . . say fifteen pounds of bees left. The survival of the strongest.

"I insulate the hives then. Wrap them up in tar paper, put Cellotex on top of the inner core. Leave ventilation, air, an opening to go in and out. Bees will come out in winter on a warm day, come out and fly a little bit. They have to come out an empty themselves out too. They eat honey in there and get filled up a bit."

Some people in these parts still read the moon for messages, planting to the configurations of the cosmos. What of Gust Klenke and the bees? What do they say of the seasons, the times?

"They can tell weather," he says. "If it's going to rain, they head back for the hive early. They come in before you know what the weather is. They go with the weather. If the weather is early [spring] they go by that. They can tell to a certain extent if the weather is going to be nice. They start to move in there. They get excited. Cold weather, they cluster up tighter and things like that. They can probably tell that ahead of time. Full moon? Not that I know of. It's night. But outside temperatures make a difference with them."

Inside the tiny cluttered shack (another beehive of his own?) he explains the extracting machine. "I got an extracting machine. First I take a knife then and skim the top right off. Then I set the whole frame right in here, spin it out on one side, reverse it, spin it out on the other. Then it runs out there in a gallon jar. I wait till the wax goes to the top, strain it, then bottle it. Before I had an extracting machine, I'd squash it . . . let it drain through a cloth. Once you got the honey, then there's just the bottling, labeling and selling."

Gus and the bees . . . going on how many years now?

Fifteen or twenty, in a big way. Otherwise I used to have a few hives around from the time I could crawl. I gave most of the honey away then. It was only worth three to five cents a pound in those days . . . ninety cents a pound today."

But this fascination with bees? How did it come about?

Gust smiles the smile of a mischievous boy. "When I was a kid, I used to have fun with the humble bees. I used to tease them in the straw stacks. I was just interested in them, seeing what they were doing. You know how kids are. I'd pester them, see if they would sting me. I'd see them pulling a straw, and I'd hang on one end and they would hold the other. I'd get a kick out of that. There wasn't too much to read up on, on bees at that time. One of our neighbors raised strawberries. I'd help her. She had ten or thirteen beehives, and that's where I got more or less interested in the bees. She had bees in a shed, though, inside a chicken house. And she gave me one of them hives. That one was mine, so I used to go and look at it, watch it. I was ten or twelve, I suppose. This was in Sevastopol. That's where I was born. We had a farm in Sevastopol, eighty acres, all hand worked. There used to be a lot of bees around in them days, lots of farming.

"Farming has changed today. Hay, years ago, wasn't cut till after blossom. Now, they cut it just before. They cut it green. You had more feed for bees then, with the blossoms. There would be seventy-five to eighty hives in one spot then. Not now; it's out of the picture.

"This year is a good year for honey, though. New weeds coming in here. There's a new yellow flower all over I haven't seen before. Like I say, what happens in nature? I don't know. Things take a cycle I guess. I thought them new weeds was mustard, but they wasn't. A different plant altogether.

"Sprays kill a lot of bees off. You got to look out for that. Kills them off. And there ain't no farming on the land anymore. They're planting it in trees, they aren't farming it. Or they're building. Years ago that was always pasture. That's gone by. And you got too many people nowadays who don't want bees around. They're afraid of them. They don't keep them. The orchards . . . there's still some. We work together. Orchard people need the bees, I need the blossoms. But a lot of the smaller orchards are going out. They don't care anymore."

Blossoms and carburetors are one hell of a combination. But often it takes a native, the know-how of a native man, to make meaning of things, to merge his own way of life with whatever he finds near.

"I always monkeyed around with machines on the farms. I always helped people fix them. When tractors started coming in, people didn't know much about that. I'd help them out. When cars started coming out, gasoline. I always liked to monkey around with that. But now, with the new cars, so many things added on to them, they're hard to work on.

"I started in the cheese factory business, too, back in Sevastopol, 1912, 1914. Started here in Ellison Bay, 1917, 1918, moved up here after the First World War. The Gilbert Olson house, down near you, that was my factory. I lived in the house across the road there about ten years. I was in the cheese business about fifteen years. I started when I was about eighteen, nineteen, and kept at it till about thirty-five years of age. In the cheese factory we had gas engines and things like that I took care of."

"Is there a mechanics to beekeeping?"

"The bee business is problems too, all the way. It's always something. Always something you got to figure some way out of it. It's exactly like the machine. Every hive you open is different. You got a problem every time you open a hive. But there's always some way out of it, some way to fix it."

"The same as life?" I wonder to myself. Besides bees and "monkeying around" with engines, how does a Gust Klenke maintain a smooth running life of his own?

"I just don't worry about things anymore. Something comes along, and it goes. I'm not happy with everything that happened in my life, but I can't complain. Helping friends, helping people. That's what it's all about, ain't it? If you can't help people, then there's nothing to it. You were put here to do something, I suppose, even if it's the wrong thing at times. I like it better here than any place. More quiet. People are easy to get along with.

"I think there's a higher power that regulates these things. If you go contrary to what He's set out, you pay for it. Kind of a plan. You either got to live toward that plan or you pay for it. That's my idea, even if I don't go to church. I know when I'm doing right and when I'm doing wrong. I know this much: If I do something that harms my neighbor, I ain't doing right. Same as if you eat things you're not supposed to, you're going to pay for that in your health. You harm your neighbor, you can't expect him to be good to you."

The daily life of Good Man Gust Klenke?

"I get up, not as early as I used to, four or five in the morning. Now, about seven. Then I have things planned, certain things I got to do with the bees. You plan your life around that, doing what you have to do. Somebody wants something done, you go to work then on that. I don't really have any set plans. The whole day goes like that, from one thing to another. I don't have to punch no clock.

"I work till I got things to do and then go to bed. I read the news, see what's going on in certain things in the news. Some of this, some of that. World affairs . . . I can't keep up with. That's so twisted up now you don't know who to believe. But it'll all straighten itself out somehow. They tell us the end is coming pretty soon, but I don't know. I don't know how it can keep on like it is if we don't destroy ourselves."

Tourists occasionally find Gust, sometimes deliberately seek him out. The garage, for all its glorious dereliction, invites curiosity.

"I wonder once in a while if the tourists know whether they're coming or going. I can't keep up with that. That wears me out. They want to be all over, do everything at one time. I don't think they're ever satisfied.

"Am I satisfied? I haven't thought about it. I'm satisfied bein' here, what I'm doing. If you don't get things muddled up, you're satisfied."

As for Mother Nature, the DNR, the environment, the way things are, the way they were? "You can't do what you please anymore," claims Gust. "People telling you what you can and can't do. That's the whole thing, if you don't get it all mixed up. A lot of things they're doing now, they're turning it all around, getting it out of shape. You can't do that.

Planting fish where they don't belong, chemical sprays bothering people and animals and everything else.

"I'm very wrong, maybe, but as farms get bigger, there's more pollution. With small farms you wouldn't have all these big problems. Now with one hundred, two hundred head of cattle in one spot—it's too much."

Peace of mind for an old bee man? "When I get out by the bees, I forget everything else. Other things don't bother me. That's one of the reasons I got out by the bees. I don't have those other problems there."

"And fiddle playing? What was that all about?" And why has the old man stopped playing?

"Oh, fiddling was just fiddling, that's all. When I was a kid every house seemed to have musical instruments around. Everybody played something. You had to entertain yourself somehow. My dad was a band guy. He played in Milwaukee. We had a band for several years, played around the dance halls here. I was twelve or thirteen. Played waltzes, two-steps square dances, things like that. Didn't have none of this jitterbug stuff. It was all right. Kids, you know . . . you got out, you played. We played at a dance hall in Institute. Valmy had one up above a tavern. Baileys Harbor . . . I don't know if it burned down or not. Carlsville, they still have one I guess. It was Schram's in Baileys Harbor [now the Frontier Saloon]. It's a long time ago I played there.

"In Ellison Bay we played one time, or twice. Mike Anderson's tavern or saloon. They had a dance hall up above where Earl and Rita are [Sister Bay Bowl]. I think it burned down. I always played with a band, not alone. "The last time? Maybe thirty years ago. [Silence] Yeeeeeeeep. I doubt if I can still play it. If you're going to play it, you got to play right along; otherwise you're going to get out of it, like anything else."

As we leave the extracting house, I recall Darlene Cooper telling me once how she's been after Gust to play the fiddle again, how she told him she would bring her guitar over, how Gust just smiled his little boy's smile, which probably meant "no." But I would give anything to see that, to hear Gust take up the fiddle again.

I am reminded also of a story about Gust once playing for a local get together at the old Ellison Bay Schoolhouse: Gust fiddling while some of the people played cards, danced, or just listened. When someone from the local church popped in, and equated dancing/fiddling/card playing with sin (as they usually do) quite a row was started . . . a fiddling man being the work of the devil, I suppose. And goodness triumphed over evil in this instance, I'm sorry to say, for the story goes that Gust put his fiddle away that night and never played again.

"You want to see some bees?" he asks. I follow his slouch-and-slide steps toward the trunk of his car containing a wonderful assortment of what might be defined as junk, but to Gus, all the tools of his trades, parts and pieces of the whole. He scatters things around till he comes up with a Congo-type headpiece with a veil, and a bellows device which he calls a smoker. He stuffs the smoker with old burlap, lights it, and pumps it till the smoke starts coming out good and strong. Back into his stream of silence, Gust collects his gear and moves out. I figure we're going to some of his hives in a distant field somewhere, but Gust walks toward the front of his own house, disappearing inside for a moment. He returns a few seconds later with yet another congo helmet, which he hands to me. "We're going to check the hives behind the house."

I find it hard to believe this scene: me and old Gust on his front steps in Ellison Bay preparing for some kind of safari for bees in his backyard, donning gear that somehow has the era of the 1920's about it. He's tying a net around him that hangs down from the Congo headpiece, while explaining to me, "You can't run bees without a smoker and a veil . . . well, you can, some days."

We look like two characters out of an old newsreel. I feel like a doughboy in World War I preparing for trench warfare. All we need now is a swarm of bees and the two of us hotfooting it out of there to add a Chaplinesque touch.

But Gust is cool. He knows exactly where he's at. Though I may be a trifle concerned about my introduction to beekeeping, Gust is calmly telling me what a good health food honey is. "It's easy to digest," he says. "It's pre-digested. You can't eat too much honey. It's energy, mostly. It has a few minerals and things like that are good for you — vitamins — and I think it steps up your circulation a bit."

Stalking the hives behind the house, I can see and hear the air alive with bees. Gust walks in the midst of them, smoking them out. I hang back a bit, amazed to see him moving into it all, like it's his rightful place to be. He moves the boxes on the hives, taking out a frame to show me.

"A hive like this I would say has 60 to 75,000 bees," he explains — bees clustering to the combs, flying, filling the air with their buzzing. "Now this here is the starting of a queen cell," he says, pointing to a different structured cell, cutting it out with his knife. "Like this, you just cut it off.

"Now this is a worker brood. This is drone brood . . . they're bigger cells. The queen is large too, looks like a peanut shell."

Gust checks the sky, notices the sun shining. It's the almost perfect day for bees and the old man who tends them. "Now today, see," he tells me, "You wouldn't need no nets or anything else. The bees are so busy they won't even bother us. These are Italian bees, the main ones around here. Most of them are Italian. They produce the most honey and are the easiest to get along with. They understand the winter better."

I try listen to Gust, his voice now over the sound of the bees, studying the fascination of their hives, wary of the possibility of getting stung.

Gust, the sincerest of teachers, goes over each truth carefully, loving what he knows, wanting and willing to pass it on in this way.

"The smoke chases them away, you see. Makes it easier for me to work. It gets in their eyes. A bee has five eyes so he can look all over, around. Now this pollen, they change that over and make food for young bees out of that. They fly two, three, four miles to pick it up. That's good for you too. You eat it, just like that . . . high protein. Honey—I eat it right out of the hive. That's the way I like it best, when it's good and fresh. Just take the comb to you and eat it. Nothing better than fresh honey right out of the hive . . . yeeeeeep."

I am wearing a short sleeved shirt, my hands are bare, my net is unfastened. I am vulnerable to the danger in bees, but no longer mindful of that. I move as I must into the humming silence, listening to the old man, merging with him into the bees, knowing he knows there are things that cannot be understood in any other way but being part of them.

"Mysteries? I suppose there are some things you don't understand. I imagine it was supposed to be that way."

Charles Peterson: The Painter of Ephraim

It is a setting lost in time, and we are all drawn to it to satisfy some deep need of place, of past, of peace within ourselves.

> Notebook entry: Chick Peterson, "Ephraim Winter." Where are we? In reality, this place doesn't exist anymore. Not the way it was. It can still be found in summer, though the scene grows more and more cluttered/infected with motels and condos north of the Village Hall . . . the purity returning briefly again around Anderson Dock. The purity of the past/present seen most perfectly in winter. The painter, Chick Peterson, knows this.

If there is a soul to this county, it lies within the white village of Ephraim. And if there is a man living here who singularly evokes the spirit of this county past—water, land, village, the older ways of men wresting a living from the land, fearlessly working the waters, or quietly being themselves at a local auction, an old fashioned fish boil in the village in winter—it is the artist Charles (Chick) Peterson, who skillfully renders a way of life real to us once more, reflecting those human values which appear (in our own time) to be more evident in the past.

"I enjoy history of all sorts," he will tell you. "I find myself intrigued with the lives and personalities of the past . . . those things, too, which were formerly functional and vital to their lives, such as a piece of farm machinery, old boats. This stimulates my imagination. Out of that come some of the spectral figures in my paintings."

He lives and paints behind the village proper, on the upper road (Moravia), a short distance from the white steeples of the local Lutheran and Moravian churches which set the tone of Ephraim, day and night, in all seasons, especially winter, and remain the focal point of visitors and natives alike traveling north down highway 42, viewing the beauty of Ephraim across the water with a reverence and hope that some things will never change.

His home, studio, and gallery also borders Anderson Lane, where the painter himself, late on a summer afternoon, might walk down toward Anderson Dock (another famous Ephraim landmark) to sail his boat, *Aquarelle*, toward Horseshoe Island, into yet another famous land/ watermark—the Ephraim sunset.

What we see, then, is a man perfectly in place. And though he may not feel it entirely appropriate to be compared to, say a Norman Rockwell, there are the similarities of knowing who and where you are, and painting this. And there is an unexplainable, perhaps even unexamined, comfort—among visitors, natives, observers, collectors of his work—that a Charles Peterson resides in Ephraim, in Door County, quietly, meticulously going about his work, painting (preserving) those things he lives amongst, remembers, imagines, reveres—things which have meaning for us all.

Though he is of this place now, his personal history begins elsewhere.

Born in Elgin, Illinois, in 1927, he describes his background as "lower working class. My dad was a watch factory machinist. During the Depression he worked as a service station attendant. In WWII he went back to work at Elgin when they began making time devices for aerial bombs."

While we are all part of our past, the artist especially, knowingly or unknowingly, seems marked by his early years and is forever giving shape to those forces.

"I have, as you are well aware, a rather clean style to my work. Precise. Orderly. I laughingly think of this as my Scandinavian background. I equate this with the Swedish farms I saw when I was there. They not only put all their farm machinery in the barns, out of view, but raked the grounds! Both of my parents were entirely Scandinavian. My mother was a native Swede. I suppose my work is part of that tradition.

"I had a terrific boyhood! Boy Scouting was a big movement in my time. I was very active in that. Our leader had an absolute talent in extracting effort from kids. We had the feeling it was a distinct privilege to work for him. He just died this last year at ninety-six. Parlasca was his name. His real appeal was Indian lore. He was probably the foremost authority on Indians in the Midwest. I finally became a semi-professional dancer because of his influence. I worked for two years as an instructor of Indian dance at Culver Military Academy. But that came later. I was out of graduate school then.

"Scouting held a group of us together until we graduated from high school. It was a great influence on me. So was Parlasca, a man who was never satisfied. He absolutely demanded our best effort. It really worked for some of us.

Though Chick always drew, he did not study art in high school. It was only after high school, in what he calls a "post graduate course—while waiting for the draft to get me"—that he took some courses. "I had a love of art," he says, but he admits the kind of art being done in high school did not interest him. "I think what happened is my mother had talked to the art teacher, Claudia Abell, and she told my mother, 'You tell that boy to take art, and he can draw anything he wants.'

"I was drawing adventurous stuff—horses, outdoor life . . . the kind of stuff I do now, I suppose. I did a lot of army trucks and airplanes, that kind of stuff, since the military life was so vital at that time. I enrolled in the Navy in 1945. I got to the Pacific theater while the war was still on. By the time I got to the Philippine Islands, the Japanese had surrendered. I was on an L.S.T. that took marines to Japan as occupation forces."

After his discharge in 1946, Chick explains, "Like most kids, I wasn't very sure who I was, what I wanted to be. I was just groping for something to do. It's incredible when I think of it. In Elgin there was this little publishing company, the D. C. Cook Publishing Co., and I walked in there and asked if they needed an artist. And they did! So suddenly I was an artist!" He laughs. "I learned a little about the process of art and then applied at the American Academy of Art in Chicago, the summer of 1947.

"That same summer I had the opportunity to go to Europe with Parlasca and teach Indian dancing at the Boy Scouts International Jamboree in Paris. Teaching Indian dancing on a ship at sea, a moving incline, was very interesting.

"When I got back to Elgin, I discovered I had been replaced by a camera at the book company, and the American Academy still had no room for me. I was then hired as an apprentice at the Leo Burnett advertising agency in Chicago."

Portrait of the artist as a young man: the influences of a traditional Swedish family in the Midwest, boyhood in Elgin, the Boy Scouts and Parlasca, who expected the best, his first art teacher, the navy, the sea his first employment as an artist, application to the American Academy of Art, apprenticeship at the Leo Burnett ad agency.

> Notebook entry: I am seeing him, I am hearing him describe the next phase of his life, and I can see the road ahead, how it will all end, and I don't like to know what's coming . . . I'm already scratching things out the way the artist himself might work and abandon early sketches in search of better insights toward a completed work of art. I feel there is more to him, to all this. And I want more. For him. For the reader. For myself.

Change. The indisputable factor governing all our lives. At this very moment I am changing my thoughts about Chick Peterson, changing the direction I feel this story should go. The sailor taking another tack, the artist conceiving a different dimension, another line, a better rhythm. Something truer to reality? Or his own imaginings?

Ephraim . . . Door County . . . past and present? Summer/ winter? True to time? What does this say? How does Chick Peterson make this place his? What is the role, the makeup of the artist anyway? One part conjurer? One part prophet? How many parts fabulist? Just how real is real? A framed print, "Ephraim Winter" begs for my attention. Sitting here in Peterson's modern studio in old (new?) Ephraim, I see myself surrounded by his paintings and drawings that speak of this village, this county, though he admits that the specifies of place in many of his paintings do not actually exist. Things must be changed to fit the artist's conception in the interests of truth to the purpose of the painting. (To reinvent the truth, what a writer might call poetic license.) A truth to the spirit of things perhaps.

Gray-haired, bearded, neatly trimmed, casually and carefully dressed, a sense of orderliness about his person, Chick Peterson is a confessed workaholic. He cannot wait to wake in the morning and paint each day. Tall, cool, somewhat distant at first, with a strange mixture of boyishness about him, there is a dignity to his presence that takes command. He is a quiet man, witty, with a clarity and brightness to his eyes in laughter and contemplation. Erudite. He would not be a man late for work with his respect for time.

He is telling me in precise detail of those trying times in Chicago, working at the ad agency, attending the American Academy of Art. Ironically, both he and the portrait artist, Jim Ingwersen of Sister Bay, attended the American Academy at the same time, yet neither man knew of the other.

"Jim and I were there at the same time, but I didn't know him. Sometime, though, if I set my psyche high, I think I can see him there."

This was also his first real contact with a big city: "Night in Chicago was a discouraging experience. I'm just repelled by cities. I'm a basically shy person, and Chicago was overwhelming to me. I had a pretty protected life at home."

> Notebook entry: His discouragement with place (Chicago) seems directly connected to his experiences at the ad agency and the American Academy. Chick Peterson baring his own soul now, the soul of all young artists possessing a certain, untried talent, suddenly forced to look at themselves, their work in the light of other artists.

"The art school was a revelation to me. For the first time, working with professionals, I realized how little I knew. It was truly discouraging for me, in that I saw the world as filled with marvelous technicians at art. Up until that time I was free to dream myself an artist. Suddenly, going down to that gloomy city at night, I saw some splendid technicians, saw the need to improve. I don't mean to stress the discouragement. The chance to work fulltime at art was exhilarating, but there was the sense of questioning whether I was qualified. It goes back to the commercialism of art. As soon as I went to the American Academy, I was intending to make my living at art. At the Academy I was dealing with practicing commercial artists for the first time. I saw what kind of proficiency was necessary for a commercial career. And it had taken them years to achieve what they were doing.

"Illustration was my aim. I had been impressed by N. C. Wyeth and others, and my outdoor life as a kid contributed to my adventurous, story-telling kind of art."

After six months, Chick quit the Burnett agency to attend art school fulltime, completing his study two years later in 1950. "And then a new form of education took place—applying for work. That education was as rich as school itself. Very pragmatic. Hard stuff. If they could use you, they'd use you."

Education, both in the real world (working in Cedar Rapids for the Stamats Publishing Co.) and in the world of the university (a B.S. and M.F.A., eventually leading to a teaching position) marks the next phase of his life. At Stamats Publishing Company, "I did illustrations. It was a very good job. It was very lonely, but educating. I was given a manuscript for this magazine, and I could pick some aspect to illustrate. And then I could watch the whole process, from photoengraving to printing. The entire process. It was very satisfying work."

By 1951, '52, though, after a year's stint doing layouts for Hart, Schaffner and Marx, "I was quite disenchanted with commercial art. It was not very satisfying."

Through the suggestion of a friend, Ray Barnhart, Chick enrolled at Marietta College in Ohio where, he gleefully admits, "I felt like I had come home. It seemed to me I had found it. They had every idea that I had ever encountered. I had access to faculty life, and I realized that world was where I belonged. I decided to teach. I loved the scholarly life. From there I went on to Ohio University for an M.F.A. I achieved Phi Beta Kappa and finished with honors."

Judging from his boyhood leadership abilities, his interest in personal achievement, his love of ideas and the pursuit of excellence, Peterson would seem a fine teacher. He proved to be, teaching for five years at a state college in West Virginia, and then returning to Marietta College, for fourteen years as head of the Art Department.

Marietta College "was a one-man art department, which was right down my alley. My first challenge was to administer to the studio aspect of the college, which I did by introducing some subjects that had not been taught there before—primarily etching, ceramics, lithography, and sculpture. They also had an existing program in painting and design plus art history, which meant that as an art teacher, I was covering the standard areas of a liberal arts curriculum all by myself, which was very exhilarating. I was so cranked up that I also had time to do my own painting! It's just inconceivable now. I also remodeled a house and raised a family!"

The move to Door County came in 1973, after resigning his teaching position (having shaped the art department, increased the staff, and developed an annual juried show of national significance) and moving to Ephraim with his wife, Sue, and their three daughters.

"I had a sabbatical in 1968, '69, which we spent here in Ephraim. I proposed painting for a year rather than going on for a degree. And that was the first time I painted in a substantial way since graduate school. I was curious as to whether I could find it challenging and whether it would grow. I found it would. It was a very exhilarating year. The response from people here was so supportive. I realized I could make a living painting."

> Notebook entry: "Ephraim Winter" . . . Home again . . . Beginnings and endings. Time present/time past. Peterson bringing all the forces, experiences that shaped him . . . home to Ephraim now . . . to recreate himself, in a sense, in his watercolors.

And it all comes together. . . . "I have always felt confident in my own ability," he tells me, trying to explain honestly why he prefers spending his time on his own work rather than visiting the exhibits of others. "It just doesn't interest me." Yet he does not deny his indebtedness to certain painters through the years. "I've been immensely impressed by Hopper, by Winslow Homer. So I have been influenced by other artists, but at the same time I've never felt I'm the product of a teacher or teachers. I feel largely self-taught. But that's not fair because it suggests everything I've learned, I've learned on my own."

The spectral figures in some of Peterson's paintings intrigue me. On the studio wall behind him hangs a beautiful painting of an old fashioned Door County fish boil. Yet what the eye sees first is an old fishing tug, *Margaret,* and a Door County setting of shore, trees, water and sky that could be anywhere along the county's coastline yet nowhere specifically. (Again, this artist's goal is to capture the essence of this place rather than the particular. And in the choice of 'his particulars' lies a common, recognizable truth.) While the eye lingers over the scene, still another picture begins to emerges: the haunting ghost figures of fishermen and their families, enjoying a fish boil. The artist reimagining, re-establishing the past in a sense that even the past of landscape and structure is not enough, not true enough. He must work in yet another layer of memory to intensify the time to make it all flow in watercolor, in a harmony akin to dream or reverie. Then another grain of truth: "One of those figures, that man over there, I believe is one of the Weborgs," he says.

"It's probably foolish of me to paint these things in watercolor—the medium is so elusive, difficult to control. It's really a double composition, the spectral figure. I think what you see has to grab and hold the viewer. All the spectral figures are seen eventually, and they also have to be well composed. In a way I see them as a separate composition which has to effortlessly merge with the entire composition. In addition, it's a watercolor. So this act of faith is excruciatingly urgent. I spend an enormous amount of time in a painting like this.

"My hope is to achieve these things as simply as possible. The other thought, which is counterproductive, is the agony of whether all that technical involvement is worthwhile. Should it be done? I won't know until it's finished.

"The choice of subject is perilous. I believe that the way one treats any subject is the way one justifies the way of doing it. It's how you do it, more than what you paint. I'll have many, many insights into this I can't see—composition as well as subject matter. Many new insights as I go. But I'm always limited by the choice of medium—watercolor. It's important in my choice of subject. But I'm so delighted in the technical difficulty that I'm willing to risk it. I'm even eager to risk it. Thank God it's morning," he laughs, "so I can get back out there to work!"

Notebook entry: A return to the heart and soul of the artist. He is in his element. Let him go . . .

"I was raised among working people. I admire people who do their work effortlessly, whatever it is. I suppose it's the appeal of an honest way of life. It's part of what has always appealed to me about country living. Here in Door County I'm impressed very easily by the forthright, hardworking people here. So often in the city you find a certain defensiveness, unwilling to face you man to man. I like the forthright, more direct character of the people working here. I admire honest livelihood. I'm impressed by the fishermen, too. These guys go out every day and risk their lives in these boats. And the farm people, too, clearing the rocks out of their fields. By contrast, the people in the city — theirs is primarily a secondary production, not raising anything, only engaged in services.

"I think people dominate my paintings. What interests me is nature, and man's experience in nature. A piece of land alone is not enough to hold my interest. I think my interest is with individual people, though I don't do portraits of them *per se*. I generalize people, I know. The people I like to paint are mostly earlier Door Countyites, working people who were independent. That's the part of this place that strikes me. A lot of our county has lost this fierce independent spirit.

"I certainly make use of the subject of the County—for example, this Door County church I'm beginning right now. It's out on double E, yet the people who look upon my work for identifiable Door County scenes may not find them. I shift things around. I'm often changing the subject for a variety of requirements—composition as well as the storytelling aspect of my art. This composition I'm working on has come from a lot of different sources. The actual church I'm working on did not come to me till the actual composition. That composition involved some activities which may never have occurred in that actual church. And to express my view of this rather complicated subject, I have eliminated part of the church. And I have placed it on its land in a different way as a means of analyzing its human message, which interests me in a certain way. So I shift it around to improve its message.

"I'm fascinated by human experience. I suppose I've always been an illustrator at heart. That's what interests me, and that's why I paint."

> Notebook entry: The eye is the heart of the painter. He is what he paints? Try another tack. Start with the sea . . . the fascination of water . . .

"I don't know. My real life as a teacher was very rational—ideas, art history. But when I quit teaching I gave up intellectuality and began painting what pleases me. It's a Walter Mitty thing, I suppose. I sail vicariously, but I also sail. I've always loved sailing, loved boats, particularly sailboats. I do a lot of sailing myself when the weather's sufficiently rough. I also found the subject technically challenging. I have to virtually reinvent the method of painting water every time I set out. I really have to stick my neck out. I have to risk failure every time I set out in the watercolor medium. But I revel in the technical difficulty!

"Water . . . I think it's a very useful subject. At the same time, it interests me technically. I can get very enthusiastic about water itself because of its energy, its constant change, its moods. It's always been very useful to me in storytelling because I can create almost any imaginative mood with water. Every mood from placid, mirror-like calm, lyrical, to the most terrifying threat. It's a relief from weather on a sultry day, but on other days it can kill you—the water surging under the ice on a cold winter day."

He points to a painting of a Cape Ann doryman out lobstering (recently completed for Sturgeon Bay minister Phil Sweet), then opens his sketchbook to show the process that went on in completing the painting. "I tried it first with sail, without sail, a variety of positions . . . I'm looking for composition, just groping for an idea. So I made, in effect, 1, 2, 3, 4, 5 pages, and on the 6th page, after the 17th layout, it finally went togeher for me. Some of these I took time to work out in light and dark values . . . tension, thrust, trying to convey something of the life this man had at the turn of the century. You just go by feeling that you've finally got it. So often you go by faith."

Notebook entry: How it ends in faith. The faith of the painter?

"I had a rather strict Lutheran boyhood. I believe in the existence of a supreme force. There are certainly forces at work far beyond human control. I like to think there is the possibility of being reincarnated. All these things . . . you just hate to see them disappear. It's easier for me to relate human associations with the divine as an involvement with nature. I feel, perhaps, a broad, more universal power here."

The painter of rural Door County churches: is the faith of the painter sought (expressed) in his subject? The painting that hangs in the Ephraim Moravian Church—"Jesus and the Fishermen"—was given to the church in 1978 on its 125th anniversary by the artist, Charles Peterson, who lives just down the road from it. It's a painting of four fishermen and their boats near the Ephraim shore (Biblical? Door County historical?) and Jesus, the Fisherman, extending his arm toward them, toward it all. In the background, a Door County scene instantly recognizable: Ephraim's harbor and the bluff.

"I've often been moved by the emotional stimulus of a piece of music. Romantic music, heroic music, impresses me. A lot of the Christian literature is inspirational to me. In this theme of the fishermen, I see Christ as a virile and physically strong individual, as he must be to lead fishermen. He's a workingman. He's a fisherman. Strong. You think of the fishermen here, a Tim Weborg or someone–not a limp-wristed person—gathering his men. These are fierce men. I wanted to present that kind of feeling. And it struck me I would place Him here, in Eagle Harbor, stemming as it does from commercial fishermen."

Notebook entry: Now Ephraim itself, the elusiveness of place. The village of all seasons, but especially Ephraim in winter . . .

"For me, I can get tuned in on this life far better here than in a city. The isolation, the quiet, is better for me. It's clear the place is aesthetically pleasing. It has all the things that have attracted people for the last century—the lake, the trees, the hill, the solitude—and, on the contrary, the increasing force of tourism is an alarm for some people. That's a touchy area, isn't it? I value Ephraim because it does give me the chance to withdraw and lead a quiet, conventional life.

"I mostly find myself drawn to the lake . . . I suppose by reason of the fact I do my walking after working hours, when the light is fading. Mostly I just walk for the pleasure of it, delighting in what I see. You know, I've sailed across this bloody harbor a thousand times, around

Horseshoe Island and back again, and I never tire of it. I suppose I feel at peace in Ephraim.

Ephraim sunsets. . . .

"I never paint a sunset . . . or butterflies. They are far superior to anything I can contribute, whereas the choice of an old farmyard needs some clarification, and that I can provide. Providing order . . . that's the function of composition."

Anderson Dock . . . "I've done it 200 times. And I have just begun to scratch the surface."

Winter . . . "As a reclusive artist, I love the winter for the solitude and the long, uninterrupted concentration. As an artist, I also see a lot of moods to the season, almost as broad as water. It presents every kind of mood because of its involvement in human experience."

Ephraim Winter . . . We look at his new print, "Ephraim Winter," signed and numbered (124/850), the "Peterson Print," which is on its way to becoming a tradition of its own with the issue of one or possibly two prints each year around December. The tradition began in 1979 with "Home for Christmas," of which 1,000 were printed, 500 signed. All of them are now gone.

"Ephraim Winter" . . . what's to be seen? What remains? Notice how the artist, head in hand, voice slightly fading, reflects on winter, on Ephraim, on place . . . slowly absorbed into his own painting . . .

"The past of Ephraim, Ephraim around the turn of the century, some of the solitude I enjoy so much here, the single purity of winter here, physical health to me—it's linked to Ephraim's past when life was more basic, less a resort area. People either produced material things, their own food and shelter, or they didn't survive. I think that's getting close to my view of life—and it ought to be that, so it looks beautiful: harmony within the design. Even though I was not here, I hope it is faithful to the spirit of life at that time. I think of old man Wilson waving out the kitchen door, the old Wilson house with the light on in the window. . . ."

Tim Weborg: Final Notes on a Fisherman's Life

A morning much like this morning, near the end: darkness and daybreak, autumn on the edge of winter, land and water, a man making his way in the midst of it all.

A cold, overcast morning in fall some years ago. October weather. Dark October movements in a man. That time of the year when the tourists flee like geese. When the landscape turns on itself, prepares for the bareness, the emptiness of winter, reminding the outsider, the native, of the isolated truths of his own precarious existence.

That time of the year, the season between seasons, from late October to first snow, the cold, wet steel time occasionally embraced by fog, a time no tourist will ever know the disoriented depths of unless he's lived a life here, year after year, with no thought of getting out.

On such a morning I am reminded of someone closing the door, and I await the sound of the latch. I am reminded of the fisherman, and all the fish trapped in nets.

I walk my road toward the lake wrapped in fog. All sounds are muffled, yet held closer to the ear . . . a dog's bark, a jay's cry, the fog horn, the chug of a fishing tug going out (Tim, I wonder?) moving through Death's Door just beyond me.

On such days I am reminded of a man's inability to do anything but live out the day.

Once on such a morning I arose in the early darkness, drank black coffee, packed a small lunch, and found my way towards the harbor in Gills Rock, where I knew fisherman Tim Weborg would be preparing his boat for the day's run, to see him in his setting, to see what his life was like, to see how a native, a man from a family of fishermen, fit into the scheme of things.

I was not anxious to go out with him that morning. Any excitement I may have experienced the day before had changed to foreboding once I faced the dark day with the wind coming up. For I was again caught up in one of the blacker moods of daily life which seem to lie in wait for me this season. Neither life nor work nor art was going well. At that time there was still that separation at that time. Life in Door County was alienation at best. What the hell was I doing sentenced to the desolation of this deadly landscape when I could be alive and well experiencing both a real and fictitious life in Chicago? Santa Fe? Rhodes?

And what did I know or care about the life of the fisherman, except that somehow the romance of life near water has always inspired me? Fishermen are an old, old metaphor for men. An old, old story. And the fact that they existed, as of old, right here, only moments from my door, was romance enough for me to redeem my sedentary ways of late, discover some form of identity, record and possibly discover a meaning for men there. Go back to water, where it all begins.

OCTOBER NOTES . . . THE FISHERMAN

Details of the fishing tug . . . the shape of an old shoe . . . functional and beautiful in its own way: it is what it does . . . ample working space inside . . . an old fashioned comfort about it, like an artist's studio . . . a certain solitary strength.

Scene before going out . . . Tim Weborg coming down the hill. His house behind him . . . the harbor, the boat, the bay all set before him. This could be Scandinavia, or anywhere in the world . . . in all these places, this same story with each day . . . fishermen moving down to the seas. Darkness of morning. Lights in the fish shanty.

Inside the boat (the *Freitag Brothers*) . . . putting on the lights, preparing to start the engine . . . the smell of oil, oil, oil . . . Tim placing his lunch bucket on the rack . . . the sound of the engine starting . . . Harvey Hansen, his partner, coming on the scene.

Tim, young, stocky, bullnecked . . . Harvey, older, thin, very still. Neither man seems to speak to the other . . . no small talk, no weather talk . . . nothing. Each man seems to know what he must do. Does the deafening sound of the engine drive them to silence? Putting on their slicks, their waders, their rubber shoes. The two men carrying a wooden fish box of crushed ice . . . in silence, without consulting one another, instinctively performing the deed.
Hansen wiping the mist from the front window . . .
The bell "tink" signaling the start . . .
Tim forcing a lever . . .
The *Freitag* moving out . . .

Talking with Tim last evening, some years since the October Notes, exploring once again, more personally, the fisherman's life. There is consistency in this way of life: man, boat, harbor, work are all the same. He has a new partner, Jeff Weborg, but Tim is the same, still at it, still a young man, thirty-six, but now the father of two daughters.

Fishing for him in the beginning?

"Ever since the summer months when I was ten years old, just going along for the fun of it with my dad and his brother. Once you get started you can't stop. The family goes back three generations in commercial fishing. It's like father and son. It gets in your blood. It's hard to leave. You have to love it. Right after high school, I went fishing full time.

"I always said I'd be a commercial fisherman someday; I had it in my heart. I loved it. All my brothers are in it. Some left other jobs and came back home because dad needed them.

"I was going to go in the Navy—because that meant water too—but then I broke my neck. I was to be confined to a wheelchair for the rest of my life; that's what they said, the rest of my life. 1961 . . . I was eighteen years old. A ski jumping accident at Nor-Ski Ridge [now Omnibus]. I was in thirteen tournaments that winter. I'm wired in the neck now. See this? All wires. I lost two inches of my neck. My head is right on my shoulders. I was six foot one, and now I'm five foot eleven and a half. With the wires and muscles, I'm all fused together.

"I'm one of the fortunate fellows to be alive, to be as strong as I am. I went through a lot of hair-raising experiences. Why I'm still here, no one knows. I was in a circular bed at St. Vincent's Hospital with forty-five pounds of weight hanging from the top of my head for two months. Then I went to give my girlfriend a little goodnight peck, and I moved like this; that's when I found out I could move again, my neck was okay.

"So I just dressed up and walked out of the hospital before anyone knew what happened. I said, 'I'm going home. Get me a cab.' They tried to get me back in bed. The nurses couldn't believe I got out of bed. Well, they convinced me. I was put in a bed without traction for a while. Then they let me go home for a week.

"But I didn't go home. I got in my car, threw my neck collar in the back seat, went to the V-Bar and started dancing. I just kept on going from one place to another, having a hell of a time. The hospital was looking for me, but I didn't know it. They wanted me back right away for surgery. The hospital was afraid that the neck would settle. My spinal cord could have been severed and killed me. The X-rays showed this. I was supposed to keep the neck collar on. They had the sheriff, the whole county looking for me. When I found out, I drove straight to Green Bay, three in the morning. 'Doctors and nurses,' I said. 'Here I am. I'm not drunk. I drove here all the way from Gills Rock.'

"I was scheduled for surgery at seven a.m. The doctor said there was a 50-50 chance for pulling through. Eleven hours I was in surgery. It was unreal when I woke up. I had a body cast on right down to the legs where you bend. They pulled out the quarters, the halves, the chips of the crushed vertebrae, and then put in stainless steel wires. The muscles have grown in . . . and this is what's supporting my neck."

OCTOBER NOTES . . . THE FISHERMAN

Sights from the fishing tug in darkness, plying the waters of Death's Door . . . lights from the shore at Gills Rock . . . a yard light on nearing Northport . . . the Coast Guard Station on Plum Island . . . the first ferry crossing from Washington Island, the red light . . . the light on Pilot Island . . . the sound of the bell buoy.

Tim leaning out the side opening, teasing the gulls already following the boat in the graying morning, synchronized with its movement as if part of the vessel, its work, its destination . . . the relationship of air to water to earth (to man).

Once out of Death's Door, the tug begins to rock and dip and settle like a gull into the greater always changing movement of the lake water . . . everything is about to be different here . . . but nothing has changed.

Tim, never resting, getting the boat straight for the work to begin . . . Tim moving, balancing, lunging into the matters at hand.

Darkness has filtered into a wooly, desolate gray with a dull and constant light of its own.

"Jeff and I are partners now," Tim explains. "Harvey's retired. The *Freitag* was built in 1952. 42 feet in length, 13 foot beam, 4½ foot draft, net tonnage—fifteen tons. We fish all the time except Oct. 25 to Dec. 1. Five weeks of closed season to give the whitefish a chance to spawn.

"I'm usually up around 5:30 in the morning. No breakfast at all. My grandfather would always get up and make his breakfast of side pork and cornbread. A lot of the fishermen eat, but I don't. If I take a break once I'm out there, I'll eat something around nine o'clock. I have sandwiches . . . peanut butter and jelly. Two sandwiches, that's all . . . a few cookies, a pint of milk. Some days I get only the peanut butter and jelly sandwiches in—like these last few days with the nets full of trash fish, alewives and smelt.

"I'm usually on the boat about ten till six in the morning and underway at six. I have a helper, Rick Johnson, running the boat now. Jeff, my partner, has his own boat. We're out straight north of Gills Rock now, on a range straight north of Table Bluff. Right now we're lifting seventeen to twenty fathom.

"From six a.m. we're out there. Today, let's see . . . we came in 2:30, close to three o'clock in the afternoon. Other days, with less junk and stuff, you could get in at eleven. Six days a week we fish. When we get a bad day, we have to go out on Sunday.

"We dress the fish on the water. Ice them. We carry ice on the boat. When we get back in, there's more work. Reeling nets, mending nets, weighing the fish up, packing them in the wooden crates, tagging them for shipment. I'm always in the shed . . . work is never done.

OCTOBER NOTES . . . THE FISHERMAN

Reaching the first buoy, marking the placement of the nets . . . the tug rocking, the two men both now in front of the boat, Tim reaching out for the buoy with a gaff hook, pulling it aboard along with the rest of the rig, positioning the net for the net lifter, from roller to lifter pen, then the lifter, the cleaning table, and the steel net box.

Few whitefish . . . Tim untangling fish from the net . . . the utter silence shared by the two fishermen in the midst of labor.

The constant tossing of the boat . . . the struggle to even remain standing, to maintain any sense of balance with the boat heaving, seemingly sinking at the point where the nets are lifted . . . as if the lake itself were in a tug-of-war with the fishermen, pulling everything back to the water.

The smell of the engine . . . oil, oil, oil . . . an uncomfortable mixture of cold and hot . . . a semblance of hell on water . . . opposites everywhere . . . and harmony.

Hansen occasionally following up a large fish with a hand-held green net.

After pulling all the nets, then setting them . . . again . . . for the next time. . . .

Living/fishing amidst the elements: rain, snow, sleet. "In winter, there's wind, cold, ice . . . good fishing in the lake, but very dangerous. You can set the nets, and in one storm lose the whole rig—all your investment. Lose it all. People don't realize what's all involved in it. When these nets are gone, you're out of it. One box of gill net is twelve hundred feet long. We lift ten boxes a day like that, costing somewhere around $350 to $400 a box, including twine. Twine is up to $36 a pound now. And we have somewhere near two hundred boxes of nets, with the old equipment, about thirty-five boxes brand new, fishable condition.
"The main danger for us is icing down. If you have very long runs, as you're running in the spray, it coats layer upon layer of ice. It builds up. The boat is just like a ball of ice. Some of the boats are insulated; we're not. Once you lose your boat, you can ice down and sink out there. We do have a coal furnace running in winter.

"In December, I'm in Sand Bay. We have a pier, too, in Rowleys Bay. December is a real good month. One year, south of Baileys Harbor, we set four boxes of nets, got 3500 pounds of whitefish on four boxes of nets, which is amazing. They hung like bananas and grapes.

"When the fish are there, commercial fishing is just about the best dollar you can make. When they're not there, it's bad. Like Las Vegas — when you lose it, you really lose it.

"My dad [Wallace Weborg] has always managed to make a good living here. In 1955, though, the whitefish were gone, the rig lay idle in the shed over ten years. My dad fished on Lake Winnebago then. Fished sheephead, a rough fish. In '65, we began setting the pond nets again. The whitefish have always run in cycles. My dad's seventy-five years old now, retired. He smokes fish. But he'd love to go back to fishing again. 'Fish is in my blood,' he says."

OCTOBER NOTES . . . THE FISHERMAN

Pulling nets . . . setting nets . . . the ritual . . . the monotony . . . a life made upon water? Setting the nets now out the back opening of the tug . . . Tim swaying, maintaining a balance against the tension of the net unraveling, pulling, almost fed to the waters.

The boat dipping, rising, into the gray sky . . . airborne? float? What has become of the horizon? Where is the dividing line? Circles . . . vertigo . . . where is the net going? What is the pattern? Everything veering away, from one side of the boat to the other. Fishermen (farmers?) working a mobile area just as one works a fixed field of twenty acres on land. (The tilling of the waters?)

The body beginning to express a tiredness in trying to hold still. . .

Still, the fisherman is satisfied in his work. "Just the challenge of fighting the old wild blue yonder. And there's the beauty of Door County. I love it from the sea: feeding the gulls, coming in, seeing the beautiful landscape from the water, especially the changing of the seasons. It's just great to be out there.

"It's not an easy life. It's a tough life. You have to be a man of steel to put up with much of it. You are just beat at times, and yet you have to go back into it. There are times you get disgusted and mad, but that too passes and bang, you're right into it again.

"Physically, the joints hurt, give way. There's the bending [Tim, all 230 plus pounds of him, standing on the land, bending, swaying, heaving, going through the motions of a man's dance on water], always the bending back and forth like this. And you stand at attention, straight like this; the boat's moving, but you're at attention picking fish; the nets are moving, but this is like you can't stop. The sea is with you. You can't sit down, you can't take a break: this is what standing at attention means, sometimes twelve, thirteen hours, going like this all day with the pressure going down on your hips, your joints. Without the lubricant for the bones, the joints begin to wear out. Guys like Ralph Larson . . . this is why you see them so bent up, using canes. Then you get trouble with your arthritis."

OCTOBER NOTES . . . THE FISHERMAN

Coming back . . . afternoon . . . a light rain falling (that haiku? No sky at all, no earth at all, and still . . . water, only water?) Cleaning the fish . . . washing down the boat . . . eating lunch. Hansen almost asleep, dozing at the wheel . . . Tim throwing out fish guts to a cloud of frenzied gulls. His childish delight in this strange communication. They know all about each other, the fisherman, the fish, the gull. No boundaries . . . no attachment . . . one. . . .

Slipping in Death's Door . . . the waters quiet once again . . . the boat sets still.

Gliding in, the engine stilled . . . silence . . . SILENCE . . . nothing. . . .

"I'm the fourth generation, but it goes back to Norway, so I'm fifth. Just about all my life is fishing. TV is sleeping medicine. I get pretty weak at night. I'm not as fast as I used to be. Since I have been married now for nine years, I've given up scuba diving. An asthma attack almost killed me last spring. After the neck, the Doc said no water skiing, no motorcycle, no snowmobiling. It's a miracle I'm here. In 1961, I went waterskiing anyway—another close call. I had several car accidents before that, several I just skimmed through alive. Why I'm here, I don't know.

"A snowmobile accident in 1973. I'm still paralyzed by that in my face. I hit a tree at seventy miles an hour in a blinding snow blizzard. Two hairline cracks in the lower back. I was full of blood. I drove home, though, walked into the house and said, 'Call Doc Farmer.' I was in shock. That was the only way I could run that machine across the ice— in shock.

"Then on January 27, 1977, I went through the ice on a snowmobile into 120 feet of water, straight north of Table Bluff, in Death's Door. It was around 8:30 at night. I had a compass in my pocket, but I could not find the trail back. The wind shifted and it blew. The time was up when I was supposed to be back in Gills Rock. A southwest wind had opened up the ice, and the right ski of the snowmobile went through. And I went through. I was in the water like this, pounding the ice with my arm, smashing it. My arm was black and blue. I didn't panic. When the snowmobile went under, that was it. I knew when I got back to solid ice I would be okay. The gloves, being wet, froze to the ice, and I pulled myself out like a deer would be pulling himself up. It was ten below zero. Once I got up, I was even more scared because of the trip back home and being wet. When I got out, I stood up, and I could see Table Bluff. I lay down again and crawled over 1,000 yards before I was sure I was on solid ice. I ran when I could. I climbed up on the rocks at eleven p.m. From my feet to my knees I was numb.

"It's hard to believe why a person is still here, why I'm still healthy and strong. It's really a miracle that a guy can come through life this way. I'm sort of glad I didn't have any sons, so that they wouldn't go through what I've been through. You think your folks don't know it, but they know it all. It all had to happen to me the way it did."

OCTOBER NOTES . . . THE FISHERMAN

Whatever you do, the less it requires of the physical, of love, of danger, risk, the threat of death, the less you have lived the life of the fisherman . . . the less you have lived.

The romance of the fisherman . . . no more. Instead, the reality of men at work; the reality of landscape beyond land; the reality of a way of life prevailing.

Tim, a little warmed now with brandy and beer, relishes the role of story teller. His voice echoing, taking total command in the telling, starting slowly, of average pitch, then raising suddenly to a shouting level of intensity till the words spew forth, caught alive, almost pulsing before his outstretched hands. A man moving through life by sheer physical force. A man wanting to be lifted to the heavens on skis . . . wanting to rise from the road in fast cars . . . wanting the freedom of movement in water, wanting to fly, wanting to *be* "the wild blue yonder."

"Oh, more or less I'm a believer. Yeah, out there, I ask Him a lot of times for a lot of favors . . . to try and calm the seas. He's never let me down when He could have many a time.

"I'll take the water over land anytime. I love water. I could live on water twenty-four hours a day. The sea doesn't bother me. I just love being out there. I'll fish for the rest of my life. I don't know what else I would do. I just wouldn't be happy any other way.

"It's scary at times, when the land just doesn't look right to you, when nothing seems to be there. You got to believe in your time and your compass course. There's no other way.

OCTOBER NOTES . . . THE FISHERMAN

The journey ended. . . the run complete. Lying in bed at night, arms, legs, back, neck aching from a day at sea . . . muscles still fighting for balance in a whole universe set free and dizzily dancing . . . giving way, anchors loose, flying fish, seining stars . . . a full moon bobbing like a buoy in the first falling snow . . . a turning sleep beneath the waves. The foghorn bemoaning the darkness and danger of the hour . . . and both the dream and the knowing within me that the fishermen will rise now and be with the water again. . . .

It all happens the way it is. . . .

There is no other way. . . .

I began yesterday, or years ago, with winter here in Door. Looking out my window now, the setting is much the same. Transformations of all sorts continue.

Without reason, I head out to walk with winter to the lake. Snow covers the ground. I think of the good friends gone, buried beneath this earth nearby. The bare branches of maple and birch entangle the silver sky. I smell the coming of fresh snow. The living and the dying.

I walked through the field past Charley Root's old house, now abandoned, awaiting the crying wind and weathering of still another winter. The barn has almost disappeared. The house, too, gives way to earth and the elements. Yet the rainbow of his flower garden holds a silent force beneath the snow. No one is home. His history here is ended. With luck, the land will continue to tell the story.

Winter, I've come to know, turns a man most inside himself. Even outside, as I am now, feeling cold, hearing birds and wind in an afternoon growing darker as the fields and trees turn lighter . . . even now, in the midst of all this moving before me, I am more inside than out.

And though I still harbor the deadlines of the time outside me, I have begun to savor the life within. I can write whole books now, stories and poems in the snow. I can paint a hundred watercolors in an afternoon's storm. I can live anywhere in the world on a winter's night walk, yet still follow my fresh tracks home.

Yes. I have not come to terms with living in this place. No. I'll stay for now. Yes. I should be moving on. No. Nothing ever ends.

At times I am haunted by a vision of all the people in this book gathered in the same room. What would they think? What would they say? And would they wonder why one man, a writer, an outsider, needs to express his life through theirs?

I am continually reminded of a line from Henry Miller. "Who were they [these people] if not myself?"

There is no mystery. I see only a oneness, a constancy in all their lives, examined or unexamined, lived upon a landscape, a place of reverence and wonder, that has made a difference in the quality of their living.

I suspect we have lost this, are losing it everywhere, even here. In all areas where the separation of man from nature, from small community, has separated man from himself.

No mystery. Simplicity.

Walking now toward the quiet lake at the end of my road, I see and feel the water fighting the final grasp of ice. I toss a pebble, record a final movement. . . .

I suspect we will lose all this. I know the battle is being waged within the County this very moment. The space is getting smaller. The landscape is up for grabs. We are all interested in land values, not the value of this land. We are all more concerned with ourselves than the preservation of a natural mystery, a landscape we need for our own spiritual survival.

It's not "them" but us. "Who were they, if not myself?"

So I begin once again in winter, adrift in a maze of contradictions. What can any man do? I write, I listen, I tell stories. I keep on walking. Hating the inevitable diminishment of a quality of peace I have come to love to hate—but longing to experience until the internal rhythm and movement of it all here is gone.

I could have ended this book where I began. Any one of the people could have brought the Way of Door full circle, for the weaving of each life in this place I see as whole, be it Charley and his dogs, or Freddie and his dance.

I see it all, a slow dance to Door. A circle ever extending itself . . . a pebble tossed in water.

We all begin and end there. Water. The fisherman. And begin again.

For the Way of Door is water most of all. The nearness of it. How it heightens the light. How it softens the edges. How it entreats us all to be with it. How it turns earth and the heavens and us in the endless dance.

Words of the Tao float back to me: "Man at his best, like water, serves as he goes along: Like water he seeks his own level, the common level of life . . . Loves living close to the earth, living clear down in his heart, loves kinship with his neighbors. . . . The pick of words that tell the truth, the even tenor of a well-run state, the fair profit of able dealing, the right timing of useful deeds. . . . And for blocking no one's Way no one blames him. .

Be living, not dying."

In darkness now above that is light upon the earth, I retrace my steps in snow to where I began.

A Note from the Publisher

Norb Blei and I began work on this edition of *Door Way* back in 2010, just before the series of health problems which finally took his life. He wanted another hardback; I argued for a cheaper paperback which would outmaneuver the used copies for sale on web bookstores and give his words a wider circulation. He reluctantly agreed. I scanned pages of the original edition to text and carefully edited each chapter, as a close comparison of this edition with the cloth *Door Way* will show. Norb proofed the revisions and set to work on a preface for the new edition. Then came the health problems, and that preface — along with God knows how many projects in process — never did get finished. My stock of *Door Way* diminished to zero, and Norb died.

But *Door Way* is one of the ten or twelve books I am most proud to have published, a portrait of Door County at a particular point in time, and a well written narrative of a life which in many ways resembles my own. A week before his departure, I visited Norb and promised to push ahead with this book. He apologized for never finished the preface, asked me to write a brief note of explanation and get *Door Way* back in print. A few distractions in my own life — like a trip to Outer Mongolia — slowed the process a bit, but with the help of Marcy Olson and the good folks at Thomson-Shore, we now have books. Mission accomplished, good buddy. FURTHUR.

—David Pichaske